Economics and Politics Revisited

COMPARATIVE POLITICS

Comparative Politics is a series for researchers, teachers, and students of political science that deals with contemporary government and politics. Global in scope, books in the series are characterized by a stress on comparative analysis and strong methodological rigour. The series is published in association with the European Consortium for Political Research. For more information visit www.ecprnet.eu

The series is edited by Nicole Bolleyer, chair of comparative political science, Geschwister Scholl Institute, LMU Munich, and Jonathan Slapin, professor of political institutions and European politics, University of Zurich.

OTHER TITLES IN THE SERIES

Coalition Agreements as Control Devices
Coalition Governance in Western and Eastern Europe
Heike Klüver, Hanna Bäck, and Svenja Krauss

Voters under Pressure
Group-Based Cross-Pressure and Electoral Volatility
Ruth Dassonneville

Minority Governments in Comparative Perspective
Edited by Bonnie N. Field and Shane Martin

The Government Party
Political Dominance in Democracy
R. Kenneth Carty

Reimagining the Judiciary
Women's Representation on High Courts Worldwide
Maria C. Escobar-Lemmon, Valerie J. Hoekstra, Alice J. Kang, and Miki Caul Kittilson

The New Kremlinology
Understanding Regime Personalization in Russia
Alexander Baturo and Jos Elkink

Coalition Governance in Western Europe
Edited by Torbjörn Bergman, Hanna Bäck, and Johan Hellström

Beyond Turnout
How Compulsory Voting Shapes Citizens and Political Parties
Shane P. Singh

Economics and Politics Revisited

Executive Approval and the New Calculus of Support

Edited by

TIMOTHY HELLWIG
AND
MATTHEW SINGER

ecpr

OXFORD
UNIVERSITY PRESS

OXFORD
UNIVERSITY PRESS

Great Clarendon Street, Oxford, OX2 6DP,
United Kingdom

Oxford University Press is a department of the University of Oxford.
It furthers the University's objective of excellence in research, scholarship,
and education by publishing worldwide. Oxford is a registered trade mark of
Oxford University Press in the UK and in certain other countries

Published in the United States of America by Oxford University Press
198 Madison Avenue, New York, NY 10016, United States of America

British Library Cataloguing in Publication Data
Data available

Library of Congress Control Number: 2023935112

ISBN 978–0–19–287166–4

DOI: 10.1093/oso/9780192871664.001.0001

Printed and bound by
CPI Group (UK) Ltd, Croydon, CR0 4YY

Foreword

Martin Paldam

Both economics and political science know potential relationships that seem obvious but explain less than we would like. A couple of examples show the problem. One is the *Phillips Curve*: when unemployment falls, wage increases rise.[1] Another is the *Democratic Transition:* when income rises, countries become more democratic.[2] Both of these relations are perfectly true, but the fit is not as good as we would like. That is, it is easy to find periods in many countries where they fail. This makes people say that the relations do not hold, but, lo and behold, after a period they reappear. They are modest but robust in large data sets, and thus they vary in small ones.

The booming literature on the replication crisis in the social sciences has the main message that it is often possible to mine a data set to make it confess as desired by the priors of the researcher. Mining can also overfit relations to make them better than they are. Mining is done by trying many ad hoc control variables, by adding dummies for exceptional periods, etc. Mining becomes more difficult the larger the data set is, but a great deal can still be done. Results of data mining do not replicate. Consequently, only results that have been repeatedly and independently replicated should be believed. Such replication will also reveal overfitting and make relations modest but honest.

This book deals with the linkage between economic performance and leader support which is another relation that is obviously true but has a modest fit. The economic voting model rests on the responsibility hypothesis that the government is responsible for the economy. It seems evident that the approval rate falls for a government that has handled the economy poorly. There are indeed many cases which could be interpreted as just that. However, both vote functions and popularity functions—the latter the focus of this book—have limited

[1] The Phillips Curve follows from demand and supply, which is the first thing the student of economics learns. In large datasets the correlation between the rate of unemployment and the rate of wage rises is about—0.4.

[2] The Democratic Transition follows from the agricultural and religious transitions that undermine the power of the two main pillars of the traditional political system. In large datasets the correlation between income and any of the standard democracy indices is about 0.6.

explanatory power. It is easy indeed to point to cases that are exceptions to economic voting.

Many potential complications contribute to the modesty of the relation. Seven such complications are:

(i) Voting is about politics, so surely the economy cannot be the only explanation. Politics is a notoriously complex activity that is difficult to catch with numbers. In contrast, large statistical offices with networks of data-collection agents compile economic data. Several international organizations try to make the definitions used universal, and they publish large international data sets. There is no office of similar size collecting political data, though many private polling firms collect information, which is less general and coordinated. In addition, political events are very diverse.[3]

(ii) The large recent literature on populism shows that economic mismanagement is often the result of governments trying to give everybody (or at least too many) what they want. Poor people want subsidies, and rich people want tax cuts. The combination of the two leads countries into trouble, but it often takes a couple of decades. The stories of the debt burdens of many countries, including the United States, France, and Japan, show just how slowly these things happen. Italy, Greece, and Argentina illustrate how difficult things become when fewer and fewer want to hold the debt, while voters still have some confidence in their populists.

(iii) The economy is a complex entity generating much data. A boom is when most trends in the data rise, and a slump is when they fall. However, mostly some trends go up, and others go down. This has led to the distinction between sociotropic and egotropic voting. The government tries to steer the whole economy, not the economy of voter *V*, thus *V* should hold the government responsible for the society and vote on a sociotropic basis. It is a problem that *V* mainly knows her own economic situation and that of her friends. Thus, she may vote informed by egotropic motivations. It has been found that the variable people know best is unemployment. They also know inflation, but only when it is high. Many other variables have been tried with mixed results.

[3] Part II in Paldam (2021) shows that the Democratic Transition is a well-determined path as a function of income. Changes in the political system take place as jumps generated by seemingly random triggering events, which are largely political and very diverse. The transition path is an attractor for the jumps.

(vi) The link from a poor economic performance to the decisions of the government is often weak. Many governments make great efforts to blame others when things go less well. The best to blame are foreigners, including certain international organizations such as the EU and the IMF.[4] However, sometimes events from abroad are indeed crucial. Many governments are in minority and depend upon other parties that may not want them to be too successful. Thus, governments can pass blame.

(v) The reward for economic success is less than the punishment for a similar economic fiasco, with a ratio of 1 to 3. This is the grievance asymmetry. It means that the average government—that has success in some fields, but fiasco in others—will experience a fall in popularity. The grievance asymmetry causes a cost of ruling, as has indeed been found.

(vi) Economic voting has consistently been found to have a short time horizon, like one to two quarters. Here the reader should recall item (ii) above. Such myopia is no problem for the political scientist, who, like former British Prime Minister Harold Wilson, knows that 'a week is a long time in politics'. However, economists prefer theories where agents maximize over an infinite time. Given the rate of discount and the uncertainty of the world, it may still be a handful of years. One observation follows: when people answer at polls, they have at most a minute to think. That surely gives a short time horizon. Elections, however, come after a campaign that has normally been quite hectic for at least a month. The news media, and many conversations between people, have covered politics and the candidates. Thus, we expect decisions about votes to have a longer time horizon and to reflect a more complex judgement.

(vii) Finally, as noted in some of the chapters in this volume, there is the problem of issue voting. Sometimes an issue comes to dominate an election. It may even be a politician, who is the issue, so that the like/dislike of the voters for a candidate comes to dominate all other considerations. This is, of cause, particularly important in presidential systems.

[4] Its charter states that the job of the IMF is to make the international monetary system work. It means that it should cure balance of payments crises. Such crises occur when countries spend more than they produce and cannot finance the debt produced. When the IMF lends, it demands that countries tax more and spend less. This is a nasty job, especially in poor countries, but somebody should do it! Moreover, it provides governments with a wonderful scapegoat.

These considerations can be discussed in many details. This has been done in the past and in the volume at hand. The field developed in waves. There was a large wave in the 1980s and 1990s that culminated with Lewis-Beck (1988), and the predecessor of the present volume in 1991. The volumes by Lewis-Beck and Paldam (2000) and by Dorussen and Taylor (2002) seemed to have exhausted the wave. Then it was largely dormant for a time, but now it has started again. For an old researcher in the field of economic voting, it is wonderful to see a new book in the field, which updates and revises so many old findings. The literature is still struggling with most of the problems mentioned, but I think that it is clear both that there is an underlying vote and popularity function, and that they explain too little. We really want to be able to forecast elections.

However, if we could forecast election outcomes perfectly, elections would be a formality. This would reduce voting substantially. With less voting the outcome would probably change, and our predictions would have to include that effect too. Thus, a complex game between forecasters, voters, and politicians would result. There are already many tactical games played in politics, but the fraction would surely rise. This is not what we want to be central in democracy.

References

Dorussen H., Taylor, M., eds (2002). *Economic Voting*. London and New York: Routledge/ECPR studies in European Political Science

Lewis-Beck, M. (1988). *Economics and Elections: The Major Western Democracies*. Ann Arbor, MI: University of Michigan Press.

Lewis-Beck, M., and Paldam. M., (2000). Special issue: Economics and Elections. *Electoral Studies* 19 (2/3)

Nannestad, P., and Paldam, M. (1997). The grievance asymmetry revisited: A micro study of economic voting in Denmark, 1986–1992. *European Journal of Political Economy* 13, 81–99.

Norpoth, H., Lewis-Beck, M., Lafay, J.-D., eds (1991). *Economics and Politics: The Calculus of Support*. Ann Arbor, MI: University of Michigan Press.

Paldam, M. (2021). *The Grand Pattern of Development and the Transition of Institutions*. Cambridge and New York: Cambridge University Press.

Preface and Acknowledgements

The origins of this volume are numerous. In the most immediate sense, its genesis was quite serendipitous. It can be traced to late 2019. At that time, Tim was approached by Indiana University's Office of the Vice President for International Affairs with a request to hold an academic event in conjunction with IU's bicentennial celebration of 2020. As part of the festivities marking the university's 200th birthday, the IU president was to travel to Europe to visit partner institutions, meet with alumni, and hold a reception at IU's Gateway office in Berlin. Charged with developing a one-day scholarly event, Tim proposed a workshop comprising papers on public support for governments across Europe. The idea would be to invite scholars based in Europe, along with some from North America, to travel to Berlin to present research on this common theme with the hopes of eventual publication. Unfortunately, the COVID-19 pandemic did not accommodate our plans. What we hoped would be a temporary annoyance, of course, developed into something far graver, and our plans to convene in Berlin were shelved.

But like Churchill at Yalta, we decided not to let a good crisis go to waste and convened a virtual workshop in June 2020 in place of an in-person event. While less stimulating than an in-person event, meeting over zoom did make it possible to invite more participants and increase the number of countries covered. Although we were unable to benefit directly from their support, we thank Ally Batten, Hannah Buxbaum, and Shawn Reynolds of IU's international office, as well as Frank Hess and Heather Duemling from IU's Institute for European Studies, for endorsing the project at its early stages.

More fundamentally, however, this volume would not be possible without the Executive Approval Project (www.executiveapproval.org). From modest beginnings, the EAP has developed over the years into one of the largest cross-national over-time data sources in the study of democratic performance and is now the go-to source for data and insights on job approval ratings for presidents, prime ministers, and governments. The EAP owes much of its current success to the leadership of our fellow team members, Ryan Carlin, Jonathan Hartlyn, Greg Love, and Cecilia Martínez-Gallardo. The project originated at the University of North Carolina at Chapel Hill where Jonathan and Ceci were on the faculty and Ryan was a PhD candidate. Greg's methodological and technical skills have been instrumental in growing and standardizing the data. The project relies on the efforts of countless research assistants and on-the-ground partners—a sampling of whom are contributors to this volume. While the two of us are formally editors of this volume, it is truthfully an EAP project writ large. We could not have succeeded without Ryan, Jonathan, Greg, and Ceci's contributions and feedback along the way.

Lastly, with respect to its central concern—the influence of economics on political support—this book has had a longer development still. Both of us have long been interested in the economy's place in representative democracy. Our research addresses such questions as whether the economy drives politics, under what contexts, and relative to what else. These too are the questions that motivate this volume. As a PhD candidate twenty years ago, Tim was browsing through the stacks at the University of Minnesota's Wilson Library and came across *Economics and Politics: The Calculus of Support*, edited by Helmut Norpoth, Michael Lewis-Beck, and Jean-Dominique Lafay. A few years later, Matt was introduced to the topic of instability in economic voting by his classmate Liz Zechmeister at a reading group that she invited the first-year graduate student to join, which quickly led to him reading the Norpoth et al. volume. Both Matt and Tim were hooked by the arguments laid out in the book. Each chapter of the book considered how the economy shaped vote- or popularity-functions in different countries. Anchoring the volume was Martin Paldam's captivating essay on the 'instability dilemma' characterizing these 'VP' functions. With his observation that the relationship between economics and government support was at once unstable and highly significant, Paldam helped chart a course for decades of scholarship on why, when, and where 'the economy matters'. These questions continue to frame inquiry in the current volume. We thank Martin Paldam and the editors and contributors to the original *Economics and Politics* for providing the motivation. We can only hope that the current volume will be as influential as its predecessor published over thirty years ago.

We also extend our thanks to Oxford University Press. Thanks to Susan Scarrow and Jon Slapin as editors of OUP's Comparative Politics series for their sage advice and feedback on our proposals, Dominic Byatt for his early endorsement of the project, Ryan Morris for taking over as its shepherd, and the reviewers for helping us sharpen the manuscript's message. We also thank our home institutions for their support of our work. At UConn, funds from the Alan R. Bennett Honors professorship allowed Matt to hire undergraduate research assistance to generate data on party-system characteristics and he is grateful to Katherine Smith for her work in generating that data set and for

Alan's ongoing support of our programme. Tim thanks Calista Stafford and Gracie Symington for research assistance and IU's Center of Excellence for Women and Technology's Emerging Scholars programme for support.

Finally, we extend our appreciation to our families for their ongoing support as we worked on this project and had to disappear for various zoom meetings to coordinate with each other or with the larger EAP team. Our thanks go out to Tana, Claire, and Owen Hellwig and Cara, Mary, Andrew, Whitney, and Annie Singer for letting us be fascinated with these questions and to give us space to chase the answers.

Timothy Hellwig
Matthew Singer

Contents

List of Figures

List of Tables

List of Contributors

Luís Aguiar-Conraria, associate professor, University of Minho

John Bartle, professor, University of Essex

Éric Bélanger, professor, McGill University

Paolo Bellucci, professor, University of Siena

Ryan E. Carlin, professor, Georgia State University

Sebastian Dellepiane-Avellaneda, senior lecturer, University of Strathclyde

Kathleen M. Donovan, support specialist, Redistricting Data Hub

Bruno Fernandes, PhD candidate, University of Minho

Emiliano Grossman, associate professor, Sciences Po, Paris

Isabelle Guinaudeau, CNRS associate researcher, Center for European Studies and Comparative Politics, Sciences Po

Jonathan Hartlyn, Kenneth J. Reckford Distinguished Professor, University of North Carolina at Chapel Hill

Timothy Hellwig, professor, Indiana University

Airo Hino, professor, Waseda University

Olivier Jacques, assistant professor, Université de Montréal

Mark A. Kayser, professor, Hertie School, Berlin

Paul M. Kellstedt, professor, Texas A&M University

Ellen Key, assistant professor, Appalachian State University

Panos Koliastasis, postdoctoral researcher, University of Athens

Matthew J. Lebo, professor and chair, University of Western Ontario

Arndt Leininger, assistant professor, Chemnitz University of Technology

Michael S. Lewis-Beck, F. Wendell Miller Distinguished Professor, University of Iowa

Gregory J. Love, professor, University of Mississippi

Pedro C. Magalhães, principal researcher, University of Lisbon

Cecilia Martínez-Gallardo, associate professor, University of North Carolina at Chapel Hill

Anthony McGann, professor and head of school, University of Strathclyde

Vincenzo Memoli, associate professor, Università degli Studi di Catania

Hanako Ohmura, professor, Kwansei Gakuin University

Lluís Orriols, associate professor, Universidad Carlos III de Madrid

Brandon Beomseob Park, assistant professor, Soongsil University

Pedro Riera, associate professor, Universidad Carlos III de Madrid

Xavier Romero-Vidal, research associate, Centre for the Future of Democracy, University of Cambridge

Henrik Bech Seeberg, associate professor, Aarhus University

Matthew Singer, Alan R. Bennett Professor, University of Connecticut

Mary Stegmaier, associate professor and VP international, University of Missouri

John Yfantopoulos, professor of health economics, University of Athens

1

Introduction

Instability and Government Popularity in the Twenty-first Century

Ryan E. Carlin, Jonathan Hartlyn, Timothy Hellwig, Gregory J. Love, Cecilia Martínez-Gallardo, and Matthew Singer

Support from the governed is essential for making democracy work.[1] Democratic leaders who enjoy high levels of support can advance their policy agenda, but public disdain can lead to gridlock or even regime change. For policymakers, executive approval is an asset when trying to quell minority uprisings, gain an upper hand in inter-branch negotiations, and claim a mandate for policy change. Given its central importance for democratic governance, the approval of presidents, prime ministers, and governments is a central concern for scholars and policymakers alike. If elections are potent but rare opportunities for public control, then surveys of public sentiment between elections provide a continual accountability mechanism, capturing public reactions to policy reforms and changing environments.

How do publics evaluate the job performance of political executives? Scholars, journalists, and pundits alike have long converged on a single answer: the economy. A rising economy improves the popularity of the government, but if the economy turns south, so do the government's prospects. This economy–popularity link is not only an empirical regularity but, in the view of most observers, is normatively attractive. It produces a virtuous circle linking changes in economic conditions to public evaluations of government performance to mandates to pursue economic policies for positive and sustainable outcomes which, in turn, bolster job ratings, and so on.

The real world, however, is rarely that simple. In his classic essay in the pathbreaking volume *Economics and Politics: The Calculus of Support* (Norpoth, Lewis-Beck, and Lafay, 1991), Martin Paldam challenged this conventional

[1] For research assistance, we are grateful to Katherine Smith and Calista Stafford and to funding from the Alan R. Bennett Professorship at the University of Connecticut and to the Office of the Vice Provost of International Affairs at Indiana University.

Ryan E. Carlin et al., *Introduction.* In: *Economics and Politics Revisited.* Edited by: Timothy Hellwig and Matthew Singer, Oxford University Press. © Ryan E. Carlin et al. (2023). DOI: 10.1093/oso/9780192871664.003.0001

wisdom. Across established Western democracies, evidence of the so-called 'popularity function'—whereby the economy and other systemic factors translate into political support—was remarkably mixed. Paldam pointed out that despite much case-study evidence linking economic outcomes to government support, the strength of these ties varied widely, and pooled cross-national models revealed no consistent relationship. To Paldam (1991), the connection between the economy and government support was 'on the one hand unstable and, on the other hand, highly significant' (1991, 28). He urged scholars to 'analyze periodicity more systematically' and to 'identify the periods where the functions work best and periods where they break down' (29). As Anderson (2007, 275) astutely notes, Paldam's 'instability dilemma' changed the research paradigm's fundamental question. Where it once was 'How can we best identify a relationship we know exists?' it now became 'How can we best make sense of a relationship we know to be unstable'?

Predicting government popularity from economic trends is no less fraught today than thirty years ago. Taking stock a decade and a half ago, Anderson (2007) found the empirical record so varied over time and space, and contingent on so many political and institutional factors, that he questioned, provocatively, whether the 'economic vote' exists at all. In a more recent critical review Kayser (2014) arrives at a similar conclusion. Others, however, have offered a more charitable view. Nadeau, Lewis-Beck, and Bélanger (2013), for example, show economic assessments are frequently tied to 'economic reality'. Hellwig and Marinova (2017) make the case for not throwing the baby out with the bathwater. Rather than abandoning the research programme, researchers should revisit the measures, models, and untested assumptions that characterize the extant literature. For Carlin et al. (2021), the instability that we see can reflect the rational response of the public to the institutional and information environments. In short, the extent to which economic bases of political support exist, and explanations for why they appear so elusive, remain contested.

This volume seeks to reassess the impact of economic conditions on political support among established democracies for the twenty-first century. It is motivated by an overarching question: *Has the economy's role as a driver of popularity changed over time?* Although a large literature examines why the economy's effect varies across countries, its focus has been on institutional features that are largely static.[2] Yet the political economy of advanced capitalism today is very different from what it was thirty years ago, and this

[2] The United Kingdom's recent experience with coalition politics, as discussed in the Chapter 3, is an exception.

has reshaped party systems in many countries. But does this matter for popularity? Have non-economic markers of system performance—like corruption, immigration, or security—supplanted the economy's role in recent decades? Have other factors—such as group identity or partisan dispositions—blunted or redirected the economy's sway over support for government leaders? Or has economic instability and rising inequality following the Global Financial Crisis kept the public's attention on the economy despite these other changes?

To address these questions, contributors to this volume analyse public opinion data collected by the Executive Approval Project (EAP; www.executiveapproval.org). The project's Executive Approval Database (EAD) compiles and assembles survey marginals from thousands of individual public opinion polls from hundreds of polling firms into single measures of leader approval that are comparable across countries and over time. For many countries, the EAD series span decades, reaching from the 1980s (or earlier) to the present. These data are exceptional in many respects, but two are integral to this volume. The first is country coverage. The EAD makes it possible for scholars to assess popularity functions for more governments in more countries than ever before. Extant research into popularity functions has focused largely on a small subset of democracies, with the United States, Britain, and France receiving a disproportionate degree of attention (see Lewis-Beck and Stegmaier, 2000). The EAD includes time-series measures of executive approval for more than fifty countries based on data from hundreds of polling firms and thousands of individual public opinion polls. Twenty of those countries are examined in this volume—eleven in depth.

The second EAD comparative advantage is that it provides high frequency series for time-series analysis. This makes it possible to estimate *popularity* functions, eschewing the small-N problem plaguing *vote* functions (where sample size is constrained by the number of elections). High-frequency data also allow analysts to characterize the dynamic processes governing public support for governments.[3] Our goal is that this book and the data it features will serve as the go-to source for academics, journalists, pollsters, and students seeking to understand why some governments enjoy the support of the public while others do not.

We begin with a survey of the cross-national research on government popularity, identifying a set of emerging economic and political factors that might be challenging the economy's role as the chief driver of popular support for

[3] For a recent example, see Carlin et al. (2018), who assess the cyclical properties of presidential approval in eighteen countries. Also see Chapter 2 of this volume.

democratic governments. Among them we highlight economic issues that are newly salient, non-economic issues that compete for the public's attention, partisan polarization, and populism. We then provide a first comparison of the link between the economy and government popularity in twenty countries over thirty years. Echoing Paldam thirty years on, we show that the relationship varies considerably across countries. Yet we also document substantial variation in the economy–approval relationship within countries over time, which has received much less attention. In most countries considered here, the economy's effect on approval has weakened over time. In some places, however, its effect has grown over time, while in yet other places we observe a declining role for the economy in the first decade of the century only to see a rebound after the Great Recession. This variation sets the stage for the chapters that follow.

Differences in the economy's political impact may be traced to the public's capacity to assign responsibility for changes in economic performance, by the salience of economic factors, and by the willingness of the public to update their assessments of public officials. Traditionally, the literature on cross-national variation has focused on political and economic factors that shape attributions of responsibility. Yet some chapters in this volume question the importance of these contexts. Specifically, those that look at fragmented party systems and coalition government, factors that should diffuse responsibility for the economy, find inconsistent evidence that these factors shape how the public responds to the economy. Instead, the analyses in this volume focus the attention on how the evolving issue agenda and the degree to which the electorate is anchored by either polarization or partisanship shape the process by which leaders are held accountable.[4]

Confronting the Instability Dilemma: Context, Issue Salience, and Partisanship

The instability dilemma identified by Paldam has fuelled a large literature on economic voting and vote-popularity (VP) functions (Stewart and Clarke, 2017; Lewis-Beck and Stegmaier, 2018; Magalhães, 2020 provide recent reviews). While debates persist, we identify three general tendencies. First, most single case studies find at least *some* impact of the economy on leader support. Second, macro trumps micro. While voters sometimes hold leaders

[4] But see chapters on France and Portugal on how the distribution of authority within semi-presidential systems alters the bases of executive approval.

accountable for their personal financial situation, most studies find that voters are more likely to blame the government for the state of the national economy than for their personal economic circumstances (Fiorina, 1981; Kinder and Kiewiet, 1981; Lewis-Beck, 1988; Markus, 1988).[5] Third, public reactions to 'the economy' are not only about economics. Non-economic considerations also influence how the public makes sense of economic information (Duch, Palmer, and Anderson, 2000; De Boef and Kellstedt, 2004; Gerber and Huber, 2010; Carlin et al., 2021). Thus, the correlation between economic perceptions and political attitudes is in part a spurious reflection of underlying partisan loyalties or endogenous attempts by government supporters to justify their support for the incumbent, especially in cross-sectional survey data (Kramer, 1983; Wlezien, Franklin, and Twiggs, 1997; Anderson, Mendes, and Tverdova, 2004; Evans and Anderson, 2006; Healy et al., 2014; Evans and Chzhen, 2016). Aggregate trends in consumer confidence are more exogenous and tend to mirror economic outputs on average, but even they are shaped by partisan loyalties (Lee and Singer, 2021).

Other topics, though, remain grounds for debate. Engaging with democratic theory, scholars continue to discuss whether voters *should* reward politicians for expected policy outcomes or hold them accountable for what they have *already* delivered (Barro, 1973; Ferejohn, 1986; Fearon, 1999; Ashworth and Bueno de Mesquita, 2014). Others address whether the public *actually* is more forward- or backward-looking, with the balance of evidence pointing to a public that employs a mixture of retrospective assessments and prospective anticipation to evaluate leaders.[6] Also at issue is whether some groups are more responsive to economic fluctuations than others (e.g. Weatherford, 1983; Singer, 2013b; 2016; Fossati, 2014; Marx, 2016), whether individuals benchmark economic performance against other yardsticks (e.g. Besley and Case, 1995; Kayser and Peress, 2012; Aytac, 2018; Park, 2019), and whether they rely more on their own observations of the economy or on media coverage of official reports (Kayser and Leininger, 2015). Several chapters in this volume assemble new data to examine these core questions.

[5] The weak connection between pocketbook finances and vote choice often reflects the public being less likely to blame the government for personal economic outcomes than it is to blame it for national economic conditions (e.g. Feldman, 1982; Tilley et al., 2018; Baird and Wolak, 2021). Yet recent studies find that personal—and group—financial standing warrant renewed attention as drivers of public opinion (Ansolabehere, Meredith, and Snowberg, 2014; Healy, Persson, and Snowberg, 2017; Singer, 2018; Visconti, 2019; Green, Hellwig, and Fieldhouse, 2022).

[6] For the classic argument that the electorate is backwards looking, see Fiorina (1981). For evidence that voters are future looking, see Mackuen, Erikson, and Stimson (1992). It may be, however, that the evaluations matter under different circumstances (Nadeau and Lewis-Beck, 2001; Singer and Carlin, 2013).

But while these debates rage on, these studies share an assumption that a positive association between economics and politics is good for accountability and, hence, for making representative democracy work. Popular control of elected policymakers requires sanctions when they perform badly. If the economy is in fact the *sine qua non* of policymaker performance in advanced democracies, it follows that the absence of an economy-to-politics connection is evidence of substandard democratic performance. In cases where the economy has no effect on public sentiment, then, democrats might hope this non-finding could be chalked up as an exception rather than a rule.

Yet as analyses of vote and popularity functions expanded beyond a select few cases like Britain and the United States, and as scholars pooled data from multiple countries, the robustness of the economy–government support relation was called into question. Some viewed Paldam's (1991) finding of an unstable relationship between the economy and incumbent vote share as an indictment against the role of elections in democratic accountability. Adding fuel to the flames, Nannestad and Paldam (1994) surveyed the expanding set of studies and concluded that, on balance, VP-functions manifest 'a lack of stability'. Cheibub and Przeworski (1999) further problematized the economy–political support relationship, finding that leader re-election was only weakly tied to economic outcomes, a result they deemed 'both surprising and dismaying' (229).

In the face of these surprises, others took on the task of identifying what could explain these findings. In what follows we highlight three sets of these factors: context, issue salience, and political dispositions. We note that because much of the valuable research on the economy–political support nexus has focused on the conditioning role of the institutional context, the focus has largely been on spatial variation. This has meant that temporal bases of variation have received less attention (exceptions include Kirchgassner, 1991; Nadeau, Niemi, and Yoshinaka, 2002; Remmer, 2003; Singer, 2013a; Dassonneville and Lewis-Beck, 2019; Donovan et al., 2020). A central objective of this volume, then, is to re-centre our concerns on time and temporal change. As we note in our review of these three factors, dynamics may be shifting in ways that are likely to change the economy–politics link.

Responsibility-based Explanations for Instability in the Economy–Political Support Nexus

One strand of research set out to solve the instability dilemma by identifying sources of cross-national variation. Powell and Whitten (1993) identified a set of institutional factors—coalition government, bicameralism, opposition power-sharing, and party cohesion—that shape the ability of citizens to assign responsibility for economic outcomes. In contexts where institutional veto-points or party-system fragmentation diffuse power, they noted, it is more difficult for rational citizens to apportion responsibility for economic outcomes across political actors. The core notion of 'clarity of responsibility' has now been applied and modified many times over, representing a major step forward in specifying the connection between the economy and election outcomes. Extensions of this initial insight include examining party-system effects, government types, and constitutional regimes (e.g. Bengtsson, 2004; van der Eijk et al., 2007; Duch and Stevenson, 2008; Hellwig and Samuels, 2008; Hobolt, Tilley, and Banducci, 2013; Singer, 2020, Duch and Falcó-Gimeno, 2022).

Beyond institutional arrangements, responsibility attributions may also be shaped by beliefs about the relative capacity of governments to execute policy. Many models of the mass political economy are vestiges of an earlier era; one in which governments could fine-tune the economy through monetary and fiscal policies (Hibbs, 1977). Fundamental changes to post-industrial economies, however, have made this view increasingly untenable. Greater dependence on global financial flows, investment, and trade has shrunk the influence of domestic policymaking on economic outcomes. This makes it difficult to disentangle who is in control of the economy and may lead the public to discount the economy when evaluating leaders, especially in situations where it is strongly integrated into a global economy (Hellwig, 2007; 2015; Campello and Zucco, 2016). In this context, assigning responsibility may require the public benchmark their country's performance against global trends or that they focus on a more limited set of economic indicators that politicians can control.

Political elites and the media can also shape the narrative about responsibility attribution. Leaders may attempt to claim credit for outcomes that have occurred on their watch or to divert blame to others when the economy is bad. Leaders may also affect the attribution of responsibility by engaging in activist economic policies that foreground state action and by making those policies a central part of their appeal (Carlin and Hellwig, 2019). Coverage of political events also shapes the process of attribution; as the media assigns credit/blame to the government, public responses to the economy become stronger (Damstra et al., 2021)

Along with reducing instability, the clarity of responsibility approach to economic voting has the potential to restore the centrality of elections as mechanisms of accountability. The normative appeal of the VP-function stems from its simplicity. Citizens receive information about the state of the economy, they attribute responsibility for some share of these outcomes to the government, and then evaluate politicians accordingly. This mechanism of citizen control—or what V.O. Key (1964) characterized as the ability to act as a rational 'god of vengeance and reward'—appears central to democratic representation. If a complex institutional environment or an interconnected multilayered economic system makes it difficult to discern who is responsible for economic conditions, then a rational public should de-link evaluations of the economy from evaluations of incumbents.[7]

Yet despite the empirical and normative successes of taking the political context into account, this research agenda is limited in its capacity to understand systematic change within countries over time. Institutional factors contributing to the clarity of responsibility are largely static. Explaining change over time from the perspective of responsibility attributions requires change in context. For instance, the distribution of parties in government can change over time and alternating periods of coalition and single-party or of majority and minority government should thus reshape patterns of economic accountability (e.g. Nadeau, Niemi, and Yoshinaka, 2002; Duch and Stevenson, 2008; Hobolt, Tilley, and Banducci, 2013). But despite their prominence in the cross-national literature, party system and coalitional variables are unlikely to be sufficient to explain the over-time variation that we document below, especially over the long term.

Issue-based Explanations for Instability

The evolving salience of political issues represents another source of change in the economy–political support nexus. Though economic fluctuations are key drivers of citizen well-being, scholars recognize this is not always the case. Indeed, Paldam (1991, 13) identified a list of 'highly relevant non-economic factors' that include the personality of politicians, changes in party structure, foreign policy crises, scandals, and polarizing issues like abortion or nuclear power plants. More recent scholarship provides evidence that non-economic issues emerge and compete with the economy for space on the public agenda. Some voters prioritize other aspects of government performance, such as foreign policy, or train their sights on particular issues, like protecting the

[7] Studies have questioned whether the public can evaluate how much control governments actually have over outcomes (e.g. Hayes et al., 2015; Achen and Bartels, 2016; Campello and Zucco, 2016). Yet studies have consistently found that the economy–government support relationship is weaker in contexts where it is difficult to identify who's to blame, suggesting that the public can take into account the responsibility of government actors over outcomes and discount their influence accordingly (e.g. Carlin and Hellwig, 2020; Duch and Stevenson, 2008).

environment (Singer, 2011b; 2013a; de Vries and Giger, 2014). When these issues gain in salience, the economy plays a smaller role.

Both the public's interests and choices made by political actors shape the relative importance of the economy vis-à-vis other concerns. The public focuses its attention on issues that are easily accessible and personally impactful. As a result, the public's attention to the economy is shaped by media coverage compared to other issues, recessions that drive the public and media's attention, and personal economic vulnerabilities or weak safety nets that make some groups particularly vulnerable and therefore attuned to economic swings (Bloom and Price, 1975; Soroka, 2006; Kelleher and Wolak, 2006; Singer, 2011a; 2011b; Dassonneville and Lewis-Beck, 2014; Lobo and Pannico, 2020). Wars, terrorist attacks, corruption scandals, natural disasters, and public health crises, in contrast, can shift the attention of the public and the media away from the economy (Brody, 1991; Krosnick and Brannon, 1993; Edwards et al., 1995; Singer, 2013a; Bol et al., 2021, Singer, 2021). Vote-seeking elites, of course, can also leverage these other issue concerns to improve their chances in electoral contests (Druckman and Holmes, 2004; Vavreck, 2009; Hart, 2016; c.f. Eshbaugh-Soha and Peake, 2005).

There also is evidence that non-economic factors have grown in importance. According to Inglehart (1977; 2008), rising affluence and generational replacement have fuelled value change in Western societies. Since the 1970s, concerns about economic well-being and security have been supplanted by environmental quality, changing social norms and values, and transparent and open governance. At the same time, changing economic circumstances and weakened safety nets created newly vulnerable individuals who coalesced around cultural issues that protected their social standing rather than matters of markets and redistribution. These shifts in mass values contributed to shifts in elite behaviour. While parties on the left turned away from redistributive politics and towards social issues, many conservative parties responded with a renewed emphasis on traditional cultural issues. An ascendant values-based axis of political competition identified by such labels as libertarian-authoritarian (Norris and Inglehart, 2019), integration-demarcation (Kriesi et al., 2008), or GAL-TAN (Hooghe and Marks, 2018) has the capacity to supplant one centred on economic concerns. If the economy has become less salient in political competition, then its importance as a basis of evaluating political leaders' performance should also be diminishing in countries where these trends are most pronounced.

But a values-based popularity function may also be incomplete. Increasing volatility in commercial and financial markets can magnify the public's attention on the economy. The Global Financial Crisis placed economic management back at the head of the political agenda in many countries (Bartels, 2013; Singer, 2013a; Dassonneville and Lewis-Beck, 2014). Changes to how capitalism works may also reshape *which* aspects of the economy receive the public's attention. The growth of a more diverse post-industrial economy, coupled with labour market dualization and informal and gig sectors, have made for greater wage heterogeneity over time (Berlingieri et al., 2017). As a result, growth in one sector is less apt to spill over to others. The implication for government popularity is clear. If 'the economy' means evermore different things to voters, then national economic indicators may have little bearing on collective evaluations of the executive's job performance. Recent work finds factors like economic insecurity and occupational unemployment are among the strongest movers of voters' evaluations and choices (Lindvall and Rueda, 2014; Marx, 2016; Helgason and Mérola, 2017; Hutter et al., 2018).[8] In sum, shifts in issue salience and heterogeneity in national economies may encourage scholars to consider more targeted indicators of economic performance to capture what is salient to the electorate.

Political Dispositions and Instability

A third approach to the instability dilemma focuses on the degree to which government popularity is anchored in political dispositions. Of these anchors, partisanship dominates. Partisans tend to view the world through rose-tinted glasses when their preferred party or candidate is in a position of power but trend gloomy when other parties are in charge.[9] Furthermore, partisans are likely to stick with their preferred team even when they perform badly and to resist pressures to switch party allegiance. This dynamic has been widely demonstrated with regards to scandals (Anderson and Tverdova, 2003; Anduiza et al., 2013, Eggers, 2014; Solaz et al., 2019; Fumarola 2020), but it also applies to the economy. Illustrating this implication of partisanship for leader evaluations, Kayser and Wlezien (2011) show that partisan attachments vary inversely with the influence of economic considerations on incumbent party vote intentions (see also Donovan et al., 2020; Ellis and Ura, 2021). Where partisan attachments are weak, as they were in many European countries in the 1980s, voters have more room to focus on the economy. The opposite is

[8] Asset ownership has also risen in electoral importance as wealth has supplanted income as a gauge of material well-being (Lewis-Beck and Nadeau, 2011; Hellwig and McAllister, 2019; Adler and Ansell, 2020).

[9] Observers of American politics argue that a sense of disdain for one's least-liked party may be stronger than attachment to one's favoured party (e.g. Abramowitz and Webster, 2016).

true when partisan bonds are strong (see also van der Brug, van der Eijk, and Franklin, 2007; Dassonneville, 2016; Jung, 2018).

Whether political systems are experiencing de-alignment and personalization or a prolonged process of realignment remains a subject of debate (e.g. Hooghe and Marks, 2018; Garzia et al., 2022). Continued political de-alignment opens space for the public to respond to economic fluctuations free from partisan blinders. But in many countries a renewed salience of partisan frames and the rise of negative partisanship is contributing to disdain towards out-partisans. The resulting bias may reduce the public's willingness to use performance in office to update leader evaluations.

Polarization's effects are also debated. If polarization generates partisan loyalties and makes it hard for individuals to see the flaws in their own side or the virtues of their opponents, then evaluations of leader performance may remain rigid even as outcomes change. Alternatively, polarization may sharpen the economy's influence. If parties adopt similar positions on economic policy, the public has little reason to believe that changing leaders will affect economic policies or, in turn, outcomes. Absent meaningful alternatives, the public is unlikely to focus their attention on the economy when voting (Hellwig, 2012; Stiers and Dassonneville, 2020). Polarization around economic issues may thus focus the public's attention on economic management whereas it is polarization around non-economic or cultural issues—and not polarization per se—that limits the effect of the economy on performance evaluations.

The evidence that polarization leads to approval ratings that are more stable and less responsive to outcomes is most clearly established in the US case. Donovan et al. (2020) show polarization has increased partisan-motivated reasoning when it comes to evaluations of the US president, reducing the connection between economic outcomes and approval. Economic performance and salient political events have continued to affect government support in the United States (Newman and Otto, 2021), but their effects are much more muted than in the past. Cross-national studies have also furnished evidence that the economy's role in elections is larger when parties take divergent economic positions (Hellwig, 2012; Gélineau and Singer, 2015). The degree to which this applies to executive approval, however, remains an open question.

Finally, there is evidence that the influence of the economy may depend on the type of leader. It is likely no coincidence that polarizing populist leaders like Narendra Modi, Victor Orbán, and Donald Trump experience time-invariant approval ratings, seemingly unaffected by changing conditions. Carlin and Love (2020) find that populist leaders have high and remarkably stubborn levels of *dis*approval and that this disapproval is less sensitive to shocks in economic growth relative to non-populists. Where populists have taken power, the economy's effect on approval may be diminished.

Is It Still the Economy? Of Time and Government Popularity

Our understanding of the sources of variation in the economics–politics connection has grown considerably since Paldam's classic essay. In the thirty years that followed its publication, scholars have identified circumstances where the economy's effect is modest or missing. In this chapter, we have identified three major groups of factors explaining the instability dilemma that have, on balance, become more relevant over time: the conditions that impact attribution of responsibility to the executive, issue salience, and partisan predisposttions.

So, what do these developments portend for popularity functions? On the one hand, shifts in the salience of political issues and the strengthening of partisan anchors in many countries imply that the economy's influence on government popularity—or what Paldam (1991) calls the 'e-fraction'—has weakened and that it is largely conditioned by the more diffuse political component (the 'p-fraction'). Anecdotally, the empirical record of several recent elections highlights the relative lack of importance of economic concerns. For example, President Trump's approval in the United States was only weakly improved by the strong economy in 2019 and his candidacy for re-election in 2020 was little affected by the COVID-recession. Elections in Denmark in 2015 and 2019 were conducted against the background of a relatively strong economy and yet in each case the incumbent coalition was defeated. The same thing occurred in 2017 in New Zealand where the governing National Party lost despite a solid record of economic stewardship. And in Germany in 2017, though the strong economy resulted in a victory for Chancellor Angela Merkel's Christian Democrats, the party's vote share fell, nonetheless.

To move beyond these anecdotes, this section provides a helicopter assessment of the relationship between economic conditions and executive approval to document that there is change over time that merits explanation. Our analysis trades precision for breadth, ceding the former to the detailed country chapters that follow. We focus on countries that meet two criteria. The first is based on country attributes. Explanations for public support vary widely from one country to the next and can be based on culture, norms, tradition, history, and a host of other factors resistant to precise measurement. To minimize the variance in these often-unobserved factors and to align with the focus of the original *Economics and Politics* volume (Norpoth, Lewis-Beck, and Lafay,

1991), we restrict our examination to countries attaining a certain level of economic stability and political democracy, as determined by membership in the Organization for Cooperation and Economic Development (OECD) by the end of the 1990s. The second criterion is data availability. To examine changes in the drivers of popularity, we select countries for which we can construct reliable measures of president/prime minister/government job approval at quarterly (or more frequent) intervals from 1990 (or earlier) to the present day.

These two criteria yield twenty countries: Australia, Austria, Canada, Czech Republic, Denmark, France, Germany, Greece, Ireland, Italy, Japan, Korea, Mexico, New Zealand, Poland, Portugal, Spain, Sweden, the United Kingdom, and the United States.[10] Data for our measure of public evaluations, *Approval*, are from the Executive Approval Dataset 2.0 described in the next chapter. We use a standard measure of executive approval equal to the percentage of respondents with positive views towards the executive's performance for the respective quarter.[11]

Table 1.1 reports contemporaneous correlations between *Approval* and *Objective Economy*, a variable constructed by standardizing and combining quarterly GDP growth, inflation, and unemployment (Carlin et al., 2021). These simple correlations do not control for electoral cycles, leadership change, or other factors, nor do they consider the lag structure of the relationship. They also cannot address dynamics of collective opinion, a topic addressed in Chapter 2. The bivariate correlations nonetheless provide a starting point for our inquiry. The first column provides a measure of association for the entire time series, 1990–2018. The evidence of an economy–popularity link is mixed, with a positive and statistically significant association between the economy and approval in half (ten out of twenty) of the countries.

The remaining columns in Table 1.1 report contemporaneous correlations in approximately ten-year increments. We divide time into three periods around two seminal events: the September 11, 2001, terrorist attacks in the United States—an event that reshaped the electoral agenda and made terrorism more salient around the globe—and the 2008 Global Financial Crisis. Fewer observations per cell make it more difficult to reject the null of no correlation. Nevertheless, it seems clear that the average correlation was much

[10] Countries that meet the first criterion but not the second are Belgium, Finland, Hungary, Iceland, Luxembourg, the Netherlands, Norway, Switzerland, and Turkey.

[11] For France, Korea, Mexico, and the United States, *Approval* refers to evaluations of the president. For the remaining countries, *Approval* refers to evaluations of the prime minister or government. An alternative measure incorporates approval and disapproval into a measure of relative approval; however, in some cases this would reduce series length. While the EAD has both a smoothed and an unsmoothed version of this series, we use the unsmoothed series to capture small shifts in approval.

Table 1.1 Executive approval and the objective economy: contemporaneous correlations

	All 1990*–2019	Period 1 1990–9/11, 2001	Period 2 9/11, 2001–2008 Crisis	Period 3 2008 Crisis—2019
Australia (1990–2018)	**0.23**	**0.46**	**−0.40**	**−0.33**
Austria (1990–2019)	0.13	−0.29	0.07	−0.06
Canada (1990–2018)	**0.58**	**0.80**	0.04	−0.07
Czech Republic (PM) (1998–2018)	−0.00	−0.11	**0.44**	0.30
Denmark (1990–2019)	0.08	0.08	0.11	0.16
France (Pres) (1990–2019)	**0.27**	**0.76**	0.01	**−0.31**
Germany (1990–2019)	**0.41**	**0.72**	**0.55**	**−0.35**
Greece (1998–2019)	**0.47**	0.25	−0.05	−0.11
Ireland (1990–2018)	**0.23**	**0.66**	0.20	0.17
Italy (1995–2018)	**−0.45**	**−0.50**	0.12	**−0.47**
Japan (1990–2019)	0.16	0.09	0.18	0.29
South Korea (1990–2018)	−0.16	−0.25	−0.25	**0.35**
Mexico (1990–2019)	0.03	**0.63**	0.28	**−0.36**
New Zealand (1990–2019)	−0.01	0.10	**0.55**	**−0.44**
Poland (PM) (1996–2018)	**0.26**	0.27	**0.37**	**0.32**
Portugal (PM) (1990–2018)	**0.24**	−0.14	−0.04	**0.52**
Spain (1990–2019)	**0.70**	**0.81**	0.27	**0.34**
Sweden (1990–2019)	0.07	**0.49**	**−0.50**	−0.21
United Kingdom (1990–2019)	**0.31**	**0.37**	**0.46**	**0.37**
United States (1990–2019)	−0.01	−0.17	0.20	**−0.23**
Mean *r*	0.18	0.25	0.13	−0.01
Share positively signed, p<0.05	10/20	9/20	5/20	5/20

* or earliest available.
Source: Executive Approval Project, World Bank, IMF, and OECD.
Notes: Cells report Pearson r correlation coefficients. Boldface type are statistically significant at $p < 0.05$. Observations are, for column 1, ≥ 97 for columns 2–4, ≥ 28.

stronger in the pre-9/11 era than in subsequent periods. The bivariate correlation is significant and positive in nine of twenty countries between 1990 and 2001 compared to just five during the 2000s as well as since the Global Financial Crisis. The average bivariate correlation falls from 0.25 to −0.01 over those three decades as well.

Trends in the economy–approval relationship aside, a more fundamental and definitive conclusion is that the correlation between the objective economy and approval is far from robust. This may be because other factors—like competing issues or partisan-motivated reasoning—have blunted the economy's effects. Or it could be due to slippage between objective economic outcomes and how the public experiences the economy. Researchers increasingly examine the interplay between government popularity and the public's subjective economic assessments. Use of subjective indicators bypasses questions of which economic indicator is most important or how the public processes mixed economic outcomes, or how it absorbs the process by which macroeconomic information is filtered and processed by the media and other actors. Accordingly, we replicate our analyses substituting the objective economy for the subjective one, using consumer confidence survey data from the EU, OECD, and other sources.[12]

Results are reported in Table 1.2. The first column shows that over the period 1990–2018 there is a positive and statistically significant correlation ($p < 0.05$, two-tailed) between the economy and *Approval* in three-quarters of the country cases. Though the strength of the association varies considerably, this suggests that on balance popular support tracks views of the economy, albeit to different degrees.

The remaining columns again report correlations by decade. On average, correlations were stronger in the pre-9/11 era than in subsequent periods. The bivariate correlation is significant and positive in 58 per cent of the countries (ten of the seventeen for which we have data) between 1990 and September 11, compared to 40 per cent (eight of twenty) during the 2000s and 35 per cent (seven of twenty) since the Global Financial Crisis. But these trends mask heterogeneity across countries. The importance of the economy has declined for eleven countries: Australia, Austria, Canada,[13] France, Germany, Ireland, Italy, Mexico, Spain, and Great Britain, while consumer sentiment has had a growing influence in just three: the Czech Republic, Denmark, Japan. For a second group, the relationship is strong before 9/11, fades in its aftermath, and rebounds after 2008. This group includes two countries beset by Europe's sovereign debt crisis, Greece and Portugal, as well as Sweden and South Korea. Finally, we see the strongest connection between the economy and evaluations of the executive in New Zealand and the United States in the middle period, which is surprising given the presumed salience of terrorism and wars in the latter case.

Thus, while there have always been countries where support for elected leaders did not correspond to economic factors, the number of countries

[12] We standardize the series to create a common measure. Details on the sources and measures of consumer confidence series are provided in Chapter 15.

[13] Trends for Canada based on the macro economy since the consumer confidence series is short.

Table 1.2 Executive approval and the subjective economy: contemporaneous correlations

	All 1990*–2019	Period 1 1990–9/11, 2001	Period 2 9/11, 2001–2008 Crisis	Period 3 2008 Crisis—2019
Australia (1990–2018)	**0.33**	**0.36**	−0.35	0.17
Austria (1995–2019)	**0.28**	**0.84**	0.23	0.23
Canada (2010–2018)	0.01	–	−0.04	0.14
Czech Republic (PM) (1998–2018)	0.00	**−0.51**	**0.42**	**0.39**
Denmark (1990–2019)	0.35	−0.14	−0.06	**0.42**
France (Pres) (1990–2019)	**0.63**	**0.80**	**0.56**	0.06
Germany (1990–2019)	**0.58**	**0.80**	**0.79**	−0.27
Greece (1997–2019)	**0.65**	**0.45**	0.12	**0.31**
Ireland (1990–2018)	**0.64**	**0.72**	**0.60**	**0.40**
Italy (1995–2018)	**−0.41**	0.07	−0.06	**−0.32**
Japan (1990–2019)	**0.21**	0.15	0.07	**0.54**
South Korea (1999–2018)	**0.49**	0.54	0.10	**0.48**
Mexico (2001–2019)	**0.51**	–	**0.47**	0.20
New Zealand (1990–2019)	0.06	−0.01	**0.54**	−0.15
Poland (PM) (2000–2019)	**0.30**	–	0.15	0.27
Portugal (PM) (1990–2018)	**0.40**	**0.57**	−0.13	**0.58**
Spain (1990–2019)	**0.43**	**0.76**	0.23	0.06
Sweden (1995–2019)	**0.39**	**0.68**	−0.15	**0.50**
United Kingdom (1990–2019)	**0.48**	**0.70**	**0.65**	0.25
United States (1990–2019)	**0.28**	0.21	**0.43**	−0.18
Mean *r*	0.33	0.41	0.23	0.20
Share positively signed, p<0.05	15/20	10/17	8/20	7/20

* or earliest available.
Source: Executive Approval Project, World Bank, IMF, and OECD.
Notes: Cells report Pearson r correlation coefficients. Boldface values are statistically significant at $p < 0.05$. Observations are, for column 1, ≥ 97 for columns 2–4, ≥ 28.

in which leader popularity is divorced from the economy appears to have increased with time. There is no universal pattern, however. Multiple mechanisms are at work. But there is little debate that the association between the economy and leader approval varies over time. Tables 1.1 and 1.2 are only a first cut. A full understanding of the dynamics of public support and the relative importance of the economy and other drivers requires more fine-grained analysis. The central task of this volume is to understand the bases of these differences and uncover the reasons for change over time. To do so, in the following chapters we present eleven single-country studies and a summary cross-national analysis. The next section previews these contributions.

Overview of the Book

As a collection, the chapters take us further than any previous volume in understanding the factors shaping executive approval in advanced democracies. This effort would not be possible without the Executive Approval Database (EAD). Accordingly, Chapter 2 provides readers with a primer on this essential resource. First, we offer an explanation for the study of executive approval as a concept of central concern to system support, regime resilience, and political stability, distinguishing it from measures of vote intention. We then describe the structure of the data, how they are compiled, and how users can customize the indicators—in terms of content and aggregation—to fit their needs.

The country case studies in Chapters 3–13 constitute the heart of the volume. Each chapter is written by scholars who both have deep knowledge of their country case and are skilled analysts of macro public opinion. Each chapter does four main things: i) it describes the country's landscape and identifies how its distinct political, economic, and cultural features may be reflected in popular support; ii) it situates the analysis following a review of findings from existing scholarship; iii) it advances a set of claims about the drivers of approval *and their change over time*; and iv) it tests claims and contending arguments using the EAD. So, while chapters tend to have a common framework, they vary in emphasis, based on key features of the country in question.

Chapters take different approaches to modelling change. In terms of the three approaches identified above—the clarity of responsibility, issue salience, and political predispositions—chapters on Britain, France, Portugal, and Japan pay particular attention to the first dimension. Most of these cases, but not all, show that differences in political alignment shape the public's response to the economy. The first chapter finds at best partial support for the clarity of responsibility hypothesis. John Bartle, Sebastian Dellepiane, and Anthony McGann provide an analysis of popular support for the British prime minister. Britain is unique in that power in the Westminster model is concentrated in the government. Adding to this high clarity setting has been a tradition, beginning with Margaret Thatcher's election in 1979, of long interrupted periods of single-party government. The Conservative Party led the government for seventeen years until 1997, followed by thirteen years of

Labour in charge. The authors show that this unique set of factors gives the economy an outsized role in driving public opinion towards the prime minister. The British political system, they argue, is characterized by stability and continuity. While there has been some institutional change, no development has altered the basic story of responsiveness and accountability. Consistent with arguments about the economic drivers of the clarity of responsibility, the authors find that the move towards central bank independence modified the relationship between interest rates and approval. Yet the extraordinary (for Britain, at least) coalition government period between 2010 and 2015 did not modify the relationship between policy advantage and approval as the clarity of responsibility model would predict.

The next two chapters, on France and Portugal, focus on the nature of presidential–legislative relations in semi-presidential systems and find more evidence that institutional arrangements condition executive approval. Although France and Portugal both feature popularly elected presidents, the role of the president in each system is very different with important implications for executive approval dynamics. Emiliano Grossman and Isabelle Guinaudeau's chapter on presidential popularity in France highlights the importance of two factors: the nature of the dual executive and the 'cost' of ruling. The authors observe a seemingly inexorable trend of French presidents having the will of the people at their backs when first elected, but then gradually falling out of favour. This secular decline in support, they assert, is exacerbated by a re-assertion of executive power in the office of the president. This point gets to the heart of the constitutional design of the Fifth Republic. While devised to have a strong president, the Constitution also separates the executive in two, relegating the day-to-day matters of governing and domestic policy to the prime minister so that the president can stay 'above politics'. The implication is that the prime minister is institutionally responsible for the health of the economy while the president represents the state on the world stage. Grossman and Guinaudeau, however, find that this separation is increasing irrelevant. Intriguingly, they find that the drivers of presidential approval vary across eras, from the early years of the Fifth Republic, to its post-1981 maturity, to the current era.

Like France, the Portuguese constitution also stipulates two executives. Unlike France, however, the weight of power is concentrated in the prime minister, with the president having a more ceremonial role. In their chapter, Luís Aguiar-Conraria, Bruno Fernandes, and Pedro Magalhães ask whether this distinction nevertheless matters for popular support. Extant research, they point out, identifies a puzzle: if the Portuguese president has evolved to being 'above parties' and serving as a moderating lever on partisan policy, why do studies find his popularity to be so sensitive to economic conditions? To address this question, the authors draw insights from the asymmetric effects of growing and contracting economies, from the cost of ruling, and from how term limits shape policy behaviour. The result is a novel finding that the influence of the economy on prime ministerial and presidential approval depends not only on partisan alignment of the dual executive, but also on the president's (lack of) re-election incentives. More broadly, the chapter provides new insights into how the constitutional rules of the game matter.

The chapter on Japan demonstrates that approval ratings reflect discrete policy changes put in place by governments. The case of Japan is notable in many respects, not least of which is that government approval is *more* closely linked to economic evaluations in recent decades than in previous times (see also Table 1.2, this chapter). This, as Hanako Ohmura and Airo Hino note, may be due to shifts in the government's policy regime facilitated by a political context that concentrates power in the executive. In late 2012 the government of Shinzo Abe took a concerted effort at reigniting Japan's sluggish economy. The policy regime, known as the 'three arrows', emphasized (i) aggressive monetary policy, mainly by way of easing; (ii) fiscal consolidation and stimulus; and (iii) a strategy aimed at short-term growth. This more activist regime may well have activated the economy in the minds of the public. Also notable in terms of over-time change is the fact that while support for Japan's ruling party generally predicts government job approval, the relationship ebbs and flows over time. Both these findings speak to the importance of individual actors' abilities to shape—or manipulate—public sentiment.

A second set of chapters—on Italy, Spain, Canada, and Germany—call our attention to how shifts in issue salience fundamentally affect public evaluations of the executive. The analyses of Italy and Spain, in particular, demonstrate that the economy is not the only performance gauge on which prime ministers are evaluated. Examining the Italian case over a tumultuous twenty-year period, Paolo Bellucci and Vincenzo Memoli show that economic perceptions are weakly associated with government approval, despite reductions in party-system fragmentation since earlier waves of studies, although the public does seem to sanction the government for raising inequality. Instead, political factors matter more as government scandals bring down approval levels, and the effect is magnified by the amount of media coverage accorded to governments. They further indicate that perceptions of freedom of expression, association, and media are positively associated with higher job performance for the prime minister. Finally, they report evidence that the 2008 Great Recession increased the salience of both corruption and inequality for the Italian public. All told, Bellucci and Memoli's study illustrates the mix of factors on which prime ministers are evaluated and how their importance varies over time.

Similarly, Xavier Romero, Lluís Orriols, and Pedro Riera's study of Spain also highlights the relative importance of non-economic factors. The authors demonstrate that the economy shapes the approval of Spain's prime ministers consistently since the 1980s but that its effect varies as the economy's performance changes. In particular, the economy–approval relationship is stronger during the volatile periods in the 1990s and again after the financial crisis of 2007–2008 whereas it became weaker during the periods where the economy was more stable. The economy's *stronger* influence in the latter time period goes against the predictions of attributions of responsibility models that would have expected increased party-system fragmentation in Spain to suppress the economy's effect. But one cannot understand movements in approval in Spain with the economy alone. Notably, prime ministers tend to receive a 'rally round the flag' bump in the wake of terrorist attacks and also benefit when public mood aligns with the government's priorities.

Analysis of government popularity in Canada also stresses the importance of issue salience and reveals the importance of how the public perceives policy. As with many other countries covered in this volume, Éric Bélanger and Olivier Jacques show that the economy's influence on federal government approval has weakened over time. Perhaps more notable, however, they also find that fiscal policy components—individual and corporate income taxes, as well as budget balance—have an independent effect on approval. The authors note that the effect of the budget balance has changed over time. Prior to the early 1990s, Canadians rewarded their governments for running deficits, ostensibly reflecting support for popular social policies. Around the early 1990s, however, the public became more hawkish on the budget, rewarding the federal government for budget control efforts. Bélanger and Jacques suggest that the government's attention to austerity as sound economic management, put forward since the 1990s, has convinced many Canadians that balanced budgets are preferable to runaway spending.

The chapter on Germany focuses on how the media's delivery of economic information shapes executive ratings. Mark Kayser and Arndt Leininger argue that a heretofore overlooked source of instability in popularity functions is the actual data employed by analysts who tend to link movements in aggregate public opinion to movements of economic indicators. However, national statistics offices routinely revise these data making the economic information that scholars base their work on different from the data disseminated by the media and available to the public at the time of the survey. Analysts use revised data; survey respondents use 'vintage' data. Correcting this mismatch, Kayser and Leininger show that the impact of GDP growth on chancellor job approval is stronger and more robust when growth is based on these real-time 'vintage' estimates. Intriguingly, they further show that growth's positive influence weakens over time and that the gap between revised and real-time estimates is greater in 2010–2019 than in previous decades. If the authors are right in their claims that the media, as information provider, is to blame for the size of this gap, then the implication is that media effects may well have increased over time.

The last set of country chapters, on Greece, Denmark, and the United States, share a concern with how party positioning conditions the relationship between the economy and executive approval. In the first-ever study on prime ministerial approval in Greece, Panos Koliastasis and John Yfantopoulos probe the effects of the political *and* economic context on the public's approval of the prime minister's job in office. The Greek case allows us to consider the impact of wide-ranging economic and political upheaval on approval ratings. Greece's sovereign debt crisis in 2007 ushered in a period of pronounced economic decline, austerity, and rollbacks of social welfare, and, ostensibly, a lack of policy control on the part of national leaders in an effort to satisfy the demands of European and international lenders (the 'Troika'). Economic change fuelled political upheaval in a system notable, until then, for reasonably predictable politics—alternating between PASOK on the left and New Democracy on the right. In spite of unprecedented economic upheaval and party-system change, however, the authors find that the limits imposed on domestic governments by international financial institutions reduced the importance of perceived economic trends in the post-Memorandum era.

With a dynamic multi-party system, the Danish case contributes to our understanding of how shifts in conflict and cooperation among elites are reflected in citizen evaluations of government performance. Henrik Seeberg observes that in recent years Denmark has seen falling party polarization and a weakening of partisanship-based and cleavage-based political behaviour. This has created greater space for the economy to matter for executive approval as a valence issue even as its salience relative to non-economic issues has fallen. With an increasingly volatile electorate, more people are willing to change their mind about the government based on its performance.

The last country chapter addresses the most-studied case, the job approval of the president of the United States. The nature of American politics has changed drastically and several times over since Mueller's (1970; 1973) pioneering studies of public opinion during the 1950s and 1960s. The United States' role in the world has shrunk and its politics has become more partisan and more polarized. Surveying this landscape, Kathleen Donovan, Paul Kellstedt, Ellen Key, and Matthew Lebo examine presidential approval ratings from the 1970s through to the Trump Administration. Consistent with the general message of this volume, they show that the influence of economic sentiment on approval has weakened in recent times. Leveraging unique data on in- and out-partisans and updating their analysis of earlier presidencies with new data, the authors convincingly show that partisan attachments rendered economic fluctuations almost meaningless during the Obama and Trump presidencies. One implication of these findings is that if this trend continues into the Biden years and beyond, we may witness a permanent disconnect between system performance (as gauged by economic sentiment) and evaluations of policymakers. Donovan et al.'s chapter speaks to the need to slow or reverse the march towards greater tribalism and polarization that has beset American politics if we are to return to a more rational, and more accountable, form of democracy.

The final two chapters in the volume step back from country-specific approval dynamics to consider the big—comparative—picture. Chapter 14 begins with a return to the beginning, to *Economics and Politics: The Calculus of Support*, and traces developments in the study of executive popularity to today and beyond. In 'Economics and Approval: Past, Present, and Future', Mary Stegmaier, Brandon Beomseob Park, and Michael Lewis-Beck (one of the co-editors of the original *Economics and Politics* volume) revisit Paldam's classic chapter 'How Robust Is the Vote Function'. After taking stock of what we have learned in the intervening thirty-plus years, they assess the relative influence of economic and political factors—what Paldam memorably deemed the 'e' and 'p' fractions—on government popularity based on the country-specific evidence compiled in this volume. Drawing on Arend Lijphart's (1971) typology and considering whether the country case study chapters are consistent with classic economic-voting theories, they classify the lion's share of this volume's country chapters as theory *confirming*, either *fully* (Japan, Britain, Portugal, and France) or partially (Spain, Greece, Canada, Italy, and Denmark). The US case is theory *infirming*, in that the economy is shown to have weak and inconsistent effects, while the German study, with its comparison of vintage and revised data, appears both as a *deviant* and partially confirming case. Thus, while they recognize that the strength of the economy–politics relationship varies, they argue that economics remain a common driver of leader support in this sample. They conclude, however, by reflecting on other factors that may become impactful in the future and that may change this relationship.

Lastly, Chapter 15 reviews findings from the country chapters to offer an over-arching comprehensive assessment of the economy and executive approval. Synthesizing insights from the eleven country chapters, Timothy Hellwig and Matthew Singer advance a set of possible explanations for persistent instability in popularity functions. They revisit the three sets of factors introduced above: context, issue saliency, and political dispositions. Examining executive approval in twenty countries over three-plus decades, they find evidence that the VP function is shaped more by issue salience and political dispositions than by macro political and economic contexts. In particular, political elites have the capacity to shape approval dynamics through their messaging and the degree of polarization on non-economic issues. These results echo those from the country chapters: changes to the public agenda and to the electorate's willingness to be persuaded are fundamentally reshaping the nature of political accountability in countries where they have occurred.

References

Abramowitz, A., and Webster, S. (2016). The rise of negative partisanship and the nationalization of U.S. elections in the 21st century. *Electoral Studies, 41*(March), 12–22.

Achen, C., and Bartels, L. (2016). *Democracy for Realists.* Princeton, NJ: Princeton University Press.

Adler, D., and Ansell, B. (2020). Housing and populism. *West European Politics, 43*(2), 344–65.

Anderson, C. (2007). The end of economic voting? Contingency dilemmas and the limits of democratic accountability. *Annual Review of Political Science, 10,* 271–96.

Anderson, C., Mendes, S., and Tverdova, Y. (2004). Endogenous economic voting: Evidence from the 1997 British election. *Electoral Studies, 23,* 683–708.

Anderson, C., and Tverdova, T. (2003). Corruption, political allegiances, and attitudes toward government in contemporary democracies. *American Journal of Political Science, 47*(1), 91–109.

Anduiza, E., Gallego, A., and Muñoz, J. (2013). Turning a blind eye: Experimental evidence of partisan bias in attitudes toward corruption. *Comparative Political Studies, 46*(12), 1664–92.

Ansolabehere, S., Meredith, M., and Snowberg, E. (2014). Mecro-economic voting: Local information and micro-perceptions of the macro-economy. *Economics and Politics*, *26*(3), 380–410.

Ashworth, S,. and Bueno de Mesquita, E. (2014). Is voter competence good for voters? *American Political Science Review*, *108*(3), 565–87.

Aytac, S. (2018). Relative economic performance and the incumbent vote: A reference point theory. *The Journal of Politics*, *80*(1), 16–29.

Baird, V., and Wolak, J. (2021). Why some blame politics for their personal problems. *American Politics Research*, *49*(5), 478–89.

Barro, R. J. (1973). The control of politicians: An economic model. *Public Choice 14*, 19–42.

Bartels, L. M. (2013). Political effects of the Great Recession. *The ANNALS of the American Academy of Political and Social Science*, *650*(1), 47–76.

Bengtsson, Å. (2004). Economic voting: The effect of political context, volatility and turnout on voters' assignment of responsibility. *European Journal of Political Research*, *43*(5), 749–67.

Berlingieri, G., Blanchenay, P., and Criscuolo, C. (2017). The great divergence(s). https://doi.org/10.1787/953f3853-en.

Besley, T., and Case, A. (1995). Incumbent behavior: vote-seeking, tax-setting, and yardstick competition. *The American Economic Review*, *85*(1): 25–45.

Bloom, H. S., and Price, H. D. (1975). Voter response to short-run economic conditions: The asymmetric effect of prosperity and recession. *American Political Science Review*, *69*(4), 1240–54.

Bol, D., Giani, M., Blais, A., and Loewen, P. J. (2021). The effect of COVID-19 lockdowns on political support: Some good news for democracy? *European Journal of Political Research*, *60*(2), 497–505.

Brody, R. (1991). *Assessing the President: The Media, Elite Opinion, and Public Support*. Stanford, CA: Stanford University Press.

Campello, D., and Zucco Jr, C. (2016). Presidential success and the world economy. *The Journal of Politics*, *78*(2), 589–602.

Carlin, R. E., Hartlyn, J., Hellwig, T., Love, G. J., Martínez-Gallardo, C., and Singer, M. M. (2018). Public support for Latin American presidents: The cyclical model in comparative perspective. *Research & Politics*, *5*(3), 2053168018787690.

Carlin, R. E., & Hellwig, T. (2019). Policy regimes and economic accountability in Latin America. *Comparative Political Studies*, *52*(13–14), 2032–60.

Carlin, R. E., and Hellwig, T. (2020). The world economy, political control, and presidential success. *The Journal of Politics*, *82*(2), 786–99.

Carlin, R. E., Hellwig, T., Love, G. J., Martínez-Gallardo, C., and Singer, M. M. (2021). When does the public get it right? the information environment and the accuracy of economic sentiment. *Comparative Political Studies*, *54*(9), 1499–533.

Carlin, R. E., and Love, G. L. (2020). Populist popularity: Plebiscitarian vs. polarizing perspectives. Presented at the Conference of the World Association for Public Opinion Research-Latin America, December 2020, Salamanca, Spain.

Cheibub, J., and Przeworski, A. (1999). Democracy, elections, and accountability for economic outcomes. In *Democracy, Accountability, and Representation*, A. Przeworski, S. C. Stokes, and B. Manin, eds. New York: Cambridge University Press. 222–50.

Damstra, A., Boukes, M., and Vliegenthart, R. (2021). To credit or to blame? The asymmetric impact of government responsibility in economic news. *International Journal of Public Opinion Research*, *33*(1), 1–17.

Dassonneville, R. (2016). Volatile voters, short-term choices? An analysis of the vote choice determinants of stable and volatile voters in Great Britain. *Journal of Elections, Public Opinion and Parties*, *26*(3), 273–92.

Dassonneville, R., and Lewis-Beck, M. S. (2014). Macroeconomics, economic crisis and electoral outcomes: A national European pool. *Acta politica*, *49*(4), 372–94.

Dassonneville, R., and Lewis-Beck, M. S. (2019). A changing economic vote in Western Europe? Long-term vs. short-term forces. *European Political Science Review*, *11*(1), 91–108.

De Boef, S., and Kellstedt, P. M. (2004). The political (and economic) origins of consumer confidence. *American Journal of Political Science*, *48*(4), 633–49.

De Vries, C. E., and Giger, N. (2014). Holding governments accountable? Individual heterogeneity in performance voting. *European Journal of Political Research*, *53*(2), 345–62.

De Vries, C. E., and Hobolt, S. B. (2020), eds., *Political Entrepreneurs*. Princeton N.J.: Princeton University Press.

Donovan, K., Kellstedt, P. M., Key, E. M., and Lebo, M. J. (2020). Motivated reasoning, public opinion, and presidential approval. *Political Behavior*, *42*(4), 1201–21.

Druckman, J. N., and Holmes, J. W. (2004). Does presidential rhetoric matter? Priming and presidential approval. *Presidential Studies Quarterly*, *34*(4), 755–78.

Duch, R. M., and Falcó-Gimeno, A. (2022). Collective decision-making and the economic vote. *Comparative Political Studies*, *55*(5), 757–88.

Duch, R. M., Palmer, H. D, and Anderson, C. J. (2000). Heterogeneity in perceptions of national economic conditions. *American Journal of Political Science*, *44*(4): 635–52.

Duch, R. M., and Stevenson, R. T. (2008). *The Economic Vote*. New York: Cambridge University Press.

Edwards III, G. C., Mitchell, W., and Welch, R. (1995). Explaining presidential approval: The significance of issue salience. *American Journal of Political Science* *39*(1), 108–34.

Eggers, A. C. (2014). Partisanship and electoral accountability: Evidence from the UK expenses scandal. *Quarterly Journal of Political Science*, *9*(4), 441–72.

Ellis, C. R., and Ura, J. D. (2021). Polarization and the decline of economic voting in American national elections. *Social Science Quarterly*, *102*(1), 83–9.

Eshbaugh-Soha, M., and Peake, J. 2005. Presidents and the economic agenda. *Political Research Quarterly*, *58*(1), 127–38.

Evans, G., and Andersen, R. (2006). The political conditioning of economic perceptions. *The Journal of Politics*, *68*(1), 194–207.

Evans, G., and Chzhen, K. (2016). Re-evaluating the valence model of political choice. *Political Science Research and Methods*, *4*(1), 199–220.

Fearon, J. D. (1999). Electoral accountability and the control of politicians: Selecting good types versus sanctioning poor performance. In *Democracy, Accountability, and Representation*, A. Przeworski, S. C. Stokes, and B. Manin, eds. New York: Cambridge University Press. 131–53.

Feldman, S. (1982). Economic self-interest and political behavior. *American Journal of Political Science* *25*(3), 446–66.

Ferejohn, J. (1986). Incumbent performance and electoral control. *Public choice*, *50*(1–3), 5–25.

Fiorina, M. P. (1981). *Retrospective Voting in American National Elections*. New Haven, CT: Yale University Press.

Fossati, D. (2014). Economic vulnerability and economic voting in 14 OECD countries. *European Journal of Political Research*, *53*(1), 116–35.

Fumarola, A. (2020). The contexts of electoral accountability: Electoral integrity performance voting in 23 democracies. *Government and Opposition*, *55*(1), 41–63.

Garzia, D., Ferreira da Silva, F., and De Angelis, A. (2022). Partisan dealignment and the personalisation of politics in West European parliamentary democracies, 1961–2018. *West European Politics*, *45*(2), 311–34.

Gélineau, F., and Singer, M. M. (2015). The economy and incumbent support in Latin America. In *The Latin American Voter: Pursuing Representation and Accountability in Challenging Contexts*, R. E. Carlin, M. M. Singer, and E. J. Zechmeister, eds. Ann Arbor, MI: University of Michigan Press. 281–99.

Gerber, A. S., and Huber, G. A. (2010). Partisanship, political control, and economic assessments. *American Journal of Political Science*, *54*(1), 153–73.

Green, J., Hellwig, T., and Fieldhouse, E. (2022). Who gets what: The economy, relative gains and Brexit. *British Journal of Political Science*, *52*(1), 320–38.

Hart, A. (2016). *Economic Voting: A Campaign-Centered Theory*. New York: Cambridge University Press.

Hayes, R. C., Imai, M., and Shelton, C. A. (2015). Attribution error in economic voting: Evidence from trade shocks. *Economic Inquiry*, *53*(1), 258–75.

Healy, A., Kuo, A. G., and Malhotra, N. (2014). Partisan bias in blame attribution: When does it occur? *Journal of Experimental Political Science*, *1*(2), 144–58.

Healy, A. J., Persson, M., and Snowberg, E. (2017). Digging into the pocketbook: Evidence on economic voting from income registry data matched to a voter survey. *American Political Science Review, 111*(4), 771–85.

Helgason, A. F., and Mérola, V. (2017). Employment insecurity, incumbent partisanship, and voting behavior in comparative perspective. *Comparative Political Studies, 50*(11), 1489–523.

Hellwig, T. (2007). Economic openness, policy uncertainty, and the dynamics of government support. *Electoral Studies, 26*(4), 772–86.

Hellwig, T. (2012). Constructing accountability: Party position taking and economic voting. *Comparative Political Studies, 45*(1), 91–118.

Hellwig, T. (2015). *Globalization and Mass Politics: Retaining the Room to Maneuver.* New York: Cambridge University Press.

Hellwig, T., and Marinova, D. M. (2017). Dead ends and new paths in the study of economic voting. In *Oxford Research Encyclopedia of Politics.* https://doi.org/10.1093/acrefore/9780190228637.013.190

Hellwig, T., and McAllister, I. (2019). Party positions, asset ownership, and economic voting. *Political Studies, 67*(4), 912–31.

Hellwig, T., and Samuels, D. (2008). Electoral accountability and the variety of democratic regimes. *British Journal of Political Science, 38*(1), 65–90.

Hibbs, D. A. (1977). Political parties and macroeconomic policy. *American Political Science Review, 71*(4), 1467–87.

Hobolt, S., Tilley, J., and Banducci, S. (2013). Clarity of responsibility: How government cohesion conditions performance voting. *European Journal of Political Research, 52*(2), 164–87.

Hooghe, L., and Marks, G. (2018). Cleavage theory meets Europe's crises: Lipset, Rokkan, and the transnational cleavage. *Journal of European Public Policy, 25*(1), 109–35.

Hutter, S., Kriesi, H., and Vidal, G. (2018). Old versus new politics: The political spaces in Southern Europe in times of crises. *Party Politics, 24*(1), 10–22.

Inglehart, R. (1977). *The Silent Revolution: Changing Values and Political Styles among Western Publics.* Princeton, NJ: Princeton University Press.

Inglehart, R. F. (2008). Changing values among Western publics from 1970 to 2006. *West European Politics, 31*(1–2), 130–46.

Jung, D. J. (2018). Does partisanship hurt electoral accountability? Individual-level and aggregate-level comparisons of Western and postcommunist democracies. *East European Politics and Societies, 32*(1), 168–201.

Kayser, M. A. (2014). The elusive economic vote. In *Comparing Democracies, 4: Elections and Voting in a Changing World,* L. Leduc, R. Niemi, and P. Norris, eds. Thousand Oaks, CA: Sage. 112–32.

Kayser, M. A., and Leininger, A. (2015). Vintage errors: Do real-time economic data improve election forecasts? *Research & Politics, 2*(3), 2053168015589624.

Kayser, M. A., and Peress, M. (2012). Benchmarking across borders: Electoral accountability and the necessity of comparison. *American Political Science Review*, *106*(3), 661–84.

Kayser, M. A., and Wlezien, C. (2011). Performance pressure: Patterns of partisanship and the economic vote. *European Journal of Political Research*, *50*(3), 365–94.

Kelleher, C. A., and Wolak, J. (2006). Priming presidential approval: The conditionality of issue effects. *Political Behavior*, *28*(3), 193–210.

Key, V. O., Jr. (1964). *Politics, Parties, and Pressure Groups*. New York: Thomas Y. Crowell.

Kinder, D. R., and Kiewiet, D. R. (1981). Sociotropic politics: The American case. *British Journal of Political Science*, *11*(2), 129–61.

Kirchgässner, G. (1991). Homo oeconomicus: Das ökonomische Modell individuellen Verhaltens und seine Anwendung in den Wirtschafts- und Sozialwissenschaften. *Die Einheit der Gesellschaftswissenschaften*.

Kramer, G. H. (1983). The ecological fallacy revisited: Aggregate-versus individual-level findings on economics and elections, and sociotropic voting. *American Political Science Review*, *77*(1), 92–111.

Kriesi, H., Grande, E., Lachat, R., Dolezal, M., Bornschier, S., and Frey, T. (2008). *West European Politics in the Age of Globalization*. Cambridge: Cambridge University Press.

Krosnick, J. A., and Brannon, L. A. (1993). The impact of the Gulf War on the ingredients of presidential evaluations: Multidimensional effects of political involvement. *American Political Science Review*, *87*(4), 963–75.

Lewis-Beck, M. S. (1988). *Economics and Elections: The Major Western Democracies*. Ann Arbor, MI: University of Michigan Press.

Lewis-Beck, M. S., and Nadeau, R. (2011). Economic voting theory: Testing new dimensions. *Electoral Studies*, *30*(2), 288–94.

Lewis-Beck, M. S., and Stegmaier, M. (2000). Economic determinants of electoral outcomes. *Annual Review of Political Science*, *3*(1), 183–219.

Lewis-Beck, M. S., and Stegmaier, M. (2018). Economic voting. In *The Oxford Handbook of Public Choice*, R. Congleton, B.Grofman, and S. Voigt. New York: Oxford University Press. 247–65.

Lindvall, J., and Rueda, D. (2014). The insider–outsider dilemma. *British Journal of Political Science*, *44*(2), 460–75.

Lijphart, A. (1971). Comparative politics and the comparative method. *American Political Science Review*, *65*(3), 682–93.

Lobo, M. C., and Pannico, R. (2020). Increased economic salience or blurring of responsibility? Economic voting during the great recession. *Electoral Studies*, *65*, 102141.

MacKuen, M. B., Erikson, R. S., and Stimson, J. A. (1992). Peasants or bankers? The American electorate and the US economy. *American Political Science Review, 86*(3), 597–611.

Magalhães, P. (2020). Public opinion and executive approval. In *The Oxford Handbook of Political Executives*, eds. R. B. Andeweg, R. Elgie, L. Helms, and J. Kaarbo, eds. Oxford: Oxford University Press. 637–45.

Markus, G. B. (1988). The impact of personal and national economic conditions on the presidential vote: A pooled cross-sectional analysis. *American Journal of Political Science 32*(1), 137–54.

Marx, P. (2016). The insider–outsider divide and economic voting: Testing a new theory with German electoral data. *Socio-Economic Review, 14*(1), 97–118.

Mueller, J. E. (1970). Presidential popularity from Truman to Johnson. *American Political Science Review, 64*(1), 18–34.

Mueller, J. E. (1973). *War, Presidents, and Public Opinion*. New York: Wiley.

Nadeau, R., and Lewis-Beck, M. S. (2001). National economic voting in US presidential elections. *The Journal of Politics, 63*(1), 159–81.

Nadeau, R., Lewis-Beck, M. S., and Bélanger, É. (2013). Economics and elections revisited. *Comparative Political Studies, 46*(5), 551–73.

Nadeau, R., Niemi, R. G., and Yoshinaka, A. (2002). A cross-national analysis of economic voting: Taking account of the political context across time and nations. *Electoral Studies, 21*(3), 403–23.

Nannestad, P., and Paldam, M. (1994). The VP-function: A survey of the literature on vote and popularity functions after 25 years. *Public Choice, 79*(3), 213–45.

Norpoth, H., Lewis-Beck, M. S., and Lafay, J.-D. (1991). *Economics and Politics: The Calculus of Support*. Ann Arbor, MI: University of Michigan Press.

Norris, P., and Inglehart, R. (2019). *Cultural Backlash: Trump, Brexit, and Authoritarian Populism*. New York: Cambridge University Press.

Newman, B., & Otto, A. (2022). Polls and Elections: The economy and events still matter (At least a little): Partisans' presidential approval in the Trump era. *Presidential Studies Quarterly, 52*(1), 208–23.

Paldam, M. (1991). How robust is the vote function?: A study of seventeen nations over four decades. In *Economics and Politics: The Calculus of Support*, H. Norpoth, M. S. Lewis-Beck, and J.-D. Lafay, eds. Ann Arbor, MI: University of Michigan Press. 9–31.

Park, B. B. (2019). Compared to what? Media-guided reference points and relative economic voting. *Electoral Studies, 62*, 102085.

Powell Jr, G. B., and Whitten, G. D. (1993). A cross-national analysis of economic voting: Taking account of the political context. *American Journal of Political Science 37*(2), 391–414.

Remmer, K. (2003). Elections and economics in contemporary Latin America. In *Post-Stabilization Politics in Latin America: Competition, Transition, Collapse*, Carol Wise and Riordan Roett, eds. Washington, DC: Brookings. 31–55.

Singer, M. M. (2011a). Who says 'it's the economy'? Cross-national and cross-individual variation in the salience of economic performance. *Comparative Political Studies*, *44*(3), 284–312.

Singer, M. M. (2011b). Economic voting and welfare programmes: Evidence from the American states. *European Journal of Political Research*, *50*(4), 479–503.

Singer, M. M. (2013a). The global economic crisis and domestic political agendas. *Electoral Studies*, *32*(2), 404–10.

Singer, M. M. (2013b). Should nervous workers make incumbents worry about their own job prospects? Evidence from developing countries. *European Journal of Political Research*, *52*(2), 143–63.

Singer, M. M. (2016). Informal sector work and evaluations of the incumbent: The electoral effect of vulnerability on economic voting. *Latin American Politics and Society*, *58*(2), 49–73.

Singer, M. M. (2018). Personal economic struggles and heterogeneous government approval after the Great Recession. *Public Opinion Quarterly*, *82*(3), 524–52.

Singer, M. M. (2020). Conditional accountability for the economy, insecurity, and corruption across Latin American party systems. *Latin American Politics and Society*, *62*(4), 126–52.

Singer, M. M. (2021). It's NOT the economy when people are dying: Accountability for household economic and health outcomes during the pandemic. *Journal of Elections, Public Opinion and Parties*, *31*(supplement 1), 155–66.

Singer, M. M., and Carlin, R. E. (2013). Context counts: The election cycle, development, and the nature of economic voting. *The Journal of Politics*, *75*(3), 730–42.

Solaz, H., De Vries, C. E., and De Geus, R. A. (2019). In-group loyalty and the punishment of corruption. *Comparative Political Studies*, *52*(6), 896–926.

Soroka, S. N. (2006). Good news and bad news: Asymmetric responses to economic information. *The Journal of Politics*, *68*(2), 372–85.

Stewart, M., and Clarke, H. (2017). Economic voting. In *The Routledge Handbook of Elections, Voting Behavior and Public Opinion*, J. Fisher, E. Fieldhouse, M. N. Franklin, R. Gibson, M. Cantijoch, and C. Wlezien, eds. London: Routledge. 192–204.

Stiers, D., and Dassonneville, R. (2020). Retrospective voting and the polarization of available alternatives. *Canadian Journal of Political Science/Revue canadienne de science politique*, *53*(1), 99–115.

Tilley, J., Neundorf, A., and Hobolt, S. B. (2018). When the pound in people's pocket matters: How changes to personal financial circumstances affect party choice. *The Journal of Politics*, *80*(2), 555–69.

Van der Brug, W., Van der Eijk, C., and Franklin, M. (2007). *The Economy and the Vote: Economic Conditions and Elections in Fifteen Countries*. Cambridge: Cambridge University Press.

Vavreck, L. (2009). *The Message Matters: The Economy and Presidential Campaigns*. Princton, NJ: Princeton University Press.

Visconti, G. (2019). Economic perceptions and electoral choices: A design-based approach. *Political Science Research and Methods*, *7*(4), 795–813.

Weatherford, M. S. (1983). Economic voting and the 'symbolic politics' argument: A reinterpretation and synthesis. *American Political Science Review*, *77*(1), 158–74.

Wlezien, C., Franklin, M., and Twiggs, D. (1997). Economic perceptions and vote choice: Disentangling the endogeneity. *Political Behavior*, *19*(1), 7–17.

2

The Executive Approval Database

Conceptual and Empirical Bases

Ryan E. Carlin, Jonathan Hartlyn, Timothy Hellwig, Gregory J. Love, Cecilia Martínez-Gallardo, and Matthew Singer

Writing in the introduction to *Economics and Politics*, Lewis-Beck identifies 'the perennial first question' as 'Do voters respond to the economy?' (1991, 1). Tackling this question requires a temporal measure of the public's response that captures the dynamics of the economy and key events, but also minimizes concerns about the endogeneity inherent to cross-sectional data (Kramer, 1983). Paldam (1991) identifies two such measures: *vote* for the government—a 'V-function' with elections as the unit of analysis—and government *popularity*—a 'P-function' with more frequent units of analysis (e.g. annual, quarterly, monthly). A distinguishing feature of this volume is its exclusive use of P-functions.[1] Unlike the vote, popularity functions allow us to gauge how citizens update their response to economic outputs over time and help account for the diversity of executive institutional arrangements. A variety of popularity indicators have been employed in P-function research in different countries and eras, reflecting the accessibility, length, and methodological soundness of different time-series data at a given time and place. But any broadly comparative study of the economic reward/punishment hypothesis or related issues requires a measure of incumbent popularity that is valid and reliable across an array of contexts and gauged relatively frequently. Such an indicator has been hard to come by.

The Executive Approval Database (EAD; Carlin, Hartlyn, Hellwig, Love, Martinez-Gallardo, and Singer, 2016; 2019) was created to resolve this problem. Its annual and quarterly executive popularity estimates provide numerous analytical advantages. Generating these estimates, however, requires addressing several conceptual, methodological, and measurement problems. Below we identify these hurdles and describe how the Executive Approval Project

[1] Indeed, this is the only collection of studies ever published which exclusively features popularity functions; not even the original *Economics and Politics* (1991) volume was as singular in focus.

Ryan E. Carlin et al., *The Executive Approval Database*. In: *Economics and Politics Revisited*. Edited by: Timothy Hellwig and Matthew Singer, Oxford University Press. © Ryan E. Carlin et al. (2023). DOI: 10.1093/oso/9780192871664.003.0002

overcomes them. We begin with a conceptual question about the nature of executive approval before diving into more technical questions of methods and measurement. Along the way we outline key decision points allowing readers to judge the validity of the EAD's measures. Towards the end of the chapter, we discuss the properties of the dataset and the specific countries examined in this volume.

What Is Executive Approval?

Although dozens of studies have employed approval estimates from the EAD, very little has been done to conceptualize approval as a measure of support for the executive or to compare it to other similar indicators. We include ourselves in this critique. A clear discussion of the concept is long overdue. Here we identify the inter-related conceptual, methodological, and practical foundations upon which executive approval and, indeed, the EAD stand.

Executive approval is, first and foremost, a form of political support. As conceived by David Easton, *political support* refers to the way in which people evaluatively orient themselves to some object through either their attitudes or their behaviour (1975, 436). In our conception, approval is a current *attitudinal* indicator of support that can reflect favourable or unfavourable, positive or negative orientations towards an object of study—in this case the political executive. This conception distinguishes approval, an evaluative/attitudinal form of support, from other indicators of political support such as trust, vote intentions, or past vote choice.

A closely related concept is political trust. But unlike approval, measures of trust have both an evaluative *and* a behavioural component. Trust connotes an 'intention to accept vulnerability based upon positive expectations of the intentions or behaviour of another' (Rousseau et al. 1998, 395) in some specific domain (i.e. trust to tell the truth or to head the government but not, say, to perform brain surgery). Hardin (2000) expresses the encapsulated nature of trust as 'A trusts B to do X' (26). In this inherently relational conception, Van der Meer (2017) argues the trustor must evaluate (a) the trustee's ability to act in the trustor's interest or at least benignly; (b) whether the trustee can be held accountable for untrustworthy behaviour; and (c) the predictability of the trustee's behaviour. When the trustee is not the trustor's peer with whom she interacts personally, the trustor can still indirectly evaluate the trustee's competence, care, enforceable commitment/accountability, and predictability (Van der Meer, 2017). Upon this strong evaluative foundation, the trustor takes the behavioural decision to trust or distrust the trustee in some specific domain(s). Survey researchers rarely define the domain in practice, however. Given this conceptual ambiguity, we regard political trust indicators as inferior to more purely evaluative indicators of performance and only use them in our estimates of executive approval when data scarcity dictates.[2]

Another popular alternative gauge of popular support is provided by vote intentions. Vote intentions are mostly indicators of *behavioural intent*. They interrogate intended vote behaviour rather than an attitude, which entails evaluation of a leader. As such, vote intention measures are more sensitive to temporal factors. Presidential systems and some parliamentary systems have (fairly) predictable election dates, while other parliamentary systems lack a fixed election schedule. Vote intentions are, arguably, more behavioural when an election is imminent and more attitudinal in a purely hypothetical election. In the latter, answers to vote intention questions may better approximate specific form of political support, in Easton's terms. As with political trust, vote intentions contain a mixture of attitudinal and behavioural aspects. Unlike political trust, however, the meanings and drivers of vote intentions should vary significantly across countries and within countries over time. Case and small-*n* studies of parliamentary systems may be able to reduce the magnitude of these distortions. But for a broadly comparative project such as ours, this measure of support is problematic for several additional reasons.

A first and central concern attached to vote intentions is cross-contextual equivalence: identifying a measure of executive support that can serve as a common denominator across a wide range of regimes. Heterogeneity in constitutional designs across countries produces an array of political executives, some of which emerge from parliamentary elections while others are directly elected and may be term limited. Presidential systems fuse head of state and head of government into a directly elected president who serves for a fixed term. By contrast, in parliamentary systems the government is headed by a prime minister who, as *primum inter pares*, serves at the pleasure of parliament, while the head of state—even if elected—is tasked with largely ceremonial duties. Semi-presidential systems, in turn, divide power between a president directly elected to a fixed term and a prime minister with responsibility to the legislature (and, in president-parliamentary regimes, responsible to the president, as well). Whereas vote intentions for presidents seek to grant an individual a mandate to govern, vote intentions for parliament seek to grant a party a mandate to form government and to elect a prime minister. In short, the

[2] These cases are documented on the EAP website, http://www.executiveapproval.org.

'executive' as the object of political support is context-specific, and indicators should reflect that. While approval directly reflects evaluations of the performance of (context-specific) executives, vote intentions are often mediated by the relationship between executives and their party (direct in the case of presidential and indirect in parliamentary systems). Vote intentions and executive approval may also diverge when the executive is not up for re-election, e.g. when term limited by constitutions or intra-party rules.

In the case of the EAD, we include approval for heads of state, typically presidents, so long as they are directly elected in competitive elections and hold more than ceremonial law-making power (Siaroff, 2003; see also Hellwig and Samuels, 2008). Prime ministers and their governing cabinets form the executive branch in parliamentary systems and so together they are conceived as the political executive in our dataset. Finally, the complexity of semi-presidential systems leads us to conceive of the 'executive' as the president and the prime minister, both separately and as a governing unit.

A second, related concern with vote intentions as measures of political support across a range of countries is, that as measures of behavioural intent, they may be more sensitive to differences in electoral and party-system structures than a purely attitudinal indicator like executive approval. Inherently, vote intention is a measure relative to other parties or candidates within a given context, rather than focused on the executive.[3] A prime minister thus may be broadly popular among the electorate but possess lower vote intention numbers (e.g. well below 50 per cent) if governing in a fractured party system with post-electoral coalitions compared to a similarly popular prime minister in a majoritarian system. Moreover, unpopular prime ministers can face leadership battles from within their own parties. In these cases, approval is arguably a more valid barometer of prime minister security and power than party vote intentions. Likewise, in systems with fixed terms for the executive, vote intention questions asking about potential behaviour in a polling booth months or years away is likely to mix both current evaluations of the executive's performance and expectations of future outcomes and actions. And, in turn, these mixtures of current evaluations and future expectations shift across the electoral cycle. In sum, even in parliamentary regimes, measures of vote intention and executive approval do not necessarily measure the same thing. Empirically, they may not always track each other closely, as we show below.

[3] Concern about how the relative character of vote intentions biases popular support has given rise to a variety of solutions, perhaps most prominently the concept of 'electoral utilities' (van der Eijk et al., 2006).

These concerns for cross-contextual equivalence and the sensitivity of vote intention measures to institutional variation, both between and within countries, have led us to focus on attitudinal indicators of executive approval as a reliable measure within and across systems. Our decision has been widely validated as an increasingly large body of research that relies on approval data has established the importance of executive approval for both politics and policy. Formal theories of government stability in parliamentary systems, for example, argue 'public opinion' matters a great deal for cabinet stability (inter alia, Laver and Shepsle, 1998; see review in Magalhães, 2020). More widely, empirical work in a range of countries demonstrates how strong approval ratings endow presidents with the necessary political capital to advance their legislative agendas (Canes-Wrone and De Marchi, 2002; Calvo, 2007), to refrain from legislating by decree (Shair-Rosenfield and Stoyan, 2018), to manage their government coalition (Martínez-Gallardo, 2014), to weather scandals and avoid impeachment (Pérez-Liñán, 2007), and to alter term limits (Corrales, 2018).

Moreover, there are also practical reasons to use executive approval. For one, the scarcity of vote intentions data in presidential systems is more acute than the scarcity of approval data in parliamentary systems. In presidential systems, where elections are only held *de jure* (if not always *de facto*) at specified intervals, vote intentions are rarely polled outside of campaign season. Over time, as access to survey data has become more widespread across the globe, more research has relied on approval data to measure support for the executive. As an empirical matter, approval appears more sensitive to economic fluctuations than vote intentions *regardless of the democratic regime type* (Pickup, 2010).

In sum, our choice to use executive approval is driven by important theoretical, empirical, and practical considerations suggesting approval measures are most appropriate across a broad range of political systems.

Conceptualizing and Measuring Mass Executive Approval over Time and Space

In constructing the first large cross-national dataset of public evaluations of incumbent political executives, the Executive Approval Project's data collection and processing effort seeks to resolve several thorny challenges. We discuss them in turn, beginning with our approach to measuring executive approval as a latent concept and following with more practical issues associated with data collection.

Executive Approval as a Latent Concept

A first key challenge in measuring executive approval is that, like many concepts in the social sciences, it is not directly observable. Instead, approval is typically approximated through questions in public opinion surveys. These surveys, however, have a range of methodological issues—including variations in survey question wording, survey house effects, item effects, and response effects—that cause measures to diverge from each other and the concept they are trying to measure and need to be resolved in order to more accurately evaluate executive approval across countries and over time.

Our solution to these methodological issues is to treat executive approval as a *latent construct*, rather than a phenomenon that can be directly observed from responses to any particular survey question. In this we build on work by Erikson, Mackuen, and Stimson (2002) in *The Macro Polity.* They measure 'policy mood' as a latent construct estimated by aggregating numerous survey marginals on a wide variety of domestic policy issues for the United States.[4] We view executive approval as a similar latent construct that can be gauged via myriad combinations of question wordings and response choices—none of which perfectly measures 'executive approval' but each of which partially taps the concept. Therefore, to create an index of executive approval that reflects approval over time we collect time series of all available survey marginals of items that tap the public's evaluation of the executive and then extract their common variance to measure the underlying latent variable.[5] Leveraging readings from multiple indicators rather than relying on a single series has several methodological advantages.

First, temporal variation helps mitigate the measurement problem inherent in survey research questions when it comes to effectively gauging underlying concepts. In the case of the United States, for example, early research equated presidential approval with a positive answer to Gallup's traditional job approval question: 'Do you approve or disapprove of the way [the incumbent] is handling his job as president?' Despite the widespread use of this item, scholars criticized the wording of the question as 'unfocused' because it did 'not relate to any concrete action by respondents' (Neustadt, 1960). Mueller

[4] *The Macro Polity* authors rarely, if ever, use this technique to create a macro 'executive approval' series. Perhaps this owes to the fact that the Gallup measure of presidential approval has become the industry standard in the United States. Thus, they do not contend with the issues of question wording and missingness that confront comparativists. In *Tides of Consent* (2004), Stimson crafts a 'generic approval' indicator that combines approval of presidents, senators, governors, Congress, and trust in government.

[5] Only general evaluations are included, issue- or area-specific evaluations are excluded.

(1970, 19) agreed but noted that '[w]hatever the peculiarities there are in this question, they are at least constant' over time. Temporal changes reflect changes in attitudes, not particular aspects of the measurement instrument such as question wording or individuals' interpretations of survey items. By focusing on how series with a constant measurement vary over time, we can isolate the latent attitude from its measurement.

Second, covariation across time series improves measurement reliability. Sampling theory tells us that any given survey or series can be an outlier. Moreover, we should expect systematic errors owing to survey house effects (non-random differences in measures of approval unique to each polling firm) as well as item effects (variations in question wording biasing results in one direction or another). Employing multiple indicators also resonates with a core measurement principle in the psychometric tradition: any single measure is less reliable than multiple measures of the same concept.

Our approach addresses a significant related problem: survey response effects. As Zaller and Feldman (1992) remind us, 'survey questions do not *simply* measure public opinion. They also shape and channel it by the way they frame issues, order the alternatives, and otherwise set the context of the question' (582, emphasis in original). Responses reflect respondents' comprehension of the question; their strategies and cues to retrieve information about it from their memory; their ability to judge, integrate, and infer from this information and to map it onto a response choice (Tourangeau, Rips, and Rasinski, 2000). Error, biases, and multiple and conflicting considerations are around every corner of this process. Hence, the perfect survey question is a unicorn; all are flawed but aggregating among several closely related items across different surveys allows the signal to stand out from the noise.

Overall, these conceptual and methodological issues support our treatment of executive approval as a latent construct. Focusing on changes in approval series over time enables us to effectively diminish house effects, survey response effects, and other issues of measurement. Whether the various time series indeed tap the same underlying construct becomes an empirical question. If so, we can use the communality in their dynamics to estimate a weighted average of executive popularity. Not surprisingly, scholars have referred to these as 'macro-approval' measures (Carlin and Martínez-Gallardo, 2019, 17) or as 'latent popularity' (Campello and Zucco, 2020, 140). In this volume, we use both terms as well as their shorthand versions—'approval' and 'popularity'—interchangeably.

Challenges in Data Collection

A second set of challenges in measuring executive approval relates to data collection. Two major obstacles stand out. The first is largely practical: how to identify and then access executive approval data—both academic and commercial—across countries, over time, in multiple languages. Academic surveys are typically archived in national and international repositories and available to researchers. Unfortunately, they tend to be relatively infrequent. Though commercial survey houses often meet market demands for more timely readings of executive approval, they are under no obligation to share their data; they may even have to honour client wishes that the data remain private. Whenever possible, the Executive Approval Project seeks to establish collaborative relationships with commercial pollsters. Otherwise, we must rely on internet and social media searches to piece together data series, often from national news media sources. Countries with long-established commercial and academic polling industries have years of rich, publicly available data—over seventy years in the cases of the United States and the United Kingdom. Many newer democracies, especially in Latin America, have seen an explosion in their polling industries in the past thirty years (Carlin, 2021) while others, particularly in Africa and South Asia, have yet to develop a significant polling industry and are not included in our dataset (EAD 2.01, 10 October 2019; see http://www.executiveapproval.org/). All the underlying data and the resulting latent measures of approval are freely available for download from the project's website. And we are indebted to scores of scholars who have generously contributed data they have collected for their own purposes; we acknowledge them on our website.

Therefore, the first task in producing reliable over-time estimates of executive approval is significant archival work and a non-trivial investment in relationships with pollsters and scholars who might be willing to share their data. The geographic and temporal scope of the EAD is inherently limited by these factors. In recent years, the Executive Approval Project has relied on some twenty Country Teams to facilitate relationships with local pollsters and to manage data collection. The remainder of the work falls to the project's Core Members and their research assistants.

A second key challenge of data collection stems from the divergent conceptualizations and measurements of approval by commercial firms and academic polls operating within a specific country. The aforementioned study of macro-opinion in terms of 'policy mood' has been criticized as having an empirical foundation that is vulnerable to the shifting questions of pollsters (Page and

Shapiro, 1992). Specifically, if the questions used to measure policy mood are driven more by survey firm interest than by the actual relevance of the issue in the body politic, then they may feature vastly different question formulations and may not, when aggregated, correlate with a single latent dimension.

We avoid many of these issues by focusing on a clearly defined concept, outlined above, built upon attitudinal measures of support for the incumbent executive. Our data collection efforts for the EAD focus on a comparable set of items specifically asking about the 'approval', 'favourability', or 'ratings' of the executive's 'management', 'job', 'performance', or 'image'. This relatively restrictive set means the source data for our approval series are likely to reflect a unidimensional construct of public support for the executive.

It is important to note that our definition of executive approval varies slightly based on system type. Executive approval in presidential systems is straightforward. In parliamentary systems, we conceptualize prime minister approval to include government approval where available. As alluded to above, for systems with two politically relevant national executives, such as the semi-presidential regimes of France and Portugal, we collect all available marginals for each executive and produce separate approval series for each office. For some semi-presidential systems there is additional polling asking about 'government' performance and we calculate a separate government series where available. Finally, for researchers wanting a global evaluation of executive actors in semi-presidential systems, the EAD includes an executive series generated by using all survey marginals asking about approval of any executive actor (president, prime minister, or government).[6]

Overall, the EAD 2.0 is generated from more than 46,000 survey marginals drawn from 762 survey series (with the same question wording and response options by the same firm) covering over 600 political executives in forty-seven countries. The two countries with the largest number of marginals are the United States and the United Kingdom (7,876 and 4,079, respectively), accounting for 25 per cent of the survey marginals used to construct the EAD.[7] Figure 2.1 displays the marginals (bars) and number of series (dots) used for each country in the EAD 2.0.

[6] Grossman and Guinaudeau (this volume) discuss the use of these measures under periods of cohabitation.

[7] Greece, Japan, Italy, Czech Republic, Ukraine, and Turkey each have differences in their polling industries that cause their input series to be slightly different than described above. Additionally, the Germany series pre-unification is only West Germany. Following unification, a key polling source was based on separate sampling frames for East and West Germany, which we combine using weights for the relative population of each of the regions. Further details regarding these countries can be found in the Executive Approval Dataset Codebook at http://www.executiveapproval.org

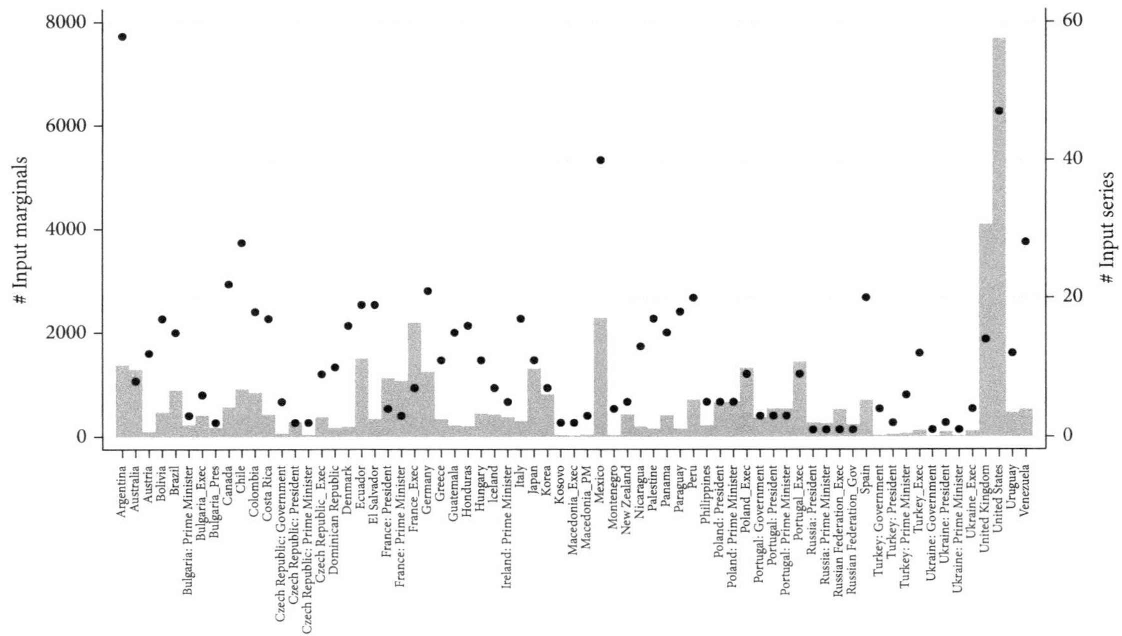

Figure 2.1 Number of survey marginals (bars) and series (dots) by country

Source: Executive Approval Database 2.0.

Producing a valid, reliable, and continuous measure of executive approval from surveys still presents a number of methodological pitfalls, even with a carefully structured data collection of survey marginals from similarly worded questions. One such pitfall comes from house effects, the concern that different polling firms may have a systematic left or right (pro- or anti-incumbent) tilt in their polls; issues may also emerge due to differing sampling frames, response modes, response categories, or question wording. Moreover, these differences may not be limited to between-house effects, but also within firms whose response categories and/or sampling frames change over time. If one were to simply pool all questions without acknowledging and addressing house effects, the resulting measure of approval may be significantly biased and with low reliability.

A second challenge is the frequent lack of overlap across different survey series from the same country over time. We can illustrate this with the United Kingdom, where fourteen pollsters either currently publish measures of prime minister/government approval or have regularly done so in the past. Yet, these series differ in their temporal coverage and continuity.[8] Some begin in the 1930s while others have only begun in the last year or two. National Opinion Polls were only fielded from the 1960s until the 1980s while Gallup started in the 1930s but has not asked consistently about leader approval since 2000. Additionally, the United Kingdom highlights the heterogeneity of question wording across firms. Polling questions tapping prime minister approval have included questions such as: 'Do you approve or disapprove of the government's record to date?', 'Are you satisfied or dissatisfied with [name] as prime minister?', 'Are you satisfied or dissatisfied with the way the government is running the country?', and 'Do you have a favourable or unfavourable view of [name of prime minister]?' The number of response options (approve/disapprove, strongly approve/somewhat approve/somewhat disapprove/strongly disapprove, etc.) also vary by firm and/or time period. These questions all likely tap into a similar latent dimension of leader approval and discarding information would be exceedingly inefficient. Yet, making use of these similar questions requires finding a way to combine them temporally in a consistent and reliable manner.

In all, we require a method to create a continuous latent measure of executive approval that addresses house effects and temporal and minor question-wording inconsistencies. To do this, the Executive Approval Project turns

[8] Where gaps are long, the output series is shortened, excluding certain periods of time. For shorter temporal gaps—less than 6 consecutive quarters of input data—the EAD generates an approval series via linear interpolation.

to the dyads-ratio algorithm, developed by Stimson (1991). The algorithm, implemented in various iterations of the WCALC and other software,[9] is built on the idea that if a given time series is a valid measure of approval, then the ratio between any two values in the series is a *relative* measure of approval. The approach converts all series into ratios between each observation in each series and then the algorithm assesses the common variance among the resultant ratio series. From this, reliability measures for each series are produced and serve two purposes: (1) they are used to weight each series in generating the latent measure of approval and, (2) they indicate whether a unidimensional construct is supported and how strongly the input series correlate with it. By design, each latent approval measure included in the EAD 2.0 (and 1.0) conforms to a single dimension on which most series load very highly (> 0.70). Two related steps are used to produce the data. First, since the input series are converted to unit-less ratios, the resulting output lacks units. However, the final step of the algorithm uses the weighted values of the original series to recode the ratios back into levels of approval.

Finally, we employ exponential smoothing to help remove any residual sampling variance from the series. For some measures of policy mood, such smoothing can have a meaningful impact on the resultant series. However, because the EAD 2.0 employs similarly worded questions for all survey marginals and has high frequency input series for most countries, the difference between smoothed and unsmoothed data is negligible. Quarterly data from the EAD 2.0 with and without smoothing correlate at $r = 0.99$ or greater.

While the dyads-ratio algorithm is a long-established and validated method for combining disparate survey series, it is not the only one. Other approaches have been proposed over the past two decades, including aggregate Bayesian item-response theory (McGann, 2014) and Bayesian latent trait models (e.g. Claassen, 2019; see also Solt, 2020). While previous research has shown some differences in the production of measures of policy mood depending on the aggregation approach, this is much less of a concern regarding executive approval. The EAD is substantially less sensitive to the choice of aggregation methods because of the relatively coherent nature and high frequency of the input series.

To illustrate how issues of differing temporal coverage of input series and variations in house effects are addressed, we provide a graphical example of the United Kingdom. The top three panels in Figure 2.2 show how combining

[9] The EAD 2.0 uses an R version of the algorithm by Stimson and updated by Patrick English. https://github.com/patrick-eng/bootstrap.dyads. For a more detailed discussion of the history and mechanisms of the dyads-ratio approach, see Stimson (2018).

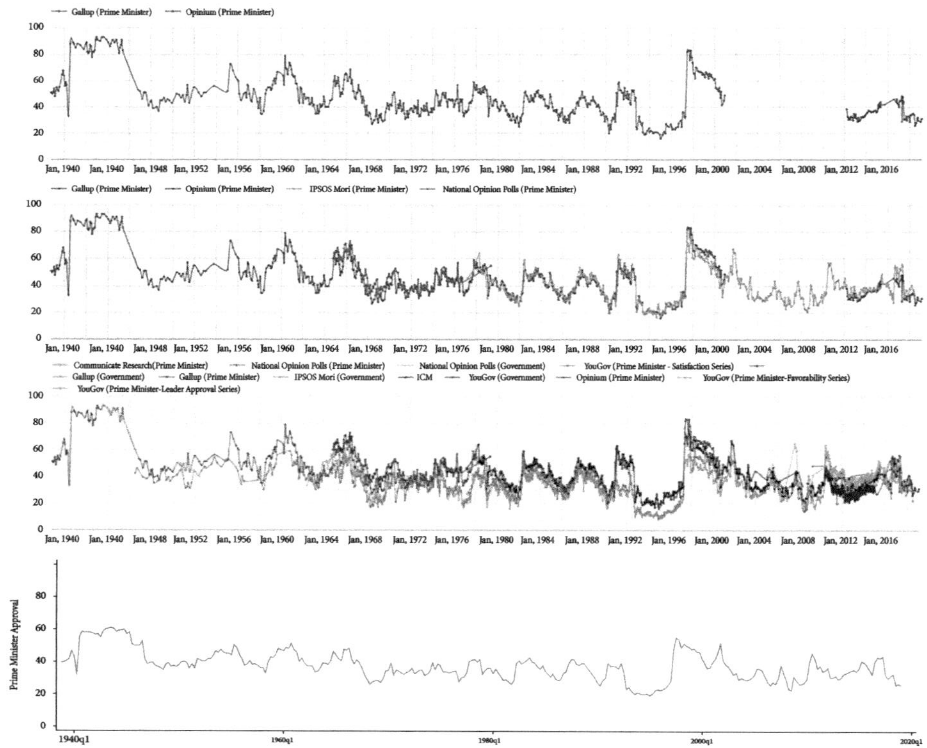

Figure 2.2 Combining input series and the resulting latent measure of executive approval in the United Kingdom

Source: Executive Approval Database 2.0.

different series dramatically increases the temporal coverage of the data. The first panel graphs the long-running but now discontinued Gallup survey and the recently produced Opinium polls regarding opinions of the prime minister. Neither series is ideal by itself; the Gallup poll has great historical depth but stops in 2000 while the Opinium series is only available for a relatively short window starting in 2010. Furthermore, because they do not overlap we cannot tell if they measure the same concept. The second panel adds series from National Opinion Polls and from IPSOS Mori. These two polls overlap with the Gallup and Opinium series and seem to move together, while diverging slightly. The third panel repeats this exercise for all available surveys in the United Kingdom asking about the prime minister or the government. In general, the series seem to rise and fall together (with occasional outliers). Yet any single series is much too thin to provide adequate high frequency coverage across the entire time span. Moreover, the divergence across series at any given point in time also highlights that raw survey marginals for many single series may suffer house effects and noise from random sampling error. By combining the common changes in these disparate, yet conceptually related, series, the EAD generates a latent measure that is logical, coherent, and reliable. The final panel graphs the latent measure which now covers the entire time period and has controlled for the house and measurement effects while still capturing variation in approval that exists over time.

Approval and Vote Intention: United Kingdom and Germany

In our theoretical conceptualization of executive approval, we make a clear distinction between measures of approval and vote intention questions. Above we lay out our arguments for why these two measures, approval and vote intention, are conceptually distinct and should be empirically distinct. In practice, however, comparisons have been difficult because, for most countries, there has not been a cohesive and consistent global data collection effort for vote intention that parallels what the Executive Approval Project has done for approval. There are, however, two significant cases in Europe for which we do have monthly estimates for vote intention for the prime minister's party and prime minister approval from the EAD: the United Kingdom and Germany.

We use these two cases to compare vote intentions and approval ratings. Figure 2.3 shows the trends in prime ministerial approval and vote intentions since 1980 in the United Kingdom; Figure 2.4 graphs approval of the German chancellor since 2000. The UK data come from the new dataset,

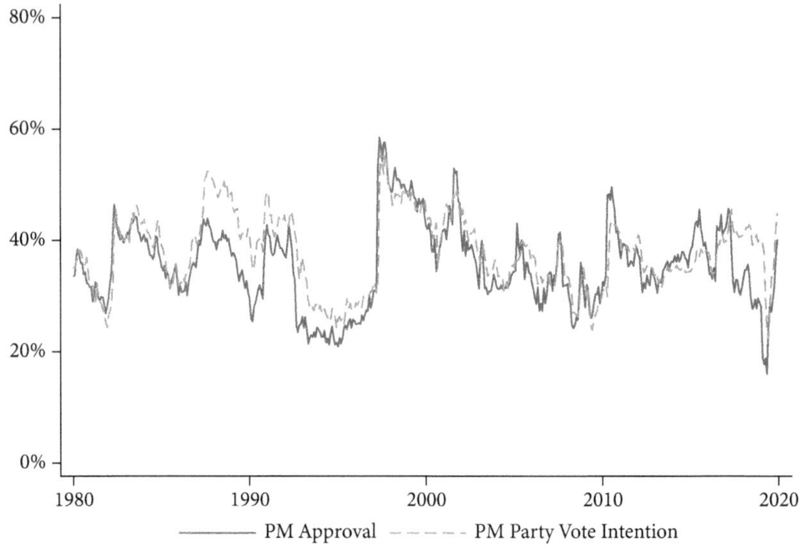

Figure 2.3 Prime minister approval and vote intention for the prime minister's party in the United Kingdom
Source: Executive Approval Database 2.0 and Bailey, Pack, and Mansillo (2021).

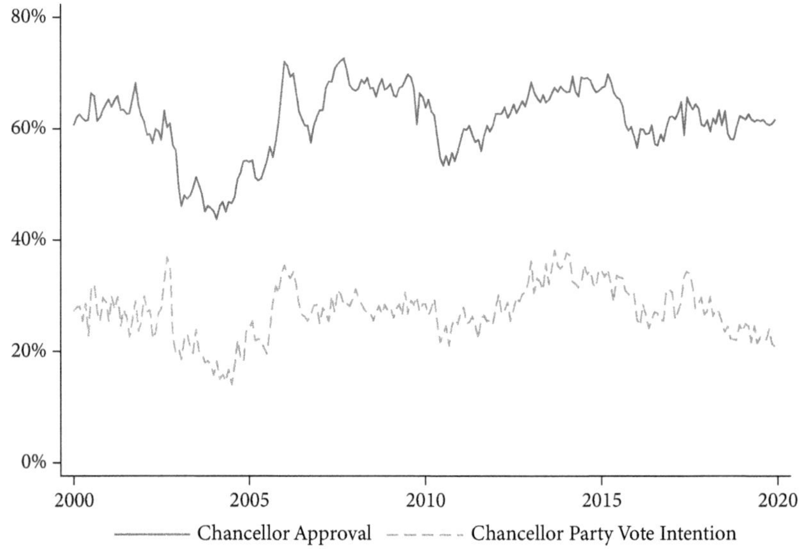

Figure 2.4 Chancellor approval and vote intention for the chancellor's party in Germany
Source: Executive Approval Database 2.0 and *Politbarometer*.

PollBasePro, by Bailey, Pack, and Mansillo (2021) that contains daily estimates of vote intentions for Labour, Conservative, and Liberal Democrat parties. We aggregate these measures into monthly averages for the sitting prime minister's party. For Germany the data come from a single source, the (almost) monthly *Politbarometer* poll from the GESIS data archive.

Figure 2.3 makes clear that approval and vote intention in the United Kingdom are empirically related; yet, at times they become considerably delinked from each other. During the premierships of Margaret Thatcher (1979–1990) and John Major (1990–1997), the Conservative Party was substantially more popular (measured by vote intentions) than either leader. But during the tenures of Tony Blair (1997–2007) and Gordon Brown (2007–2010), Labour was essentially as popular as either prime minister. And, in the post-Brexit period, we see a large gap form between vote intention and approval, as the Conservative Party remained moderately popular even as Theresa May (2016—2019) was deeply unpopular.

The gap between approval and vote intention in Germany (Figure 2.4) is starker. In part due to the multi-party governance system in Germany, chancellors, both Gerhard Schroder (SPD, 1998–2005) and Angela Merkel (CDU/CSU, 2005–2021), have been significantly more popular than their parties. In recent years Merkel's party, the CDU/CSU, has seen its popularity fall while Merkel remained a popular leader. As in the United Kingdom, approval for German chancellors is often more volatile than support for their party. Of course, if the government coalition members in Germany were stable under either the SPD or the CDU/CSU chancellorships, then approval and vote intention would be more closely linked. However, Merkel appears to have leveraged her personal popularity into a stable government, despite having governed with differing coalition partners. The approval of the chancellor may, therefore, play a central role in the shaping and maintenance of German governments.

Overall, the United Kingdom and Germany display somewhat different relationships, mostly in levels, between approval and vote intention reflecting their different party systems. Yet both cases highlight that while clearly related, the two measures are empirically distinct, and these distinctions hold important implications for both theory and measurement.

Quarterly Approval Estimates

Using the measurement approach laid out above, EAD 2.0 has broad geographic and temporal coverage. Although this book focuses only on OECD countries with long polling series, in this section we compare basic trends in approval for the subset of cases in the book with countries in the entire EAD 2.0 dataset.

Figure 2.5 shows the extent of the EAD 2.0's quarterly coverage over the past seventy years for the countries examined in Chapter 1 and in the following chapters. The lines are the smoothed estimates of public approval of the executive with the vertical ticks identifying national executive elections (direct or indirect). Looking over the figure, the pattern of honeymoons following elections is a notable feature in many countries (Müller and Louwerse, 2020), with the effect most pronounced in presidential systems (highlighting the results of Carlin et al., 2018). We also see, and Dickey-Fuller tests support, that for many countries the approval series appear to be stationary around a long-term mean in the mid-40s.

The established advanced industrial democracies, which are the bulk of cases in this book, have patterns of approval that are similar in some respects to the countries in the full EAD 2.0 dataset. On average, political executives in the full dataset enjoy a mean approval rating of 44.7 per cent. Pooled mean approval for all countries has remained quite stable between 43 per cent and

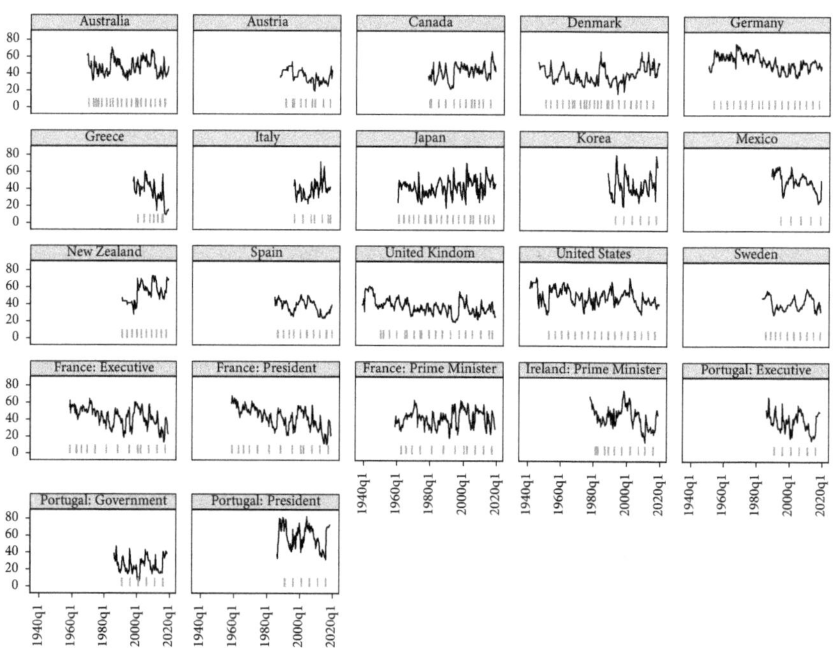

Figure 2.5 Quarterly executive approval estimates from the EAD 2.0, for cases in this book

Source: Executive Approval Database 2.0.

45 per cent since the 1970s. At the country-level, Ukraine's leaders are on average the least popular (22 per cent for president) followed by Peru's presidents (28 per cent). While the Russian president is, on average, the most popular leader in the dataset (66 per cent), it is important to note that the data coverage almost entirely overlaps with Vladimir Putin or Dmitry Medvedev's time in office. The next most popular set of presidents, on average, including some alternation in power across political parties, are found in the Dominican Republic (58 per cent). With regard to the subset of countries in this volume, mean approval is 44 per cent, just slightly lower than for the full EAD 2.0. Similarly, this volume's subset of cases also displays large variation across cases. On average, the Portuguese government is the least popular (25.1 per cent), while the Portuguese president is the most popular (58.6 per cent), followed by the New Zealand prime minister (53.4 per cent).

However, executive approval in new democracies tends to exhibit greater volatility, often around elections, than in older polities (Figure 2.6). Variance of approval in the full dataset is 182.3, with most of it occurring within countries (average: 127.7) though we see substantial between-country variance as well (average: 65.5). Unlike with mean approval ratings, though, we observe a steady increase in the variance in approval over the past six decades. In the

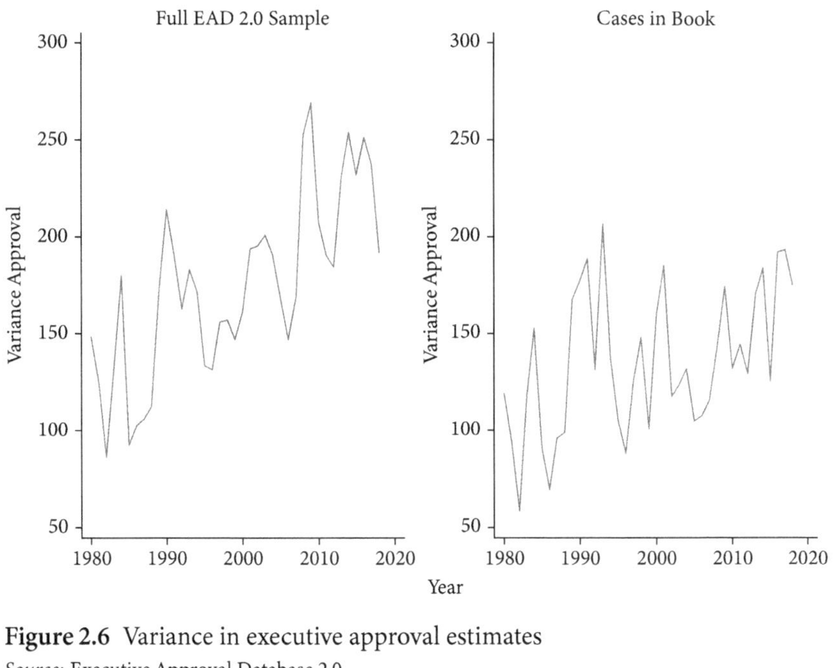

Figure 2.6 Variance in executive approval estimates
Source: Executive Approval Database 2.0.

1960s variance in approval was 111.9, whereas in the most recent decade, 2010–2019, the variance of approval had nearly doubled to 221. Of course, part of this rise is likely attributed to newer democracies entering the dataset in more recent decades. Yet even if we restrict the sample only to those countries that have approval data starting in 1990, we also observe a general increase in the variance in approval over time, particularly in the past decade. Since 1990 variance in approval in these countries has increased an average of 1.8 per year. The average within-country variance from 2010 to 2015 was 46 per cent greater than the amount of variance in the 1995–2000 period.

Although the cases in this book have similar mean levels of approval, the variance in government approval in these countries is substantially lower than in the full EAD 2.0 (overall: 143, within-country mean: 104). The variance in approval within this set of largely advanced industrial democracies has increased over time, but at a much slower rate than in the full sample. Figure 2.6 highlights the increase in variance over time in the full EAD 2.0 and the sample of countries covered in this volume (Chapters 3–13 for individual countries and the cross-national analyses reported in Chapter 15). The left panel shows all countries in the EAD 2.0 and the right panel features only those countries and executives examined in the following chapters in this book. While approval volatility has been increasing in both samples, it has done so less than in the least established democracies.

Concluding Reflection

This chapter began by echoing the call issued by foundational works in the economic voting canon that gauging dynamics of the public's response to the economy requires time-series measures. In some countries, widespread public polling about the executive has been commonplace for decades, whereas in other countries it is only a recent phenomenon (if it exists at all). Even when polling firms regularly ask about the leader's popularity, and publicly report their results, the task of generating a continuous valid measure of approval remains challenging: question wording varies across countries, polling agencies, and time periods; sampling varies with distinct frames and frequencies; some pollsters exit the market and new ones enter.

Whereas previous work on executive approval either ignored or relied on stopgap measures to deal with these challenges, the Executive Approval Project addresses them directly. As a result, the EAD has created valid, highly comparable, and reasonably long time series of approval for several dozen countries.

Comparative projects such as the current volume grounded in advanced democracies, a special issue focused on Latin America cases (Carlin and Martínez-Gallardo, 2019), and numerous articles have been possible because of the EAD. We hope that more and more scholars will use these data to focus on the causes and consequences of executive approval. Government approval is shaped in different ways by institutions, processes of everyday politics, and crises. In turn, it can drive political calculations, the policymaking process, and election outcomes. Yet scholars have not had the tools to study these dynamics in more than a handful of countries at a time. We hope and expect that scholars will employ the EAD 2.0 and future releases broadly in their comparative research well into the future.

References

Bailey, J., Pack, M., and Mansillo, L. (2021). PollBasePro: Daily estimates of aggregate voting intention in Britain from 1955 to the present day. APSA Preprints. doi: 10.33774/apsa-2021-2hbgw.

Calvo, E. (2007). The responsive legislature: Public opinion and law making in a highly disciplined legislature. *British Journal of Political Science*, *37*(2), 263–80.

Campello, D., and Zucco, C. (2020). *The Volatility Curse: Exogenous Shocks and Representation in Resource-rich Democracies*. Cambridge: Cambridge University Press.

Canes-Wrone, B., and De Marchi, S. (2002). Presidential approval and legislative success. *Journal of Politics*, *64*(2), 491–509.

Carlin, R. E. (2021). Surveys and the study of Latin American politics. In *Oxford Research Encyclopedia of Politics*. New York: Oxford University Press. doi.org/10.1093/acrefore/9780190228637.013.1668.

Carlin, R. E., and Martínez Gallardo, C. (2019). Outliers of presidential approval: Dynamics, levels, and rates. *Revista Latinoamericana de Opinión Pública* 9(2), 7–27.

Carlin, R. E., Hartlyn, J., Hellwig, T., Love, G. J., Martínez-Gallardo, C., and Singer, M. M. (2016). Executive Approval Database 1.0. Available for download at http://www.executiveapproval.org.

Carlin, R. E., Hartlyn, J., Hellwig, T., Love, G. J., Martínez-Gallardo, C., and Singer, M. M. (2018). Public support for Latin American presidents: The cyclical model in comparative perspective. *Research & Politics*, *5*(3), 2053168018787690.

Carlin, R. E., Hartlyn, J., Hellwig, T., Love, G. J., Martínez-Gallardo, C., and Singer, M. M. (2019). Executive Approval Database 2.0. Available for download at http://www.executiveapproval.org.

Claassen, C. (2019). Estimating smooth country–year panels of public opinion. *Political Analysis*, *27*(1), 1–20.

Corrales, J. (2018). *Fixing Democracy: Why Constitutional Change Often Fails to Enhance Democracy in Latin America.* Oxford: Oxford University Press.

Easton, D. (1975). A re-assessment of the concept of political support. *British Journal of Political Science, 5*(4), 435–57.

Erikson, R. S., MacKuen, M. B., and Stimson, J. A. (2002). *The Macro Polity.* Cambridge: Cambridge University Press.

Hardin, R. (1999). Do we want trust in government?. In *Democracy and Trust*, M. Warren, ed. New York: Cambridge University Press. 22–41.

Hardin, R. (2000). Trust and society. In *Competition and Structure: The Political Economy of Collective Decisions: Essays in Honor of Albert Breton*, G. Galeotti, P. Salmon, and R. Wintrobe, eds. New York: Cambridge University Press. 24–46.

Hellwig, T., and Samuels, D. (2008). Electoral accountability and the variety of democratic regimes. *British Journal of Political Science, 38*(1), 65–90.

Kramer, G. H. (1983). The ecological fallacy revisited: Aggregate- versus individual-level findings on economics and elections, and sociotropic voting. *American Political Science Review, 77*(1), 92–111.

Laver, M., and Shepsle, K. A. (1998). Events, equilibria, and government survival. *American Journal of Political Science, 42*(1), 28–54.

Lewis-Beck, M. S. (1991). Introduction. In *Economics and Politics: The Calculus of Support*, H. Norpoth, M. S. Lewis-Beck, and J.-D.Lafay, eds. Ann Arbor, MI: University of Michigan Press. 1–8.

Magalhães, P. (2020). Public opinion and executive approval. In *The Oxford Handbook of Political Executives*, R. Andeweg,R. Elgie, L. Helms, and J. Kaarbo, eds. Oxford: Oxford University Press. 627–45.

Martínez-Gallardo, C. (2014). Designing cabinets: Presidential politics and ministerial instability. *Journal of Politics in Latin America, 6*(2), 3–38.

McGann, A. J. (2014). Estimating the political center from aggregate data: An item response theory alternative to the Stimson dyad ratios algorithm. *Political Analysis, 22*(1), 115–29.

Mueller, J. E. (1970). Presidential popularity from Truman to Johnson. *American Political Science Review, 64*(1), 18–34.

Müller, S., and Louwerse, T. (2020). The electoral cycle effect in parliamentary democracies. *Political Science Research and Methods, 8*(4), 795–802.

Neustadt, R. (1960). *Presidential Power.* New York: John Wiley and Sons.

Page, B. I., and Shapiro, R. Y. (1992). *The Rational Public: Fifty Years of Trends in Americans' Policy Preferences.* Chicago, IL: University of Chicago Press.

Paldam, M. (1991). How robust is the vote function? A study of seventeen nations over four decades. In *Economics and Politics: The Calculus of Support*, H. Norpoth, M. S. Lewis-Beck, and J.-D. Lafay, eds. Ann Arbor, MI: University of Michigan Press. 9–31.

Pérez-Liñán, A. (2007). *Presidential Impeachment and the New Political Instability in Latin America*. Cambridge: Cambridge University Press.

Pickup, M. (2010). Better know your dependent variable: A multination analysis of government support measures in economic popularity models. *British Journal of Political Science*, *40*(2), 449–68.

Rousseau, D. M., Sitkin, S. B., Burt, R. S., and Camerer, C. (1998). Not so different after all: A cross-discipline view of trust. *Academy of Management Review*, *23*(3), 393–404.

Shair-Rosenfield, S., and Stoyan, A. T. (2018). Gendered opportunities and constraints: How executive sex and approval influence executive decree issuance. *Political Research Quarterly*, *71*(3), 586–99.

Siaroff, A. (2003). Comparative presidencies: The inadequacy of the presidential, semi-presidential and parliamentary distinction. *European Journal of Political Research*, *42*(3), 287–312.

Solt, F. (2020). Modeling dynamic comparative public opinion. Paper presented at the Annual Meeting of the Southern Political Science Association.

Stimson, J. A. (1991). *Public Opinion in America: Moods, Cycles, and Swings*. Boulder, CO: Westview Press.

Stimson, J. A. (2004). *Tides of Consent: How Opinion Movements Shape American Politics*. New York: Cambridge University Press.

Stimson, J. A. (2018). The dyad ratios algorithm for estimating latent public opinion: Estimation, testing, and comparison to other approaches. *Bulletin of Sociological Methodology/Bulletin de Méthodologie Sociologique*, *137*(1), 201–18.

Tourangeau, R., Rips, L. J., and Rasinski, K. (2000). *The Psychology of Survey Response*. New York: Cambridge University Press.

Van der Eijk, C., Van der Brug, W., Kroh, M., and Franklin, M. (2006). Rethinking the dependent variable in voting behavior: On the measurement and analysis of electoral utilities. *Electoral Studies*, *25*(3), 424–47.

Van der Meer, T. (2017). Political trust and the 'crisis of democracy'. In *Oxford Research Encyclopedia of Politics*. New York: Oxford University Press. https://doi.org/10.1093/acrefore/9780190228637.013.77

Zaller, J., and Feldman, S. (1992). A simple theory of the survey response: Answering questions versus revealing preferences. *American Journal of Political Science*, *36*(3), 579–616.

3

Executive Approval in Great Britain

Continuity and Change

John Bartle, Sebastian Dellepiane-Avellaneda, and Anthony McGann

Democracy is said to be unique among political systems because it guarantees that there is a relationship between what the people want and what government says and does (May, 1978). This is because the executive is accountable for the policies it pursues and the outcomes it delivers. This proposition naturally gives rise to the expectation that the public's approval of leaders is conditional on the delivery of policies that fit their values, and conditions that improve their well-being (Erikson et al., 2002). If democracy is to fulfil its promise, voters should respond by rewarding the executive for good times and punishing them for bad times (Key, 1966). Since leaders want to win re-election, they anticipate the public's response and deliver policies that honour their values, and conditions that improve their welfare. Mutual responsiveness means that policy preferences, evaluations of conditions, policy, and performance conditions are to some degree endogenous (Budge, 2019).

The expectation that executives are judged by their ability to deliver favourable conditions is particularly high in Britain, where the political system and its institutions produce 'clarity of responsibility' (Powell and Whitten, 1993). Parliament is sovereign and the legislature weakly bicameral (Lijphart, 1999). The plurality electoral system that is used for elections to the House of Commons encourages voters to think of as a choice between two major parties (Bartle, 2021). The largest party in the Commons has won a majority in eighteen out of twenty-one elections from 1945 to 2019. Peacetime coalitions are rare. The Commons provides only a weak check on the executive because the majority of Members of Parliament (MPs) share the same electoral incentives as the government. The 'fusion' of the executive and legislature means that for most purposes government and Parliament are the same thing (Bagehot, 2001). To be sure, the House of Lords is not controlled by the government and can delay non-money bills. The Lords, however, has no power over money

John Bartle et al., *Executive Approval in Great Britain.* In: *Economics and Politics Revisited.* Edited by: Timothy Hellwig and Matthew Singer, Oxford University Press. © John Bartle et al. (2023). DOI: 10.1093/oso/9780192871664.003.0003

bills. Governments can also use the Parliament Acts 1911 and 1949 to pass bills without the Lords' consent after one year (King, 2010).

Government responsibility is also enhanced by Britain's unitary system that hoards power in *national* political institutions. The Westminster Parliament may devolve power to other institutions in Scotland, Wales, and Northern Ireland but it can always take those powers back. The legal constraints imposed by membership of the European Convention on Human Rights (ECHR) and the Human Rights Act 1998 (HRA) are weak. Parliament can abolish the HRA and withdraw from the ECHR. The UK Supreme Court cannot declare acts of Parliament unconstitutional and often defers to the executive. Since their governments have enormous power most Britons naturally regard governments as universal problem solvers (King, 2000). If there is anywhere where we should expect to find a *law-like* relationship between conditions and approval of the executive, it is Britain.

The British political system has a reputation for continuity and stability, represented by institutions like the monarchy and the House of Lords. Crucially, elections to the Commons are based on the plurality rule and single-party government predominates. We might suppose this means that the public's responsiveness to government is a constant. Beneath this veneer of continuity, however, there have been significant changes. British society has been transformed by immigration. Technological change and deindustrialization have eroded the working class. The population has moved from the cities to the suburbs. These changes have compelled the parties to forge new social coalitions. Election outcomes have varied enormously. Nevertheless, the periodic alternation of parties in government has not guaranteed policy that matches public preferences (Bartle et al., 2019; McGann et al., 2023). The party duopoly was challenged by the electoral rise of the Liberal Democrats from 1970 to 2010. This culminated in a hung parliament and a coalition between the Conservatives and the Liberal Democrats. From 2010 to 2015 the British electorate dealt with the challenge of how to allocate rewards or punishments between coalition partners.

The two major parties have also been challenged by the growth of nationalism in Scotland from 1998. Devolution made government responsibility for conditions in Scotland, Wales, and Northern Ireland fuzzier (McGann et al., 2019). Other changes produced abrupt shocks that reverberated through time. Referendums have caused chaos in the party system. The 2014 referendum on Scottish independence led to the collapse of Labour in Scotland and the hegemony of the Scottish National Party in Scotland (Johns, 2018). In England, Eurosceptic and populist parties like the United Kingdom Independence Party and the Brexit Party also challenged the duopoly. The national referendum on membership of the European Union in 2016 forged new identities of 'Remainers' and 'Leavers'. It restructured party coalitions as former Labour-voting Leavers deserted the party and middle-class Remainers supported 'Remain' parties (Sobolewska, 2021). Polarization around this issue might be expected to reduce the impact of conditions on approval. Somewhat less dramatically, but no less importantly, in May 1997, Labour established the Monetary Policy Committee of the Bank of England and gave it control over interest rates. This altered the government's ability to control monetary policy and the national economy (Dellepiane-Avellaneda, 2012).

In this chapter we examine what drives executive approval in Britain between 1980 and 2015. We examine what is inferred about executive approval from studies. We formulate hypotheses, introduce our data, and produce a general model of executive approval. We show that governments are rewarded for making people feel good about the economy and punished for making them feel bad. Executive performance is also evaluated based on their ability to manage 'events'. Other factors such as the electoral cycle, the cost of ruling and policy also play a role. We then examine whether some of the changes outlined above affected the public's responsiveness to executive performance. We find that increased independence of the Bank of England weakened the relationship between interest rates and approval. The coalition government, however, did little to alter the fundamental dynamics of monthly approval. We finally speculate about the future drivers of approval.

Previous Studies of Government Support in Britain

Great Britain is the ideal testbed for the proposition that executive approval depends on their ability to deliver policy that aligns with the electorate's values and improve their welfare by securing favourable conditions (Erikson et al., 2002). This makes it surprising that there have been few studies of executive approval in Britain. There has been just one brief study in a book published forty years ago (Alt, 1979) and one paper in a major political science journal (Hudson, 1985). British scholars have instead focused on the proportion of the electorate that express an intention to vote for the governing party (Sanders et al., 1987; Clarke et al., 1990). This has generally been assumed to be a synonym for executive approval.

The focus of British political science on vote intentions (or 'popularity functions') is unsurprising. The data are widely available in almost continuous time series from the 1940s (King and Wybrow, 2001). These series provide evidence about support for all parties, so vote intentions are excellent predictors of election outcomes (Wlezien et al., 2013). The neglect of executive approval has made it difficult to compare findings with presidential systems such as the United States or understand how institutions affect responsiveness. Just as importantly, vote intention is *not* a synonym for approval (Hudson, 1985). Voters may disapprove of the government but vote for it because the other parties are worse. Others may approve of the government and vote for another party because the governing party has little chance of winning in their constituency under the plurality rule. The correlation between executive approval as measured by the Executive Approval Project (EAP) team and intention to vote for the government in Britain between 1980 and 2015 is 0.85 (N=444). This is very high, but it is not perfect. It is a stretch to infer what drives approval from studies to vote intention or popularity. Nevertheless, this is exactly what we must do to establish what is already known or thought to be known about what drives approval in Britain.

What Drives Support for British Government?

Most research in the 'popularity functions' tradition assumes that intention to vote for the governing party is influenced by three variables: the economy, an autonomous electoral cycle, and events (Goodhart and Bhansali, 1970; Frey and Schneider, 1978; Pissarides, 1980; Sanders et al., 1987; Clarke et al., 1990). Curiously, most studies pay little or no intention to the role of policy in driving government popularity, and none have incorporated indicators of policy. We address this striking omission below.

The Objective Economy

There are many indicators that voters could use to assess whether conditions are better or worse and shape evaluations of executive performance. The British state delivers many services. It seems plausible that the electorate factor in a range of considerations, including the performance of the National Health Service (NHS), the quality of education, and national security (Fiorina, 1981). Most studies, however, have devoted most attention to economic conditions (Miller and Mackie, 1973; Pissarides, 1980; Chrystal and Alt, 1981; Sanders et al., 1987; Clarke et al., 1990). This is partly a simple matter of data availability. Economic data has a market value because those who make money value it. The condition of the economy is recorded in many indicators and economic data is available in monthly, quarterly, and annual time series. The economy provides readily quantifiable and easily interpretable indicator of whether things are 'better' or 'worse' and whether the executive should be 'rewarded' or 'punished'. Economic prosperity is also a precondition for all the other services that government provide in cradle-to-the-grave welfare systems such as Britain. Few disagree with Harold Wilson's famous assertion that: 'All political history shows that the standing of a government and its ability to hold the confidence of the electorate at a general election depend on the success of its economic policy' (Goodhart and Bhansali, 1970, 45).

The earliest studies of government popularity found that rising unemployment and/or inflation are associated with reductions in popularity (Goodhart and Bhansali, 1970; Frey and Schneider, 1978; Pissarides, 1980). Later studies suggested that other indicators such as exchange rates and public-sector borrowing influenced government popularity (Sanders et al., 1987). Yet these models—just like those elsewhere—were plagued by instability (Paldam, 1991; Sanders, 2005). Variables that were significant in one period were insignificant in the next. This instability of the popularity functions caused much debate. Many analysts informally concluded that this instability reflected the sad—but very real—fact that 'things change'. Others demanded a renewed search for truly law-like relations (Budge, 2019).

Subjective Economic Expectations

Early studies of popularity functions noted that objective economic indicators needed to be translated into subjective perceptions before they could influence vote intentions (Hudson, 1985; Sanders et al., 1993). Attention shifted to subjective perceptions measured in representative national surveys. Among the family of perceptions variables expectations have received far more attention than retrospections. To a degree, this is simply because expectations point the way to a profitable future. Market research companies are largely uninterested in retrospections. In an ideal word we would have access to continuous retrospective economic perceptions series, but these are simply not available. Objective economic data provide the best—but far from perfect—indicators of retrospective evaluations. Theoretical developments in macroeconomics also shifted attention to expectations. The 'rational expectations' revolution suggested that rational agents were forward-looking (Shaw, 1984). The major debates in the popularity functions literature focused on whether expectations about national conditions ('sociotropic') or household finances ('egocentric') were more important. Egocentric expectations were central to the 'Essex model' that correctly forecast victory for the Conservative party in the 1992 general election (Sanders, 1991; Price and Sanders, 1993). The success of this model was taken to confirm the proposition that voters were primarily motivated by egocentric considerations. Pre-election polls indicated the public's preference for Labour's policy of increasing taxes and spending rather than the Conservative policy of tax cuts. Most surveys of vote intention also suggested that Labour would be the largest party at that election. Yet still the Conservatives won. Some concluded that Britain was a 'nation of liars' that professed their good intentions to pollsters while voting for tax cuts in the privacy of the polls (Crewe, 1992). Others suggested that the Conservatives' victory owed more to doubts about Labour competence (King, 1998).

The Electoral Cycle

It has long been suspected that there were systematic forces that influenced government popularity that had nothing to do with conditions or the well-being of the electorate. As with students of politics in the United States (Stimson 1976) and elsewhere (Carlin et al., 2018), scholars of British politics are familiar with the 'mid-term blues': the proposition that governments experience a brief 'honeymoon' immediately after an election when support is unusually high, followed by a steady decline in support until around six months before the next general election, and finally a surge in support in the six months or so before an election (Miller and Mackie, 1973). This 'decline-recovery' pattern has also been observed in elections to local authorities, and Westminster by-elections (Rallings and Thrasher, 1997; Norris, 1990).

The earliest British studies suggested this autonomous cycle reflects the tendency of survey respondents to view opinion polls as a referendum on governments (Pissarides, 1980). In the mid-term respondents signal discontent by withdrawing support (Miller and Mackie, 1973). As the next election approaches responses to vote intention questions reflect 'real' choices. Other theories suggest that governments make decisions that disappoint various groups. Over time a 'coalition of minorities' emerges and government support declines (Mueller, 1970). The most widely accepted explanation is an 'elite leadership' theory (Brody, 1991). New governments are insulated from criticism. If the opposition criticize them immediately after an election, they appear like bad losers. Defeated parties become introspective and provide less effective opposition. The media are also less critical as they focus on the policies of the new government. Public discourse becomes more favourable to the government. Over time, things change. Oppositions oppose. Bad news is more newsworthy. Media coverage becomes more critical (Zaller, 1992). The public follow these cues and support for the government declines. The British media system accentuates this trend. Broadcasters are subject to statutory regulation by the Office of Communications to ensure 'due impartiality' (Kuhn, 2007). These rules are important in the run-up to elections. Broadcasters increasingly frame politics as a choice between incumbents and opposition. As coverage becomes more balanced, government popularity increases.

The Costs of Ruling

There are other autonomous forces that influence government popularity. While support for the government tends to rally in the run-up to the general election, it rarely returns to the level at the previous general election. Governing parties across space and time tend to suffer a loss of vote that appears to have nothing to do with conditions (Nannestad and Paldam, 2002; Sanders, 2005; Wlezien, 2017). Theories of the electoral cycle do not explain this phenomenon. Some analysts attribute it to 'grievance asymmetry': the proposition that voters focus place more weight on negative developments, resulting in excessive punishment (Stokes and Iverson, 1966; Soroka, 2014). Others suggest that the phenomenon is rooted in something more tangible: the tendency of governments to move towards their polar positions. This results in an increasing 'gap' between the electorate's preferences and government policy (Soroka and Wlezien, 2009). The emergence of such a gap is likely because there are few checks and balances, other than elections in the British system. It follows that if the major opposition party is uncompetitive (as was true of both Labour between 1980 and 1987 and the Conservatives between 1997 and 2005) the need for government moderation is reduced. Policy gaps are very likely to open up (Bartle et al., 2019).

Events

Political scientists are wary about claims that 'events' drive support or vote intentions (Bytzek, 2011). The goal of political science is to produce empirical generalizations that hold across both space and time (Budge, 2019). Most of the things that we commonly refer to as 'events', however, are unique to a particular time and to a particular place. The 'ideal type event' is both unique and unpredictable. Political scientists are also sceptical about events because their impact depends on how well the government 'manages' them or provides reassurance. If events are managed well and the public reassured, they boost support. If they are not, they reduce support. Without an objective way of operationalizing how well 'managed' an event is, there is no way to predict how the event will affect approval. We can merely observe the effect as evidenced by the coefficients in our models. If they are positive, the event was well-managed. If they are negative, they were not well managed and the public was not reassured that the government was in control.

Notwithstanding these reservations, popularity functions studies regularly incorporate event variables (Sanders et al., 1987; Sanders, 2005). This is not simply because events are important in themselves but because including such variables can often clarify the impact of more systematic forces such as economic expectations.

Policy

The electorate want competence *and* policy that honours its values (Erikson et al., 2002, 30–1). If governing parties were fully responsive to public preferences, policy would match those preferences (Erikson et al., 2002). Yet there are good grounds for believing that governments will 'overshoot' the electorate's 'ideal point'. Parties need to satisfy their members (Strøm, 1990). They are also often uncertain about public preferences and fall back on ideology (Budge, 1994). As we have previously suggested, governments sometimes have a competence advantage over their competitors and are unlikely to be punished in elections for deviating from the 'ideal point' (McGann et al., 2023). Yet, if we can measure 'distance' over time this would improve our ability to understand the dynamics of support and approval.

Despite the theoretical importance of policy, no study of 'popularity functions' to date has directly incorporated measures of policy distance. This is in part because this variable raises theoretical problems. 'Thermostatic models' show that public preferences respond 'negatively' to policy (Wlezien, 1995). Similarly, some macro-level models suggest that policy can respond to public preferences (Erikson et al., 2002). 'Feedback' and endogeneity make it difficult to draw casual inferences. Even if these problems can be overcome neither public preferences nor policy are easily measurable on the same metric.[1]

Data and Measures

In this section we describe the data used to produce our general model of executive approval in Great Britain for the thirty-five years from 1980 to 2015. We also briefly outline our error correction approach to modelling approval.

There are excellent data on executive approval in Britain stretching back to 1938 (Gallup Opinion Polls, 1977a, 1977b; King and Wybrow, 2001). The EAP estimates are based on nineteen separate series and 2,918 separate monthly observations from 1938 to 2020. The EAP team have used the dyads-ratio algorithm to build a continuous time series (Stimson, 1999). Their analyses suggest that the individual series produced by the different houses tap the same construct. Both those items that refer to the 'prime minister' and those that refer to 'government', load highly on the extracted series. It also makes no difference whether approval is measured by items that refer to 'approval' or 'satisfaction'. Both tap the same construct, which we label 'executive approval'.

The EAP estimates of executive approval are displayed in Figure 3.1. We divide the series into three periods. The estimates between 1938 and 1961 are based on irregular readings by just Gallup. There are many months when there are no readings at all. We have least confidence in the EAP estimates for this period and represent approval before 1961 by a dotted line. From 1961 to 2015 the monthly estimates are based on at least two polls, and from 1962, usually from more than one survey house. We have confidence in these estimates but cannot model approval over that period because we do not have

[1] It is difficult to measure 'policy distance'. The natural dimension is a general left-right dimension (Budge, 1994). Both the electorate's ideal point and policy are not easy to estimate. To be sure, we have lots of data on public preferences and we can use the dyads-ratio algorithm to extract the latent dimension (Erikson et al., 2002; Bartle et al., 2011). The underlying data is sparse, so we can only confidently infer the annual average left-right position of the electorate (the 'policy mood'). Since executive approval fluctuates within the space of a few months the two measures are not commensurable. Even greater problems attend the measurement of 'policy'. We could use spending (distinguishing between left-wing spending on social programmes and right-wing spending on security programmes). Spending is a lagging-indicator, and there is often some slippage between planned and actual spending. Government spending data, moreover, is not published monthly. Any indicator of policy relevant to approval would require a great deal of interpolation. Alternatively, we could use words as indicators of policy. The parties produce many of these, but words are not action (McGann et al., 2023). Many of the big set-piece declarations such as the budget speech (Hakhverdian, 2010) and Queen's speech (Jennings and John, 2009) take place in particular months. In the summer recess when Parliament is not in session, the number of words produced declines. Even if we were able to measure policy preferences and policy, we would still be left with the problem of how to calibrate these measures on the same metric to estimate 'distance' (Erikson et al., 2002).

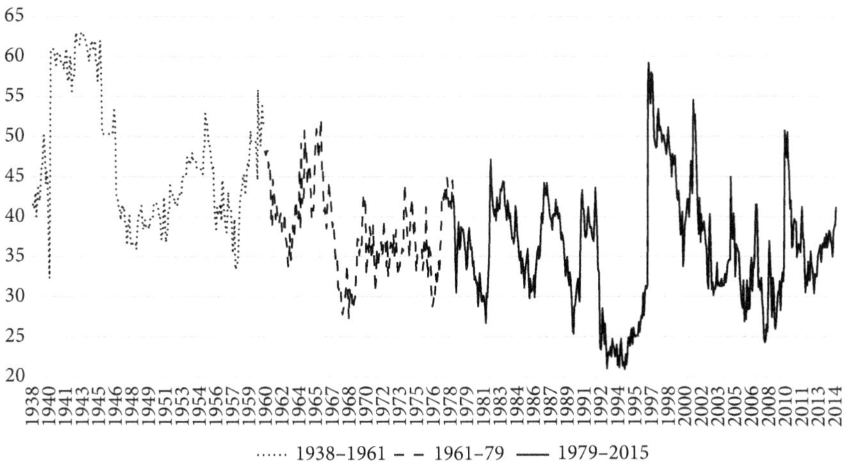

Figure 3.1 Executive approval in Britain, 1938–2015
Source: Executive Approval Project estimate.

data on egocentric economic expectations until 1980. We represent approval between 1961 and 1980 by a dashed line. The approval series from 1980 to 2015 is based on multiple indicators every month and can be modelled using economic expectations data. We represent approval in these thirty-five years by an unbroken line.

To capture the effect of the economy in our models, we use both objective and subjective economic measures. Objective economic data are supplied by the Bank of England.[2] We measure unemployment using estimates of unemployment benchmarked to the labour-force survey measure using the Chow-Lin method. We also include measures of inflation, interest rates, and stock market prices from the same source. All four indicators are widely reported and provide a readily understood measure of the national economy. Moving to the subjective economy, monthly sociotropic expectations data are available from 1974 until the present day. As previously noted, egocentric expectations are only available from 1980 to 2015. Survey houses have collected expectations data using different question wordings and response categories. We convert responses into ratios (positive expectations as a share of the sum of positive and negative expectations) and estimate two expectations series using the dyads-ratio algorithm (Stimson, 1999). The separately estimated sociotropic and egocentric expectations series correlate modestly

[2] The data is drawn from the dataset 'A millennium of macroeconomic data', available at: https://www.bankofengland.co.uk/statistics/research-datasets.

(Pearson's R=0.40, N=443). This suggests that they pick up distinct perceptions. Both exert independent effects on executive approval, so this limits our analyses of approval to the thirty-five years between 1980 and 2015.

Our models also include control for the cycle by including two variables: one counting the number of months since the last election and the same variable squared. If there is a cycle of decline-recovery, the coefficient for the number of months since the last election should be negative and months squared should be positive. To measure the costs of ruling we include a variable counting the *total* number of months since a turnover of party control, we also add another indicator measuring the total number of months that the prime minister has been in office. This innovation is partly because approval of the prime minister is used to estimate executive approval and partly because it is intuitively plausible to suggest that long-serving prime ministers might exert a drag on approval. We expect both coefficients to be negative.

The identification of events involves a (perhaps unnerving) degree of discretion. We identified events that affected approval simply by eyeballing the approval series in Figure 3.1. As a rule of thumb, we assumed that monthly variations of eight points or more are unlikely to be the product of systemic economic or cyclical influences. We examined historical records to identify events that might account for these punctuations. We also followed the cues provided by both studies of government popularity (Sanders et al., 1987; Clarke et al., 1990; Sanders, 2005) and policy advantage (Green and Jennings, 2012).

These considerations lead us to whether various 'events' had an impact net of economics, the political cycle, and costs of ruling. Selected events include economic crises: the ERM crisis in September 1992 ('Black Wednesday'), the petrol crisis of September 2000 and the financial crash following the collapse of a bank in November 2007 ('Northern Rock'). We also include a variable representing the apparent positive effect of the bank rescue unveiled in October 2008 by Gordon Brown.

The inclusion of events variables also allows us to incorporate other things that are universally desired. These include events relating to national security such as the Falklands War in 1982, the first Gulf War in 1990/1 and the second Gulf War in 2003. All had a successful outcome and seemed to boost approval. If these events have a significant effect this may be either because the government managed them well and provided reassurance or simply because the electorate tend to 'rally around the flag' in response to 'threats'.

We include more regular event variables representing turnovers of power from one party to another and changes in prime minister. These variables are crucial because they allow us to estimate a single model across time and set aside the difficult issues about the periodicity of our models (Paldam, 1991). We expect both to increase approval. We also include variables representing Conservative and coalition governments. Our expectations here are based on intuition. Since the Conservative party have been in power far longer than Labour, we expect it has gained a higher reputation. Our expectations about the coalition are based on intuition that the electorate would view power-sharing with suspicion.

We have already noted that it is not possible to measure the gap between policy preferences of the electorate and policy of the government. Nevertheless, we have a large amount of data about how well regarded the parties are in relation to policy domains. From 1950 onwards, the survey houses have asked respondents to say which party would be best to deal with either 'issues' or 'problems' (King and Wybrow, 2001). These questions relate to a wide range of issues including the economy (prosperity, unemployment, inflation, and taxation), public services (the NHS, schools and education, welfare) and security (crime, defence, and immigration). The issues have changed over time and the wordings of questions have changed to reflect contemporary discourse. Nevertheless, the electorate's responses to these diverse questions track each other over time. This suggests that responses to such questions capture a general policy advantage (Green and Jennings, 2012).

We separately analyse all the available 'best party' data across all issues for all three major parties using the dyads-ratio algorithm (Stimson, 1999). We label the first extracted dimension 'policy advantage'. When there is one party in power, policy advantage is represented by that party's score. When the Conservatives and Liberal Democrats are in coalition between 2010 and 2015, the advantage is the sum of the two parties' scores.

Hypotheses

Our survey of the popularity functions literature enables us to formulate three 'core hypotheses' about executive approval relating to: the electoral cycle and costs of ruling, the economy, and events.

Electoral cycle and costs of ruling: Approval declines with each month in a parliament (H1a) and increases with months squared (H1b) ('electoral cycle'). Approval declines the longer a government (H1c) and prime minister (H1d) is in power ('costs of ruling').

The economy: Increases in unemployment (H2a), inflation (H2b), and interest rates (H2c) all reduce approval, while increases in the stock market (H2d), egocentric economic expectations (H2e), and sociotropic expectations (H2f) increase approval.

Events: H3. Discrete events affect approval. 'Regular' events also affect approval: turnover of government (H3a) and changes of prime minister (H3b) increase approval. Conservative governments have higher approval than Labour (H3c) and coalition governments have lower approval than Labour (H3d).

Our final hypothesis that goes beyond the usual three core hypotheses is:

Policy: Increases in government policy advantage increase approval (H4).

Our hypothesis about the costs of ruling associated with prime ministers represents an original contribution to the study of executive approval—though this is in part necessitated by the incorporation of prime ministerial approval in the executive approval series. The addition of stock market as an indicator of economic welfare is similarly original, as far as we are aware. Our major innovation, however, is the addition of an indicator of policy advantage that tries to gauge the impact of policy considerations on approval.

Methods

Except for events, most series in our models suggest the possibility of unit roots.[3] Accordingly, we employ an error correction model specification (Enders, 2006). These models allow us to examine both the short-run effects (Δx) and long-run effects (x_{t-n}) of variables on changes in executive approval.[4]

Variables may exert an influence with a lag. We use information criteria to select the most appropriate lags for each continuous explanatory variable. This evidence suggests that lags of four months for unemployment, three months for stock markets, two months for interest rates, four months for sociotropic

[3] The Dickey-Fuller tests produced the following results (test-statistics in brackets) approval, (−3.963), unemployment, lags 4 (−2.159), inflation (−0.803), stock market, lags 3 (−2.407), interest rates, lags 2 (−0.257), sociotropic expectations, lags 4 (−3.776), egocentric expectations (−4.426), and policy advantage, lags 2 (−3.251)

[4] In recent years there have been debates about the applicability of the error correction model (DeBoef and Keele, 2008; Enns et al., 2016; Grant and Lebo, 2016). The issues are not resolved. The findings laid out here are similar in terms of both the sign and significance to the b-coefficients generated by simpler specifications.

expectations and two months for governing party policy advantage, are appropriate. Both inflation and egocentric expectations are lagged just one month. We lagged some events variables as necessary. We also log continuous variables (inflation, unemployment, stock market, expectations, and governing party policy advantage). This tames heteroscedasticity but increases the size of the estimated b-coefficients and adds a degree of complexity to interpretation of results.

Empirical Results: A General Model of Executive Approval

Political science is about the search for law-like relations that exist across both space and time (Budge, 2019). It makes sense to assess what drives approval over as long a period as possible. In this section we focus on 1980 to 2015 since we have relevant quality economic expectations data. This produces a time series of 431 months.

The results from our general error correction model are displayed in the first column of Table 3.1. The error correction term is significant and correctly (negatively) signed. Turning to our first core hypothesis, the coefficients for those variables designed to control for the electoral cycle are correctly signed and statistically significant, providing support for both H1a, and H1b. The coefficient for the number of months since the general election is significant and negative (b=−0.07) and the coefficient for months squared is significant and positive (b=0.001). In a typical forty-eight-month parliament approval falls by 3.36 points for reasons that have nothing to do with economic conditions. Similarly, the coefficients for total number of months that the government is in power (b=−0.03) and total number of months that the prime minister is in office (b=0.01) are significant and negatively signed, confirming H1c and H1d. The Labour government from 1997 to 2010, for example, was in power 156 months. Longevity reduced Labour's approval by 4.68 points net of all other factors. If the party had still been led by Tony Blair in 2010, these costs would have been even greater. We interpret these findings as reflecting the unobserved impact of a policy gap that is not fully captured by policy advantage (McGann et al., 2023). It may also reflect grievance asymmetry, or initially inflated expectations about what governments can do (Wlezien, 2017; Stimson, 1976).

We now turn to our second core hypothesis about the economy. The 'family' of H2 hypotheses receives partial support in relation to the objective economy. The coefficients on both lagged unemployment (b=1.37) and

Table 3.1 Models of executive approval, 1980–2015

	General Model		Bank of England		Coalition	
	B	(SE)	B	(SE)	B	(SE)
Error Correction	−0.32*	(0.03)	−0.32*	(0.03)	−0.31*	(0.00)
Electoral cycle and costs of ruling						
Months since election$_t$	−0.07*	(0.03)	−0.06*	(0.03)	−0.07*	(0.03)
Months since election squared$_t$	0.001*	(0.00)	0.001*	(0.00)	0.001*	(0.00)
Govt months in power total$_t$	−0.03*	(0.00)	−0.02*	(0.00)	−0.03*	(0.00)
PM months in powert otal$_t$	−0.01*	(0.00)	−0.01*	(0.00)	−0.01*	(0.00)
Economics						
ΔUnemployment$_t$	2.31	(7.40)	0.52	(7.64)	1.78	(7.42)
Unemployment$_{t-4}$	1.37*	(0.62)	1.73*	(0.62)	1.35*	(0.62)
ΔInflation$_t$	−0.24	(0.69)	−0.05	(0.69)	−0.30	(0.69)
Inflation$_{t-1}$	1.17*	(0.28)	1.62*	(0.32)	1.16*	(0.28)
ΔStock market$_t$	−3.67	(2.44)	−4.24°	(2.42)	−3.79	(2.45)
Stock market$_{t-3}$	2.88*	(0.44)	2.18*	(0.50)	2.85*	(0.44)
ΔInterest rates$_t$	3.70*	(1.41)	3.46°	(2.10)	3.62*	(1.41)
Interest rates$_{t-2}$	−0.29	(0.36)	−1.39*	(0.67)	−0.28	(0.36)
ΔEgocentric expectations$_t$	3.21*	(1.04)	3.23*	(1.03)	2.96*	(1.05)
Egocentric expectations$_{t-1}$	3.69*	(0.77)	4.01*	(0.77)	3.61*	(0.78)
ΔSociotropic expectations$_t$	3.01*	(0.41)	3.00*	(0.40)	3.04*	(0.41)
Sociotropic expectations$_{t-4}$	0.66*	(0.29)	0.86*	(0.29)	0.67*	(0.29)
Events						
Exchange Rate Mechanism crisis$_{t-1}$	−6.36*	(1.87)	−5.92*	(1.86)	−6.36*	(1.88)
Petrol$_t$	−5.61*	(1.90)	−5.21*	(1.88)	−5.48*	(1.90)
Northern Rock$_t$	−5.82*	(1.85)	−6.01*	(1.83)	−5.82*	(1.85)
Banking rescue$_{t-1}$	9.18*	(1.90)	8.94*	(1.88)	9.17*	(1.90)
MPs expenses$_{t-1}$	−3.12°	(1.89)	−3.31°	(1.87)	−3.21°	(1.89)
Falklands$_t$	5.77*	(1.10)	5.49*	(1.09)	5.74*	(1.10)
Gulf War 1$_t$	2.88*	(1.13)	3.42*	(1.13)	2.89*	(1.13)
Gulf War 2$_t$	4.23*	(1.36)	4.35*	(1.35)	4.21*	(1.36)
Brighton bomb$_t$	4.22*	(1.83)	3.93*	(1.81)	4.11*	(1.84)
9/11$_t$	13.51*	(1.90)	13.41*	(1.88)	13.49*	(1.90)
7/7 bombings$_t$	4.01*	(1.85)	3.83*	(1.83)	4.03*	(1.86)
Change in government$_t$	13.77*	(1.14)	13.43*	(1.14)	13.69*	(1.14)

Change prime minister$_{t-1}$	1.95*	(0.89)	2.09*	(0.88)	2.31*	(0.92)
Conservative government$_t$	1.02	(0.75)	2.62*	(0.92)	1.00	(0.75)
Coalition government$_t$	−4.12*	(0.98)	−2.25*	(1.08)	−3.85	(10.33)
Government policy advantage						
ΔAdvantage$_t$	6.83*	(1.39)	6.68*	(1.37)	7.84*	(1.56)
Advantage$_{t-2}$	4.89*	(1.00)	5.28*	(1.02)	4.69*	(1.06)
Bank of England independence$_t$			−0.45	(1.71)		
Interaction terms						
ΔInterest rates$_t$ × Bank of England			0.36	(2.68)		
Interest rates$_{t-2}$ × Bank of England			1.93*	(0.77)		
ΔGovernment policy advantage$_t$ × coalition					−4.74	(3.52)
Government policy advantage$_t$ × coalition					−0.05	(2.87)
Constant	−42.35*	(5.32)	41.99*	(5.26)	−41.23*	(5.44)
Adjusted R^2	0.59		0.60		0.59	
N	431		431		431	

Source: Author's estimates.
Note: °p<0.10, * p<0.05 (two-tailed test), standard errors in parentheses.

inflation (b=1.17) are statistically significant but, unexpectedly, *positively* signed. Interest rates have a statistically significant (b=3.70) short-term influence on approval. This is also contrary to expectations. Approval increases as interest rates rise. We must reject H2a, H2b, and H2c. The stock market has a statistically significant and correctly signed positive long-term effect on approval (b=2.88), providing support for H2d. This variable may provide the surest indicator of the health of the economy since efficient markets incorporate all the available data and are forward- looking. Overall, only one of the four hypotheses about the impact of objective economic indicators is correct (H2d). Since objective indicators provide evidence about the past, these findings may suggest that the electorate is focused on the future. It is tempting to suggest that these results are simply because we have included subjective expectations that mediate the impact of objective indicators. This is not the case. If we omit expectations and policy advantage, the coefficients for the objective economic indicators are scarcely altered.

The findings displayed for the general model in Table 3.1 provide overwhelming support for H2e and H2f: governments are rewarded for making people feel good about the economy and punished for making them feel bad.[5] Egocentric expectations exert both a statistically significant short-term effect (b=3.21) and long-term effect (b=3.69). Sociotropic expectations also exert statistically significant short-term (b=3.01) and long-term (b=0.66) effects. The size of the short-term coefficients are very similar but egocentric expectations exert a stronger long-term effect. This confirms the importance of the 'pocketbook' factor and provides a compelling reason for confining our analyses of the dynamics of approval between 1980 and 2015.

We now turn to the third core hypothesis about the impact of events. Each event included in the models has a statistically significant influence on approval. All the coefficients are consistent with expectations. Economic crises such a 'Black Wednesday' in 1992, the petrol crisis in 2000 and collapse of Northern Rock bank in 2007 all exert a strong negative effect. The coefficient for the banking rescue in October 2008 suggests that well-managed events can have a positive impact. The electorate may not have believed Gordon Brown's claim that he 'saved the world'—but they appear to have believed his actions made their lives better.[6]

The coefficients for the Falklands War in 1982, the first Gulf War in 1991, and the second Gulf War in 2003, suggest that these events boosted approval. So did the Brighton bomb attack of 1984 and the so-called 7/7 bombings of 2005. The MPs expenses scandal in 2009 also had a (marginally significant, $p<0.1$) negative effect on approval, even though the revelations of wrongdoing by MPs affected *all* parties at Westminster. The most striking finding, however, relates to the 9/11 attacks (b=13.51). These developments had a massive impact on approval of the British government. This may have reflected a simply 'rally around the flag' or approval for Tony Blair's decision to stand shoulder to shoulder with the United States.

[5] The sociotropic expectations series is apparently easier to model than egocentric expectations. It responds to inflation and the stock market plus events like the ERM debacle.

[6] At Prime Minister's Question Time on 10 December 2008 Brown said: 'We have not only saved the world.' See https://hansard.parliament.uk/commons/2008-12-0/debates/08121022000005/OralAnswersToQuestions.

The coefficients in the first column provide handsome support for the less unique events. The coefficient for turnover of government is large and significant (b=13.77), confirming H3a. The coefficient for change of prime minister is far smaller (b=1.96) but statistically significant and confirms H3b. Together with evidence about the costs of ruling associated with governments and prime minister, these findings confirm the importance of the parliamentary system. Changes of government have more effect on policy than changes of prime minister. The coefficient for Conservative governments is positively signed but not significant, so we reject H3c. The coefficient for the coalition (b=−4.12), on the other hand, is correctly negatively signed and significant, confirming H3d. Disraeli's quip that 'England does not love coalitions' has some truth to it (McLean, 2012).

Before we close our discussion of events it is worth noting that the addition of events helped to clarify the impact of other variables—including cyclical effects, the costs of ruling, and economic expectations. They are not just important in themselves—they are necessary to observe other systematic influences.

Finally, policy advantage matters a great deal to executive approval. The coefficients for both the short-term (b=6.83) and long-term (b=4.89) effects of this variable are statistically significant, positively signed, and substantively important, confirming H4. Policy advantage captures a whole slew of issues.[7] We take this finding as providing support for the policy gap hypothesis. Economic considerations are an important component of this indicator since it incorporates unemployment, inflation, taxation, and borrowing. Yet it also incorporates other issues that have been neglected in studies of executive approval. These include security (crime, terrorism, immigration, and defence), the public services (NHS, education, and transport), and foreign policy (defence, peace).

The findings laid out in the first column of Table 3.1 suggest that the three core hypotheses derived from the popularity functions literature: cyclical effects and the cost of ruling, economics, and events are also relevant to the dynamics of approval. Like others before us, we are impressed by the impact of economic expectations. Governments are undoubtedly rewarded for making people feel good and punished for making them feel bad about the economy. But policy matters too, and policy means more than economics. It is difficult to establish precisely how much of approval is the result of economics

[7] Future studies might distinguish between advantage on economic and non-economic issues, but the available evidence suggest that evaluations of party policy advantage are synoptic.

(the 'e-fraction') and how much is the result of politics (the 'p-fraction') (Paldam, 1991). We would have to allocate events to either economics or politics. Since non-economic events matter—as we demonstrate—then the size of the 'e' and 'p' fractions must vary over time. Both economics and politics matter and it is misleading to frame research as a tournament, especially since this also ignores cyclical effects and the costs of ruling.

Have the Forces Driving Approval Changed over Time?

Our general model in Table 3.1 provides our best shot at producing a general law of approval across time. Studies of popularity functions in Britain and approval elsewhere, suggest that findings depend on the periods chosen for analysis (Miller and Mackie, 1973; Paldam, 1991). In the British case, unique popularity functions are sometimes estimated for different parliaments, even if the same party remains in power—effectively throwing away relevant evidence. Yet there are few good reasons to expect that the fundamental drivers of approval should differ from one government to the next if the institutions of democracy are unchanged. We prefer to assume a degree of continuity and produce a general model that incorporates our three core hypotheses and indicator of policy advantage, over as long a period as possible.

When the institutions in a democracy are stable it makes a great deal of sense to assume that the drivers of approval do not change. While some of the fundamentals of the system have been stable—particularly the electoral system for elections to Westminster—the last thirty-five years have witnessed important changes that may have modified the clarity of responsibility in the British constitution. One such development was the establishment of the Monetary Policy Committee (MPC) in 1997 that gave the Bank of England operational control of interest rates (Dellepiane-Avellaneda, 2012). From 1997 onwards chancellors and governments were able to influence interest rates indirectly by setting inflation targets. All the decisions on interest rates were made by the nine-member MPC, only four of whom were directly appointed by the chancellor. The government's responsibility for monetary policy was weakened, if not entirely extinguished. This might be expected to modify the impact of conditions on evaluations of the government.

Another potentially important development, was the Conservative-Liberal Democrat coalition from 2010 to 2015, the first peacetime coalition since 1931. This represented a very significant deviation from the norm of single-party government. Few living voters would have experienced a power-sharing coalition before. The Conservative party was the senior partner with 306 seats in the Commons and eighteen seats in the cabinet, while the Liberal Democrats had fifty-seven seats in the Commons and five seats in cabinet. David Cameron, the Conservative leader, became prime minister and Nick Clegg, the Liberal Democrat leader, became his deputy. Advocates of the Westminster system claim that parliamentary sovereignty and single-party government enhance accountability. Powerful governing parties can be held responsible. Under the coalition, power and responsibility were diffused.

To test whether these two changes modified the drivers of approval we use interaction terms. To gauge the effect of Bank of England independence we included another dummy variable for independence from May 1997 and then multiplied both interest rates and its first difference by this variable. The results are displayed in the third column of Table 3.1. The main short-term effect remains significant (at $p<0.1$) but its interaction term is insignificant. The main long-term effect for interest rates is negative ($b=-1.39$ and significant at $p<0.05$), while its interaction effect with central bank independence is positive ($b=1.93$), and statistically significant at $p<0.05$. It seems that before central bank independence governments were punished for rising interest rates. After independence rising interest rates have a positive effect on approval. This change may be because governments were no longer held responsible for interest rates. It may also be because from 1997 increases in interest rates were likely to signal that there was a recovery and good times would follow, while a reduction in interest rates signalled bad times ahead. Whatever the case, central bank independence appears to have modified the relationship between approval and one of the most important economic instruments.[8]

To gauge the effect of the coalition we again simply multiply both government policy advantage and its first difference by the dummy variable for the coalition and examine the resulting coefficients to establish whether the effects of these variables varied under coalition conditions. The results are displayed in the fifth column of Table 3.1. The main effects of government policy remain positive. The coefficients for the corresponding interaction terms are negative ($b=-4.74$ for the first difference and $b=-0.05$ for the long-term effect). Both coefficients, however, are statistically insignificant. The coalition, on this evidence, does not appear to have modified the fundamental dynamics of monthly executive approval.

[8] Since interest rates were held at 0.5 per cent during the period of the coalition it is possible that this finding is the result of some very peculiar circumstances. If we run the same model from 1980 to 2010, however, we obtain very similar results.

Other evidence suggests that the electorate simply reacted against the coalition for other reasons. This is illustrated by the negative coefficient (b=−4.12) for coalitions in the first column of Table 3.1. The vote intentions series for this period shows that support for the Liberal Democrats plummeted within a few weeks of entering the coalition. This decline lasted for five years. In 2015 it resulted in a massive reduction in the Liberal Democrat vote, from 23 to just 7.9 per cent, and the loss of forty-nine of the fifty-seven seats held five years before (Bartle, 2021). This in part reflected the general tendency of voters to punish junior parties in coalitions (Kluver and Spoon, 2019). It also reflected the fact that many Liberal Democrat voters in 2010 were essentially anti-Conservative voters who had temporarily lent their votes to the third party. The Liberal Democrats willingness to enter a coalition with the Conservatives undoubtedly shocked many such voters. This produced a step-shift in Liberal Democrat fortunes.

Conclusion

The British political system promotes a simple clarity of responsibly. The buck stops with the executive. This chapter provides evidence that the British electorate hold their governments accountable for conditions. Perceptions of the economic future matter and are crucial to understanding the dynamics of executive approval. Governments are rewarded for making people feel optimistic about their economic futures and punished for making them feel bad. They are also rewarded for managing events and providing reassurance of control. Policy advantage plays a role too. Nevertheless, the electoral cycle also plays a role. So do the (two) 'costs of ruling'. These unconditional influences may discourage the executive from responding to the electorate. Why bother responding to the electorate if you are going to lose anyway? So might an uncompetitive opposition. Why respond to the electorate if the major opposition are unelectable? (Bartle et al., 2019; McGann et al., 2023). The British system provides rough—but far from perfect—accountability.

The British political system is characterized by stability and continuity. There has been some institutional change, and there is some evidence that the electorate has responded to change in reasonable ways. Central bank independence seems to have modified the relationship between interest rates approval. The coalition government from 2010 to 2015, on the other hand, did not modify the relationship between policy and approval. Future coalition governments might modify behaviour as voters gain experience of multi-party governments. While the two-party system reasserted itself in 2017 and 2019, coalitions are always possible given the plurality electoral system (Bartle, 2021). If a more proportional system was adopted for Westminster elections, this would modify the dynamics of approval in the longer term as the electorate learned the new rules of the game. Change is also possible without electoral reform. The social coalitions within the two major parties have undergone change as 'Leavers' moved to the Conservatives and 'Remainers' moved to Labour. The divisions between 'remain' and 'leave' partly reflect wider divisions about social and cultural issues (Sobolewska, 2021). This shift in the nature of party coalition may result in parties defined by their attitudes towards cultural change. The British electorate may become less responsive to economic conditions—just like its US counterpart (see Chapter 13).[9]

Finally, the United Kingdom's recent decision to 'take back control' by leaving the European Union may increase the electorate's responsiveness to the executive. The British government can no longer blame the European Union for its woes. The reassertion of national sovereignty should encourage voters to pay more attention to the activities of their executive branch. British governments might find the British electorate even more watchful—and even more vengeful—in the future.

References

Alt, J. E. (1979). *The Politics of Economic Decline.* Cambridge: Cambridge University Press.

Bagehot, W. (2001). *The English Constitution.* Oxford: Oxford University Press.

Bartle, J. (2021). The two-party system: All else is embellishment and detail. In *Breaking the Deadlock: Britain at the Polls 2019*, N. Allen, and J. Bartle, eds. Manchester: Manchester University Press. 89–122.

Bartle, J., Dellepiane-Avellaneda, S., and Stimson, J. A. (2011). The moving centre: Preferences for government activity in Britain, 1950–2005. *British Journal of Political Science, 41*(2), 259–85.

Bartle, J., McGann, A., and Dellepiane-Avellaneda, S. (2019). Policy accommodation versus electoral turnover: Policy representation in Britain, 1945–2015. *Journal of Public Policy, 38*(2), 235–65.

Brody, R. (1991). *Assessing the President: The Media, Elite Opinion and Public Support.* Stanford, CA: Stanford University Press.

[9] Regrettably, we are not able to examine any post-2016 changes because of gaps in the economic expectations series.

Budge, I. (1994). A new spatial theory of party competition: Uncertainty, ideology and policy equilibria viewed comparatively and temporally. *British Journal of Political Science, 24*(4), 443–67.

Budge, I. (2019). *Politics: A Unified Introduction to How Democracy Works.* London: Routledge.

Bytzek, E. (2011). Questioning the obvious: Political events and public opinion on the government's standing in Germany 1977–2002. *International Journal of Public Opinion Research, 23*(4), 406–36.

Carlin, R. E, Hartlyn, J., Hellwig, T., Love, G. J., Martínez-Gallardo, C., and Singer, M. M. (2018). Public support for Latin American presidents: The cyclical model in comparative perspective. *Research & Politics.* https://doi.org/10.1177/2053168018787690.

Chrystal, K. A. and Alt. J (1981). Some problems in formulating and testing a politico-economic model of the United Kingdom. *Economic Journal, 91*(363), 730–6.

Clarke, H. D., Mishler, W., and Whiteley, P. (1990). Recapturing the Falklands: Models of Conservative popularity, 1979–83. *British Journal of Political Science, 20*(1), 63–81.

Crewe, I. (1992). A nation of liars? Opinion polls and the 1992 election. *Parliamentary Affairs, 45*(4), 475–95.

DeBoef, S., and Keele, L. (2008). Taking time seriously. *American Journal of Political Science, 52*(1), 184–200.

Dellepiane-Avellaneda, S. (2012). Gordon Unbound: The heresthetic of Central Bank Independence in Britain. *British Journal of Political Science, 43*(2), 263–93.

Enders, W. P. (2006). *Applied Econometric Time Series.* Hoboken, NJ: John Wiley & Sons.

Enns, P. K., Kelly, N. J., Masaki, T., and Wohlfarth, P. C. (2016). Don't jettison the general error correction model just yet: A practical guide to avoiding spurious regression with the GECM. *Research & Politics.* https://doi.org/10.1177/2053168016643345.

Erikson, R. S., MacKuen, M. B., and Stimson, J. A. (2002). *The Macro Polity.* New York: Cambridge University Press.

Fiorina, M. P. (1981). *Retrospective Voting in American National Elections.* New Haven, CT: Yale University Press.

Frey, B. and Schneider, F. (1978). A politico-economic model of the United Kingdom. *Economic Jounral, 88*(350), 243–53.

Gallup Opinion Polls. (1977a). *The Gallup International Public Opinion Polls, Great Britain,* 1937–1975, *Volume* 6. Santa Barbara, CA: Greenwood Press.

Gallup Opinion Polls. (1977b). *The Gallup International Public Opinion Polls, Great Britain, 1937–1975, Volume 2.* Santa Barbara, CA: Greenwood Press.

Goodhart, C. A. E., and Bhanslai, R. J. (1970). Political economy. *Political Studies, 18*(1), 43–106.
Grant, T and Lebo, M. J. (2016). Error correction methods with political time series. *Political Analysis, 24*(1), 3–30.
Green, J. and Jennings, W. (2012). Valence as macro-competence: An analysis of mood in party competence evaluations in Great Britain. *British Journal of Political Science, 42*(2), 311–43.
Hakhverdian, A. (2010). Political representation and its mechanisms: A dynamic left-right approach for the United Kingdom, 1976–2006. *British Journal of Political Science, 40*(4), 835–56.
Hudson, J. (1985). The relationship between government popularity and approval for the government's record in the United Kingdom. *British Journal of Political Science, 15(*2), 165–86.
Jennings, W., and John, P. (2009). The dynamics of political attention: Public opinion and the Queen's Speech in the United Kingdom. *American Journal of Political Science, 53*(4), 838–54.
Johns, R. (2018). Squeezing the SNP: the election in Scotland. In *None Past the Post: Britain at the Polls 2017,* N. Allen and J. Bartle, eds. Manchester: Manchester Univesity Press. 100–20.
King, A. (1998). Why Labour won – at last. In *New Labour Triumphs: Britain at the Polls*, A. King, ed. Chatham, NJ: Chatham House. 177–208.
King, A. (2000). *Does the United Kingdom Still Have a Constitution?* London: Sweet & Maxwell.
King, A. (2010). *The British Constitution.* Oxford: Oxford University Press.
King, A., and Wybrow. R. (2001). *British Political Opinion, 1937–2000: The Gallup Polls.* London: Politicos Publishing.
Kluver, H., and Spoon, J. J. (2019). Helping or hurting? How governing as a junior coalition partner influences electoral outcomes. *Journal of Politics, 82*(4), 1231–42.
Kuhn, R. (2007). *Politics and the Media in Britain.* London: Palgrave.
Lijphart, A. (1999). *Patterns of Democracy: Government Forms and Performance in Thirty-six Countries.* New Haven, CT: Yale University Press.
McGann, A., Dellepiane-Avellaneda, S., and Bartle, J. (2019). Parallel lines? Policy mood in a plurinational democracy, *Electoral Studies, 58*(1), 48–57.
McGann, A., Dellepiane Avellaneda, S., and Bartle, J. (2023). Responsive government for realists? Public opinion and policy responsiveness in the Netherlands and the UK. *Economics and Politics, 35*(1), 333–55.
McLean, I. (2012). England does not love coalitions: The most misused political quotation in the book. *Government and Opposition, 47*(1), 3–21.
May, J. D. (1978). Defining democracy: A bid for coherence and consensus. *Political Studies, 26*(1), 1–14.

Miller, W. L., and Mackie, M. (1973). The electoral cycle and the asymmetry of government and opposition popularity: An alternative model of the relationship between economic conditions and government popularity. *Political Studies, 21*(2), 263–79.

Mueller, J. (1970). Presidential popularity from Truman to Johnson. *American Political Science Review, 65*(1), 18–34.

Nannestad, P., and Paldam, M. (2002). The costs of ruling: a foundation for two theories. In *Economic Voting*, H. Dorussen and M. Taylor, eds. London: Routledge. 17–44.

Norris, P. (1990). *British By-elections: The Volatile Electorate.* Oxford: Clarendon Press.

Key. V. O. (1966). *The Responsible Electorate: Rationality in Presidential Voting, 1936–1960.* New York: Belknap Press.

Paldam, M. (1991). How robust is the vote function? A study of seventeen nations over four decades. In *Economics and Politics: The Calculus of Support*, H. Norpoth, M. S. Lewis-Beck, and J. D. Lafay, eds. Ann Arbor, MI: University of Michigan Press. 9–31.

Pissarides, C. (1980). British government popularity and economic performance. *Economic Journal, 90*(359), 569–81.

Powell, G. B., and Whitten, G. D. (1993). A cross-national analysis of economic voting: Taking account of the political context. *American Journal of Political Science, 37*(2), 391–414.

Price, S., and Sanders, D. (1993). Modelling government popularity in post-war Britain: A methodological example. *American Journal of Political Science, 37*(3), 317–34.

Rallings, C., and Thrasher, M. (1997). *Local Elections in Britain.* London: Routledge.

Sanders, D. (1991). Government popularity and the next general election. *Political Studies, 62*(2), 235–61.

Sanders, D. (2005). Popularity function forecasts for the 2005 British general election. *British Journal of Politics and International Relations, 7*(2), 174–90.

Sanders, D., Ward, H. and Marsh, D. (1993). The electoral impact of press coverage of the British economy, 1979–87. *British Journal of Political Science, 23*(2), 175–210.

Sanders, D., Ward, H., Marsh, D., and Fletcher, T. (1987). Government popularity and the Falklands war: A reassessment. *British Journal of Political Science, 17*(3), 281–313.

Shaw, G. (1984). *Rational Expectations: An Elementary Exposition.* Brighton: Wheatsheaf Books.

Sobolewska, M. (2021). A changing electorate: New identities and the British 'culture war'. In *Breaking the Deadlock: Britain at the Polls 2019*, N. Allen, and J. Bartle, eds. Manchester: Manchester University Press. 123–47.

Soroka, S. (2014). *Negativity in Politics: Causes and Consequences*. Cambridge: Cambridge University Press.

Soroka, S. and Wlezien, C. (2009). *Degrees of Democracy*. Cambridge: Cambridge University Press.

Stimson, J. A. (1976). Public support for American presidents: A cyclical model. *Public Opinion Quarterly 40*(1), 1–21.

Stimson, J. A. (1999). *Public Opinion in America: Moods, Cycles, and Swings*. Boulder, CO: Westview Press.

Stokes, D. E., and Iverson, G. R. (1966). On the existence of forces restoring party competition. *Public Opinion Quarterly*, *26*(2), 159–71.

Strøm, K. (1990). A behavioural theory of competitive parties. *American Journal of Political Science*, *34*(2), 565–98.

Wlezien, C. (1995) The public as thermostat: Dynamics of preferences for spending. *Americcan Journal of Political Science*, *39*(4), 981–1000.

Wlezien, C. (2017) Policy (mis)representation and the cost of ruling: US presidential elections in comparative perspective. *Comparative Political Studies*, *50*(6), 711–38.

Wlezien, C., Jennings, W., Fisher, S., Ford, R., and Pickup, M. (2013). Polls and the vote in Britain. *Political Studies*, *61*(1), 66–91.

Zaller, J. R. (1992). *The Nature and Origins of Mass Opinion*. Cambridge: Cambridge University Press.

4

The Cost of Ruling above Everything Else

Explaining Presidential Popularity in France

Emiliano Grossman and Isabelle Guinaudeau

In 2007, Nicolas Sarkozy was elected president on an ambitious reform platform. He scorned his predecessor Jacques Chirac for his failure to enact any major change. In 2012, his successor François Hollande promised to return to a 'normal presidency', where the head of state would no longer be omnipresent in policymaking. From 2017, Emmanuel Macron in turn returned to a more activist style of governing. At certain moments of their respective terms, these presidents had to deal with major crises including the Iraq War, the Great Recession, the Fukushima disaster, the terrorist attacks in Paris in 2015 and the coronavirus outbreak in 2020.

Despite these contrasted styles and contexts, Sarkozy, Hollande, and Macron experienced strikingly similar fates with respect to their popularity: a sharp peak in the aftermath of the election quickly followed by a sudden drop that was only the beginning of a seemingly inexorable erosion process, leading to even lower levels. This pattern of decreasing executive popularity, sometimes referred to as the 'cost of ruling', is not unique to France (Mueller, 1973; Stimson, 1976; Paldam and Skott, 1995; Nannestad and Paldam, 2002; Palmer and Whitten, 2002; Stevenson, 2002; Wlezien, 2017; Thesen et al., 2019). Yet, it seems particularly strong under the French Fifth Republic and, as we show, tends to dominate other possible drivers of (un)popularity, in particular the economic determinants reassessed in this volume.

The correlations presented in Table 1.1 in the introduction to this volume depict a sharp decline over time in the relationship between the French public's subjective perceptions of macro-economic conditions, as captured by the consumer confidence index, and approval of the political executive over the last decades. Indeed, France provides the sharpest decline of all those observed. Yet, there is some uncertainty as to what the consumer confidence

Emiliano Grossman and Isabelle Guinaudeau, *The Cost of Ruling above Everything Else.* In: *Economics and Politics Revisited.* Edited by: Timothy Hellwig and Matthew Singer, Oxford University Press. © Emiliano Grossman and Isabelle Guinaudeau (2023). DOI: 10.1093/oso/9780192871664.003.0004

index captures and the extent to which it reflects effective economic outcomes.[1] Subjective views may be biased depending on levels of information and the way individuals filter and process it, so that the causal relationship with presidential assessment can be bidirectional (De Boef and Kellstedt, 2004; Enns et al., 2012; Vaillant and Flambard, 2014). In addition, the findings produced by past multivariate analyses are, at best, mixed.

Among the countries covered in this volume, France also stands out with its semi-presidential regime adopted in 1958. The Fifth Republic was conceived to divide executive responsibility between a powerful and directly elected president, who was to focus on 'high politics' and to remain above partisan controversies and day-to-day politics, and a government subject to assembly confidence and in charge of the problems of the day (Shugart, 2005; Elgie, 2010). This could have been expected to blur responsibilities, making it comparatively difficult for citizens to assign blame and praise for economic outcomes. Yet the reality is more complex. As we shall see, the institutions and practice of the Fifth Republic turn the president, except in periods of cohabitations (as divided government is called in France), into a 'man of providence' expected to take charge of the country. This is coupled with a widespread belief that the president alone can get things done. This results in an unusually strong concentration of responsibilities in the hands of the president.

We argue that this is precisely where the crux of the Fifth Republic lies: power is so heavily concentrated in the hands of the president that she pays a comparatively strong price for it in terms of popularity. This cost-of-ruling effect is such that economic considerations may only exert residual influence. Blame for perceived or real failures to meet policy expectations is concentrated on the president. And even improving economic conditions are unlikely to offset the decline in popularity. Given the growing centrality of the presidential figure over time, this cost of ruling is likely to have become even stronger. To assess these expectations, we use a unique data series on executive popularity, objective and subjective economic conditions, and political cycles to re-examine the determinants of presidential popularity over the past four and half decades.

These observations shed light on what could be called the decline of French presidents. Popularity is an important determinant of policymaking capacity. In France, Magni-Berton (2008) observes that governments adopt fewer laws in times of unpopularity, because they have to negotiate more with veto

[1] On the correlation between objective and subjective economic indicators in the French context, see Bélanger and Lewis-Beck 2004, 232.

players. We have shown elsewhere that a certain level of executive popularity is a precondition for mandate responsiveness (Grossman and Guinaudeau, 2021). The literature suggests that this factor also shapes governments' incentives: degradations in popularity tend to prompt them to short-term spending to try to regain support (Frey, 1997; Pommerehne et al., 1981; Haynes and Stone, 1990), although the latitude for strategic spending is shrinking in times of fiscal competition and budget austerity. Against this background, the lows in executive popularity reached in recent years have caught the attention of many observers of French politics.

We proceed as follows. We next introduce our theoretical framework and our central assumptions. We then describe the data and our empirical strategy. The findings presented in the third section provide strong evidence for our argument. The cost of ruling shapes presidential popularity much more than economic performance, even if we find a significant effect of inflation and consumer confidence. Cohabitations used to limit cost of ruling, yet they no longer occur. The final section discusses these results and draws out their implications for understanding the popularity of French executives.

Theory: Sources of (Un)Popularity

Research on popularity functions tend to cluster around two main perspectives. The first of these centres on *economic explanations*. In the tradition of V.O. Key's (1966) reward-punishment model, executives are rewarded for good economic performance (e.g. decreasing unemployment and/or low inflation rates, sometimes also growth in real income) with higher levels of popularity—and sanctioned for bad ones, with growing unpopularity (Paldam, 1981; (Hibbs et al., 1982; Norpoth and Yantek, 1983; Ostrom and Simon, 1985). An alternative perspective emphasizes cyclical patterns marked by honeymoon periods in the aftermath of the election of a new president followed by steady declines in popularity over the course of the term. This is often referred to in the comparative politics literature as the *cost of ruling*.[2] The unique concentration of power in the hands of the president in the French context leads us to expect a predominance of the cost of ruling—at the expense of economic considerations. In this section we first point to the mixed evidence as to the impact of economic factors before developing our argument about the ever-increasing cost of ruling in France.

[2] Cuzán (2015) speaks of the 'law of shrinking support'.

The Limited Explanatory Power of Economic Determinants

Economic factors, typically gauged in terms of inflation and unemployment, have been at the core of popularity functions since their origins (Goodhart and Bhansali, 1970; Lafay, 1984; Monroe, 1984). This relationship has been increasingly questioned over the last decades, in view of considerable variation across contexts (Paldam, 1991; see Bellucci and Lewis-Beck, 2011 and the introduction to this volume for a critical discussion). Economic determinants were also scrutinized in studies of executive popularity in France (e.g. Lafay, 1984).

According to the Constitution of the Fifth Republic, presidents exert executive powers in consultation with the prime minister. This division of authority has led some authors to research the consequences of economic performance on executive approval with a focus on prime ministers rather than presidents (Lewis-Beck, 1980; Boya, 2017). In theory, the president was indeed supposed to remain above party politics and to focus on the highest national concerns, leaving the prime minister to take responsibility for the handling of day-to-day problems. In practice, however, presidents use their full political weight, derived from their direct election, to take leadership and stage themselves as the main person in charge—a practice that has been present since the origins of the Fifth Republic but, as we will see, has become reinforced over time. The dividing line between presidential and prime ministerial prerogatives is clearer in times of cohabitation when both office holders come from different parties. This happened twice under François Mitterrand's presidency after he lost the legislative elections (1986–1988 and 1993–1995) and once after Jacques Chirac's dissolution of the Assembly (1997–2002).[3] The president's influence was then reduced following the sanction of lost legislative elections, and institutionally given that she is no longer backed by a parliamentary majority allowing her to pass her policies. In these instances, the prime minister then took leadership on day-to-day policymaking, while the chief of state mainly focused on foreign policy and defence, where her role is preeminent according to Article 5 of the Constitution.

As a matter of fact, the effect of economic indicators on presidential popularity is at best mixed, regardless of the partisan affinity with the prime minister.

[3] The 2022 legislative elections left Emmanuel Macron without a ruling majority. They did not, however, result in a cohabitation as the presidential coalition remains the biggest force in the National Assembly and other parties are neither willing, nor able to form an alternative majority. This unprecedented situation will make the vote of any bill conditional upon the construction of a parliamentary majority.

Some authors find an impact, mostly for unemployment, while the effect of inflation appears to be more ambiguous (Lewis-Beck, 1980; Hibbs and Vasilatos, 1981; Conley, 2006). Inflation attracted public attention in the 1970s and 1980s, but it has remained at low (and decreasing) levels since.[4] Unemployment is a more salient problem, but it has also become a structural one, as the unemployment rate has remained between 7 and 10 per cent since the 1980s. Most fluctuations within this range occurred in the 1980s, 1990s, and 2000s, with unemployment repeatedly reaching the symbolic threshold of the two-digit figure, which may have had consequences on executive approval.

But while many studies found an association between economic outcomes and government support, several studies do not find any impact of macroeconomic conditions (Pommerehne et al., 1981; Turgeon et al., 2015), or only moderated by media coverage (Gerstlé and François, 2011). Still others point to the comparatively stronger relevance of other factors, including political events, electoral cycles, and cohabitation (Norpoth, 1984; Anderson, 1995; Conley, 2006; Boukari and Farvaque, 2019). 'Rally-round-the-flag' events (Mueller, 1973; Baum, 2002; Hetherington and Nelson, 2003; Conley, 2006) may indeed be more relevant to presidential popularity ratings given the president's constitutional prerogatives (Turgeon and Bélanger, 2017).

In a nutshell, past literature suggests that popularity functions focusing on the economy perform less well in France, pointing to the need to look for alternative explanations.

Concentrating Power and Blame

The key to understanding the dynamics of French presidential popularity may lie instead in one of the most striking features of the Fifth Republic: the unique power concentration in the hands of French presidents. This is mainly due to the distinctly French variety of semi-presidentialism (Elgie, 1999; Shugart, 2005) in which French presidents disproportionately suffer from blame-attribution for any development, triggering dissatisfaction. This is reflected in decreasing popularity and electoral prospects the longer a president is in power.

[4] It remains to be seen the extent to which the return of inflation in 2022 will impact presidential popularity.

This pattern, which has been observed across time and countries (Carlin et al., 2019; Nannestad and Paldam, 2002; Wlezien, 2017), is conventionally referred to as the cost of ruling. It translates into a typical cycle of popularity characterized by a high in the honeymoon period immediately after a presidential election followed by a steady degradation as the electoral cycle advances, albeit with an end-of-term upturn as the next election approaches and the president intensifies re-election-oriented efforts (Stimson, 1976). The mechanisms accounting for this law are subject to debate (see Wlezien, 2017 for a review). Stimson (1976) interpreted it as the result of a psychological effect in which popularity diminishes as time passes and the disproportionately high expectations addressed to newly elected executives meet reality and generate disappointment. Mueller (1973) pointed instead to the cumulation over time of the dissatisfaction of successive decisions' minorities, with the effect of undermining executive popularity. A further mechanism—that might reinforce the previous ones—pertains to 'grievance asymmetry' and voters' tendency to focus on negative developments such as failure, crises, or scandals (Mueller, 1973; Paldam and Skott, 1995; Nannestad and Paldam 2002; Palmer and Whitten, 2002; Stevenson, 2002; Soroka, 2014; Naurin et al., 2019; Thesen et al., 2019). A more recent argument posits that a longer time in office allows executives to shift policy away from median voters' wishes, with negative feedback on executive popularity (Wlezien, 2017).

The unique concentration of power in the hands of the president makes the French executive particularly conducive to cost-of-ruling effects. And Figure 4.1, below, certainly points to the pattern just described. The fathers of the Constitution tailored the presidential function to the needs and goals of Charles de Gaulle, poised to become its first president. The new Constitution was designed to respond to years of parliamentary and governmental instability under the Fourth Republic, as well as weak executives and an inability to pass unpopular reforms. The Algerian War was an additional contextual constraint. With France on the brink of civil war, De Gaulle appeared as the saviour, standing above conflicting interests and proposed a system providing the president with considerable powers. These powers derive first and foremost from the president's direct election (since 1965) as well as from a majoritarian electoral system which, at least until the mid-1980s, facilitated the construction of solid parliamentary majorities.

These institutions allow the president to play a central role in cabinet formation, portfolio allocation, policy agenda-setting, and reshuffles (Guinaudeau and Persico, 2021). When the president and the prime minister come from the same party, the latter tends to be far less visible and to leave leadership to the president. This can be exemplified by Nicolas Sarkozy's refusal to take on 'the ridiculous role of demanding that the prime minister reduces unemployment'. He famously declared: 'It is up to me to react. [. . .] The prime minister is a collaborator, I am the boss.'[5] Presidents have not hesitated to use government reshuffles, and even to change their prime ministers, to improve their popularity (Grossman, 2009), even though this does not always prove effective. This provides the French president with unique leverage: her constitutional prerogatives hugely outweigh those of heads of state in parliamentary systems, while the majoritarian voting system long guaranteed that she could rely on a parliamentary majority. The legislative procedures defined in articles 44.3 and 49.3 of the Constitution allow the executive to pass legislation even in the absence of such a majority.

Successive presidents have tended to reinforce personalization, presenting themselves as saviours, trying to combine charisma, competence, and leadership. Initiated by De Gaulle himself, his successors have tried to stick to his style. This may be due in part to the two-round electoral system, in which candidates have to cater to their own constituency in the first round to enter the second round where, two weeks later, they must obtain a majority without any political agreement being passed in between with other political forces. Candidates typically bridge these divergent imperatives by putting forward their personal qualities as charismatic leaders and problem handlers, along with making ambitious electoral promises. This tends to generate high expectations that then lead to huge disappointments once in office (Grossman and Sauger, 2014). This intuition is close to 'expectation gap' which Stimson (1976) assumes to nourish the costs of ruling. Concentration of power in the hands of the president may also activate multiple other mechanisms assumed to contribute to the pattern of cost of ruling. The president is likely to be the one blamed by successive minorities for dissatisfying policy outcomes or by citizens for grievance. The French peculiarities just discussed make it likely that responsibility for disappointments is unambiguously attributed to the president. The cost of ruling is therefore likely to be stronger than elsewhere, reducing the impact of other factors.

If the cost of ruling targeted at the main person in charge is the driving mechanism, then periods of divided government should act as an important moderator. Cohabitation crucially upsets the balance of power between president and prime minister, turning power, responsibility, and public attention away from the former and towards the latter (Baumgartner et al., 2014; see also

[5] 'Pour le chef de l'État, Fillon est un "collaborateur"', *Le Figaro*, 23 August 2007.

Aguiar-Conraria, Fernandes, and Magalhães in this volume). While an argument centred on clarity of responsibility would lead us to expect less impact of economic performance during cohabitations (Lewis-Beck, 1997; Hellwig and Samuels, 2008), the cost-of-ruling mechanism implies that presidents should be more popular during these periods.

Yet, the synchronization of legislative and presidential electoral cycles since 2002 means cohabitations de facto no longer occur. The presidential election takes place first, focusing the bulk of public attention over months of dramatic campaigns in which each candidate develops an individual personal programme. This reduces the stakes of the legislative elections that take place a few weeks later, leaving parties' legislative programmes largely unnoticed, in the shadow of the president's ambitious campaigns. Until 2022 (see footnote 3), these elections have consistently given the newly elected president a solid parliamentary majority. This may have further reinforced the above-mentioned cycles of presidential popularity. Presidents intervene more and more in day-to-day problem-solving and reforms, often eclipsing the prime minister, at the risk of having to take the blame for any kind of unsatisfactory outcome.

Hypotheses

Based on the above discussion, we formulate the following expectation as to the general determinants of presidential popularity in France:

H1: Presidential popularity is heavily shaped by time in office, with high levels in the first months of the term, a degradation over the course of the term, and an end-of-term improvement (*cost of ruling*).

Heavy costs of ruling further do not leave much room for presidents to politically capitalize on good economic performance. This motivates a second expectation:

H2a: Presidential popularity does not respond to economic performance (*objective economic explanation*).

Yet, the relationship between presidential popularity and subjective perceptions of the economy may be stronger, whereby causality may go in both directions. Subjective economic assessments account better for the fact that citizens, when making up their image of the president, draw on information available to them, and this information may be filtered or biased. At the same time, intense (and growing) dissatisfaction with policy outcomes and grievances blamed on the president spill over into public beliefs about the economy. Our approach does not allow us to disentangle these effects, yet both would result in a significant relationship between subjective perceptions of the economy and executive approval:

> H2b: Subjective assessments of the economy are correlated with presidential popularity (*subjective economic explanation*).

Periods of divided government allows the public to better grasp the mechanisms at play. It has been sometimes argued that economic factors do not matter because of the difficulty of attributing responsibility between the two executives (see Lewis-Beck, 1997 on the 1995 presidential election; Lewis-Beck and Nadeau, 2000, on the 1984–1994 period; and Hellwig and Samuels, 2008 for the general argumentation). If this applies more generally, then economic factors should be more influential during periods of unified government when responsibilities are more clearly defined and the president unambiguously in charge. If, however, the economy does not significantly matter because of the overriding cost of ruling, then cohabitation should above all provide the president with a bonus in popularity and dampen the cyclical effect deriving from cost of ruling, while leaving the marginal effect of economic conditions on presidential popularity unchanged. Cohabitation may pre-emptively lower the public's expectations towards the president as well as complicate the attribution of blame and grievance as those can also be directed at the prime minister. These expectations will be explored based on the following hypotheses:

> H3a: Cohabitation dampens the impact of economic performance on presidential popularity, which has a statistically significant effect only outside cohabitations (*responsibility limitation*).
>
> H3b: Cohabitations provide presidents with a bonus in popularity and limit the degradation in their popularity over the course of the electoral cycle (*cost-of-ruling limitation*).

These expectations will be tested by means of time-series analyses on data covering sixty years of the Fifth Republic (1959–2019). As the preceding discussion has made clear, power concentration in the hands of the president is a core, constitutive feature of this political system. Therefore, we do not expect any fundamental shift over time concerning the role of the cost of ruling. Yet, the synchronization of legislative and presidential cycles has further concentrated the focus of public attention on the president (see above). This generates more and more incentives for candidates to the presidency to campaign on ambitious personal, favouring expectation gaps, while presidential leadership in daily policymaking incites citizens to focus blame for any dissatisfying outcome on the president. This cycle repeats itself at each presidential term, yet the ability of newly elected presidents to raise hopes seems to diminish, which leads to lower levels of popularity over time. Accordingly, costs of ruling may have been less strong in the 'mature' years of the Fifth Republic (1981–2002), a period marked by regular alternations in power and cohabitations, than in the early years (1959–1981).[6] These costs can be expected to have reinforced in the post-2002 period and the disappearance of divided government.

H4: The cost-of-ruling effect is stronger after 2002 compared to the 1981–2002 period (*increasing cost of ruling*).

Dependent Variable: Presidential Popularity Since the Beginning of the Fifth Republic

Our dependent variable is the monthly series for France from the Executive Approval Data, a series which constitutes the longest-running component of the Executive Approval Project data examined for the French case (and others) in Chapters 1, 2, and 14 of this volume. Before we turn to multivariate analyses, a visual inspection of the data is highly instructive: Figure 4.1 shows presidential approval rates, Figure 4.2 those for the prime minister.

Looking at the long-term dynamics of presidents, one is struck by the frequent decline over time, especially when compared to the trend for prime ministerial popularity. The first two presidents of the Fifth Republic, De Gaulle and Pompidou, benefited from very high levels of popularity. De Gaulle enjoyed a personal bonus as a charismatic wartime leader both during World War II and, again, in the context of the Algerian independence war, when he prevented a coup attempt by dissident French generals in Algeria. His former prime minister and successor, Georges Pompidou, also features significantly higher popularity figures than any of his successors (Parodi, 1971). In 1974, the election of Valéry Giscard d'Estaing marked the end of the

[6] This corresponds to historical cuts that have been explained elsewhere (Chevallier et al., 2004; Grossman and Sauger, 2009).

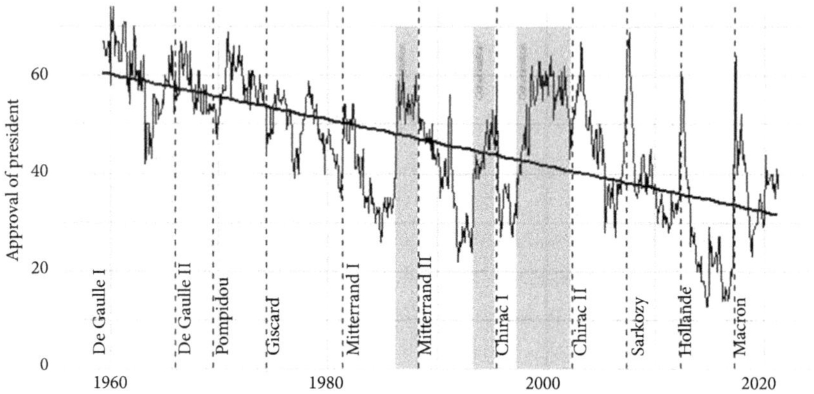

Figure 4.1 Presidential popularity since the beginning of the Fifth Republic (1958–2021)

Source: Executive Approval Database.
Note: Dashed lines indicate presidential elections, shaded areas represent periods of cohabitation, and solid vertical line represents the linear trend.

Gaullist period (Hibbs and Vasilatos, 1981). Giscard was the first president for whom we clearly observe a pattern corresponding to the cost-of-ruling assumption. He took office with lower levels of approval than his two predecessors. More importantly, he experienced a steady decline of popularity between 1975 and 1981, dropping by almost 20 per cent. He had to deal with the consequences of the oil shock as well as with growing tensions with his Gaullist allies, resulting in Prime Minister Jacques Chirac's resignation in 1976. He nonetheless benefited from a sudden rise in popularity in the run-up to the 1981 elections. As already mentioned, this cyclicality has become commonplace in the decades following.

However, Mitterrand's two presidential terms (1981–1995) marked a new and important turning point (Grossman and Sauger, 2009). First, he was the first president from the left-wing block, and his election opened a period of regular alternations in power. Second, Mitterrand's presidencies witnessed the first episodes of divided government. Following legislative elections that did not provide him with a parliamentary majority, François Mitterrand had to appoint right-wing prime ministers in 1986 (Jacques Chirac) and 1993 (Edouard Balladur). His successor Jacques Chirac later faced the same situation after calling for early elections, leading to the socialist government of Lionel Jospin (1997–2002). Figure 4.1 corroborates the expectation that cohabitation used to moderate the cost-of-ruling effect, by shifting (some) blame to prime ministers instead of presidents (Conley, 2006).

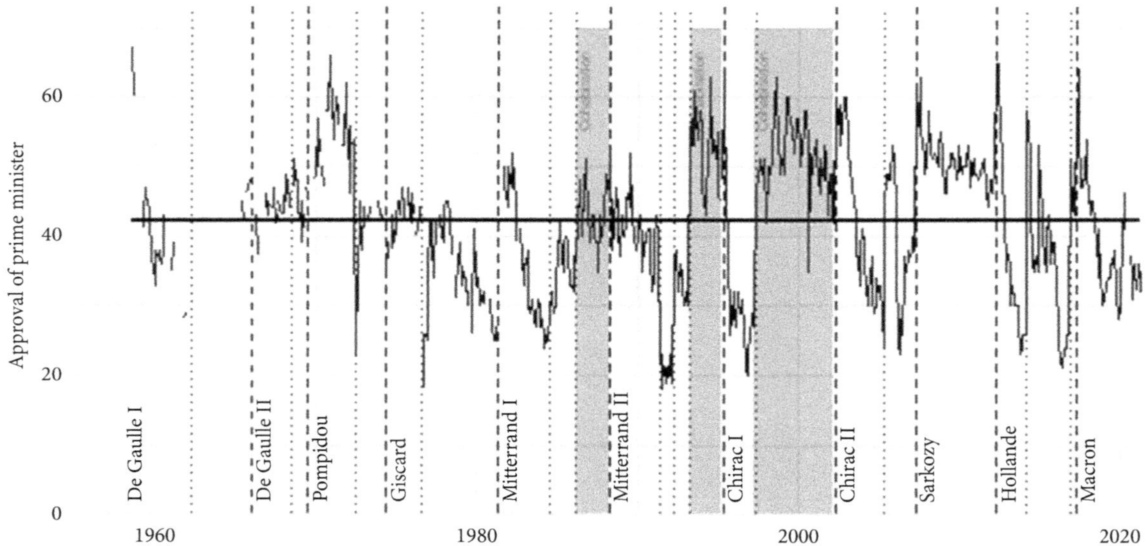

Figure 4.2 Prime minister popularity since the beginning of the Fifth Republic (1958–2021)

Source: Executive Approval Database.

Note: Dashed lines indicate presidential elections, dotted lines indicate a change of the prime minister, shaded areas represent periods of cohabitation, and solid vertical line represents the linear trend.

After 2002, presidential terms were reduced from seven to five years. Synchronization of legislative and presidential cycles made divided government less likely and further concentrated powers in the hands of the head of state. As expected, the result seems to be that honeymoons reached increasingly smaller heights with each successive presidency and, further, that presidents suffered even steeper declines in popularity (cf. Figure 4.3). Presidential popularity fell to an all-time low in the last months of François Hollande's term, with only 11.5 per cent of approval in the second quarter of 2016.

Overall, the visualizations of our dependent variable point to the cost-of-ruling argument. Figure 4.3 displays this cyclical pattern based, for each period of the Fifth Republic, on the 'average' level of presidential and prime minister popularity over the course of a presidential term. Following Carlin and colleagues (2019), we standardize them from 0 (term beginning) to 1 (term end) to adjust for varying term length. Figure 4.3 confirms that presidents tend to be most popular immediately after their election and experience a decline in popularity as time goes by. Yet, dynamics have changed over time. In the early years of the Fifth Republic, the president used to be more popular than the prime minister and enjoyed long periods of honeymoon, although approval rates tended to decline in the second half of their term. After 1981, honeymoon periods were much shorter in time: presidents seemed to suffer costs of ruling (more than their prime minister) until the middle of their term, while this dynamic reversed in the second half of the term. This pattern is likely to derive from cohabitations liberating the president from at least parts of the cost of ruling, leading to historically high approval rates. Since 2002 cohabitations no longer appear and, as expected, the president tends to pay most of the cost of ruling until the very last months of their term.

The figures not only provide preliminary support for our assumption on the moderating effect of divided government, but also corroborate a historical trend according to which presidents pay an increasing cost of ruling. This is even more striking when comparing presidential and prime ministerial popularity: the prime minister curve used, in early years, to start lower but to escape the decrease experienced by presidents. The two most recent decades witness a synchronization of presidential and prime ministerial popularity cycles, which maps on to the synchronization of election cycles, yet the decline in popularity is far less pronounced for prime ministers than for presidents. As a consequence, prime ministers tend to outperform (sometimes spectacularly) presidents.

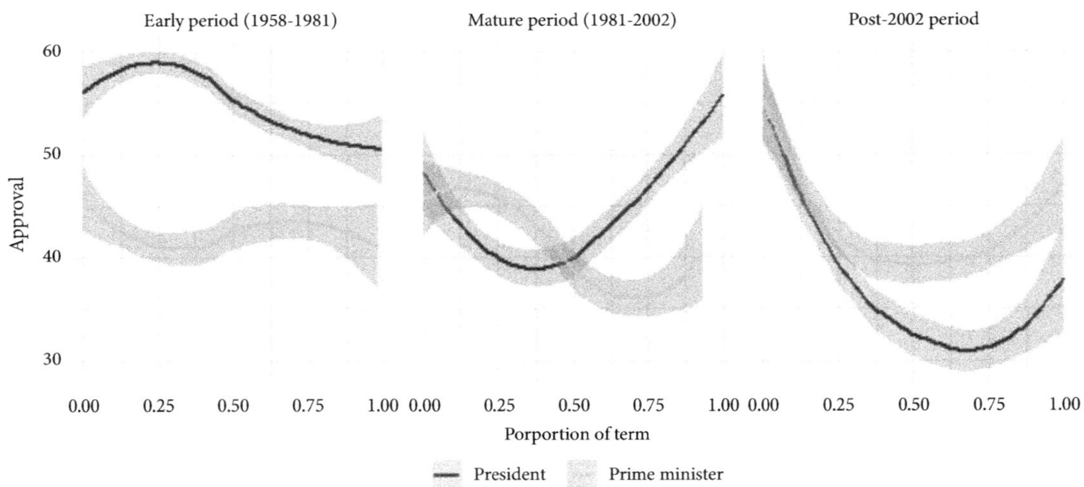

Figure 4.3 Dynamics of presidential and prime minister popularity in France, 95 per cent confidence intervals

Source: Executive Approval Database.

Explaining Popularity over Time

Based on the discussion in the previous section, we concentrate on presidents here, arguably the effective chief executive of the French Fifth Republic. We briefly present our modelling strategy and the main variables, before turning to the findings.

Model

Our dependent variable is the series on executive approval described above. An Augmented Dickey-Fuller (ADF) test and residual statistics (Ljung-Box Q) reveal a unit-root process ($p > 0.1$) and autocorrelation in the residuals. The ACFs and PACFs functions depict an autoregressive order of one lag. Given these diagnoses, we difference the dependent variable and add a lagged dependent variable, along with fixed effects for presidents. This demanding strategy ensures highly robust results that are confirmed by Ljung-Box statistics reported for each of the models in Tables 4.1 and 4.2.

The first independent variable is economic performance. Macroeconomic performance is measured by three conventional indicators. The first is the quarterly (available since 1990) inflation rate. Second, data on the unemployment rate, i.e. the percentage of unemployed workers, are available quarterly since 1975. The source for both is the French national statistical institute INSEE. Third, a variable for quarter-on-quarter GDP growth comes from OECD statistics and is available from 1958. In addition to these indicators of 'objective' macroeconomic performance, we use a measure of subjective perceptions of the economy, i.e. the Consumer Confidence Index from the OECD. As all four variables are available quarterly, we use difference from one quarter to the next and use the same value for each month in the quarter. Summary statistics for the four variables are available in Table 4.3 in the appendix.

We then test for the cost of ruling in three parallel ways. We use a political-cycle variable capturing the proportion of the term that has elapsed. This is normalized across varying lengths of term. In order to account for a possible improvement of popularity towards the end of term, as is apparent in Figure 4.1, we add a quadratic term of the cost-of-ruling variable. We also add a dummy distinguishing the three first months of each term to account for boosts in popularity during 'honeymoon' periods. A dummy for periods of divided government (cohabitation) will allow us to explore how far these periods dampen the cost of ruling and moderate the impact of economic factors. Finally, all models include a dummy for left (PS) presidents.

Findings

Our findings are presented in Tables 4.1 and 4.2 and in Figures 4.4 and 4.5. The four first models assess the relative explanatory power of economic and cost-of-ruling explanations. In line with H1, the cyclical cost of ruling has a powerful effect on presidential popularity: presidents are significantly more popular during honeymoon periods, yet their approval rates tend to deteriorate with time in office. This effect is robust across all models. The positive and significant coefficient for the squared term confirms that popularity tends to increase again towards the end of presidential terms.

Table 4.1 Presidential popularity in France

	Dependent variable			
	Δ Executive approval (president)			
	(1)	(2)	(3)	(4)
Lagged approval	−0.138*	−0.161*	−0.167*	−0.189*
	(0.017)	(0.022)	(0.027)	(0.021)
Δ Growth	0.194°			
	(0.110)			
Δ Unemployment		0.247		
		(1.248)		
Δ Inflation			−2.519*	
			(0.835)	
Δ Consumer confidence				0.616*
				(0.135)
Honeymoon	0.762	1.910*	2.345*	0.954
	(0.621)	(0.824)	(1.099)	(0.753)
Proportion of term	−6.187*	−9.329*	−11.995*	−8.248*
	(2.098)	(3.052)	(4.583)	(2.747)
Proportion (squared)	5.047*	7.982*	11.264*	6.888*
	(1.974)	(2.739)	(4.084)	(2.519)
Cohabitation	3.175*	3.841*	3.569*	3.218*
	(0.613)	(0.735)	(0.903)	(0.687)
Left-wing president	0.884°	1.307*	1.931*	0.887°
	(0.501)	(0.549)	(0.835)	(0.531)
Ljung-Box stat. (p-value)	5.396 (0.02)	6.704 (0.01)	5.603 (0.018)	7.727 (0.005)
Observations	785	533	337	562
R^2	0.095	0.115	0.150	0.141

Source: Executive Approval Project dataset
Notes: °p<0.1; *p<0.05 (two-tailed test). Cells report OLS coefficients with standard errors in parentheses. Models include fixed effects by presidents (not reported).

Given our review of conditions likely to enhance costs of ruling, H2a did not expect economic fluctuations to be a powerful predictor of presidential popularity in France. Findings are consistent with this expectation with regard to unemployment, which does not significantly shape presidential popularity. Growth has a positive impact but it is minor in amplitude: 1 per cent GDP growth is associated on average to less than 0.2 per cent increase in popularity. Inflation has a stronger—negative—impact on presidential approval. Findings indicate that a 1 per cent increase in inflation is associated, on average, to a decrease in presidential approval by 2.5 percentage points.

Subjective assessments appear to matter as well, with an average bonus of 0.6 per cent when consumer confidence rises by 1 per cent. This finding needs to be interpreted with caution given possible feedback effects. As already discussed, consumer confidence may on the one hand correct for information and perceptions biases; on the other hand, subjective perceptions of the economy may be shaped by citizens' attitude towards their executive. The data at hand does not allow us to adjudicate these two possible mechanisms.

Cohabitation generates substantive popularity bonuses, in line with H4: the popularity rate of the president is 3 to 4 per cent higher on average when the prime minister is from an opposition party. Cohabitations are the only periods in which the president is not the main and only person in charge: our findings confirm that this allows her to escape some of the cost of ruling. Left-wing presidents appear to be slightly more popular. Finally, Ljung-Box Statistics confirm that residuals are randomly distributed.

Interactions in Table 4.2 provide deeper insight into the effects of cohabitation. Constitutive terms for economic conditions suggest that outside cohabitations, their respective effect is similar to those found for the whole period (depicted in Table 4.1). The marginal effects plotted on Figure 4.4 shows that cohabitation upsets the effects of most variables of interest. Our results are—somewhat—at odds with those found by Lewis-Beck and Nadeau (2000), who compare the effect of economic variables across a set of elections and periods of unified and divided government in France. They show that the effect of economic context is strongest for presidents under unified government. We confirm this is the case at least for inflation and consumer confidence, while unemployment has an unexpected effect and growth is not significant. In line with one of our central expectations (H3b), cost-of-ruling effects—measured as the elapsed proportion of term—are present only in periods of unified government. During cohabitation, the president—no longer in charge

Table 4.2 Cohabitations and presidential popularity in France

	Dependent variable				
	Δ Executive approval (president)				
	(1)	(2)	(3)	(4)	(5)
Lagged approval	−0.139*	−0.163*	−0.168*	−0.144*	−0.134*
	(0.017)	(0.022)	(0.027)	(0.020)	(0.021)
Δ Growth	−0.031				
	(0.113)				
Δ Unemployment		1.087			
		(1.377)			
Δ Inflation			−2.991*		
			(0.948)		
Δ Consumer confidence				4.038*	3.123*
				(0.606)	(0.566)
Cohabitation	3.244*	3.874*	3.600*	3.586*	4.121*
	(0.616)	(0.735)	(0.903)	(0.677)	(1.586)
Honeymoon	0.818	1.952*	2.351*	1.193	1.247°
	(0.622)	(0.824)	(1.099)	(0.731)	(0.742)
Proportion of term	−6.014*	−9.461*	−12.081*	−8.856*	−8.284*
	(2.101)	(3.050)	(4.583)	(2.693)	(2.735)
Proportion squared	4.911*	8.062*	11.312*	7.135*	7.105*
	(1.977)	(2.736)	(4.084)	(2.466)	(2.571)
Left-wing president	0.906°	1.202*	1.922*	0.958°	0.819
	(0.502)	(0.554)	(0.835)	(0.517)	(0.567)
Cohabitation × Growth	−0.795				
	(1.328)				
Cohabitation × Unemp.		−4.621			
		(3.218)			
Cohabitation × Inflation			2.098		
			(1.999)		
Cohabitation × Cons. confidence				−5.771*	
				(1.539)	
Cohabitation × Prop. term					−1.463
					(2.308)
Ljung-Box stat. (p-value)	5.91	7.052	5.984	1.896	2.385
	(0.015)	(0.008)	(0.014)	(0.169)	(0.122)
Observations	784	533	337	561	561
R^2	0.092	0.119	0.153	0.178	0.157

Source: Executive Approval Project dataset
Notes: °$p<0.10$; *$p<0.05$ (two-tailed test). Cells report OLS coefficients with standard errors in parentheses. Models include fixed effects by presidents (not reported). Average marginal effects calculated based on the interaction terms presented in Table 4.2.

of everyday politics—experiences rising popularity. Moreover, even under this specification, the honeymoon effect and the squared version of proportion of term feature positive and significant coefficients across all models.

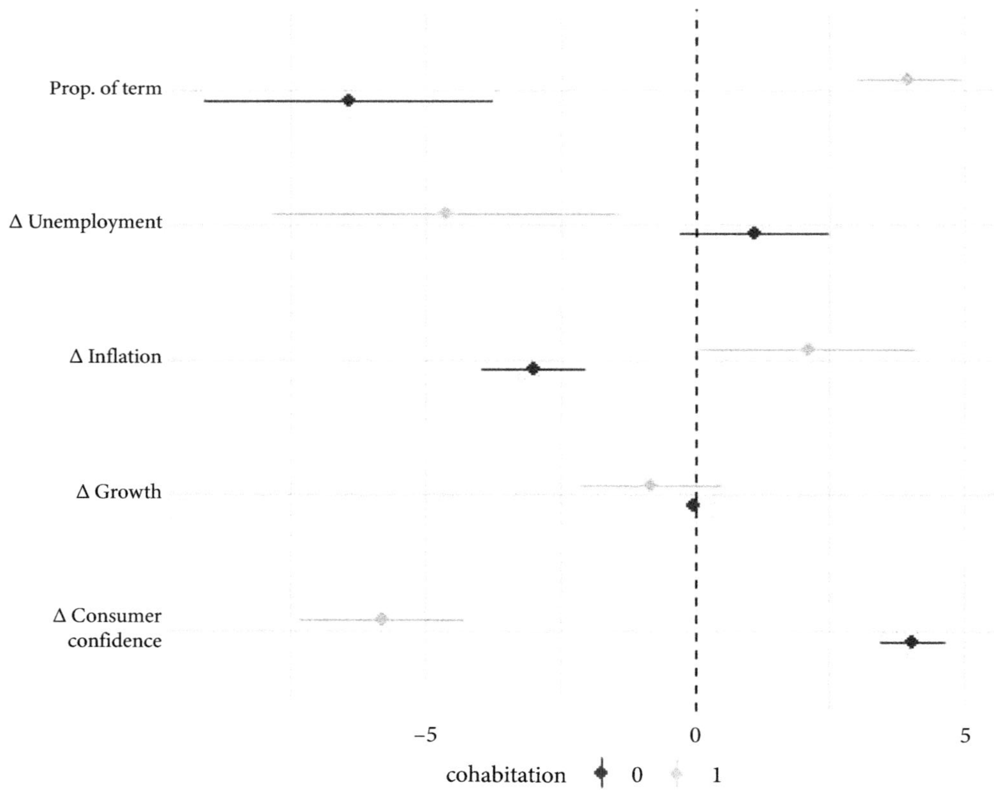

Figure 4.4 Marginal effects under unified government and cohabitation
Source: Produced using Table 4.2 estimates.

Does the effect of economic performance maybe vary over time? Economic issues had weaker salience than matters of national security and foreign policy during the early years of the Fifth Republic. Economic problems have become more salient at least since the 1970s, in the context of rising unemployment, growing inflation, and declining growth, although other topics such as education, internal security, and institutions also attract considerable attention.[7] Some of the studies reviewed suggested that the relationship between the economy and presidential popularity may not be stable. Yet, this relationship has never been analysed over a period of several decades and for all four indicators, as we are able to do it in this chapter. To assess how far the predictors of presidential popularity have changed over time, we model interactions between our main predictors and each of the three phases of the Fifth Republic.

To facilitate the interpretation of interactions, Figure 4.5 presents the marginal effect of our macroeconomic indicators on presidential popularity separately for each period, based on models (not shown) adding an interaction term to those in Table 4.2. This allows us to disaggregate the effects for each determinant for distinct periods and to examine how far the triggers of popularity have changed, at least partially over time.

Figure 4.5 shows some trends and effects, but mostly confirms that macroeconomic indicators do not strongly affect popularity in France except for inflation. Coefficients for unemployment have the expected sign only during the early and mature period, and the effect is not statistically significant. Growth shows a significant positive effect only during the early period. Inflation seems to be the most relevant indicator: it appears to have become even more of an issue for executives in the most recent period, maybe as result of independent central banks and the cross-party consensus against inflation that has emerged since the late 1980s.[8]

These findings may come as a surprise in the light of observations that unemployment is more easily perceived by the public and tends to be more salient for executive performance evaluation than inflation (e.g. Hibbs and Vasilatos, 1981; Conley, 2006). Our results should not be seen as a refutation that rising unemployment fuels public dissatisfaction, but rather as an indication that its effect is far from overwhelming. After decades of structural unemployment at high levels, this phenomenon may be regarded with

[7] See for example Grossman and Guinaudeau (2021), Figure 3.7, on issue attention in French laws and manifestos over time. See also Kriesi et al. (2008) on the emergence of new cleavages related to culture and globalization.

[8] Our inflation indicator is not available for the 'early' period. The model thus only covers the 'mature' and 'post' periods.

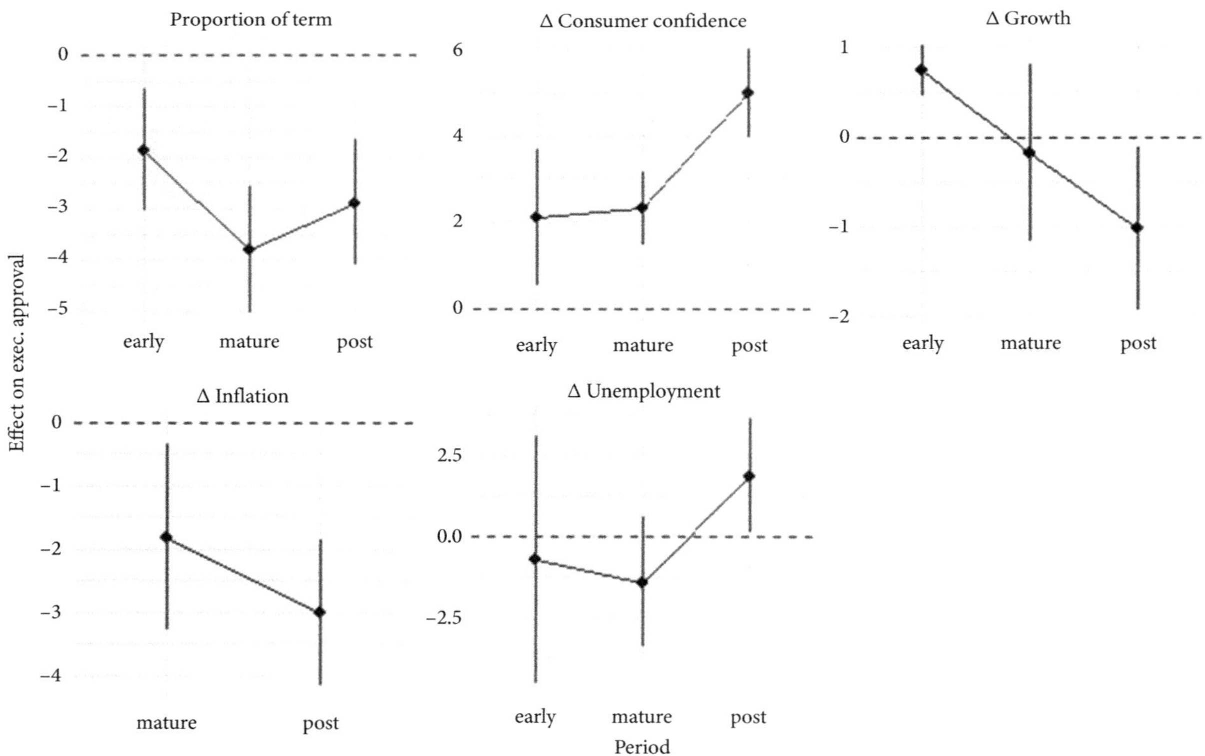

Figure 4.5 Marginal effect of economic indicators and of the proportion of the term that has elapsed on popularity (unstandardized coefficients)

Source: Executive Approval Database.

Note: average marginal effects calculated based on models similar to those in Table 4.2, interacting periods with different covariants. The periods are the same as Figure 4.2: early (1958–1981), mature (1981–2002), and post (since 2002).

more fatalism, while inflation has now long stayed at very low levels, similar to growth.

The other interesting result concerns the growing importance of consumer confidence. This indicator has clearly become a better predictor over time. At the same time, as discussed above, the subjective nature of this indicator raises some questions, as it is probably reinforced by partisan identity and is possibly 'bi-directional' in its causal effect. Put differently, while it moves with executive popularity, future work should probably test systematically the relationship of those two indicators over several lags.[9]

The variations across time and indicators call for further research on the visibility and salience of indicators (in the vein of Gerstlé and François, 2011, who unfortunately did not cover GDP growth as an economic indicator), as well as on beliefs regarding the executive's economic steering capacity.

More interestingly, and confirming Figure 4.1, our cost-of-ruling assumption holds true for all periods, as time in office (modelled as proportion of term) has the expected negative effect. This effect tends to be reinforced after the early years of the Fifth Republic. Cost of ruling results in ever lower levels of popularity given that presidents start their term at lower levels of popularity over time.

Discussion

Executive popularity is (once again?) becoming topical in an era of growing public distrust with the potential to undermine policymaking capacity. Can conventional popularity functions account for this evolution? Economic explanations have been prominently challenged by scholars who have pointed to their contrasted explanatory power and to a series of social and political transformations related to changing cleavages, constraints on the macroeconomic margins for manoeuvre at the domestic level and the rise of issue entrepreneurs and new populist challengers. In France, the relevance of economic conditions was already challenged before, with most studies concluding that political dynamics remain largely autonomous from economic ones.

This chapter argues that any explanation of presidential popularity in the French context should focus on what has been referred to as the cost of ruling. The unique centrality of the president in the French political system makes her the person in charge. To be up to this office—and, before that, to the challenge

[9] Tests for Grange causality (not shown) point to a stronger effect of consumer confidence on executive approval than the reverse but cannot exclude the possibility of a bidirectional effect.

of attracting votes in her own political constituency in the first round and to gather a majority in the second round two weeks later—presidents must profile themselves as extraordinary problem handlers standing above partisan disputes and to embody ambitious and attractive visions. This, we show, accounts for the repeated pattern of peaks of popularity at the beginning of each new presidential mandate and a steep fall thereafter. Presidents appear, in sum, to be doomed to deceive and, worse, any grievance or dissatisfaction with policy outputs or outcomes will be targeted at them. And this is unlikely to be balanced out even by comparatively good economic performance. We argue that this pattern has strengthened in the context of the growing presidentialization of the political system. Institutional reforms have limited the likeliness of cohabitations, while presidents' have increasingly claimed full leadership in policymaking.

To substantiate these claims, this chapter re-assesses the explanatory power of economic conditions and the cost of ruling over more than six decades of existence of the Fifth Republic. These analyses deliver several important lessons. First, the cost of ruling is the main driver of presidential popularity since the early 1980s. It leaves little room for the president to capitalize on good economic performance except with regard to fighting inflation. There is admittedly a correlation between presidential popularity and consumer confidence that is even higher over the most recent period. Yet, the nature of the causal relationship is unclear. It is not implausible that attitudes towards the executive carry over to consumer confidence.

Second, divided government—or *cohabitation*—importantly alters the logic of executive approval: periods of divided government see the disappearance of the cost of ruling and allow the president to benefit from a cost of ruling that now applies to the prime minister. During those periods, moreover, economic factors tend to play more in favour of the president (despite blurred responsibilities with the prime minister and government).

The synchronization of presidential and legislative cycles, which now take place within six weeks of each other, has limited the likeliness of cohabitations. Without those periods of lower exposition for presidents, the Fifth Republic henceforth features an apparently unlimited capacity to disappoint. Whether or not unemployment and inflation are successfully tackled, presidents in office get more and more unpopular as time goes by. Blame avoidance strategies are admittedly difficult to combine with the very offensive way in which presidential candidates profile themselves in electoral campaigns. They keep sticking to the image of strong presidents who have control over things and play a central role on the world stage, despite massive contradictory evidence.

The outcome of the 2022 legislative election is largely unprecedented. It remains to be seen how it will affect power concentration, cost of ruling, and presidential approval. The return of cohabitations remains rather unlikely. Yet, the absence of parliamentary majority dramatically reduces the president's room for manoeuvre, forcing him to negotiate compromises with other political forces. While this is certainly constraining in terms of policymaking capacity, it could eventually also limit presidential responsibility and cost of ruling.

Appendix

Table 4.3. Summary Statistics for Economic Indicators

	Avail. since	Missing (%)	Mean	SD	Min	Median	Max	Source
Inflation	1990	57	1.5	0.8	-0.7	1.6	3.7	INSEE
Growth	1958	2	0.7	1.8	-13.8	0.7	18.7	OECD
Unemployment	1975	33	8.3	1.9	3.0	8.8	10.8	INSEE
Consumer Confidence Index	1973	29	100.0	1.8	94.9	100.1	106.5	OECD

References

Anderson, C. (1995). *Blaming the Government: Citizens and the Economy in Five European Democracies*. New York: M. E. Sharpe.

Baum, M. A. (2002). The constituent foundations of the rally-round-the-flag phenomenon. *International Studies Quarterly*, *46*(2), 263–98.

Baumgartner, F. R., Brouard, S., Grossman, E., Lazardeux, S. G., and Moody, J. (2014). Divided government, legislative productivity, and policy change in the USA and France: Divided government and policy change. *Governance*, *27*(3), 423–47.

Bélanger, É., and Lewis-Beck, M. S. (2004). National economic voting in France: Objective versus subjective measures. In Lewis-Beck, M. S., ed., *The French Voter: Before and After the 2002 Elections*. London: Palgrave Macmillian. 231–42.

Bellucci, P., and Lewis-Beck, M. S. (2011). A stable popularity function? Cross-national analysis. *European Journal of Political Research*, *50*(2), 190–211.

Boukari, M., and Farvaque, E. (2019). Who profits from legislative activism? An analysis of presidential and prime ministerial popularity. *French Politics*, *17*(1), 64–91.

Boya, C. (2017). La présidentialisation du système français depuis 2002 à travers la fonction de popularité. *Revue francaise d'economie*, *32*(4), 95–130.

Carlin, R. E., Carreras, M., and Love, G. J. (2020). Presidents' sex and popularity: Baselines, dynamics and policy performance. *British Journal of Political Science*, *50*(4), 1359–79.

Chevallier, J.-J., Carcassone, G., and Duhamel, O. (2004). *La Ve République 1958–2004: Histoire des institutions et des régimes politiques de la France* (eleventh edn). Paris: Armand Colin.

Conley, R. S. (2006). From Elysian Fields to the Guillotine? The dynamics of presidential and prime ministerial approval in Fifth Republic France. *Comparative Political Studies*, *39*(5), 570–98.

Cuzán, A. G. (2015). Five laws of politics. *PS: Political Science and Politics*, *48*(3), 415–19.

De Boef, S., and Kellstedt, P. (2004) The Political (and Economic) Origins of Consumer Confidence. *American Journal of Political Science*, *48*(4), 633–49.

Elgie, R. (1999). *Semi-Presidentialism in Europe*. Oxford: Oxford University Press.

Elgie, R. (2010). Semi-presidentialism, cohabitation and the collapse of electoral democracies, 1990–2008. *Government and Opposition*, *45*(1), 29–49.

Enns, P.K., Kellstedt, P.M. and McAvoy, G.E. (2012) The consequences of partisanship in economic perceptions. *Public Opinion Quarterly*, *76*(2), 287–310.

Frey, B. S. (1997). *Political Business Cycles*. https://www.e-elgar.com/shop/gbp/political-business-cycles-9781858983998.html.

Gerstlé, J., and François, A. (2011). Médiatisation de l' économie et fabrication de la popularité du président français (2007–2010). *Revue francaise de science politique*, *61*(2), 249–81.

Goodhart, C. A. E., and Bhansali, R. J. (1970). Political economy. *Political Studies*, *18*(1), 43–106.

Grossman, E. (2009). The president's choice? Government and cabinet turnover under the Fifth Republic. *West European Politics*, *32*(2), 268–86.

Grossman, E., and Guinaudeau, I. (2021). *Do Elections (Still) Matter? Mandates, Institutions and Policies in Western Europe*. Oxford: Oxford University Press.

Grossman, E., and Sauger, N. (2009). The end of ambiguity? Presidents versus parties or the four phases of the Fifth Republic. *West European Politics*, *32*(2), 423–37.

Grossman, E., and Sauger, N. (2014). 'Un président normal'? Presidential (in-)action and unpopularity in the wake of the great recession. *French Politics*, *12*(2), 86–103.

Guinaudeau, I., and Persico, S. (2021). Coalition politics in France: Electoral necessity and presidential leadership beyond parties. In *Coalition Governance in Western Europe*, T. Bergman, H. Bäck, and J. Hellström, eds. Oxford: Oxford University Press. 206–46.

Haynes, S. E., and Stone, J. A. (1990). Political models of the business cycle should be revived. *Economic Inquiry*, *28*(3), 442–65.

Hellwig, T., and Samuels, D. (2008). Electoral accountability and the variety of democratic regimes. *British Journal of Political Science*, *38*(1), 65–90.

Hetherington, M. J., and Nelson, M. (2003). Anatomy of a rally effect: George W. Bush and the war on terrorism. *Political Science and Politics*, *36*(01), 37–42.

Hibbs, D. A., Rivers, R. D., and Vasilatos, N. (1982). On the demand for economic outcomes: Macroeconomic performance and mass political support in the United States, Great Britain, and Germany. *The Journal of Politics*, *44*(2), 426–62.

Hibbs, D. A., and Vasilatos, N. (1981). Economics and politics in France: Economic performance and mass political support for Presidents Pompidou and Giscard d'Estaing. *European Journal of Political Research*, *9*(2), 133–45.

Key, V. O. J. (1966). *The Responsible Electorate: Rationality in Presidential Voting 1936–1960*. Cambridge, MA: Harvard University Press.

Kriesi, H., Grande, E., Lachat, R., Dolezal, M., Bornschier, S., and Frey, T. (eds) (2008). *West European Politics in the Age of Globalization*. Cambridge: Cambridge University Press.

Lafay, J.-D. (1984). Political change and stability of the popularity function: The French general election of 1981. *Political Behavior*, *6*(4), 333–52.

Lewis-Beck, M. S. (1980). Economic conditions and executive popularity: The French experience. *American Journal of Political Science*, *24*(2), 306–23.

Lewis-Beck, M. S. (1997). Who's the chef? Economic voting under a dual executive. *European Journal of Political Research*, *31*(3), 315–25.

Lewis-Beck, M. S., and Nadeau, R. (2000). French electoral institutions and the economic vote. *Electoral Studies*, *19*(2–3),171–82.

Magni-Berton, R. (2008). Popularité, élections et marge de manœuvre du gouvernement. Une analyse de la production législative en France et en Italie. *Revue internationale de politique comparee*, *15*(2), 277–95.

Monroe, K. R. (1984). *Presidential Popularity and the Economy*. New York: Praeger Publishers.

Mueller, J. E. (1973). *War, Presidents, and Public Opinion*. New York: Wiley.

Nannestad, P., and Paldam, M. (2002). The cost of ruling: A foundation stone for two theories. In Dorussen, H. and Taylor, M (eds.) *Economic Voting*. London: Routledge. 17–44.

Naurin, E., Soroka, S., and Marwat, N. (2019) Asymmetric Accountability: An Experimental Investigation of Biases in Evaluations of Governments' Election Pledges. *Comparative Political Studies*, *52*(13–14), 2207–34.

Norpoth, H. (1984). Economics, politics, and the cycle of presidential popularity. *Political Behavior*, *6*, 253–73.

Norpoth, H., and Yantek, T. (1983). Macroeconomic conditions and fluctuations of presidential popularity. *American Journal of Political Science*, *27*(4), 785–807.

Ostrom, C. W. J., and Simon, D. M. (1985). Promise and performance: A dynamic model of presidential popularity. *American Political Science Review*, *79*(2), 334–58.

Paldam, M. (1981). A preliminary survey of the theories and findings on vote and popularity functions. *European Journal of Political Research*, *9*(2), 181–99.

Paldam, M. (1991). How robust is the vote function? A study of seventeen nations over four decades. In *Economics and Politics: The Calculus of Support.* Ann Arbor, MI: University of Michigan Press. 9–32.

Paldam, M., and Skott, P. (1995). A rational-voter explanation of the cost of ruling. *Public Choice*, *83*(1), 159–72.

Palmer, H. D., and Whitten, G. D. (2002). Economics, politics, and the cost of ruling in advanced industrial democracies. In Dorussen, H. and Taylor, M. (eds.) *Economic Voting*. London: Routledge. 66–91.

Parodi, J.-L. (1971). Sur deux courbes de popularité. *Revue française de science politique*, *21*(1), 129–51.

Pommerehne, W., Schneider, F., and Lafay, J.-D. (1981). Les interactions entre économie et politique: Synthèse des analyses théoriques et empiriques. *Revue économique*, *32*(1), 110–62.

Shugart, M. S. (2005). Semi-presidential systems: Dual executive and mixed authority patterns. *French Politics*, *3*(3), 323–51.

Soroka, S. (2014) *Negativity in Democratic Politics. Causes and Consequences.* Cambridge: Cambridge University Press.

Stevenson, R. T. (2002). The cost of ruling, cabinet duration, and the 'median-gap' model. *Public Choice*, *113*(1), 157–78.

Stimson, J. A. (1976). Public support for American presidents: A cyclical model. *The Public Opinion Quarterly*, *40*(1), 1–21.

Thesen, G., Mortensen, P. B., and Green-Pedersen, C. (2020). Cost of ruling as a game of tones. The accumulation of bad news and incumbents' vote loss. *European Journal of Political Research*, *59*(3), 555– 77.

Turgeon, M., and Bélanger, É. (2017). Institutions and attribution of responsibility outside the electoral context: A look at French semi-presidentialism. *European Political Science Review*, *9*(2), 209–31.

Turgeon, M., Bélanger, É., and Nadeau, R. (2015). French popularity functions: Different measures, different determinants? *French Politics*, *13*(3), 266–86.

Vaillant N., and Flambard, V. (2014) Economic conditions and confidence: Do changes in the consumption level affect the dynamics of confidence? *Economics Bulletin*, *35*(1), 21–9.

Wlezien, C. (2017). Policy (mis)representation and the cost of ruling: US presidential elections in comparative perspective. *Comparative Political Studies*, *50*(6), 711–38.

5

The Economy and Executive Approval in a Semi-Presidential Regime

The Case of Portugal

Luís Aguiar-Conraria, Bruno Fernandes, and Pedro C. Magalhães

Over the last two decades, several studies have enhanced our understanding of the relationship between the economy and public support for the executive in Portugal (Veiga, 1998; Veiga and Veiga, 2004a; 2007). The central finding is clear: the public approval of governments and prime ministers is affected by economic performance. This is not at all surprising. Left-right socio-economic issues have dominated the policy agenda throughout Portugal's democratic history (Tsatsanis, Freire, and Tsirbas, 2014, 527). Despite a proportional representation electoral system, party-system fragmentation in Portugal has remained relatively low and was, until recently, declining, a singular trend among established democracies (Lijphart, 2012, 75). Since 1985, cabinets have either been single-party governments (often with an absolute majority) or minimum-winning ideologically cohesive coalitions. The combination of persistently high salience of economic issues and high clarity of responsibility for outcomes makes Portugal a clear-cut candidate for a solid and stable linkage between economic performance and the executive's public approval.

Yet several blind spots remain. We know, for example, that the relationship between objective economic performance and executive approval (see Chapter 1 of this volume) or support for incumbent parties (Freire and Santana-Pereira, 2012; Lobo and Pannico, 2020) has been stronger in some periods than in others in Portugal. Despite sharply contrasting economic conditions, consecutive elections have yielded similarly hefty punishments for government parties (Magalhães, 2017). Forecasting models of incumbent party vote have been required to incorporate political variables to account

Luís Aguiar-Conraria et al., *The Economy and Executive Approval in a Semi-Presidential Regime.* In: *Economics and Politics Revisited.* Edited by: Timothy Hellwig and Matthew Singer, Oxford University Press. © Luís Aguiar-Conraria et al. (2023). DOI: 10.1093/oso/9780192871664.003.0005

for the insufficient predictive power of economic variables (Magalhães and Aguiar-Conraria, 2009). In other words, the questions of whether vote or popularity functions are stable and of the variance in public support for the incumbent explained by the economy (the 'e-fraction' of those functions), famously raised by Paldam (1991), remain relevant and intriguing for the case of Portugal.

In this chapter, we advance two arguments about how to reconcile the evidence about the simultaneous importance and instability of economic performance as a driver of executive support in Portugal. The first points to the *economic context* itself and what it should imply for the clarity of performance signals available to voters. More specifically, we investigate whether executives are more punished by adverse economic developments than they are rewarded by positive ones. Although the possibility of such *asymmetry* in the relationship between economic performance and approval has been part of the literature since its modern inception (Mueller, 1970), the relatively short democratic electoral history of Portugal has contributed to leaving that hypothesis unexamined. To address that gap, we investigate whether the relationship between economic performance and executive approval in Portugal differs depending on whether the economy is expanding or contracting.

The second relevant context, we argue, is *political* and *institutional*. In Portugal's semi-presidential system, prime ministers who head the executive coexist with popularly elected and term-limited presidents that, while not sharing governing responsibilities, hold substantive powers and enjoy high public visibility. We suggest that the unstable nature of the political relationship between prime ministers and presidents in Portugal shapes the economics–approval link. To be sure, the literature on executive approval in semi-presidential systems has already suggested this is the case, treating periods of cohabitation—when the president and prime minister come from different parties or party coalitions—as causing a switch of responsibility from one incumbent to another, and therefore a switch in which actor voters hold accountable for the economy (Hellwig and Samuels, 2008; Elgie, 2018). We argue, however, that Portugal displays different features, with different consequences. What matters in Portugal's brand of semi-presidentialism is not cohabitation per se, but rather whether these periods are characterized by a *conflictual relationship* between prime ministers and presidents. In such conflictual contexts, we argue, clarity of responsibility for policy outcomes should be obscured, and the relationship between economic performance and the approval of both entities weakened. This calls attention to the importance of institutional factors behind the 'instability dilemma' addressed in the Introduction to this volume.

Taken together, the two arguments help us understand some of the puzzling instability in the relationship between the economy and approval in Portugal, hopefully also contributing to the study of public support for prime ministers (and presidents) in semi-presidential systems similar to the Portuguese.

Public Approval and the Economy in Portugal

Economic Contexts and Asymmetry

The study of the relationship between economic performance and executive approval in Portugal has resulted in relatively few studies, but with broadly consistent results. The pioneering work of Veiga (1998), using monthly approval data from 1986 to 1996, showed that prime ministerial popularity, besides receiving a boost immediately after the election (a honeymoon effect) and declining with time (cost of ruling), was negatively affected by increases in the unemployment rate. Later, revisiting a more extended time series of similar data, Veiga and Veiga (2004a; 2007) confirmed the previous findings. Other subsequent studies using aggregate data, this time focusing on the vote function, have confirmed the importance of economic performance—particularly of unemployment and GDP growth—as drivers of incumbent support (Veiga and Veiga 2004b; 2010; Freire and Lobo, 2005; Magalhães and Aguiar-Conraria, 2009; Goulart and Veiga, 2016).

However, has economic performance been equally consequential at all times? Recently, Lobo and Pannico (2020) showed that 'economic voting' in Portugal seems to have become stronger with the economic crisis of the early 2010s. Similarly, in Chapter 1 in this volume Carlin at al. show that the relationship between objective economic indicators and executive approval in Portugal became stronger in the period that encompasses the worst economic crisis experienced by the country in decades. This suggests that crises may render economic performance more politically consequential. In fact, from a cross-national perspective, Lewis-Beck and Nadeau (2012, 475) had already detected that the economy had a greater impact on incumbent support in Southern than in Northern Europe. They concluded that '[t]he greater weight of the economic vote in the PIGS [Portugal, Italy, Greece, and Spain] countries appears almost entirely due to their poorer economic position, coupled with their less complex links between governance and policy execution'. In sum, the economy seems to 'matter more' in contexts where economic conditions are more adverse.

Why should that occur? A well-known hypothesis points to an *asymmetry* in economic voting (Mueller, 1970; Nannestad and Paldam, 1997; Bélanger and Meguid, 2008; Dassonneville and Lewis-Beck, 2014). As Evans and Andersen put it, economic downturns 'elicit shared and reasonably perceptive responses that are not powerfully affected by political conditioning' (2006, 195). Under an economic crisis, the information conveyed by the mass media is more unequivocally negative than it is positive under economic good times (Soroka, 2006) and the salience of economic issues increases, boosting the relevance of economic performance for government approval (Singer, 2011). In contrast, during periods of growth, the economy loses importance and the signals conveyed by the 'mediated economy' become less unequivocal (Evans and Andersen, 2006, 195; see also Chzhen, Evans, and Pickup, 2014 and Dickerson, 2016). The 2011 and 2015 elections in Portugal illustrate this phenomenon. In the former, a major economic crisis led to large losses for the incumbent centre-left Socialist Party. However, in the latter, a clear economic recovery failed to prevent an almost equally large punishment for the ruling centre-right coalition. Magalhães (2017) shows that while citizens' evaluations of the economy were fundamentally exogenous in relation to political predispositions during the period of economic crisis, in 2015 they were powerfully contaminated by partisanship.

This suggests that the instability in the vote function in Portugal may partially result from how buoyant or stagnant economic conditions are differentially transmitted to incumbent support. To the extent that these general ideas about the vote function also apply to the popularity function, we should see the approval of the Portuguese prime minister suffering more under economic downturns than it is boosted by economic recoveries. In other words, we should expect the relationship between economic performance and prime ministerial approval to be *asymmetric*.

Portuguese Semi-Presidentialism and its Implications

A second potential source of instability in the economics–approval link concerns the institutional and political context under which voters evaluate incumbents. The idea is far from new. The 'clarity of responsibility' argument is predicated on the notion that the relationship between economic performance and public support depends on the extent to which there is a 'perceived unified control of policymaking by the incumbent government' (Powell and Whitten, 1993, 398). In contexts where such perceived control is lacking—characterized by greater horizontal or vertical power-sharing—the economics–approval link should weaken. In such circumstances, it becomes more difficult to determine who should be retrospectively blamed or rewarded, and voters should discount economic performance as a signal of government competence (Duch and Stevenson, 2008).

In the study of executive approval in semi-presidential systems—where a popularly elected head of state coexists with a prime minister accountable before parliament (Elgie, 1999)—the notion that context affects responsibility for the economy has been present as well. However, informed by the experience of Fifth Republic France, the main focus of that inquiry has been how semi-presidentialism allows for two alternating patterns of economic accountability. Under unified government, when French presidents are supported by a parliamentary majority of their own party, they become the leaders of that majority and thus of the executive, giving the system an unmistakable presidential dynamic (Shugart, 2005). In contrast, under 'cohabitation', when presidents and prime ministers belonged to different parties, power shifted to the latter, creating a 'parliamentary' dynamic. The presence or absence of cohabitation was thought to determine an oscillation between phases when the system became de facto, respectively, parliamentary and presidential (Duverger, 1980; Lijphart, 2012).

This, in turn, generated another oscillation: on whom voters held accountable for economic performance. In the presidential phases, under unified government, the French president's approval was strongly affected by economic performance. However, in the parliamentary phases, under cohabitation, the responsibility for economic governance shifted to the prime minister. During these periods the economy's influence on presidential support dropped significantly, while the opposite occurred with prime ministerial approval (Lewis-Beck, 1997; Lewis-Beck and Nadeau, 2004).[1]

In 2002, the synchronization of presidential and legislative elections made cohabitation in France much more unlikely, ending this oscillation. However, the French experience still moulds the thinking about economic accountability in semi-presidential systems, with studies finding the same kind of oscillating pattern in countries other than France. Looking at election results in many semi-presidential systems, Hellwig and Samuels (2008) showed that presidents are rewarded and punished for the economy only under conditions of unified government, while the prime minister's party is only rewarded

[1] But see also Turgeon, Bélanger, and Nadeau (2015), who show that only prime ministerial approval is affected by economic variables, and only during cohabitation.

and punished under conditions of cohabitation. Elgie (2018), finding similar results, suggested the existence, in the study of semi-presidential systems, of 'a basic scientific consensus about the effect of cohabitation on economic voting' (Elgie, 2018, 103).

However, we propose that this pattern is unlikely to extend to a semi-presidential system like Portugal's. All presidents since 1986 in Portugal have been prominent political figures, all former leaders of their parties. Presidents enjoy important powers, including the possibility of vetoing legislation or referring bills or statutes for constitutional review. Presidents also employ 'going public' tactics, using the authority and prestige of their office to direct public attention to the issues they prioritize (Neto and Lobo, 2009; Jalali, 2011). And they even have the (mostly) unconstrained possibility of dissolving parliament in the absence of a prime ministerial resignation or a successful motion of censure. This is a power they have used with parsimony in the last four decades, but which nevertheless has been used and stands as a relevant shadow over governments.

Yet while never becoming purely parliamentary, the Portuguese system's dynamic has never become presidential either, *de jure* or *de facto*. Portuguese presidents are not the leaders of their parties. The head of the executive is always the prime minister, i.e. the party and parliamentary majority leader with whom presidents coexist. Accordingly, presidential elections in Portugal bear some traits of a 'second-order' election (Reif and Schmitt, 1980), most notably their lower level of turnout in comparison with legislative elections (Fortes and Magalhães, 2005; Franco, 2020). The implication is that, at least in Portugal, there has been no oscillation between parliamentary and presidential phases depending on cohabitation or unified government. This, in turn, suggests that an oscillation in how voters hold prime ministers and presidents accountable for the economy should be absent as well.

However, this does not mean that the relationship between presidents and prime ministers is irrelevant for the role of the economy in the V-P function. Although it does not change who runs the everyday operation of government, cohabitation has nevertheless been a source of *political conflict* between presidents and prime ministers under semi-presidentialism (Protsyk, 2005a; 2005b; Elgie, 2010). The existing literature provides clear evidence about the conditions that have favoured such conflictual relationship. Portuguese presidents can only serve two consecutive terms of office. First-term incumbents who seek re-election for a second term in office—so far, all of them—have incentives to preserve a non-conflictual relationship with prime ministers and their parliamentary majorities in order to secure the required absolute majority of the vote in their re-election bid. This has occurred even under contexts of cohabitation. Since 1986, presidents Mário Soares, Jorge Sampaio, Cavaco Silva, and Marcelo Rebelo de Sousa successfully avoided major confrontations with prime ministers during their first term, even when they belonged to different parties. By defusing the potential for conflict, some incumbent presidents have even been able to secure opposing governing parties' explicit or implicit support in their re-election bids, as in the case of the Socialist Mário Soares in 1991 or the Social Democrat Marcelo Rebelo de Sousa in 2021.

However, in their second term, the combination of cohabitation and the lack of a re-election incentive has typically led presidents to engage in a more conflictual relationship with prime ministers. As Jalali (2011, 170) puts it, while presidents' first terms are characterized by a 'considerably weaker activism (. . .), not least motivated by the need to maintain a majority for reelection', second terms typically show a rise in 'legislative interventionism' and 'guerrilla warfare' on the part of presidents. In fact, second terms have only been historically peaceful under unified government, i.e. when presidents face a government majority congruent with them in partisan terms (Freire and Santana-Pereira, 2019). However, under cohabitation, presidents in their second and last term of office have used their veto and constitutional referral powers more frequently and have engaged in more open political confrontations with the government (Magalhães, 2001; Neto and Lobo, 2009; Jalali 2011; Franco 2020).

This suggests that, by favouring inter-institutional conflict between prime ministers and presidents, *second-term cohabitations* should contribute to blur accountability for the economy. By fostering 'legislative interventionism' on the part of presidents and 'constraining the governments' capacity for political leadership' (Jalali, 2011, 169), second-term cohabitations are periods when what Powell and Whitten defined as 'clarity of responsibility'—the 'perceived unified control of policymaking by the incumbent government' (1993, 398)—is undermined. This leads us to expect that the relationship between economic performance and prime ministerial approval we hypothesized earlier should be weaker when presidents and prime ministers belong to different parties *and* the former are serving their second and last term of office.

In summary, we propose two main hypotheses. H1 is that the relationship between economic performance and prime ministerial approval should be contingent upon the economic context itself: stronger under crises and weaker under expansions (i.e. asymmetric). H2 is that it should also be contingent upon the relationship between prime ministers and presidents: stronger under peaceful coexistence, weaker under contexts that have favoured political conflicts, i.e. during (presidential) second-term cohabitations.

Data, Variables, and Estimation Strategy

Data and Variables

Our dataset encompasses two measures of approval and a set of economic and political variables. We extracted two approval ratings from the Executive Approval Project dataset (Carlin et al., 2019). Our dependent variables are smoothed versions of the quarterly approval ratings of the Portuguese president and prime minister (*Presidential Approval Rating* and *PM Approval Rating*). The data available in the Executive Approval Database 2.0 goes from the second quarter of 1986 to the third quarter of 2018.

Table 5.1 lists the prime ministers and presidents throughout this period, indicating whether presidents were serving their first or second term and whether they and the prime ministers belonged to the same or different parties. The latter two aspects are crucial to test our second hypothesis and show considerable diversity through time.

Portugal had five presidents since the promulgation of the current 1976 democratic constitution. Since the approval series begin in 1986, the first president, Ramalho Eanes, is excluded from our analysis. The last we consider is Marcelo Rebelo de Sousa, who was elected in 2016. At the time of writing, all presidents spent ten years in office,[2] serving two consecutive terms of five years. Regarding the executive branch, headed by the prime minister, several personalities have been in power since 1986. Only two parties have occupied the prime ministerial post in this period: the Socialists (PS) and the Social Democrats (PSD). Another party, the Democrat and Social Centre-Popular Party (CDS-PP), has integrated some of PSD's governments to achieve a parliamentary majority.

Figure 5.1 shows the quarterly approval rates of Portuguese prime ministers (black line) and presidents (grey line). Shaded areas represent period of cohabitation, either during presidents' first (light grey) or second term (dark grey). The data covers four presidencies and ten prime ministerial cabinets. With brief exceptions in the early 1990s and late 2015, Portuguese presidents have been more popular than prime ministers throughout the entire period.

[2] The exception is the current president, Marcelo Rebelo de Sousa, who was elected in 2016 and re-elected in 2021.

Table 5.1 Portuguese presidents and prime ministers between 1986 and 2018

Period	Prime minister (party)	President (party)	Presidential term	Cohabitation
1986–1991	Cavaco Silva (PSD)	Mário Soares (PS)	First	Yes
1991–1995	Cavaco Silva (PSD)	Mário Soares (PS)	Second	Yes
1995–1996	António Guterres (PS)	Mário Soares (PS)	Second	No
1996–2001	António Guterres (PS)	Jorge Sampaio (PS)	First	No
2001–2002	António Guterres (PS)	Jorge Sampaio (PS)	Second	No
2002–2004	Durão Barroso (PSD)	Jorge Sampaio (PS)	Second	Yes
2004–2005	Pedro Santana Lopes (PSD)	Jorge Sampaio (PS)	Second	Yes
2005–2006	José Sócrates (PS)	Jorge Sampaio (PS)	Second	No
2006–2011	José Sócrates (PS)	Cavaco Silva (PSD)	First	Yes
2011	José Sócrates (PS)	Cavaco Silva (PSD)	Second	Yes
2011–2015	Pedro Passos Coelho (PSD)	Cavaco Silva (PSD)	Second	No
2015–2016	António Costa (PS)	Cavaco Silva (PSD)	Second	Yes
2016–2018	António Costa (PS)	Marcelo Rebelo de Sousa (PSD)	First	Yes

Source: Authors.

While visual inspection suggests the two series are related, the relationship is clearly imperfect and there are even periods where trends seem to diverge, suggesting that they may be driven by somewhat different processes.

To evaluate the relationship between economic performance and the public approval of prime ministers and presidents, we chose real GDP growth as our primary economic variable (*GDP Growth*). As Goulart and Veiga (2016) note, there are conditions in which unemployment rates may become deceptive indicators of economic performance, such as when massive emigration—particularly high in the 2008–2014 period in Portugal, for example—have contributed to mask unemployment. Therefore, we use instead the quarterly year-on-year growth rate of Portuguese's real GDP.[3] This information is

[3] Chain-linked volume data, with 2016 as reference year.

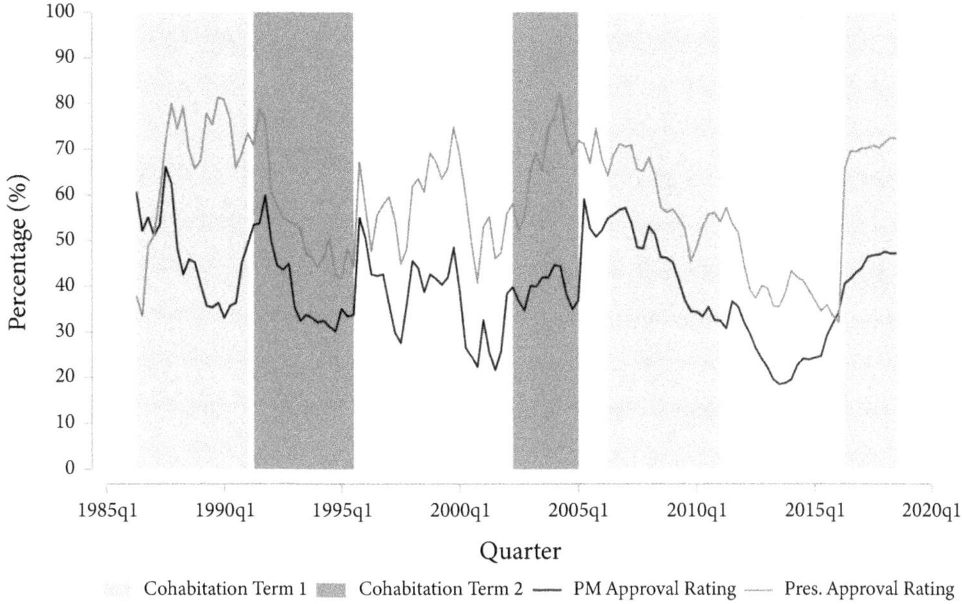

Figure 5.1 Prime ministerial and presidential approval rating, quarterly data
Source: Executive Approval Database 2.0.

conveyed by the Portuguese Central Bank, which issues long-term economic data every year. For this study, we used the 2020 version of revised estimates.

Figure 5.2 plots the evolution of the Portuguese real GDP growth since 1986, with shaded areas corresponding to recession periods. We start by observing the strong and steady economic boom that followed an earlier recession in 1983–1984, coterminous with Portugal joining the European Economic Community in 1986. This economic cycle ended in 1992–1993. Another economic boom was observed in the rest of the 1990s, at the same time Portugal was preparing to join the euro. The first decade of the twenty-first century has been marked by three economic recessions. The recession of 2011–2013 lasted several quarters: real GDP decreased sharply, unemployment reached 17 per cent—despite massive emigration—and social conditions worsened. This economic situation originated from a tight fiscal programme to reduce debt and public deficit, imposed by a bailout negotiated by the Portuguese government, IMF, and European institutions.

For the purpose of our analysis, we also collected data on several political variables:

- Honeymoon effect for president (*Honeymoon President*) and honeymoon effect for prime minister (*Honeymoon PM*). We follow

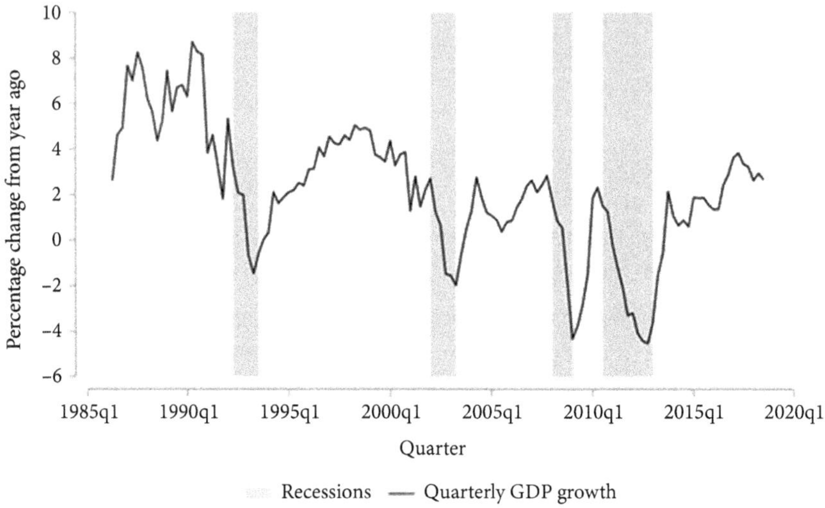

Figure 5.2 Quarterly growth rate of real GDP, percentage change from the previous year and recessions
Source: Portuguese Central Bank and FFMS Portuguese Cycles Dating Committee.

Veiga and Veiga (2004a) and coded 2 for the first quarter of each presidential (prime ministerial) term, 1 for the second quarter and 0 for others; for robustness purposes, we also estimated models where dummy variables identify the first, second, and third quarters in office.

- *Cohabitation 1st Term* and *Cohabitation 2nd Term* are dummy variables. The first is coded 1 for periods when presidents and prime ministers are from different parties and presidents are serving their first term of office, and 0 otherwise. The second is similar, with the difference that the value 1 is reserved for those periods when presidents and primes ministers are from different parties and presidents are serving their *second* term of office.
- *Unified government.* This variable is coded 1 in the cases where the president and the prime minister belong to the same political party whatever the president's term.

Estimation Strategy

We have two dependent variables we wish to explain; hence, we have two equations to estimate. If we were to estimate (e.g. by OLS) two independent equations, we would be imposing the restriction that the approval rates of prime ministers and presidents were independent. Given that one of the objects of our study is the interplay between these two political actors, imposing uncorrelated disturbances between the two equations seems to be a somewhat restrictive assumption. Therefore, we relax that assumption and estimate simultaneous equation models.[4]

Formally, we estimate a model of the type:

$$\begin{cases} y_1 = X_1\beta_1 + \varepsilon_1 \\ y_2 = X_2\beta_2 + \varepsilon_2 \end{cases}$$

Crucially, disturbances (ε_1 and ε_2) are not independent. Efficient estimation requires considering those in a structural equation setup. Also, note that we are not imposing any particular constraints on the vectors of independent variables (X_1 and X_2). In each equation we include the lagged dependent variable as an explanatory variable, allowing for autoregressive dynamics, as standard in the literature. We assessed the existence of unit roots in our dependent variables and verified that both series are stationary.[5] GDP growth is also lagged by one quarter, as also common. Initially, we also allowed for cross-influence of the lagged dependent variable. In such a case, the model would be equivalent to a vector autoregression model with exclusion restrictions. However, these cross-influences with the lagged dependent variable turned out to be not statistically significant, and we ended up excluding them from our estimations.

Results

We start by examining H1, as it relates to the shape of the relationship between economic performance (GDP growth) and prime ministerial approval measures. We hypothesized that it should be asymmetric. In Table 5.2, the results of Models 1 and 2 allow us to examine the hypothesis. Model 1 regresses prime ministerial approval (as well as presidential approval) on GDP growth lagged by one quarter, introducing specific 'honeymoon' variables and lagged

[4] The first paper to study popularity functions in Portugal, Veiga (1998), also used estimated simultaneous equation models, using the seemingly unrelated regression (SUR) method, arguing that the residuals between the popularity functions of the prime minister, the president, the parliament, and the government were correlated. The same happens, in our estimations, with the correlation between the residuals being about 0.5. With such a considerable correlation, efficiency requires simultaneous estimation.

[5] Augmented Dickey-Fuller tests were employed to check for unit roots. Test statistics are −3.252 for prime-ministerial approval and −3.077 for presidential approval. Both follow between the 1 per cent critical value (−3.500) and 5 per cent critical value (−2.888). If we consider the null of stationarity, KPSS tests provide even stronger evidence in favour of the stationarity hypotheses.

Table 5.2 Economic symmetry and asymmetry in the popularity functions of Portuguese prime ministers and presidents

	Model 1		**Model 2**	
	PM Approval	**Presidential Approval**	**PM Approval**	**Presidential Approval**
PM Approval$_{t-1}$	0.785* (0.037)		0.785* (0.036)	
Presidential Approval$_{t-1}$		0.801* (0.050)		0.800* (0.050)
Honeymoon PM	2.976* (0.958)		2.950* (0.937)	
Honeymoon president		1.498 (1.929)		1.658 (1.953)
GDP Growth$_{t-1}$	0.378* (0.134)	0.674* (0.192)		
GDP Growth Negative$_{t-1}$			−0.981* (0.277)	−0.679° (0.391)
GDP Growth Positive$_{t-1}$			0.164 (0.212)	0.677* (0.284)
Constant	6.979* (1.418)	10.186* (2.783)	7.768* (1.521)	10.227* (2.895)
Var (e.PM Approval)	20.556 (3.275)		20.220 (3.180)	
Var (e.Pres Approval)	36.723 (6.731)		36.723 (6.726)	
Cov (e.PM Approval, e.Pres Approval)	14.829 (3.129)		14.834 (3.100)	
Observations	129		129	
SRMR	0.025		0.022	

Source: Executive Approval Database 2.0.
Notes: Cells report estimates with standard errors in parentheses from simultaneous equation models. °p<0.10, *p<0.05 (two-tailed tests).

approval for each entity. Model 2 introduces a modification: following Dassonneville and Lewis-Beck (2014), we replace *GDP Growth*$_{t-1}$ with two variables: *GDP Growth Negative*$_{t-1}$ and *GDP Growth Positive*$_{t-1}$. The former is simply the value of *GDP Growth*$_{t-1}$ if negative, multiplied by −1 and zero otherwise, and the latter is *GDP Growth*$_{t-1}$ if positive, and zero otherwise.

The standardized root mean square residual (SRMR) values are in both cases below the 0.08 rule of thumb, suggesting a good fit between the models and the data.[6] The results for Model 1 show several familiar results. First, we obtain honeymoon effects for prime ministers but not for presidents.[7] Veiga and Veiga (2004a, 109 and 2007, 84), who first uncovered this contrast, did not speculate on the reasons behind it. However, one potential explanation may have to do again with the different roles of prime ministers and presidents in the political system. As Brody (1991) notes, the notion of a 'honeymoon' represents that the period of initial positive response to a new incumbent 'is limited, and beyond it a different set of processes affect the evaluation of (. . .) performance' (Brody, 1991, 28). However, while this period of suspension of criticism that executive office holders such as prime ministers are likely to get from the opposition, the media, and the public in general is indeed likely to be short, presidents without direct executive responsibilities, such as those in the Portuguese semi-presidential system, are likely to be able to deflect criticism and negative coverage for a more prolonged period. Therefore, it is not too surprising that (short-lived) 'honeymoon effects' emerge for prime ministers but not for presidents in Portugal.

Second, in Model 1, we obtain significant effects of GDP growth on both prime ministerial and presidential approval. However, Model 2, which allows for asymmetric effects of GDP growth, shows a fundamental difference between the two entities: while presidents seem equally affected by negative or positive GDP growth rates (the estimate is the same, 0.68), opinion towards the prime minister is affected only by negative growth rates (−0.98). Note that these estimates are on impact. The long-run effects are quite large, due to the implied dynamics of the autoregressive model. Imagine that the GDP growth rate is persistently negative, say −1 per cent. The estimated immediate impact is a decrease in the popularity of about one point (0.98). However, in the next quarter, popularity would decrease further, and so on. After two and a half years, the overall estimated impact of a growth rate of −1 per cent would be a decrease in the prime minister's approval of about four points.[8]

In other words, H1 is confirmed for the prime minister, but the same asymmetry is not found for presidents. The latter benefit from good times and are hurt by bad times to roughly the same extent; prime ministers, however, get

[6] The SRMR is an absolute measure of fit very common in structural equation modelling—e.g. see Maydeu-Olivares et al. (2018). The closer to zero, the better the fit.

[7] In the model where we employ dummy variables for quarters 1, 2, and 3 in office, results are similar: a significant 7-points boost in popularity for the prime minister in the first quarter, followed by (smaller) significant corrections in quarter 2 (−2 points) and 3 (−3.6 points); and no effects for presidential popularity. These results are similar across all specifications.

[8] For the president, given the autoregressive coefficient of 0.8 and the GDP growth rate coefficient of 0.68, the overall estimated impact of a 1 per cent GDP growth rate over two and half years is of about 3 points.

heavily blamed for bad times but are uncredited for good times. Again, the political and institutional role played by presidents in Portugal may contribute to explaining this difference. Their non-executive status and the incentives to secure an absolute majority for election and re-election have led viable presidential candidates to present themselves as being 'above parties', running for elections under platforms that have very low policy content, leading to a portrayal of their role as that of a non-partisan 'moderating power' (Feijó, 2021). Like French presidents under cohabitation, Portuguese presidents do not cease benefiting from the 'warm glow' of a good economy or being hurt by economic downturns (Lewis-Beck, 2004). However, the contamination of economic evaluations by partisan predispositions that, under 'good times', is likely to blur the relationship between the economy and prime ministerial approval (Evans and Andersen, 2006) is less likely to occur in the evaluation of entities that present themselves and are primarily perceived, most of the time, as 'non-partisan'.

We now turn to H2, which proposed that contexts that have favoured conflict between presidents and prime ministers should account for another aspect of the instability in the economics–approval link for prime ministers: the blurring of economic accountability during periods of presidential second-term cohabitation. To test this second hypothesis, we estimated Models 3 and 4, whose results are presented in Table 5.3. Model 3 provides an intermediate step. For prime ministers, we include lagged dependent and 'honeymoon' variables. Furthermore, we include *GDP Growth Negative*$_{t-1}$ (capturing the asymmetric relationship between economic performance and the prime minister's approval shown previously) and the three dummies capturing the three relevant political conditions that configure presidential-prime ministerial relations: *Cohabitation 1st Term*, *Cohabitation 2nd Term* (with *Unified Government* as the reference category). The specification for the presidential equation is very similar, except that, per our previous findings, the specification of the economic variable—*GDP Growth*$_{t-1}$—assumes a simple symmetrical relationship.

First, note that in Model 3, SRMR values are smaller compared to Models 1 and 2, suggesting improved fit. Second, the results show that, again, the honeymoon effects detected for the prime minister are absent in the case of the president.[9] Third, an unexpected result is that the coefficient for first-term cohabitation is positive and significant at $p<0.10$ for both presidents and prime ministers. Interestingly, this result resonates with Grossman and Guinaudeau's

[9] Results for our alternative specification of honeymoon effects are similar.

Table 5.3 Presidential and prime ministerial approval, the economy, and cohabitation

	Model 3		Model 4	
	PM Approval	**Presidential Approval**	**PM Approval**	**Presidential Approval**
PM Approval$_{t-1}$	0.769* (0.038)		0.771* (0.038)	
Presidential Approval$_{t-1}$		0.769* (0.054)		0.773* (0.053)
Honeymoon PM	3.038* (0.920)		3.073* (0.909)	
Honeymoon president		1.638 (1.869)		1.634 (1.868)
Cohabitation 1st Term	1.940° (1.037)	3.337* (1.483)	1.998° (1.109)	3.476° (1.796)
Cohabitation 2nd Term	0.069 (1.057)	1.675 (1.372)	−0.356 (1.095)	1.889 (1.558)
GDP Growth Negative$_{t-1}$	−1.066* (0.237)			
Cohabitation 1st Term × GDP Growth Negative$_{t-1}$			−1.331* (0.449)	
Cohabitation 2nd Term × GDP Growth Negative$_{t-1}$			0.511 (0.819)	
Unified Government × GDP Growth Negative$_{t-1}$			−1.138* (0.272)	
GDP Growth$_{t-1}$		0.596* (0.184)		
Cohabitation 1st Term × GDP Growth$_{t-1}$				0.566* (0.264)
Cohabitation 2nd Term × GDP Growth$_{t-1}$				0.442 (0.664)
Unified Government × GDP growth$_{t-1}$				0.651* (0.250)
Constant	8.112* (1.558)	10.529* (2.815)	8.044* (1.591)	10.250* (2.676)
Var (e.PM Approval)	19.589 (3.108)		19.046 (3.114)	
Var (e.Pres Approval)	34.984 (6.240)		35.091 (6.232)	
Cov(e.PM Approval, e.Pres Approval)	13.899 (3.074)		13.567 (3.055)	
Observations	129		129	
SRMR	0.013		0.013	

Source: Executive Approval Database 2.0.
Notes: Cells report estimates with standard errors in parentheses from simultaneous equation models. $^{\circ}p<0.10$; $^{*}p<0.05$; (two-tailed tests).

study of presidential popularity in France (Chapter 4 this volume), which shows that presidential popularity has *benefited* from cohabitation, independently of economic performance and other factors. In the case of Portugal, that premium emerges both for presidents and prime ministers, but only during first-term (peaceful) cohabitations. It is conceivable that, by generating a political climate in which governments and presidents of different parties are shown to be able to coexist peacefully, first-term cohabitations demobilize popular and partisan opposition to both entities from both partisan sides of the aisle and contribute to boosting their popularity.

In Model 4, we allow the three dummies capturing the three relevant political conditions that configure presidential-prime ministerial relations, *Cohabitation 1st Term*, *Cohabitation 2nd Term*, and *Unified Government,* to interact with our economic performance variables. This allows us to directly check the origin of the marginal effect of *GDP Growth*$_{t-1}$ for presidents and of *GDP Growth Negative*$_{t-1}$. for prime ministers. The specification effectively disaggregates one coefficient into the three that are obtained under the different relevant circumstances—*Unified Government*, *Cohabitation 1st Term*, and *Cohabitation 2nd Term*. This allows us to test H2, which suggested that the relationship between economic performance and executive approval should be contingent upon the relationship between prime ministers and presidents: stronger under peaceful coexistence than under conflictual (presidential) second-term cohabitations.

While Models 2 and 3 showed that *GDP Growth Negative*$_{t-1}$ was harmful to the prime minister, Model 4 shows that such negative value results from the aggregation of three coefficients for three different contexts. *Cohabitation 1st Term* × *GDP Growth Negative*$_{t-1}$ and *Unified Government* × *GDP Growth Negative*$_{t-1}$, are both negative, significant, and similarly sized. In other words, economic performance affects the popularity of prime ministers under conditions of first-term cohabitation or unified government, and it does so asymmetrically, as posed in H1. In contrast, the coefficient for the interaction *Cohabitation 2nd Term* × *GDP Growth Negative*$_{t-1}$ for prime ministers is far from statistical significance at conventional levels. In other words, under conditions that have been characterized by a more conflictual relationship between prime ministers and presidents, prime ministerial approval becomes insensitive to economic performance.

Similarly, Models 2 and 3 showed the coefficient *GDP Growth*$_{t-1}$ is positive for the president. Model 4 shows this results from *Cohabitation 1st Term* × *GDP Growth*$_{t-1}$ and *Unified Government* × *GDP Growth*$_{t-1}$, whose coefficients are positive, significant, and similarly sized: under conditions that favour peaceful coexistence with prime ministers, presidential approval is (symmetrically) affected by economic performance. However, like what occurs with prime ministerial approval, the interaction *Cohabitation 2nd Term* × *GDP* $Growth_{t-1}$ for presidents is not statistically significant.[10]

In sum, contextual conditions that combine a lack of re-election incentives for presidents and partisan divergence between them and prime ministers have been inimical to economic accountability: inter-institutional conflict between presidents and prime ministers makes the popularity of both entities less sensitive to economic performance, particularly in the case of the latter.

Conclusion

It has long been suspected that support for incumbent governments and parties in semi-presidential systems might be characterized by somewhat different dynamics from those observed in pure parliamentary or presidential systems. In the well-studied French case, cohabitation seemed to switch responsibility for the economy from the president to the prime minister, as the leadership of the executive moved from the former to the latter (Lewis-Beck, 1997). Other studies have even proposed this also occurs with semi-presidential systems more broadly, with cohabitation serving as the switch that makes presidents (under the former) or prime ministers and their parties (under the latter) publicly accountable for the economy.

We suggest, however, that this dynamic has not been reproduced in the case of semi-presidential Portugal, or at least not since the mid-1980s. Because cohabitation in Portugal does not switch the locus of responsibility for economic policy, it also does not switch it for economic performance from the public's point of view either. Voters strongly punish prime ministers for bad economic performance under either cohabitation or unified government. There is, however, one crucial exception: *conflictual cohabitations*, such as those that have prompted presidents to make more extensive uses of their legislative and oversight powers to place important obstacles to governments' policy agenda during presidential second (and last) terms. Under such conditions, public approval for *both* entities, prime ministers and presidents, becomes mostly insensitive to economic performance. These findings are compatible

[10] However, it has the same sign as the other interactions, suggesting the contrast between second-term cohabitations and the remaining situations is more robust for the case of prime minister than for the case of the president.

with the notion that conflicts between politically relevant presidents and the prime ministers they oppose contribute to blurring responsibility for the economy. By doing so, the study findings point to a source of instability in the Portuguese V-P function that, while rooted in institutional factors—semi-presidentialism, presidential powers, term-limits—it is far from static: it depends on the political context shaping the relationship between prime ministers, presidents, and their parties, a context that has varied significantly throughout the period under examination (see Table 5.1).

Furthermore, we also show that although the approval of both prime ministers and presidents are both affected by the economy outside of second-term cohabitations, that relationship is asymmetric for prime ministers and symmetric for presidents. Future studies may be able to establish with greater certainty the reasons for that difference. However, we speculate that it is consistent with the different roles played by both entities in the political system. As partisan entities in charge of the executive, prime ministers are affected by the economy in a way that is compatible with the higher partisan contamination of economic evaluations in good times (Evans and Andersen, 2006; see Magalhães, 2017 for Portugal), i.e. asymmetrically. Conversely, the relationship between the economy and presidential approval is less contaminated by such process, given the lower relevance of partisanship as a cue with which to evaluate presidents. The asymmetry found for prime ministerial approval addresses part of the puzzle concerning the apparent instability of the V-P function in the country (Freire and Santana-Pereira, 2012; Carlin et al., this volume). In particular, it helps accounting for the very strong connection between economic performance and prime ministerial approval during Portugal's worst economic times since the 1970s.

More broadly, this chapter makes two main contributions. First, a clearer understanding of some of the reasons why, in the case of Portugal, the link between economic performance and executive support appears unstable if approached in a way that ignores the variability introduced by economic and institutional contexts. A second contribution consists of potentially important clues to be explored in the study of semi-presidential systems that bear similarities to the Portuguese. In countries such as Bulgaria, Poland, Lithuania, Romania, Slovakia, or Slovenia, for example, popularly elected presidents are neither like the French heads of the executive nor like the mostly ceremonial figureheads that can be found in the semi-presidential systems in Austria, Ireland, or Iceland. Their powers are often relevant, and their cohabitation with prime ministers who belong to different parties has been characterized by peaceful coexistence in some cases but conflict and even policy stalemates in others (Protsyk, 2005a; 2005b; Elgie, 2010). The Portuguese case provides a few testable hypotheses about how economic performance should affect the approval of both prime ministers and presidents in such contexts.

References

Bélanger, É., and Meguid, B. M. (2008). Issue salience, issue ownership, and issue-based vote choice. *Electoral Studies*, *27*(3), 477–91.

Brody, R. (1991). *Assessing the President: The Media, Elite Opinion, and Public Support*. Stanford, CA: Stanford University Press.

Carlin, R. E., Hartlyn, J., Hellwig, T., Love, G. J., Martinez-Gallardo, C., and Singer, M. M. (2019). Executive Approval Database 2.0. Available for download at http://www.executiveapproval.org.

Chzhen, K., Evans, G., and Pickup, M. (2014). When do economic perceptions matter for party approval? *Political Behavior*, *36*(2), 291–313.

Dassonneville, R., and Lewis-Beck, M. S. (2014). Macroeconomics, economic crisis and electoral outcomes: A national European pool. *Acta Politica*, *49*(4), 372–94.

Dickerson, B. (2016). Economic perceptions, presidential approval, and causality: The moderating role of the economic context. *American Politics Research*, *44*(6), 1037–65.

Duch, R. M., and Stevenson, R. T. (2008). *The Economic Vote: How Political and Economic Institutions Condition Election Results*. Cambridge: Cambridge University Press.

Duverger, M. (1980). A new political system model: Semi-presidential government. *European Journal of Political Research*, *8*(2), 165–87.

Elgie, R. (1999). *The Politics of Semi-Presidentialism*. In *Semi-Presidentialism in Europe. Comparative European Politics*, Robert Elgie, ed. Oxford: Oxford University Press. 1–21.

Elgie, R. (2010). Semi-presidentialism, cohabitation and the collapse of electoral democracies, 1990–2008. *Government and Opposition*, *45*(1), 29–49.

Elgie, R. (2018). Regime types, presidential power, and clarity of economic responsibility. In *Political Leadership: A Pragmatic Institutionalist Approach*, R. Elgie, ed. London: Palgrave Macmillan. 85–125.

Evans, G., and Andersen, R. (2006). The political conditioning of economic perceptions. *The Journal of Politics*, *68*(1), 194–207.

Feijó, R. G. (2021). 'Moderating power' and partisan presidents: Two empirical cases. In *Presidents in Semi-Presidential Regimes*. Cham: Palgrave Pivot. 129–49.

Fortes, B. G., and Magalhães, P. (2005). As eleições presidenciais em sistemas semipresidenciais: participação eleitoral e punição dos governos. *Análise Social, XL*, 891–922.

Franco, V. S. D. (2020). *Semipresidencialismo em Portugal: Os poderes presidenciais na interação com o governo e com a Assembleia da República (1982–2016).* Lisbon: Assembleia da República.

Freire, A., and Lobo, M. C. (2005). Economics, ideology and vote: Southern Europe, 1985–2000. *European Journal of Political Research, 44*(4), 493–518.

Freire, A., and Santana-Pereira, J. (2012). Economic voting in Portugal, 2002–2009. *Electoral Studies, 31*(3), 506–12.

Freire, A., and Santana-Pereira, J. (2019). The President's dilemma: The Portuguese semi-presidential system in times of crisis (2011–16). *International Journal of Iberian Studies, 32*(3), 117–35.

Goulart, P., and Veiga, F. J. (2016). Portuguese 2015 legislative elections: How economic voting, the median voter and unemployment led to 'the times they are a'changin'? *Electoral Studies, 100*(43), 197–200.

Hellwig, T., and Samuels, D. (2008). Electoral accountability and the variety of democratic regimes. *British Journal of Political Science 38*(1): 65–90.

Jalali, C. (2011). The president is not a passenger. In *Semi-Presidentialism and Democracy*, R. Elgie, S. Moestrup, and Y.-S. Wu, eds. London: Palgrave Macmillan. 156–73.

Lewis-Beck, M. S. (1997). Who's the chef? Economic voting under a dual executive. *European Journal of Political Research, 31*(3), 315–25.

Lewis-Beck, M. S. (2004). French election theories and the 2002 results: An introduction. In *The French Voter,* M. S. Lewis-Beck, ed. Palgrave Macmillan, London. 1–11.

Lewis-Beck, M. S., and Nadeau, R. (2004). Dual governance and economic voting: France and the United States. In *The French Voter*, M. S. Lewis-Beck, ed. Palgrave Macmillan, London. 136–54.

Lewis-Beck, M. S., and Nadeau, R. (2012). PIGS or not? Economic voting in Southern Europe. *Electoral Studies, 31*(3), 472–7.

Lijphart, A. (2012). *Patterns of Democracy: Government Forms and Performance in Thirty-Six Countries.* New Haven, CT: Yale University Press.

Lobo, M. C., and Pannico, R. (2020). Increased economic salience or blurring of responsibility? Economic voting during the Great Recession. *Electoral Studies, 65*, 102141.

Magalhães, P. C (2001). As armas dos fracos: o veto político e a litigância constitucional do Presidente da República. In *Actas do I Encontro Nacional de Ciência Política*. Lisbon: Bizâncio. 489–506.

Magalhães, P. C. (2017). A tale of two elections: Information, motivated reasoning, and the economy in the 2011 and 2015 Portuguese elections. *Análise Social, 52*(225), 736–58.

Magalhães, P. C., and Aguiar-Conraria, L. (2009). Growth, centrism and semi-presidentialism: Forecasting the Portuguese general elections. *Electoral Studies*, *28*(2), 314–21.

Maydeu-Olivares, A., Shi, D., and Rosseel, Y. (2018). Assessing fit in structural equation models: A Monte-Carlo evaluation of RMSEA versus SRMR confidence intervals and tests of close fit. *Structural Equation Modeling: A Multidisciplinary Journal*, *25*(3), 389–402.

Mueller, J. E. (1970). Presidential popularity from Truman to Johnson. *The American Political Science Review*, *64*(1), 18–34.

Nannestad, P., and Paldam, M. (1997). The grievance asymmetry revisited: A micro study of economic voting in Denmark, 1986–1992. *European Journal of Political Economy*, *13*(1), 81–99.

Neto, O. A., and Lobo, M. C. (2009). Portugal's semi-presidentialism (re)considered: An assessment of the president's role in the policy process, 1976–2006. *European Journal of Political Research*, *48*(2), 234–55.

Paldam, M. (1991). How robust is the vote function? A study of seventeen nations over four decades. In *Economics and Politics: The Calculus of Support*, H. Northop, M. S. Lewis-Beck, and J.-D. Lafay eds. Ann Arbor, MI: University of Michigan Press. 9–31.

Powell Jr, G. B., and Whitten, G. D. (1993). A cross-national analysis of economic voting: taking account of the political context. *American Journal of Political Science*, *37*(2), 391–414.

Protsyk, O. (2005a). Politics of intraexecutive conflict in semipresidential regimes in Eastern Europe. *East European Politics and Societies*, *19*(2), 135–60.

Protsyk, O. (2005b). Prime ministers' identity in semi-presidential regimes: Constitutional norms and cabinet formation outcomes. *European Journal of Political Research*, *44*(5), 721–48.

Reif, K., and Schmitt, H. (1980). Nine second-order national elections—a conceptual framework for the analysis of European Election results. *European Journal of Political Research*, *8*(1), 3–44.

Shugart, M. S. (2005). Semi-presidential systems: Dual executive and mixed authority patterns. *French Politics*, *3*(3), 323–51.

Singer, M. M. (2011). Who says 'it's the economy'? Cross-national and cross-individual variation in the salience of economic performance. *Comparative Political Studies*, *44*(3), 284–312.

Soroka, S. N. (2006). Good news and bad news: Asymmetric responses to economic information. *The Journal of Politics*, *68*(2), 372–85.

Tsatsanis, E., Freire, A., and Tsirbas, Y. (2014). The impact of the economic crisis on the ideological space in Portugal and Greece: A comparison of elites and voters. *South European Society and Politics*, *19*(4), 519–40.

Turgeon, M., Bélanger, É., and Nadeau, R. (2015). French popularity functions: Different measures, different determinants? *French Politics*, *13*(3), 266–86.

Veiga, F. J., and Veiga, L. G. (2004a). Popularity functions, partisan effects, and support in parliament. *Economics and Politics*, *16*(1), 101–15.

Veiga, F. J., and Veiga, L. G. (2004b). The determinants of vote intentions in Portugal. *Public Choice*, *118*(3), 341–64.

Veiga, F. J., and Veiga, L. G. (2010). The impact of local and national economic conditions on legislative election results. *Applied Economics*, *42*(13), 1727–34.

Veiga, L. G. (1998). Popularity functions for the Portuguese prime minister, government, parliament and president. *European Journal of Political Research*, *33*(3), 347–61.

Veiga, L. G., and Veiga, F. J. (2007). Economics, popularity and vote intentions in Portugal: A longitudinal analysis with aggregate data. In *Portugal at the Polls*, A. Freire, M. C. Lobo, and P. C. Magalhães, eds. Lanham, MD: Lexington Books. 75–100.

6

Economic Retrospection in Japan

Both Partisanship and Economic Evaluations Matter

Hanako Ohmura and Airo Hino

In Japan, researchers have employed time-series data to examine the economy's political effects since 1960. During this period, Japan has followed a unique political and economic trajectory: remarkable economic growth, dramatic decline and recovery, and the continuation of democracy under the one-party dominance of the Liberal Democratic Party (LDP: *Jiyuu Minshu Tou*) and the collapse of that dominance. This changing context has potentially reshaped both the 'p-fraction' and 'e-fraction' (Paldam, 1991) elements of executive approval in Japan. First, Japan has undergone historic changes in the last three decades, such as the political upheaval of the 1993 electoral reform, the temporary displacement of the LDP's long one-party rule under the so-called '1955-system' (*Gojuugo-nen Taisei*), and its resulting partisan influence on economic voting. The objectives of the electoral reform were to: (1) curb the incentives to vote based on personal interests; (2) correct pork-barrel politics and corruption; and (3) revitalize party-oriented and policy-oriented elections (e.g. Ashibe, 1991). In other words, the electoral reform was intended to increase the clarity of responsibility for voters by redirecting their attention to political parties and policies. It led to changes in the House of Representatives' electoral system, moving from the single non-transferable vote with multi-member districts (SNTV/MMD) to a mixed system combining single-member districts and proportional representation (SMD-PR).[1]

Although these changes reduced the role of money in politics to some extent (e.g. Fujimura, 2015; Hamamoto, 2018), Japanese politics did not necessarily move towards a sharper clarity of responsibility under the party-centred and policy-centred reforms. Even though the LDP was more centralized under the leadership of Junichiro Koizumi from 2001 to 2006 and Shinzo Abe from

[1] Japan's House of Representatives has 465 members, 176 of which are elected from eleven multi-member constituencies by party-list proportional representation and 289 from single-member constituencies.

Hanako Ohmura and Airo Hino, *Economic Retrospection in Japan.* In: *Economics and Politics Revisited.*
Edited by: Timothy Hellwig and Matthew Singer, Oxford University Press. © Hanako Ohmura and Airo Hino (2023).
DOI: 10.1093/oso/9780192871664.003.0006

2012 to 2020, the clarity of responsibility has been disrupted since 1993, under the framework of coalition governments (Miyake et al., 2001; Iida, 2005). If the clarity of responsibility decreased due to the 1993 political upheaval in Japan and the new custom of repeated coalition governments, does it alter the nation's economic voting?

Alongside these political changes, there have been fundamental changes to the nation's economic model. In 1951, the Shigeru Yoshida Administration chose a lightly armed and economy-oriented policy setting at the San Francisco Peace Treaty; since then, policies have been managed in Japan in such a way as to prioritize economic growth. During the period of rapid economic expansion in the 1960s and early 1970s, support for the LDP was high; however, during the period of economic stagnation induced by the 1970 oil crisis, the seats held by the Japan Socialist Party (*Nihon Shakai Tou*) were almost tied with those of the LDP. When the bubble economy burst and the consumption tax was introduced in the late 1980s, the LDP's one-party dominance system came to an end. Similarly, the 2008 global depression prompted a government change from an LDP-led coalition to one led by the Democratic Party of Japan (DPJ). While there were demands for the end of LDP-dominated politics for a while (Nonaka, 2008), the inauguration of the second Abe administration marked a decisive turning point.[2] From 2012 onward, the Abe administration combined flexible fiscal policy with quantitative and qualitative easing (QQE). This policy orientation, known as 'Abenomics', may have significantly changed the link between the economy and politics and has come to influence economic votes. In the six national elections held under Abe's second tenure as prime minister, the LDP has consistently held more than 55 per cent of the seat share in the Diet and, despite political scandals, its approval rating did not fall far below 30 per cent (cf. Kohno, 2018).

Historically, Japan has represented a typical case of electoral accountability, where the incumbent who performs well economically enjoys high ratings and is re-elected, while those performing poorly are sanctioned (McElwain, 2015). Stimulus packages are one of the factors that have influenced Japan's economic vote. While the beginning of voting behaviour research in the 1980s has continuously revealed the mechanism of economic retrospective voting functions among Japanese voters (Hirano, 1994; Ikeda, 2000; Miyake et al., 2001), economic voting in Japan entered a new phase in the 2010s, along with

[2] Shinzo Abe also served as LDP prime minister from September 2006 to August 2007, a period known as the first Abe administration. The administration led by Abe from December 2012 to September 2019 is then the second Abe administration. When not otherwise specified, the following text refers to the second Abe administration.

the unparalleled stimulus package. An examination of the Japanese case can provide not only a typical case of economic electoral accountability, but also the implications of unprecedented aggressive economic stimulation measures on economic voting.

In this chapter, we demonstrate the generally large impact of both the electorate's partisanship and economic evaluation on cabinet approval. Through these analyses, we show that (1) both partisanship and economic evaluations significantly continue to influence cabinet approval ratings in Japan, but (2) electoral reform and the ensuing upheaval in the party system have changed economic voting via the transformation of clarity of responsibility, and (3) a major stimulus package has the potential to change the economic vote in a way that has no parallel in other countries. Whereas other contributions to this volume, such as Chapter 3 on Great Britain and Chapter 8 on Spain, raise questions about the importance of changes in the clarity of responsibility to understanding changes in the economy–approval relationship, our results demonstrate the clear importance of these factors for democratic accountability in Japan.

Partisanship and Voters in Japan: Does the Clarity of Responsibility Matter?

Under the so-called 1955-system with the SNTV/MMD electoral system, the LDP remained the dominant party in Japanese politics. Pork-barrel politics ensured the survival of one-party dominance, providing diverse economic benefits to multiple LDP candidates in an electoral district (Tatebayashi, 2004). The foundation for covering welfare by creating jobs through public works projects (Kitayama, 2003; Estévez-Abe, 2008), was made possible through profit inducements to specific industries such as construction, commerce, agriculture, forestry, and fisheries in the electoral districts (Pekkanen et al., 2006; Scheiner, 2010).

Scholars have argued that the system of one-party dominance influenced the nature of economic voting via its effect on the clarity of responsibility. Because the LDP controlled the government completely, the success/failure of the economic situation could be attributed entirely to the LDP's performance (Miyake et al., 2001; Iida, 2005). In the United Kingdom's majoritarian party system, for example, the ruling party under the parliamentary cabinet system has a similar structure for the clarity of responsibility and accountability. The clarity of responsibility may seem even higher in Japan, where there was no change of government that would have allowed executives to blame the outcomes on their predecessor in office. Japanese economic voting arguably had a distinctive feature of *invariance* of attribution.

However, the situation of one-party dominance was more complex. The signalling of the LDP's partisanship was hardly discernible. Although voters, in general, are more likely to look at the party brand under the SMD system, Japanese electorates in the 1955-system were also interested in candidate attributes: whether the candidate belonged to a group within the LDP and what benefit sharing he/she may provide. By dispersing power to the factions that send individual candidates, as opposed to concentrating it in the party's executives, the voters' evaluation of clarity of responsibility was regarded as becoming increasingly diverse and complex. Under the 1955-system, the institutional aspect of clarity of responsibility was obvious, but the substantive aspect of clarity of responsibility was marked by a degree of uncertainty.

This dispersion also meant that the diverse interests offered by LDP candidates formed a breeding ground for corruption and led to decentralization across factions within the party. This led to pressure to reform the electoral rules. In 1994, one year after the formation of an 'all but LDP' coalition government, a reform that was designed to make the electoral campaigns less expensive and foster party-based elections was implemented. The stated purpose of the change to SMD-PR was to make party labels and policies more functional and increase the likelihood of alternation of power based on policy competitions.

The clarity of responsibility might have been improved if these reforms had been adopted under an LDP administration. However, this was not the case. In tandem with the electoral reform, the LDP was ousted from power and replaced by a coalition of several parties, including the Japan New Party (*Nihon Shintou*), one of the splinter parties of the LDP. Although it was intended to promote party-based elections, the massive political upheaval of 1993–1994 instead weakened the party brand and caused greater fluidity in partisanship among voters.

In addition, the so-called twisted Parliament (*Nejire Kokkai*) that emerged in 2007 produced different majorities in the lower (House of Representatives) and upper (House of Councillors) chambers, thus blurring the clarity of responsibility (Imai and Arai, 2013). To complicate matters further, the fluidization of partisanship continued after the demise of the 1955-system; the LDP-centred Junichiro Koizumi administration from 2001 to 2006, the DPJ administrations in 2009–2012, and the second Abe administration from 2012 all contributed to the fluidization of partisanship as well as the repeated splits

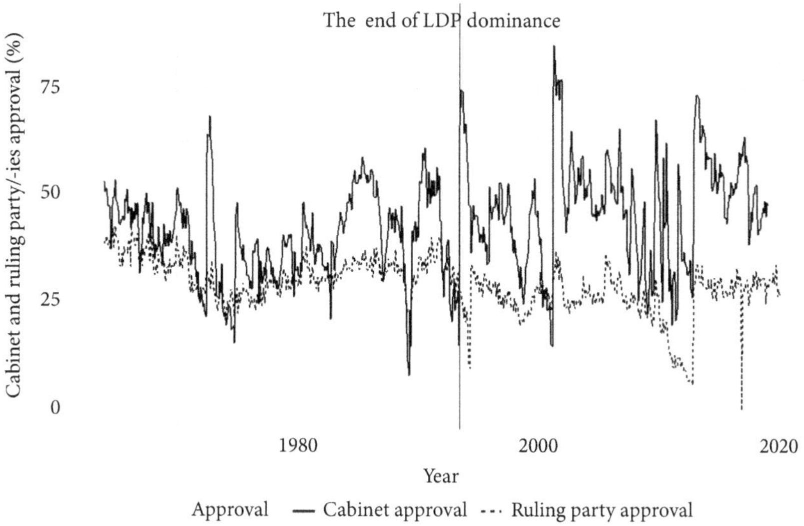

Figure 6.1 Ruling party approval and cabinet approval
Source: Executive Approval Database.

and merges of political parties in this period. Reflecting these changes in partisanship, Figure 6.1 shows a divergence in the relationship between ruling party and cabinet approval since 1993: during this period, the trend has not been a simple divergence, but rather a transition portrayed by frequent updates of ruling-cabinet approval, with significant changes at the beginning of each administration.

Against the backdrop of partisanship and attribution of responsibility, a great deal of research analysing the relationship between ruling party support and cabinet support in Japan has accumulated. In other words, the 'p-fraction' in the Japanese vote and popularity functions has been devoted to the analysis of partisanship. Iida (2005) and Maeda (2008) highlight the weakened link between the ruling party and cabinet approval after 1993, and Nakamura (2006) also examines the (in)stability of party support. These studies reveal that the ruling party's approval is the primary determinant of cabinet's approval, but the link between the two has weakened since 1993. However, connections between economic evaluations and partisan attachments and, in turn, their impact on cabinet approval have not been fully analysed.[3] In other

[3] We note that many of these studies were published in the mid-2000s and did not collect sufficient data after 1993 and that extending the period of analysis from the 2000s to the 2010s may reveal if the ties between ruling-party approval and cabinet approval are characterized by fluctuations rather than a simple downward trend.

words, much remains to be done to understand how economic voting patterns have changed under the altered clarity of responsibility.

To advance our understanding of the ruling party/cabinet approval connection in Japan, this study theoretically and empirically binds three essential components: partisanship, economic evaluations, and cabinet support. If the findings of previous studies are valid, the link between ruling party support and cabinet support would be expected to be weaker and less stable after 1993. According to the above theoretical arguments, we advance two 'p-fraction' related hypotheses:

Hypothesis 1: Ruling party approval has a positive impact on cabinet approval.
Hypothesis 2: The relationship between the ruling party approval and cabinet approval is stronger before 1993 and weaker afterwards.

Economic Status and Voters in Japan: The Effect of Economic Events and Stimulus Measures

After rejoining the international community with the San Francisco Peace Treaty in 1951, Japan under the Yoshida administration adopted a lightly armed and economy-focused policy mix designed to enhance domestic economic performance and welfare (Kusunoki, 2009). Defence spending was reduced since Japan was under the security aegis of Western countries. This politico-economic scheme worked well; Japan recorded unprecedented economic growth in the 1960s and early 1970s. Furthermore, a combination of development policy, social security, and economic stimulus measures facilitated growth rates throughout this period. The economic system was defined by a blend of social security and Keynesian economic strategies, with public works and job creation playing a significant role as social security alternatives (Kitayama, 2003; Estévez-Abe, 2008). Under this system, voters have maintained a high level of interest in business conditions at the national level and livelihood conditions at the individual level (Inoguchi, 1986; Hirano, 1994; Ikeda, 2000; McElwain, 2015; Taniguchi, 2016).

Although the economy enjoyed rapid growth until the early 1970s, it was hit by several domestic and international political-economic crises following the oil shocks of the mid-1970s. The bubble economy that burst in the late 1980s and the consumption tax first introduced in 1989 under the Noboru Takeshita administration were the underlying causes of the end of LDP dominance and the long-lasting recession in Japan. These years are known as the 'lost decades'. Even after the return of the LDP to power by forming a collation government in 1995, its rule was affected by exogenous shocks such as the 1997 Asian currency and economic crisis, the prolonged recession that spilled over from the bankruptcy of Lehman Brothers Inc. in the United States in 2008, and the Great East Japan earthquake of 2011. In particular, the recession that followed the 2011 earthquake caused the DPJ-centred coalition government, which had come to power in 2009, to lose voter trust. This, in turn, led to the LDP resuming power under the Abe cabinet in 2012. Until early 2010, however, the link between economic conditions and political support, be it sociotropic or egotropic, was still limited.

From a comparative political economy perspective, the most notable juncture was Japan's combination of QQE policy initiation by the Abe administration and the Governor of the Bank of Japan (BOJ), Haruhiko Kuroda, and a flexible fiscal policy. Fiscal stimulus was by no means limited to this period; rather, it was at the core of the political business cycle mechanism, especially during the election period (Fukumoto et al., 2020). Beginning in 2013, Abenomics was marked by a series of policies linked to price hikes and economic growth, in conjunction with monetary operations rather than the one-off introduction of fiscal stimulus. Under QQE, the BOJ set the interest rate applied to policy rate balances on current accounts, that is, the short-term policy rate at a negative 0.1 per cent and the long-term policy rate on ten-year government bonds at 0 per cent. These policy rates were left unchanged for more than ten years, which encouraged growth in corporate earnings and the housing market. Further spurring the trend, the BOJ decided to embark on purchases of Exchange Traded Funds (ETFs) and Japan–Real Estate Investment Trusts (J-REITs).[4] The BOJ had been purchasing these funds since 2010, before Abe's return to power. In April 2013, however, the BOJ implemented its policy of 'unprecedented monetary easing' (*Ijigen Kanwa*) by purchasing ETFs linked to stock market indices, one trillion yen at a time. Thus, the Nikkei Stock Average, which was at the 8,000-yen level in October 2012 before Abe took office, rose to the 30,500-yen level in September 2021 because of further purchases as part of the economic stimulus during the COVID-19 pandemic.[5]

[4] Even before its QQE policy, the BOJ had been conducting operations to guide short-term market interest rates since 1995, and in 2001 it began its quantitative easing policy by setting a target for the balance of the BOJ's current account. It was implemented and continued until 2006. Subsequently, in 2010, ETFs were purchased as part of the comprehensive quantitative easing policy, and operations in the stock market were underway.

[5] However, many studies have pointed out the negative effects of QQE, particularly negative interest rate policy, on prices (Koeda, 2019), stock markets, and REITs (Ito, 2019), and many believe that its effect on boosting the economy has been limited.

To see the connection between economic historical context and cabinet approval, i.e. the 'e-fraction', we draw a rough sketch of these series. Figure 6.2 depicts the economic historical context and the cabinet approval ratings. Figure 6.2A refers to the relationship between the business cycle and the approval rating in Japan. The period with a bold line at the bottom indicates a period of economic upturn, while no line indicates a period of recession.[6] Figure 6.2A clearly shows that cabinet approval levels rise markedly at the beginning of the economic upturn phase and remain stable during the upturn period, and vice versa. Figure 6.2B illustrates the relationship between political and economic events and cabinet approval. It shows how cabinet approval ratings fell after the onset of the economic crisis. Furthermore, it shows that cabinet approval increased significantly when Abenomics was introduced and then remained stable at that high level for an unprecedented length of time.

As suggested by the figures above, the economic situation and government popularity appears to be closely linked. The economy and its evaluations have affected political support, and a significant deterioration in the economy has resulted in sanctions against the government (McElwain, 2015; Ohmura, 2022). Since the introduction of QQE stimulus measures, cabinet approval and economic conditions appear to have entered a new phase. If economic stimulus improves government popularity, we should find that the effect of voters' subjective economic evaluations on cabinet approval in Japan has increased since 2012.

Furthermore, Figures 6.1 and 6.2 suggest that economic evaluations tend to increase during periods when partisanship are heightened. The effect of partisanship does not cancel out that of economic evaluation; instead, both are activated together to boost cabinet support, which seems to outline the patterns of economic voting in Japan since 1993. Thus, we assume that the political upheaval in 1993 did not simply change the link between ruling party support and cabinet support, but also altered the economic vote. Put differently, an interesting phenomenon may be observed in Japan after 1993, where *both* partisanship and economic evaluation have strong influences, which may be exceptional from a comparative perspective. We also note that exogenous shocks, such as an economic crisis or a major natural disaster, could cause a decline in cabinet support, as formulated in Hypothesis 4. We test the validity of these theoretical assertions on economic aspects under the following set

[6] The recession phase has been longer than the expansion phase: during the 780 months from January 1955 to December 2020, 349 months have seen economic expansion, while 431, the majority, have seen recession (Cabinet Office, 2020).

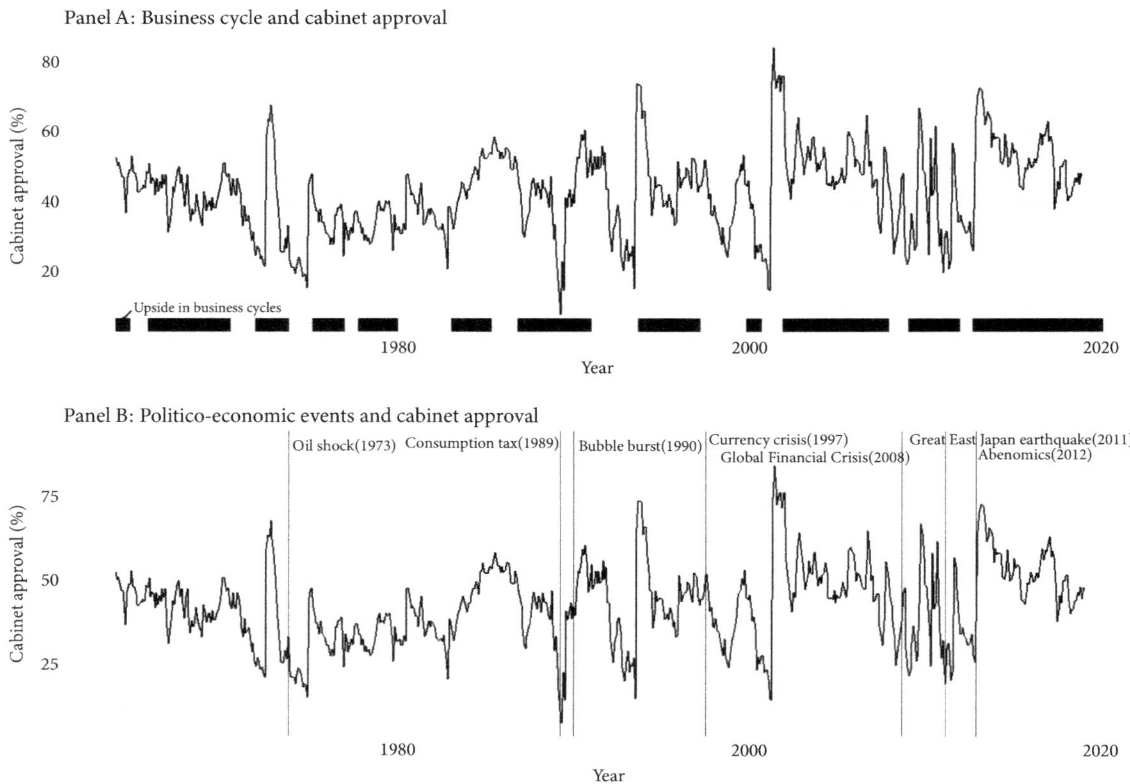

Figure 6.2 Economic status and cabinet approval, 1963–2020

Source: Executive Approval Database.

of 'e-fraction'-related hypotheses. Hypotheses 5 and 6 form the second major focus of this chapter.

Hypothesis 3: In Japan, the rise in economic evaluations contributes to an increase in cabinet approval.

Hypothesis 4: The occurrence of exogenous shocks, such as a global economic crisis or a large-scale natural disaster, deteriorates cabinet approval.

Hypothesis 5: The relationship between economic conditions and cabinet approval is stronger after the introduction of QQE during Abenomics in 2012.

Hypothesis 6: The positive influence of economic evaluations on cabinet approval has become stronger since 1993, on account of frequent changes in partisan attachments that have increased the positive influence of economic evaluations on cabinet approval.

Research Design and Data

In this chapter, we rely mainly on two types of analyses: a general error correction model (GECM) and a moving window analysis with rolling regression (RR) to test the above hypotheses. First, we proceed with the estimation of GECM (DeBoef and Keele, 2008) to comprehensively test the effects of economic evaluation and of partisanship. The GECM allows us to estimate the factors driving cabinet approval in Japan in a manner similar to those used in other chapters. In this first analysis, we estimate (1) a simple model including economic evaluations and ruling party support; (2) a model including political variables; (3) a model including both political and economic variables excluding ruling party support; and (4) a model including both political and economic variables, aiming to derive robust results.[7]

[7] On checking the order of integration (d), cabinet approval/disapproval, ruling party approval, and all economic assessments are found to be fractionally integrated ($0<d<1$). From a substantive viewpoint, considering that the cabinet's approval ratings and sociotropic evaluation (explained in the next section) are $0<d<1/2$, it becomes clear that the series is marked by frequent updates and is stationary. Reflecting the non-stationary property, other variables, including the unemployment rate, are explosive, while CPI, Nikkei225, IIP, and interest rate are located at the margin. From the variation of these d-values, it is apparent that the estimation model becomes an unbalanced equation. For the non-cointegrated, bounded, and confirmed different orders of integration, the fractional error correction mechanism (FECM) is likely to be applicable rather than the GECM/ADL, avoiding Type I error in the hypothesis test (e.g. Grant and Lebo, 2016). Accordingly, we proceed using the GECM due to its consistency with other chapters, but also conduct an analysis using the FECM to confirm that the results hold. The results are available upon request.

Second, to check for changes in economic voting over time, especially in H2 and H4–H6, we use the structural Chow test of politico-economic change (Wilcox and Wlezien, 1993; Wu et al., 2002) and a moving window model with RR (Sanders and Carey, 2002; Carey and Lebo, 2006; Maeda, 2008). The RR allows us to visualize the time-varying effects on the clarity of responsibility associated with the end of the LDP one-party rule in 1993 and the massive economic stimulus package in 2012. As discussed in the Canadian chapter in this volume, the time-varying estimators may simply stem from errors (Lebo and Box-Steffensmeier, 2008). Even if the true coefficients are constant, the estimated coefficients may exhibit random variation. The sole purpose of an RR analysis is to verify whether the coefficients are changing over time. The Chow test then assesses whether the changes over time—first a change in the clarity of responsibility in 1993 and then a change in economic policy regime in 2012—represent a structural change in the relationship between cabinet approval rating and economic evaluations.

We now describe each variable in greater detail. For our main analysis, we use the cabinet approval rating data by the Executive Approval Project.[8] Regarding the question, taking the example of Fumio Kishida's government in April 2022, the question to determine cabinet approval is 'Do you support the Fumio Kishida Government?' (Jiji Press question wording). Based on the responses, the support rate is defined as cabinet approval.[9]

To measure economic evaluations, we use data collected by Jiji Press on four types of economic evaluations since December 1963. These items concerning business and living conditions directly correspond to the concepts of sociotropic and egotropic evaluations (Kinder and Kiewiet, 1981). Business conditions are measured using responses to the question 'How do you see the national economy as a whole? Do you think it is the same as last month, getting worse, or getting better?' Living conditions are based on responses

[8] After World War II, the Allies' occupation of Japan left behind a rich foundation of public opinion surveys and a strong infrastructure in terms of public opinion departments in the media. The US Allies experimented with random sampling methods in Japan, which was a novel approach during the late 1940s, for various governance purposes (e.g. calculating the literacy rate of the country). These methods also contributed to establishing a public opinion department in each national newspaper. Journalists were taught in the so-called 'Passin School', named after Dr. Herbert Passin, who served in General Headquarters in Japan and later chaired the Sociology Department at Columbia University. Even today, national newspapers in Japan have their own public opinion departments and occasionally conduct their own nationwide surveys with random samples without outsourcing them to polling companies. See Hino and Jou (2015) for the role that the US Allies played in fertilizing the field of public opinion surveys in Japan. Of these, the data from the Jiji Press survey later became the most predominant and formed the basis of Japan's macro-political analysis.

[9] The three response categories are 'approve', 'disapprove', and 'I don't know'. In this analysis, we use the proportion of respondents who answered 'approve'.

to 'How is your present living condition compared with the same time last year? Are you feeling better or worse?' The question on business conditions is used as a sociotropic economic evaluation and the item on living conditions as an egotropic economic evaluation.[10] We then use the ruling parties' approval ratings as a partisanship indicator.[11]

Analyses also include a set of political variables. Based on the literature in Japan and elsewhere, we insert a dummy variable to measure the honeymoon effect after a new administration is inaugurated, coding months in which the government alternation occurred as 1 and other months as 0. The next variable is the effective number of parliamentary parties (ENPPs), which is calculated using seat shares (Laakso and Taagepera, 1979). Additionally, based on political corruption and political gaffes data prepared by the authors, we include a dummy variable in the model that assigns 1 to the months when corruption and gaffes by politicians of the ruling party are reported in more than one newspaper, and otherwise 0. We predict that approval ratings increase during the honeymoon period, while corruption and gaffes decrease approval ratings and increase disapproval ratings. Under a multi-party system, an increase in the ENPPs is anticipated to reduce a party's ability to gain support; thus, theoretically, an increase in ENPPs could result in a decline in cabinet support. Finally, a 1955-regime dummy is incorporated into the model, scored 1 after July 1993 and 0 before, to assess the effect of the 1955-system and its collapse.

To test the impact of objective economic conditions, we incorporate conventional economic variables such as the consumer price index (CPI), unemployment rate, the logged Nikkei Stock Average, and index of industrial production (IIP). Echoing our chapter's focus on economic stimulus measures, long-term interest rates are also added.[12] Further, we incorporate an economic crisis dummy[13] and a business cycle dummy coded 1 for business cycle expansion

[10] The choices for the business condition questions are 'I think it's definitely getting better', 'I think it's getting a little better', 'Neither', 'I think it's getting a little worse', 'I think it's definitely getting worse', and 'I don't know'. Of these, the sum of the response rates to the first two options is defined as the sociotropic evaluation. The choices for living conditions are 'I feel much better now', 'I feel a little better now', 'Neither', 'I feel a little worse now', 'I feel definitely worse now', and 'I don't know'. Of these, the sum of the response rates to the first two options is defined as the egotropic evaluation.

[11] The question to determine the ruling parties' approval rate is 'Which political party do you support?' The percentage of responses to ruling parties is defined as the ruling party's approval rate. Until 1993, the LDP maintained its one-party dominance, and the LDP's approval rating referred to the approval rating of the ruling party. Since then, coalition governments have been the norm, and the approval rating of the coalition government is calculated by adding the approval ratings of the ruling coalition parties.

[12] Data up to April 2017 was obtained from FRED; thereafter from the Bank of Japan's database.

[13] The economic crisis dummy is set as 1 and is used for the following crises: the first oil shock (October 1973), the second oil shock (January 1979), the introduction of consumption tax (April 1989), the

Table 6.1 Descriptive statistics

	N	Mean	S.D.	Median	Min	Max	Skew	Kurtosis
Cabinet app.	663	43.2	11.9	43.9	8.0	84.7	0.2	0.2
Ruling app.	663	28.9	6.2	29.3	0	43.6	−1.1	2.6
Sociotropic	658	8.4	5.1	7.6	0.4	28.4	0.7	0.1
Egotropic	658	5.2	2.6	4.5	0	15.2	1.5	1.9
CPI	663	78.6	26.3	94.2	22.3	102	−1.1	−0.4
Unemployment	663	2.9	1.3	2.7	1.0	5.5	0.4	−1
Logged Nikkei	656	9.1	0.9	9.3	7.0	10.6	−0.8	−0.3
IIP	663	100.7	19.4	103.6	55.5	124.8	−1	0
Interest	663	3.1	2.7	2.5	0.1	9.0	0.4	−1.2

Source: Executive Approval Dataset v 2.0, Jiji, FRED, the Bank of Japan.
Note: Summary statistics for variables other than dummy variables are available.

periods.[14] We will also examine economic voting after QQE by introducing a QQE dummy scored 1 for periods after January 2013.[15] Table 6.1 reports the descriptive statistics for these variables.

Empirical Results

A GECM analysis using cabinet approval as a dependent variable shows that sociotropic evaluations (ΔSociotropic) are statistically significant at the 5 per cent level in Models (1)–(3) in Table 6.2. However, the effect of egotropic evaluation is not precisely estimated. These results indicate that the cabinet approval rating is likely to rise when the sociotropic positive evaluation rises. Therefore, H3 is partially supported. While the sociotropic effect is slightly marginal, the statistical significance of the ruling party's approval rating (ΔRuling) is remarkably strong, providing solid support for H1. Furthermore,

bubble burst (March 1991), the Asian currency crisis (July 1997), the Great Financial Crisis (September 2008), the Great East Japan earthquake (March 2011), and the COVID-19 pandemic (March 2020).

[14] Data depends on the referenced dates of business conditions published by the Cabinet Office. The business cycle calculations follow Bry and Boschan (1971).

[15] To test the hypotheses in this chapter more precisely, interaction terms between economic evaluations and the ruling party approval rating, the 55-year regime dummy, and the QQE dummy are required. With marginal effects from these specifications, we can specifically deduce the economic evaluation effects with the critical politico-economic events and the change in clarity of responsibility. On the other hand, as Warner (n.d.) notes in the ECM, the need to add all interaction terms raises the issue of insufficient degrees of freedom with respect to the parameters to be measured. Also, if all interaction terms were included, the model would lose its parsimony. Therefore, in this chapter, structural changes such as the fifty-five-year regime and the introduction of QQE are examined by rolling regressions and the Chow test, and the effect of ruling party support is addressed by including it in the rolling regression equation.

Table 6.2 Estimation results of a general error correction model of cabinet approval

	Model (1) Base	**Model (2) Political**	**Model (3) w/o ruling**	**Model (4) Full**
Short-term effects				
ΔSociotropic	0.228* (0.115)	0.255* (0.114)	0.234* (0.125)	0.248* (0.118)
ΔEgotropic	0.070 (0.219)	0.079 (0.217)	0.419* (0.237)	0.199 (0.225)
ΔRuling	0.691* (0.075)	0.686* (0.075)		0.670* (0.078)
ΔENPP		−3.889 (2.377)	−4.807* (2.477)	−3.468 (2.348)
ΔCorruption		0.852 (0.635)	0.914 (0.671)	0.891 (0.645)
ΔGaffe		−0.359 (0.529)	0.063 (0.552)	−0.162 (0.523)
ΔHoneymoon dummy		3.339* (0.832)	3.524* (0.876)	3.369* (0.827)
ΔCrisis dummy		−1.089 (1.659)	−1.248 (1.731)	−1.002 (1.637)
Δ1955 era dummy		15.186* (5.832)	16.601* (6.139)	17.453* (5.818)
ΔQQE dummy			28.221* (6.103)	16.198* (6.024)
ΔCPI			0.329 (0.656)	−0.041 (0.622)
ΔUnemployment			0.516 (2.317)	0.425 (2.192)
ΔNikkei average			3.788 (5.696)	0.000 (0.000)
ΔIIP			−1.545* (0.586)	−0.664 (0.562)
ΔInterest			0.845 (1.164)	0.970 (1.100)
ΔBusiness cycle dummy			0.442 (1.302)	0.619 (1.233)
Long-run effects				
Sociotropic$_{t-1}$	0.079 (0.061)	0.081 (0.061)	0.145* (0.070)	0.119° (0.067)
Egotropic$_{t-1}$	−0.207 (0.130)	−0.180 (0.131)	0.213 (0.192)	0.092 (0.183)
Ruling$_{t-1}$	0.088° (0.046)	0.084° (0.046)		0.228* (0.055)
ENPP$_{t-1}$			1.309* (0.609)	1.209* (0.577)
CPI$_{t-1}$			0.130* (0.055)	0.142* (0.047)
Unemployment$_{t-1}$			0.690 (0.509)	0.828° (0.484)
Nikkei average$_{t-1}$			−0.597 (1.024)	0.000 (0.000)
IIP$_{t-1}$			−0.096* (0.044)	−0.119* (0.041)
Interest$_{t-1}$			0.668* (0.290)	0.535* (0.272)
Cabinet approval$_{t-1}$	−0.145* (0.020)	−0.141* (0.020)	−0.181* (0.022)	−0.214* (0.025)
Intercept	4.165* (1.233)	3.195° (1.726)	2.714 (7.130)	−4.571 (3.140)
N	642	635	625	623
Adjusted R^2	0.187	0.210	0.147	0.237
F-statistics	22.33 (p=0.000)	13.28 (p=0.000)	5.655 (p=0.000)	8.735 (p=0.000)

Source: Executive Approval Dataset v 2.0, Jiji, FRED, the Bank of Japan.
Note: ° p<0.10, * p<0.05 (two-tailed test). Standard errors are in parentheses. We use 'ecm' package in R4.0.4.

not only the short-run effect but also the long-run effect (Ruling(t-1)) is statistically significant, especially in the full model. This indicates that the ruling party's approval is a determinant of cabinet approval in the long run. As shown in the literature on Japanese retrospective voting, the main determinant of cabinet support is the ruling party/ies' support. In other words, the nature of responsibility attribution is key to retrospective voting and, by extension, economic voting. Although the causality from ruling party support to cabinet support is indisputable, we can also assert that sociotropic economic evaluation has an impact on cabinet support even after controlling for partisan effects.

Turning to other variables, we see a significant increase in cabinet support during the honeymoon period, similar to results in other countries. An additional interesting result is that both the 1955-system dummy and the QQE dummy are statistically significant at the 1 per cent level, indicating that cabinet support rose after the LDP's fall from power and after the Abe administration took office for the second time. Furthermore, Model (3) suggests that excluding the effect of ruling party support, politico-economic upheavals define cabinet support. This result reveals an upward trend in cabinet support only after 1993 and 2012, and no direct implications for economic voting can be derived. This point will be supplemented in the next RR analysis.

In the full model, the short-run effects of the economic variables are not statistically significant, but long-run effects are observed for CPI (t-1), unemployment rate (t-1), IIP (t-1), and interest (t-1). On the other hand, these results do not correspond to the theoretical assertions. Instead, the estimates suggest that increases in prices, unemployment, and long-term interest rates raise the approval rating, while economic growth lowers it. As shown in Japanese literature using aggregated data, the economic variables do not have effects consistent with theoretical expectations. For the business cycle and economic crisis dummies, the results do not support the intuitive visualization in Figure 6.2A. Therefore, we do not find support for H4.

The results of the Chow test in Table 6.3 show no statistically significant structural changes before or after the QQE, but both sociotropic and egotropic evaluations underwent structural changes both before and after 1993. In Japan, the attribution of responsibility for the economy seems to have changed along with the changes in the partisan effect on cabinet support.

The results of the moving window model estimation with RR are presented in Figures 6.3, 6.4, and 6.5 and provide further evidence for these Chow test results. Figure 6.3 shows the evolution of the coefficient on sociotropic evaluations. Until the collapse of the 1955-system, the effect of sociotropic

Table 6.3 Chow test results

	Test statistic	Critical value	*p*-value
Before/after 1993			
Sociotropic			
Break-point test	1555.70	1539.40	0.000
Egotropic			
Break-point test	1576.5	1565.60	0.000
Ruling approvals			
Break-point test	1066.87	1160.4	0.492
Before/after QQE			
Sociotropic			
Break-point test	1546.79	1586.2	0.528
Egotropic			
Break-point test	1517.69	1585.2	0.732
Ruling approvals			
Break-point test	1192.99	1222.3	0.222

Source: Authors' calculations.
Note: We use 'vars' package for the Chow test in R4.0.4.

assessment was not pronounced and showed little variance. After 1993, however, the sociotropic effect shows remarkable fluctuations. As seen with the QQE dummy since 2012, sociotropic evaluations has increased since the launch of Abenomics; the same effect is seen when controlling for the ruling party's approval effect. In addition, since 1993, the country has experienced several cyclical peaks and troughs, with a notable rise in the sociotropic effect at the start of the Junichiro Koizumi administration in the early 2000s, and at the beginning of the DPJ administration with another change of government in 2009. On the other hand, the end or collapse of those administrations was followed by a complete turnaround in the voter base that favoured the state of the economy, with voters no longer supporting the current administration and looking towards a new administration. In this light, the last years of the 2010s may be viewed as a period of sociotropic economic voting flux, during the transition of power following the resignation of Prime Minister Abe and the spread of the COVID-19 infection.

In contrast to the results with sociotropic evaluations, the effects of egotropic evaluations are not clear-cut. The period during which statistically significant effects can be observed is also limited, which is in line with the results of the ECM, where both short- and long-run effects of egotropic evaluation could not be confirmed. However, the characteristics of the transition are similar

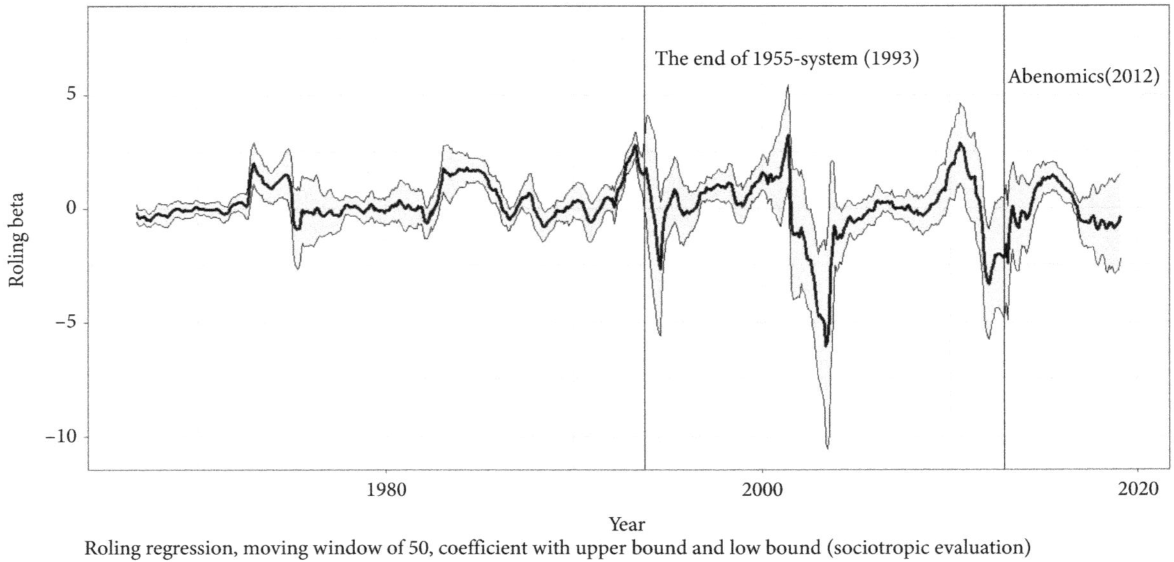

Figure 6.3 Effect of sociotropic evaluations on cabinet approval, rolling regression

Source: Produced from Table 6.2 estimates.

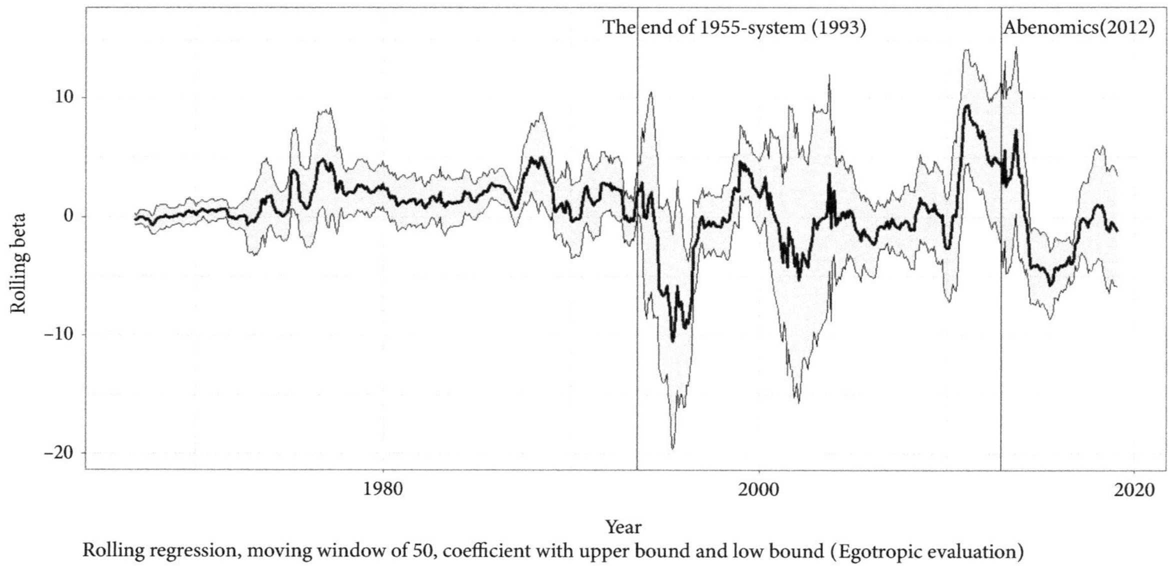

Figure 6.4 Effect of egotropic evaluations on cabinet approval, rolling regression

Source: Produced from Table 6.2 estimates.

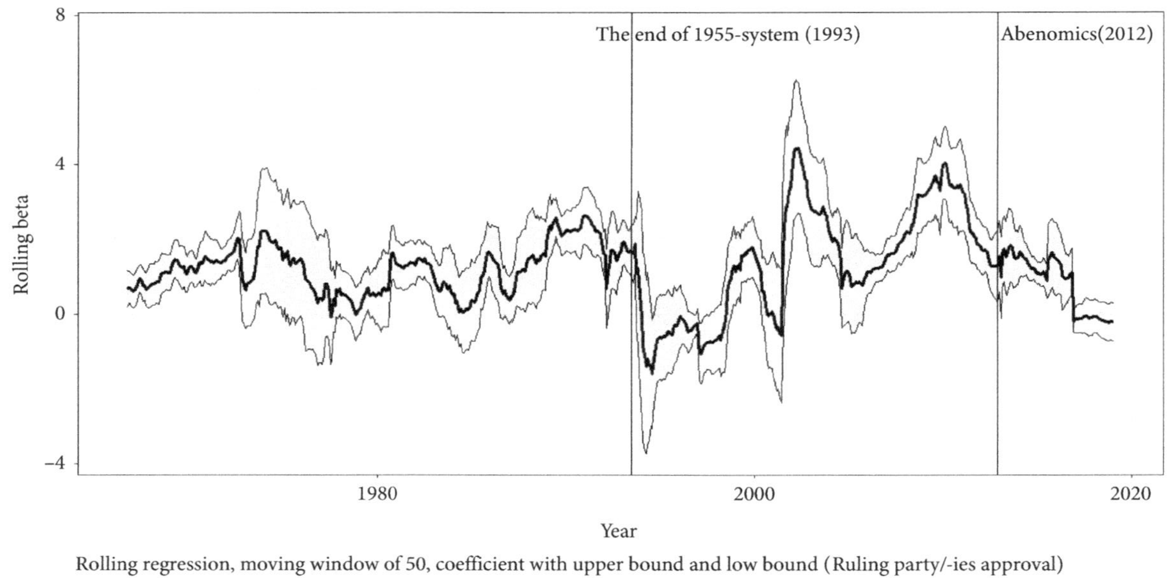

Figure 6.5 Effect of ruling party approval on cabinet approval, rolling regression

Source: Produced from Table 6.2 estimates.

to those of the sociotropic evaluation, with a near-zero effect until 1993 and large fluctuations after that. Note that Abenomics had a stable positive effect on sociotropic evaluations, while its effect on egotropic evaluations remained only temporary and marginal.

The results of the RR analysis between the ruling party support and cabinet support in Figure 6.5 also displays a divergence around 1993. The difference between the RRs suggests that the effect of ruling party support is almost stable and statistically significant even before 1993. As prior studies have repeatedly shown, the link between ruling party support and cabinet support has declined dramatically since 1993. However, our data show this not to be the case. The launch of the Koizumi administration in the early 2000s created a renewed link between the two, with support for Koizumi, the LDP, and cabinet synergizing. This tighter association also appears in 2009, when the DPJ came to power. While it was assumed that the cognitive linkage between Abe's politics and the LDP government among voters had increased since the start of the Abe administration, that linkage has not been fully confirmed. Even if this is the case, the effect of ruling party support on cabinet support has not declined consistently since 1993 and is outlined by frequent updates over the course of time. Therefore, we find little support for H2.

Finally, the overarching finding from Figures 6.3–6.5 is that while greater support for the ruling party does enhance cabinet support, the effect of economic evaluation is comparable or even greater, especially in terms of the sociotropic aspect. Figures based on the RR analyses show that the rise in partisanship does not contribute to the weakening of the economic evaluation effect; instead, it encourages that effect and increases government popularity as partisanship increases. As indicated by the Chow test, such a structural change was brought about by the 1994 electoral reforms and party-system realignment. Japanese economic voting can be regarded as a case where a change in the clarity of responsibility affected the impact of economic evaluations. Taken together, even though the transition to QQE coincided with a stronger influence of economic perceptions (and especially of the sociotropic variety), Chow test results do not fully support H5, neither for sociotropic nor egotropic economic evaluation terms. For the related H6, about the 1993 political upheaval, both the RR and the Chow test results indicate that the effects of both economic assessments have changed in tandem with a sharper clarity of responsibility. Thus, H6, our central hypothesis in this chapter, is supported.

Conclusions

Our analysis of Japan's economic voting found that the effect of economic evaluation is strong during the period when the effect of partisanship is strong, especially after 1993. The effects of partisanship and economic evaluation on cabinet approval are not trade-offs, and the effects of economic evaluation are similarly pronounced during periods when partisanship effects are strong. During periods of higher clarity of responsibility, such as the LDP's long one-party rule and the Koizumi and Abe administrations, more economic voting was observed. For economic evaluations, the effect of sociotropic evaluation was clearly predominant over egotropic evaluation, but the effect of macroeconomic indicators was either not confirmed or not consistent with the theoretical assertion.

Although our analyses do not fully corroborate the H5, rolling regression results suggest that the influence of sociotropic economic evaluations became rejuvenated after the introduction of QQE and the beginning of the Abe administration. The unprecedented monetary easing, having no parallel in any other country, piqued voters' interests in national-level economic situations and stimulated cognitive mechanisms linking the economy to politics. Nonetheless, the adoption of diverse economic policies and the longevity of their impacts on economic voting will be a significant future issue, as demonstrated by the gradual fading of this relationship in the RR estimation.

Reconnecting the main claim of this book with our findings, the effects of economic evaluations in Japan have changed over time. This transition has not been a gradual trending change, but a structural change that began with the collapse of the 1955-system and electoral reform in 1994. In this respect, Japanese economic voting is one in which 'p-fraction' attribution plays a more central role than 'e-fraction' attribution. Behind this lies Japan's politico-economic system, in which partisanship, sociotropic economic evaluation, and cabinet approval ratings are all highly intertwined. This property distinguishes the Japanese economic vote from other countries. Therefore, one limitation of this chapter's analysis is that the question of whether partisanship precedes economic evaluation, or whether economic evaluation is formed among electorates independent of partisanship, is not sufficiently clarified. Future research to uncover partisan bias may require more precise experimental designs.

References

Ashibe, N. (1991). Piecemeal thoughts on electoral reform issues [*Senkyo seido kaikaku dansou*]. *Japanese Journal of Electoral Studies* [*Senkyo Kenkyuu*], *6*, 4–19.

Bry, G., and Boschan, C. (1971). Standard business cycle analysis of economic time series. *Cyclical Analysis of Time Series: Selected Procedures and Computer Programs*. Cambridge, MA: NBER. 64–150.

Cabinet Office. (2020). *Japan's Economy 2020–2021: Rising from the Crisis of Infectious Diseases* [*Nihon Keizai 2020–2021: Kansenshou no Kiki kara Tachiagaru Nihonkeizai*], Technical report.

Carey, S., and Lebo, M. J. (2006). Election cycles and the economic voter. *Political Research Quarterly*, *59*(4), 543–56.

De Boef, S., and Keele, L. (2008). Taking time seriously. *American Journal of Political Science*, *52*(1), 184–200.

Estévez-Abe, M. (2008). *Welfare and Capitalism in Postwar Japan*. Cambridge: Cambridge University Press.

Fujimura, N. (2015). The influence of electoral institutions on legislative representation: Evidence from Japan's single non-transferable vote and single-member district systems. *Party Politics*, *21*(2), 209–21.

Fukumoto, K., Horiuchi, Y., and Tanaka. S. (2020). Treated politicians, treated voters: A natural experiment on political budget cycles. *Electoral Studies*, *67*, 102206.

Grant, T., and Lebo, M. J. (2016). Equation balance and dynamic political modeling. *Political Analysis*, *24*(01), 69–82.

Hamamoto, S. (2018). *Institutional Analysis of Party Politics in Japan* [*Gendai Nihon no seitou seiji: Senkyo seido kaikaku ha nani wo motarashitanoka*]. Tokyo: Yuuhikaku.

Hino, A., and Jou, W. (2015). Political communication research in Asia. In *International Encyclopedia of Political Communication*, volume 3, Gianpietro Mazzoleni, ed. New York: Wiley, 1–10.

Hirano, H. (1994). Political evaluation and economic evaluation: What determines Liberal Democratic Party support, cabinet support, and voting behaviour [*Seijiteki hyouka to keizaiteki hyouka: Jimintou shiji, naikaku shiji, touhyoukoudou wo kiteisuru mono*]. *Japanese Journal of Electoral Studies* [*Senkyo Kenkyuu*], *9*, 93–106.

Iida, T. (2005). Time-series analysis of the effects of party support on cabinet support: Using the ARFIMA model and time-varying parameters [*Seitou shiji no naikaku shiji heno eikyou no jikanteki henka: ARFIMA moderu to jihen parameter wo mochiita jikeiretsu bunseki*]. *Review of Electoral Studies* [*Senkyo Gakkai Kiyou*], *4*, 41–61.

Ikeda, K. (2000). Retrospective voting in the 1998 Japanese House of Councillors election: An approach from cognitive social psychology. *Japanese Journal of Electoral Studies* [*Senkyo Kenkyuu*], *15*, 109–21.

Imai, R., and Arai, K. (2013). Retrospective voting under divided parliaments [*'Nejire' Jokyoukaniokeru gyouseki hyouka to touhyou koudou*]. *Japanese Journal of Electoral Studies* [*Senkyo Kenkyuu*], *29*(1), 87–101.

Inoguchi, T. (1986). Economic conditions and policy agenda [*Keizai joukyou to seisaku kadai*]. In J. Watanuki, I. Miyake, and I. Kabashima, eds. *Electoral Behavior of Japanese Voters*. Tokyo: Tokyo Daigaku Syuppankai. 202–35.

Ito, T. (2019). Do long-term swap rate and stock price give an impact on Japanese Real Estate Investment Trust market under quantitative and qualitative easing and negative interest rate policy? *Journal of Corporate Accounting and Finance*, *31*(3), 15–19.

Kinder, D. R., and Kiewiet, D. R. (1981). Sociotropic politics: The American case. *British Journal of Political Science*, *11*(2), 129–61.

Kitayama, T. (2003). Japan as a construction state and the types of capitalism [*Doken Kokka Nihon to Shihon Shugi no Shoruikei*]. *Leviathan* [*Revaiasan*], *32*, 123–46.

Koeda, J. (2019). Macroeconomic effects of quantitative and qualitative monetary easing measures. *Journal of the Japanese and International Economies*, *52*, 121–41.

Kohno, M. (2018). *Can We Analyze Politics Scientifically?* [*Seiji wo Kagaku Suru Koto ha Kanou ka?*]. Tokyo: Chuou Kouron Shinsha.

Kusunoki, A. (2009). *Yoshida Shigeru and the Formation of Security Policy: The U.S.-Japan Concept and its Interaction, 1943–1952* [*Yoshida Shigeru to Anzen-hosyou Seisaku no Keisei: Nichibei no Kousou to Sono Sougosayou, 1943–1952*]. Kyoto: Minerva-shobou.

Laakso, M., and Taagepera, R. (1979). 'Effective' number of parties. *Comparative Political Studies*, *12*(1), 3–27.

Lebo, M. J., and Box-Steffensmeier, J. M. (2008). Dynamic conditional correlations in political science. *American Journal of Political Science*, *52*(3), 688–704.

Maeda, Y. (2008). Economy, cabinet approval, and the LDP support. *Social Science Japan Journal* [*Shakai Kagaku Kenkyuu*], *62*(5–6), 151–71.

McElwain, K. M. (2015). Inequality or growth? Subjective economic beliefs and government approval in Japan. *Leviathan* [*Revaiasan*], *57*, 72–85.

Miyake, I., Nishizawa, Y., and Kono, M. (2001). *Politics and Economy in 1955 Era of Political System:* The Analysis of Jiji-Press Data *[*55-nen taiseika no seiji to keizai: jiji seron chosa deta no bunseki*]*. Tokyo: Bokutaku-sha.

Nakamura, E. (2006). Analyzing the dynamic relationship between the Cabinet support rate and the LDP support rate using the multivariate long memory model. *Review of Electoral Studies* [*Senkyo Gakkai Kiyou*], *6*, 107–26.

Nonaka, N. (2008). *The End of the Liberal Democratic Party Politics [Jimin-tou seiji no owari]*. Tokyo: Chikuma-Shobou.

Ohmura, H. (2022). The connection between stock market prices and political support: Evidence from Japan. *Applied Economics Letters, 29*(1), 1–7.

Paldam, M. (1991). How robust is the vote function?: A study of seventeen nations over four decades. In H. Norpoth, M. S. Lewis-Beck, and J.-D. Lafay, eds. *Economics and Politics: The Calculus of Support*. Ann Arbor, MI: University of Michigan Press. 9–31.

Pekkanen, R., Nyblade, B., and Krauss, E. S. (2006). Electoral incentives in mixed-member systems: Party, posts, and zombie politicians in Japan. *American Political Science Review, 100*(2), 183–93.

Sanders, D., and Carey, S. (2002). Temporal variations in economic voting: A comparative cross-national analysis. In H. Dorussen, and M. Taylor, eds. *Economic Voting*. London: Routledge, 200–31.

Scheiner, E. (2010). *Democracy without Competition in Japan: Opposition Failure in a One-Party Dominant State*. Cambridge: Cambridge University Press.

Taniguchi, M. (2016). The multi-store model for economic voting: Rome wasn't built in a day. *Electoral Studies, 41*, 179–89.

Tatebayashi, M. (2004). *The Logic of Legislators' Activities*: Institutional Analysis of LDP Dominance in Japan *[*Giin Koudou no Seiji-Keizai Gaku: Jimin Tou Shihai no Seido Bunseki*]*. Tokyo: Yuuhikaku.

Warner, Z. (n.d.) Conditional relationships in dynamic models. Typescript, Purdue University.

Wilcox, N., and Wlezien, C. (1993). The contamination of responses to survey items: Economic perceptions and political judgments. *Political Analysis, 5*, 181–213.

Wu, H. D., Stevenson, R. L., Chen, H.-C., and Güner, Z. N. (2002). The conditioned impact of recession news: A time-series analysis of economic communication in the United States, 1987–1996. *International Journal of Public Opinion Research, 14*(1), 19–36.

7

Government Popularity in Italy

From Valence to Positional Economic Accountability

Paolo Bellucci and Vincenzo Memoli

Whether the drivers of popular approval of executives have changed overtime, and how, are the overarching themes this volume addresses. In this chapter we answer the question looking at the case of Italy, where, for an established democracy, the political system has seen unprecedented change since the 1990s. Compared to that of other democracies, research on government popularity has a relatively short tradition in Italy. Government approval was little relevant for both governing and opposition parties' electoral fortunes in the polarized multi-party system of Italy between 1948 and 1992. Voting choice was mainly driven by socio-political identities belonging to the two dominant political sub-cultures: the Catholic and the Socialist-Communist ones. The presence of mass cleavage parties and the lack of alternation in government due to the perceived anti-systemic nature of the Italian Communist Party (Bellucci, 2015) limited voters' electoral mobility. Elections were waged then on appeals to parties' traditional social bases rather than on policy issues or evaluation of governments' performance, and elections revealed more an expressive function rather than an instrumental one (Mair, 2009). Also public opinion was shaped by partisanship and for long lacked a real substantive independence, with voters mainly following partisan cues on most issues (Isernia, 2008).

Early research on economic voting in Italy recognized the limitation imposed by such a political context, pointing out how electoral accountability was significantly bound by the ideological polarization of both parties and voters (Bellucci, 1984; 1991), a finding confirmed by later comparative economic voting research (Lewis-Beck, 1988; Kayser and Wlezien, 2011). Parties' polarization and strong partisanship constituted a formidable hurdle to economic voting insofar as it inhibited voters' electoral mobility, thus affecting the electoral accountability of governments.

It is only in the early 1990s that a 'frozen' electorate began to thaw due to the transformation of the Italian party system in the wake of the fall of the

Paolo Bellucci and Vincenzo Memoli, *Government Popularity in Italy.* In: *Economics and Politics Revisited.*
Edited by: Timothy Hellwig and Matthew Singer, Oxford University Press.
DOI: 10.1093/oso/9780192871664.003.0007

Berlin Wall and of the unveiling of widespread corruption among mainstream parties (Bellucci and Segatti, 2010). The enactment of a mixed majority-proportional law (Chiaramonte, 2020) paved the way to actual alternation in government of opposing new party blocs. Voters' partisan straitjackets loosened their hold and, matched by a reduction of ideological party polarization, Italy experienced unprecedented levels of electoral volatility (Itanes, 2008).

Voting behaviour in elections held after 1994 showed a clear demarcation from the past: a drop in partisanship levels, the waning of traditional social cleavages, increasing relevance of leaders' evaluation and of valence issues (Garzia and Viotti, 2012). Economic voting and electoral accountability were then clearly evident in the electoral results, and constituted the main drives behind the alternation in government that (finally) Italy has experienced ever since (Bellucci, 2012). And government approval, as an indicator of people's support, acquired electoral relevance.

This change in patterns of voting behaviour was the result of both 'changing parties and changing partisans' which had already been observed comparatively (Dalton and Wattenberg, 2000). In Italy it was strongly affected also by the sudden entrance into politics of a media tycoon—Silvio Berlusconi—who in 1994 employed his television network to support his political bid and ushered in a growing and pervasive role of mass-media communication in electoral campaigns and beyond (Mancini, 2015). The resulting 'permanent campaign' (Farrell and Web, 2000) enhanced the visibility of governments and of party leaders, generated debates about their (in)competence, and exposed their policies on an unprecedented scale. This produced a change in the parties–government relationship. While in the earlier period of cleavage parties, governments' strength and prestige originated from the electoral strength of the parties in the ruling coalition, the prestige and strength of the parties now largely stem from their performance in government. As a byproduct, the media has systematically surveyed public opinion since the mid-1990s.

This chapter is organized as follows. In the next section we review previous studies. While earlier research relied on standard economic accountability models of approval, later analyses included political factors such as government effectiveness, scandals, and political communication. The main limitation in current research is that analyses proceeded on more or less separate tracks, a shortcoming which we address. After presenting the basic trends data on Italian governmental approval, we propose a contemporary model of government approval. Our model merges three lines of inquiry: economic accountability, government performance in the realms of corruption and inequality, and political communication. Findings support a composite explanation which highlights a diminished influence of economic valence accountability and a greater role of positional economic voting expressed by economic inequality, together with a notable impact of political communication. We conclude with the implications of our findings for future comparative research.

Previous Research on Government Popularity

The first work on popularity analysed the approval of the prime minister in the period between 1960 and 1981 (Santagata, 1985). Although data constraints limited the scope of the analysis, it showed that macroeconomic indicators—unemployment and growth—influenced popular support. These early findings were more illustrative than definitive since the small N and gaps in the series prevented the specification of full models. Moreover, political-institutional predictors were not considered. Thanks to the availability of systematic data on approval, later research allowed a better exploration of the dynamics of government popularity. The first effort to include a sizable time series covered the 1994–2006 period and encompassed two legislative elections which produced alternations in government of centre-left (1996) and centre-right (2001) party coalitions (Bellucci, 2006). The results were in line with comparable research, showing governments being held accountable for the economy. Bellucci's (2006) model shared the basic features of comparable research in the field: it adopted a reward-punishment approach (Key, 1966; Lewis-Beck and Paldam, 2000) where popularity trend is modelled as a function of consumers' sentiment, the unfolding of the electoral cycle and popularity attrition over the term (the so-called 'cost of ruling' [Nannestad and Paldam, 2002]), and external shocks (such as international events like Italy's involvement in the wars in Serbia and Iraq) that further eroded popularity. The state of the economy was measured through voters' subjective economic perceptions while the employment of objective economic indicators yielded null results.

What about, then, the electoral relevance of government approval? Individual level analysis showed government evaluations affected voting choice. In order to assess the impact of popularity on election results with aggregate national-level data, Bellucci (2010) employed his popularity model to produce an ex post forecast of election results in Italy and an ex ante forecast of the 2009 European Parliament elections. Based on the change in popularity in the quarter before the election and on a measure of past partisanship, the forecasts appeared quite successful, although a later attempt to ex ante forecast the 2018 election was dismally off track (*La Repubblica*, 2017)[1].

A second phase in the analysis of government approval in Italy broadened its scope by focusing on specific features of the Italian polity and assessing the impact of political communication and of the quality of governance. The role played by media in informing and influencing public opinion is obviously of paramount importance for the democratic process (Gunther and Mughan, 2000), although research remains systematically uncertain on their effects in terms of persuasion, framing, or attitude reinforcement among public opinion (Iyengar, 2018). The Italian media system approximates a 'polarized pluralist' model (Hallin and Mancini, 2004) with strong political parallelism of news outlets, limited pluralism, and significant state intervention. Parliament and government control over the public television network (RAI) and, until recently, Mediaset's monopoly of private TV channels are key features of Italy's media structure whose TV news coverage of ruling and opposition parties shows a clear bias according to government alternation (Durante and Knight, 2012). Bellucci and De Angelis (2013) show that this biased coverage shapes leader approval. Employing a measure of TV coverage of ruling parties (as the share of news time devoted to parties in government), they find that airtime devoted to government activity exerted a positive and significant impact in a monthly model of popularity. Both political communication and consumers' confidence exerted a direct effect on approval.[2] Further research explored political determinants of approval. Memoli (2011; 2015) focuses on quality of governance—scandals, corruption, government effectiveness—whose deterioration has been among the reasons that triggered the change of the Italian party system in the early 1990s. A first analysis on the impact of scandals—albeit limited to a short five-year period (2005–2010) and based on a model with scandals as the only determinants—found that scandals involving politicians in office impacted on the popularity of the government (Memoli, 2011). However, and confirming comparative research (Maier, 2011; Carlin, Love, and Martínez-Gallardo, 2015; Rottinghaus, 2015), not all scandals registered the same impact on approval: economic-corruption scandals were more damaging for the government popularity than sexual scandals. Later research (Memoli, 2015) considered a wider scope of political

[1] Analyses of our approval data (described below) finds a modest relationship, albeit not statistically significant due to the small N. ($r = 0.259$, $p = 0.221$), with the electoral fortunes of government parties.

[2] Bellucci and De Angelis (2013) also find TV coverage has a positive effect on government support through an analysis of thirty-six individual surveys. They uncovered a heightened influence of communication among people with lower political interest and sophistication.

determinants of approval on a longer time series. Explanatory factors included scandals (without distinguishing their nature), government effectiveness, and rule of law with findings showing approval to be responsive to any worsening of government effectiveness. Failing to find an impact of the state of the economy, Memoli (2015) inferred that public opinion approval or sanctioning of the government depended mainly on socio-political rather than economic drivers.

Recent research further supported such a claim. Malet and Kriesi's (2019) analysis found that the economy did impact on popularity in 'ordinary' times (between 1996 and 2008) but not during and after the external shock of the Great Recession (2008–2015), when executive's approval was mainly driven by political events (policy debates, scandals, cabinet crises, all measured through dummy indicators).

In summary, previous analyses on the origin of government approval in Italy have focused on three main determinants: the economy, corruption in the political system, political communication. Research, however, has not reached a consensus on whether these represent alternative explanations of government support or they need to be simultaneously considered. Neither has it been assessed whether the explanatory power of each varies over time in response to contextual changes in the polity. As the introductory chapter of this volume lays out, the balance between economic and political determinants of approval may have changed over time. Our aim now is to assess the extent to which these explanations hold for a longer time period that covers over twenty years and encompasses both an unstable consolidation of the new party system and turbulent times in the economic (the Great Recession in 2008 and the sovereign debt crisis in 2011) and social (immigration waves which burst from 2013) realms. In particular we assess a) the balance between economic and political determinants of prime minister popularity; b) whether this balance is altered over time, that is whether the drivers of approval keep their explanatory power before and after the Great Recession.

Italian Prime Minister Approval, 1995–2018

Two features of Italian post-1994 electoral politics stand out: the executives' short tenure and bipolar electoral alternation. Over the period covered by our study, Italy experienced thirteen different executives, each lasting on average twenty months, spanning over five legislatures (Table 7.1). Short tenures imply non-infrequent replacement of governments within the single legislature (with

Table 7.1 Composition and tenure of Italian executives, 1995–2018

Composition of government	Time in office (quarters)	Duration (months)	Prime minister	Popularity (average)	Standard deviation popularity	No. of parties in government coalition*
Grand Coalition	1995/1–1996/4	16	Dini	44.2	0.0	5
Elections	*1996/2*					
Centre-Left	1996/2–1998/3	29	Prodi I	35.5	7.9	4
Centre-Left	1998/4–1999/4	14	D'Alema I	40.4	4.0	7
Centre-Left	1999/4–2000/2	4	D'Alema II	41		7
Centre-Left	2000/3–2001/2	12	Amato	28	1.5	7
Elections	*2001/2*					
Centre-Right	2001/2-2005/2	46	Berlusconi II	30.6	4.7	5
Centre-Right	2005/2–2006/2	13	Berlusconi III	33	1.7	5
Elections	*2006/2*					
Centre-Left	2006/2–2008/2	24	Prodi II	39.4	6.2	7
Elections	*2008/2*					
Centre-Right	2008/2–2011/4	30	Berlusconi IV	43.1	6.5	3
Grand Coalition	2011/4–2013/2	17	Monti	51.5	13.9	7
Elections	*2013/2*					
Grand Coalition	2013/2–2014/1	10	Letta	50.4	1.3	7
Centre-Left	2014/1–2016/4	34	Renzi	45.6	10.5	4
Centre-Left	2016/4–2018/2	18	Gentiloni	39.6	2.1	5

Source: Compiled by Authors.

a statutory length of five years). Although in parliamentary democracies coalition governments are the norm, Italy's extreme ministerial turnovers reflect the difficulty of decision-making among government partners due to their ideological heterogeneity (Conti and Marangoni, 2015; Curini and Pinto, 2017). Prime ministerial turnover has been more frequent among centre-left governments whose composition has involved a larger number of parties (six on average) than with centre-right governments (four parties). Since 1994 the Italian left has been typically more fragmented and dispersed among the heirs of the Catholic and Socialist subcultures and in need of assembling larger alliances in order to be electorally competitive against the centre-right which, on the other hand, was firmly led and dominated by Berlusconi's Forza Italia party (Curini and Pinto, 2016).

The second noteworthy feature of Italian post-1994 electoral politics—bipolar electoral alternation—highlights the transition from the absence of government alternation during the so-called First Republic, 1948–1992, when all governments hinged on the Christian Democratic Party, to the systematic ousting of the outgoing coalition at each election. To date, no government has been re-elected since 1994.

Both these features pose a taxing job on public opinion. Bipolar alternation speaks, on the one hand, to a heightened expression of accountability by voters. Frequent executive replacements, on the other hand, confuse voters who, furthermore, have faced the formation of grand coalitions either when elections did not express a clear mandate (as in 2013) or when executives stepped down but parliament was not dissolved (as when the euro sovereign debt crisis hit in Italy in 2011). The public was confronted therefore with the task of evaluating the executive's performance constrained by both governments' high volatility and a blurring of ruling responsibility.

Nevertheless, approval rates over this period reveal significant differences among executives. Unsurprisingly, grand coalition governments elicited on average the largest support, either for the supposed non-partisan composition of cabinets or, more likely, for the actual large cross-party majority which initially supported them in parliament. Installed after the dissolution of the Berlusconi cabinet in 2011, Mario Monti enjoyed the highest average approval rate (51.5 per cent) but also the largest variability (with a standard deviation of 12.4) due to the sharp downward trend in approval after implementing harsh fiscal adjustments and a severe pension reform in the wake of the euro crisis (Bellucci, 2014; Culpepper, 2014). Centre-left governments enjoy on average a slightly greater approval rate (38.6) than centre-right ones (35.6), likely due to their frequent ministerial replacement. Longer tenures, indeed, entail stronger erosion of popular support, as it is shown by its variability for the centre-right Berlusconi's fourth government (2008–2011) but also for the centre-left Renzi executive (2014–2016) whose approval fell significantly over its tenure. Moreover, longer tenures may erode the link between short-term economic conditions and support, since voters accumulate knowledge over government competence (Larsen, 2021).

Figure 7.1 displays the dynamics of prime minister popularity, where the usual cyclical pattern of honeymoon, decay, and end-of-term recovery (Muller, 1973; Carlin et. al., 2018) is not overall clearly discernable. An approval cycle is evident, though, when the prime minister is able to stay in office over the entire legislative term, i.e. as with the 2001–2006 Berlusconi executive and the brief Prodi II 2006–2008 government which ended with early elections. For most executives, then, approval shows a honeymoon boost followed by a more or less intense decay. Against this background, however, Italian public opinion does not seem to express a consistent downward trend of executive approval (see for instance Grossman and Guinaudeau on France in this volume), in spite of a growing scepticism and disaffection with the political class that in 2018 eventually led to the inauguration of the first all-populist government in Europe (Garzia, 2019). The linear trend in Figure 7.1 is actually positive, and signals voters' high expectations for every new government but also severe disillusionment afterwards.

Theory and Hypotheses

To explain these approval dynamics, we consider both traditional and country-specific contextual features of the Italian political system: the state of the economy, inequality and corruption, and political communication.

Economic outcomes have traditionally been employed as the main indicators of performance of a government, whose popular support was directly linked to the ebbs and flows of economic prosperity. As discussed in the introductory chapter, reward-punishment theory of accountability that framed early comparative research has been challenged on many counts, including instability in the relationship between politics and the economy, reverse causation, and conditionality of the economy impact. Cross-national research that includes Italy (Bellucci and Lewis-Beck, 2011; Lewis-Beck and Nadeau, 2012; Talving and Braghiroli, 2017) has, however, found a comparable and stable impact of the economy on government support, while the single case studies earlier reviewed disagree over this. We are able to test again this

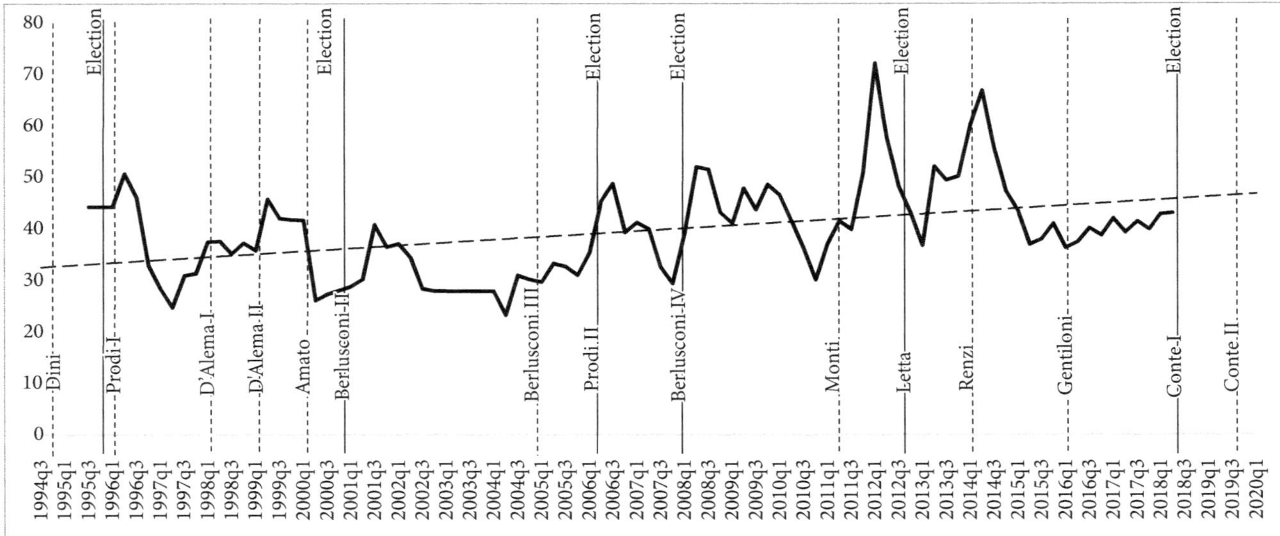

Figure 7.1 Trend of prime minister approval, Italy, 1995–2018

Source: Compiled by authors from Executive Approval Project v 2.0.

relationship over a longer time span. Our first expectation is therefore that the state of the economy—a valence issue gauged subjectively via consumer sentiment—impacts over the executive popularity, increasing it when the economy improves (H1: Economic Accountability Hypothesis).

Since the 1990s the Italian economy has grown at rates less than OECD and EU averages. Per capita income has remained below that of France or Germany, while income inequality has risen between 2008 and 2016, positioning Italy among the most unequal OECD countries, after the United States and the United Kingdom (Schadee, Segatti, and Vezzoni, 2019). Figure 7.2 charts economic trends. The impact of the double crisis, the economic one in 2008 and of the sovereign debt crisis in 2011, are visible: GDP fell in 2009 and again in 2012; unemployment which had been steadily decreasing since the mid-1990s skyrocketed after 2008. Most important, income inequality worsened, reaching two peaks in 2008 and 2012.

We then focus on economic inequality as a second economic determinant in the approval model. The first reason is that inequality may tap 'positional' economic voting, a different dimension from the valence perspective as of H1. Positional economic voting refers to voters' (desirability) preferences for competing governments' policies (Lewis-Beck and Nadeau, 2011). Dassonneville and Lewis-Beck (2020) show that income inequality affects ruling parties'

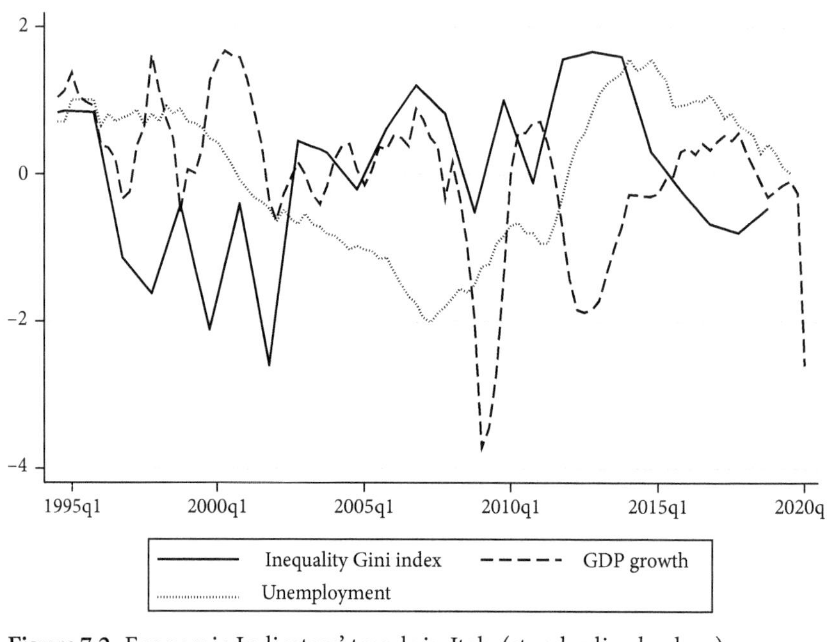

Figure 7.2 Economic Indicators' trends in Italy (standardized values)
Source: Italian Statistical Office.

electoral fortunes, but it acts more as a valence rather than a positional issue, i.e. it depresses the vote share of the government parties independently from their partisan leanings. On the other hand, Carlin et al. (2021) find support for a positional interpretation of inequality. Their analyses of presidential approval in Latin America finds that inequality mediates the impact of growth so that left-leaning presidents are punished and right-leaning ones rewarded for increasing inequality, a finding consistent with the different class interests of their electoral base. Given the uncertain policy distinctiveness of Italian coalition governments and the inter-class appeals of left and right parties (Bellucci, 2012), we expect that inequality hurts the popularity of both centre-left and centre-right governments in a similar fashion: the impact of inequality would then reveal a 'sanctioning' model rather than a 'partisan' model of accountability (Hellwig, 2012).

The second reason for focusing on inequality draws from the Great Recession. Governments presiding over the crisis across Europe were ousted at elections following waves of popular protests (Lewis-Beck, Lobo, and Bellucci, 2012; Bermeo and Bartels, 2014). Political de-alignment and party-system destabilization ensued as populist and new challenger parties rose in prominence (Hernández and Kriesi, 2016). In Italy the populist Five Star Movement (Tronconi, 2015) won 25 per cent of the votes at its first bid for parliament in 2013, increasing its share to 35 per cent in 2018. The same elections also favoured the Northern League, a former ethno-regionalist party lately refurbished as a radical right-wing populist one (Passarelli and Tuorto, 2018). Key to the populist rhetoric is opposition to supranationalism (in Europe), economic globalization, and the ensuing income inequality (O'Connor, 2017). Our expectation then is that inequality impacts negatively on prime minister approval (H2: Inequality Sanctioning Hypothesis).

The third determinant of approval we analyse is corruption. Procedural fairness and the rule of law are constitutive elements of democratic regimes and of their quality, which enhance citizens' equality and sustain economic development (Diamond and Morlino, 2005). Research has also shown that rule of law impacts popular support for institutions and political leaders. There are rewards for insuring public officials' legality of conduct and citizens' fair access to public services (Magalhães, 2020). Given its salience to the Italian case, we focus on corruption. The implosion of the traditional Italian party system in the early 1990s was precipitated by a vast judicial campaign against corruption that swept away the ruling parties (Cotta and Verzichelli, 2007), a campaign whose legacy endured long afterwards and became a signature trait for a quest to ameliorate the working of the political system (Vannucci, 2009). New parties committed themselves to fighting corruption. While many of these might be rhetorical appeals, public opinion continued to assign a high priority to the issue.[3] However, outcomes did not match popular expectations: rule-of-law indicators worsened after 2000, placing Italy below OECD standards (Memoli, 2015). Our hypothesis, then, is that a weakening of the efforts to curb corruption depresses prime ministerial approval (H3: Corruption Sanctioning Hypothesis).

Finally, we consider the impact of political communication. The role of media intermediation has been a subject of intense scrutiny by scholars of political behaviour. Yet, although a large body of literature acknowledges the importance of the information and of the media environment for public opinion, *direct* evidence of the impact of communication in studies of economic voting and popularity functions is sparse.[4] Most research has focused on the public's economic knowledge and on the source of peoples' economic perceptions. Findings show that although people have only a moderate factual knowledge of the economy (Aidt, 2000; Paldam and Nannestad, 2000), they are nevertheless able to correctly assess overall macroeconomic trends (Sanders, 2000; Duch and Stevenson, 2008). Furthermore, economic perceptions are not exclusively rooted in the economy but are also influenced by people's political leanings and media reports (Nadeau et al., 1999; De Boef and Kellstedt, 2004; Sanders and Gavin, 2004; Enns, Kellstedt, and McAvoy, 2012; Soroka, Stecula, and Wlezien, 2015). The impact of this 'mediated economy' (Stevenson and Duch, 2013) on executives' popularity appears, however, to be indirect: studies show that coverage and tone of news affect directly the evaluation of the executive's ruling competence, which in turn influences government approval (Sanders, Marsh, and Ward, 1993; Gavin, Sanders, and Farrall, 1996; Sanders and Gavin, 2004).

In the Italian case TV coverage has been shown to directly impact on government popularity. This finding has been interpreted as due to the prevailing model of the media system, which is characterized by strong political parallelism of television outlets and parliamentary oversight of public television, rather than evidence of a powerful persuasive effect of news exposure.[5] Such a

[3] Italian National Election Studies (ITANES) survey data show that (fighting) corruption was perceived as the most important problem Italy should address by 33 per cent of the voters in the 1996 legislative election, by 9 per cent in 2013 and by 14 per cent in 2018, ranking among the top priorities. ITANES data are available at www.itanes.org.

[4] For a review of research on media effects see, among others, Iyengar and Simon (2000) and Iyengar (2018).

[5] Initial findings on the impact of a then-novel television campaign inaugurated by Berlusconi in the 1994 elections showed that a persuasive effect of TV exposure was evident among people with above-average education and political interest (Ricolfi, 1994), while later re-evaluations uncovered a reverse causation effect between political choice and selective exposure to biased partisan news (Legnante and Baldassarri, 2010). The most affected by communication, however, continued to be unsophisticated voters (Barisione et al., 2010; Bellucci and De Angelis, 2013).

contentious and polarized media structure implies strong unbalanced coverage of political news and an active supply of alternative partisan frames aimed at priming voters. On the other hand, voters do react to change in control of public television ensuing government alternation, by migrating to like-minded news outlets (Durante and Knight, 2012). Parties in the ruling majority, not unexpectedly receive the largest share of coverage vis-à-vis the opposition, thus insuring a wider visibility. In the period we study, quarterly coverage of government coalition parties averages 65 per cent of total airtime with a range between 37.4 per cent and 89.3 per cent. Figure 7.3 plots trends of prime minister approval and TV coverage, showing long periods when the two series track each other ($r = 0.429, p < 0.001$). Our expectation is therefore that TV coverage devoted to government and ruling parties will have a positive impact on prime minister popularity (H4a: Political Communication Hypothesis). In order to consider the TV partisan bias in Italy's media structure we interact TV coverage with an indicator for centre-left governments. This interaction describes the likelihood that the private network and the public station controlled by the parliamentary minority will devote more time to the opposition confronting

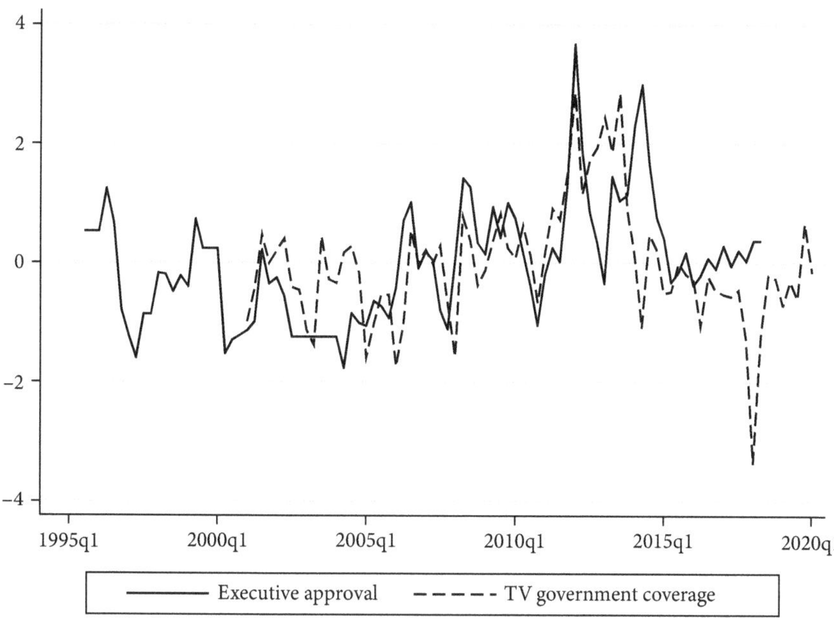

Figure 7.3 Executive approval and TV government coverage in Italy (standardized values)

Source: Compiled by authors from Executive Approval Project and Italian Regulation Communication Authority data.

an ideologically antagonist executive. Our expectation is to ascertain a negative effect on approval (H4b: Political Communication Bias Hypothesis).

Data and Methods

Our analysis employs confidence in the prime minister (per cent approving, smoothed quarterly data) between 1995 and 2018 as dependent variable, compiled and computed by the Executive Approval Project (Carlin et al., 2019).

Our model assesses the impact of several factors driving approval. For the state of the economy we rely on consumer sentiment, compiled by the Italian Statistical Office within the Joint Harmonised Programme of Business and Consumer Surveys of the European Union. The choice between employing a measure of the 'subjective' rather than of the 'objective' economy to assess government accountability has been greatly debated in the literature on V-P functions. We use subjective indicators since they have the desirable property to provide a unified global measure of the economy, which has been shown to respond closely to macroeconomic indicators (see for reviews Bellucci and Lewis-Beck, 2011; Lewis-Beck and Stegmaier, 2013).[6] The second independent variable we employ is economic inequality. We rely parsimoniously on a single measure of income inequality, employing the (quarterly interpolated) measure of the Gini index (Carlin et al., 2021) based on disposable income (Solt, 2020). Other specifications of how economic gains are distributed unequally yield similar conclusions. To tap corruption, we rely on the Word Bank Indicators of Governance, based on an aggregation of surveys of public opinion, enterprises, and experts (Kaufmann et al., 2010). The yearly values have been transformed in quarterly readings via linear interpolation, and the original values (with a range between −2.5 and +2.5) have been reverse coded such that higher values signifies more corruption. Finally, data on TV coverage of government parties comes from the Italian Communications Regulatory Authority, established in 1997. The Authority provides monthly reports of time devoted by television to political parties and leaders in news programmes. We computed the share of volume of airtime attributed to ruling parties as a measure of TV coverage of government action. Data collection began in 2001, so the models where TV coverage is included are estimated over a shorter time series.

[6] Regressing consumers' sentiment on just three macroeconomic indicators (GDP growth, unemployment, and inflation) yields an $R^2 = 0.42$.

In order to account for the dynamic properties of the series we test for their stationarity. Augmented Dickey-Fuller (ADF) and Phillips Perron tests suggest that consumer economic sentiment may be non-stationary. Therefore, we take the first difference of economic sentiment before entering the series in our models. Other series are entered in levels.

The abundance of theoretical expectations and thus of predicting variables vis-à-vis relatively short time series alerts us against overfitting a model. So we proceed to test each hypothesis separately before presenting a composite model. We consider first a baseline model which includes economic perceptions and the electoral cycle, controlling for the political leaning of governments (centre-left, centre-right, and grand coalition), then estimate a performance model which includes corruption and inequality, and finally fit a political communication model.

Results

Estimates from the baseline model of prime ministerial popularity reveal that people's economic perceptions correlate positively with approval (Table 7.2, Model 1). Economic optimism (pessimism) translates into increasing (decreasing) support for the executive, in keeping with the traditional accountability expectation. To assess its impact, consider that a one standard deviation increase in economic perceptions (3.1 percentage points) is associated on average with a change of approval of 1 point. Then, as expected, the variables tapping the honeymoon effect show a positive statistically significant impact. This would suggest that Italian prime ministers are held accountable for their management of the economy as per the standard model. However, we anticipate that this conclusion is to be revised once other determinants are taken into account, pointing to a decline of valence-based economic accountability after the Great Recession.

The performance model assesses the influence of corruption and inequality. The expectations of this policy-focused model are that increasing corruption and economic inequality would tarnish the prime minister's popularity. Estimates in Model 2 indicate this is the case, but only partially. Parameters on both series are negatively signed, as expected, but only for corruption is it statistically significant. Indeed, corruption has a greater impact than the economy: one standard deviation change in corruption would bring about a drop of prime ministerial popularity of 1.4 points. On the other hand, it is unclear if people hold the executive accountable for policy outcomes which are perceived to worsen their life conditions like income inequality.

Moving to the political communication model of approval (Model 3) we observe the strong direct impact of TV coverage on government approval we expected. A standard deviation increase of coverage (8.3 per cent of air-time) is associated to an increase of 4.5 points of popularity, an impact five times as much as that estimated for economic perceptions and three times that of inequality. The political bias hypothesis is also confirmed, as the interaction between coverage and centre-left government is negative and significant. On average this means a drop of six points in popularity attributable to TV coverage when the sitting executive is left-leaning.

Model 4 tests the viability of the previous three blocks of variables together, which implicates a reduction of the sample size because TV coverage data are available only since 2001. Estimates show that most variables retain their impact on approval, with the noteworthy exception, as anticipated, of economic perceptions. Although economic sentiment is rightly signed, it lacks statistical significance ($p = 0.19$). This means that the influence of the 'mediated economy' after 2001 is more uncertain once a full model is specified. On the other hand, the importance of other factors becomes clearer: both inequality and corruption are negatively signed and statistically significant ($p < 0.10$). Based on this model we would conclude that Italian executive approval in the recent era is mainly driven by the term cycle (the honeymoon effect), by government performance as gauged by the level of inequality and corruption, and by media exposure. Based on Model 4, which covers the 2001–2018 period, we see that one standard deviation increase of inequality and corruption brings about a similar drop of 1.2 points in popularity while a same change in standard units of TV coverage moves approval upward by 2.3 points. This also confirms political bias on TV, which in this model is estimated by a loss for centre-left governments of five points of approval (see Figure 7.4).

Our results indicate that executive approval in Italy is influenced by political communication, how people perceive the extent of corruption, and by inequality in the country (once the initial consensus for every new executive is factored in). Surprisingly, economic factors appear to have little influence on executive approval. While we find some evidence that 'the economy matters' (see Models 1 and 4), its strength and stability is uncertain, its impact is modest, and weaker compared to other factors.

Before accepting this conclusion, it is advisable to remember that the composite Model 4 is based on fewer observations than the previous ones. To assess the actual contribution of the economy as a driver of approval, we perform two further tests. First, we drop the TV coverage variable to increase the sample size. Second, we take into account the economic context by running separate

Table 7.2 OLS models of Italian prime minister approval, 1995–2018

	Model 1		**Model 2**		**Model 3**		**Model 4**	
	b	(SE)	b	(SE)	b	(SE)	b	(SE)
Economic Accountability Model								
Approval (q-1)	0.685*	(0.070)	0.741*	(0.079)	0.697*	(0.087)	0.687*	(0.075)
Economic sentiment	0.324°	(0.176)					0.247	(0.188)
Honeymoon	7.142*	(1.827)					10.169*	(2.082)
Honeymoon (q+1)	4.214*	(1.902)					3.996°	(2.100)
Performance Model								
Corruption (q-1)			−17.333°	(9.645)			−14.798°	(8.736)
Inequality (q-1)			−1.769	(2.318)			−3.737°	(1.989)
Political Communication Model								
TV coverage					0.546*	(0.169)	0.287°	(0.146)
Centre-Left government					64.275*	(19.385)	48.976*	(16.300)
TV coverage × CL government					−0.726*	(0.231)	−0.615*	(0.193)
Government (Ref: Grand coalition)								
Centre-Right	−2.966	(2.156)	−4.146	(2.812)	7.140°	(4.092)	−0.149	(3.683)
Centre-Left	−3.789°	(2.008)	−4.852°	(2.602)	−9.401°	(4.711)	−9.282*	(3.966)
Constant	14.148*	(3.841)	73.264	(77.811)	−31.316*	(14.102)	116.222°	(68.823)
R^2	0.686		0.624		0.683		0.804	
Root MSE	5.369		5.887		5.709		4.694	
N	89		83		67		67	

Source: Compiled by Authors.
Note: ° p<0.10, * p<0.05 (two-tailed tests).

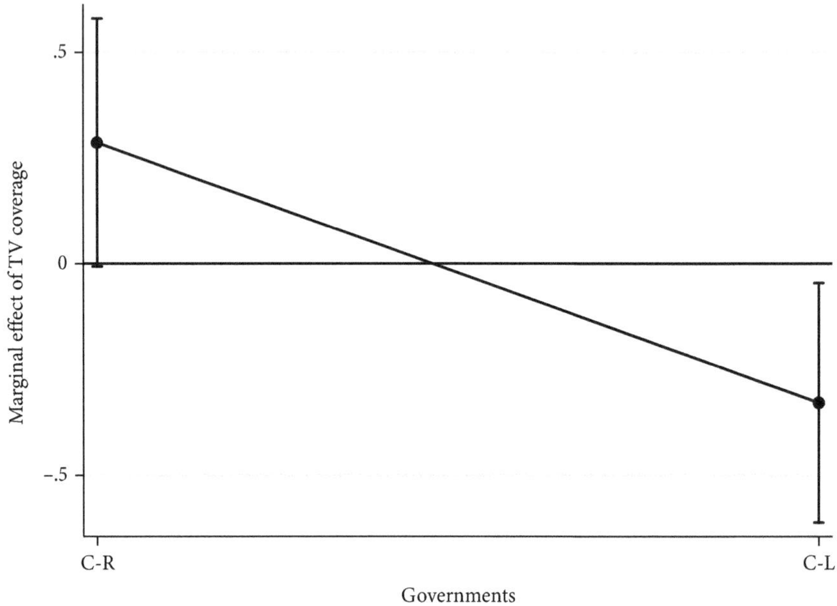

Figure 7.4 Marginal effect of TV coverage on approval of centre-right and centre-left governments (with 90 per cent confidence interval)
Source: Compiled by authors.

models for 'ordinary times' between 1995 and 2011, and for 'extraordinary times' from 2012 onward, after the inception of the sovereign debt crisis in 2012 that triggered a dramatic surge of unemployment (see Figure 7.2).

Model 5 (Table 7.3) restricts the analysis to the 1995–2011 ordinary times: the results indicate a significant negative effect of inequality. Meanwhile, the perception of corruption and the economic sentiment, albeit signed in the expected positive direction, is short of statistical significance. In Model 6—which covers the 2012–2018 period—both corruption and inequality show a statically significant impact on approval, while again the evaluation of the economy is not statistically significant. During this slump the economy does seem to have had a strong impact on the executive's popularity. But this impact is felt not through general economic evaluations (consumer sentiment) but rather by worsening inequality. The impact on the popularity of one standard deviation increase in inequality produces a drop of almost six points in this period, compared to a drop of less than two points in the period from 1995 to 2011.

In summary, despite constraints imposed by a relatively short time series, findings deliver a consistent story. The tenure cycle term effect notwithstanding, three factors appear to be important in explaining executive's approval:

Table 7.3 OLS models of Italian prime minister approval

	Model 5 1995–2011		Model 6 2012–2018	
	B	(SE)	b	(SE)
Economic Accountability Model				
Approval (q-1)	0.574*	(0.112)	0.616*	(0.207)
Economic sentiment	0.075	(0.247)	0.105	(0.283)
Honeymoon	5.094*	(2.277)	10.117*	(3.093)
Honeymoon (q+1)	1.692	(2.491)	6.586°	(3.466)
Performance Model				
Corruption	−13.256	(10.308)	−62.042*	(25.005)
Inequality	−7.564*	(3.540)	−41.185*	(13.378)
Government (Ref. Grand Coalition)				
Centre-Right	—		—	
Centre-Left	−1.308	(1.573)	1.658	(3.094)
Constant	265.658*	(119.152)	1397.2*	(451.323)
R^2	0.597		0.826	
Root MSE	5.035		4.839	
N	58		25	

Source: Compiled by Authors.
Note: ° p<0.10, * p<0.05 (two-tailed test).

corruption, economic inequality, and political communication. Corruption, which exerts a significant causal effect in most of the estimated models, is consistently a concern for public opinion, which affects the standing of the executive. To be clear, we are not concerned here with whether Italy is a corrupt country; rather, we stress how an issue which contributed to the demise of Italy's party system in the early 1990s continues to wield its legacy well beyond the events which primed voters at that time. Income inequality, which is the outcome of domestic political economy as well as of the international political economy regime for which blame is not easily attributable to sitting governments, exerts a conditional effect on approval. Its impact is particularly robust against other determinants when we estimate its influence over the period of economic crisis (2012–2018). The severity of the crisis made the state of the economy a salient issue for voters and strengthened the economic accountability of governments (Lewis-Beck and Lobo, 2017). Lastly, political communication stands out as a strong and consistent driver of popularity. We think the structure of Italy's media system might explain the direct effect of communication on approval, which is not often found in other democracies. It is surprising—and worrying—that political communication mutes the effect of the economy. This hints at the need to further deepen our understanding of the effects of political communication on government support in polarized pluralist media system democracies, and beyond.

Conclusion

The changes in voting choice patterns in Italy since the 1990s—the weakening of social cleavages and of partisanship, the personalization of political leadership, and the party-system destabilization—has heightened the importance of valence issues for voters. Party competence and ruling performance have become pivotal issues in people's 'calculus of support'. Demands for accountable government have vastly increased, and no government entering an election campaign with low approval has succeeded in remaining in office. Individual level analyses have detailed how such preoccupations explain voting choice, showing that valence evaluations are able to strengthen or weaken even long-term voters' ideological predispositions.[7] Research at the macro level has been sparser. Findings from early explanations of approval supported the economic accountability model, in which voters punish government for bad economic performance, while later research focused on 'political factors' capable of explaining the ups and downs of the executive's popularity, such as events, rule of law, and government effectiveness. A further line of inquiry explored an important institutional feature of the Italian polity: the structure of the media system. Findings were supportive of a dual impact of both the subjective economy and political communication, whose influence appeared to co-exist with no evidence of endogeneity.

This chapter merges these lines of inquiry in order to provide an assessment of the relative impact of economic (i.e. Paldam's 'e-fraction') and political (the 'p-fraction') explanations for what moves approval. We have proposed three perspectives as potential sources of approval: economic accountability, policy performance in the key realms of corruption and economic equality, and political communication. Each provides a sound explanation when taken singularly. A composite explanation that includes all three shows a diminished influence of economic accountability, and a greater role for political communication and good governance. Among performance indicators, economic inequality appears overall stronger than corruption. Controlling for period effects adds to the picture, showing that inequality is a salient explanation of approval in times of extraordinary crisis. These results seem to suggest that

[7] For a recent effort see Schadee et al. (2019).

over time the balance of the explanatory power of economic and political determinants of approval has moved towards the latter.

This conclusion needs, however, a caveat: such a finding does not mean that the subjective economy is to be left out when analysing the 'e'-part of the V-P function. After all, our 1995–2018 baseline model clearly shows the importance of the economy as a valence issue in explaining prime ministerial approval. And it does provide a parsimonious account of the ebbs and flows of popularity. Nevertheless, especially in times of profound economic crisis, positional economic voting looms as a promising approach in studying the economic determinants of government approval. The measure of inequality we employed is an objective aggregate index and, as such, we are unable to compare subjective perceptions of both the state of the economy and of inequality. We can only speculate that the salience of inequality among public opinion may have been magnified by political (and populist) entrepreneurs and political communication. And such salience may have been translated into an intensified impact on approval, especially after 2012. The implication for future comparative research is to engage the issue of how (a changing) political communication ignites or moderates the relevance of the economy for the accountability of governments.

References

Aidt, T. (2000) Economic voting and information. *Electoral Studies*, *19*, 349–62.

Barisione, M., Catellani, P., and De Sio, L. (2010). La scelta degli indecisi. In *Votare in Italia:1968–2008. Dall'appartenenza alla scelta*, P. Bellucci, and P. Segatti, eds. Bologna: il Mulino. 359–90.

Bellucci, P. (1984). The effect of aggregate economic conditions on the political preferences of the Italian electorate, 1953–1979. *European Journal of Political Research*, *12*(4), 387–401.

Bellucci, P. (1991). Italian economic voting: A deviant case or making a case for a better theory? In *Economics and Politics: The Calculus of Support*, H. Norpoth, M. S. Lewis-Beck, and J. Lafay, eds. Ann Arbor, MI: University of Michigan Press. 63–81.

Bellucci, P. (2006). All'origine della popolarità del governo in Italia. *Rivista Italiana di Scienza Politica*, *36*, 479–503.

Bellucci, P. (2010) Election cycles and electoral forecasting in Italy, 1994–2008. *International Journal of Forecasting*, *26*, 54–67.

Bellucci, P. (2012). Government accountability and voting choice in Italy, 1990–2008, *Electoral Studies*, *31*, 491–7.

Bellucci, P. (2014). The political consequences of blame attribution for the economic crisis in the 2013 Italian national election. *Journal of Elections, Public Opinion and Parties, 24*(2), 243–63.

Bellucci, P. (2015). Communists. In *The Oxford Handbook of Italian Politics*, E. Jones and G. Pasquino, eds. Oxford: Oxford University Press.

Bellucci, P., and De Angelis, A. (2013). Government approval in Italy: Political cycle, economic expectations and TV coverage, *Electoral Studies, 32*(3), 452–9.

Bellucci, P., and Lewis-Beck, M. S. (2011). A stable popularity function? Cross-national analysis. *European Journal of Political Research, 50*(2), 190–211.

Bellucci, P., and Segatti, P. (2010). *Votare in Italia: 1968–2008. Dall'appartenenza alla scelta*. Bologna: il Mulino.

Bermeo, N. G., and Bartels, L. M. (eds) (2014). *Mass Politics in Tough Times: Opinions, Votes, and Protest in the Great Recession*. Oxford: Oxford University Press.

Carlin, R. E, Love, G. J., and Martinez-Gallardo, C. (2015). Cushioning the fall: Scandals, economic conditions, and executive approval. *Political Behaviour, 37*, 109–30.

Carlin, R. E., Hartlyn, J., Hellwig, T., Love, G. J., Martinez-Gallardo, C., and Singer, M. M. (2018). Public support for Latin American presidents: The cyclical model in comparative perspective. *Research & Politics, 5*(3), 1–8.

Carlin, R. E., Hartlyn, J., Hellwig, T., Love, G. J., Martinez-Gallardo, C., and Singer, M. M. (2019). Executive Approval Database 2.0. www.executiveapproval.org.

Carlin, R. E., Hellwig, T., Love, G., Martinez-Gallardo, C., and Singer, M. M. (2021). When growth is not enough: Inequality, economic gains, and executive approval. *Political Science Research and Methods, 10*(2), 298–316.

Chiaramonte, A. (2020). An Italic obsession: Electoral reforms. *Quaderni dell'Osservatorio Elettorale-Italian Journal of Electoral Studies, 83*(1), 5–16.

Conti, N., and Marangoni, F. (eds) (2015). *The Challenge of Coalition Government: The Italian Case*. London and New York: Routledge.

Cotta, M., and Verzichelli, L. (eds) (2007). *Il Sistema politico italiano*. Bologna: il Mulino.

Culpepper, P. D. (2014). The political economy of unmediated democracy: Italian austerity under Mario Monti. *West European Politics, 37*(6), 1264–81.

Curini, L., and Pinto, L. (2016). More than post-election cabinets: Uncertainty and the 'magnitude of change' during Italian government bargaining. *International Political Science Review 37*(2), 184–97.

Curini, L., and Pinto, L. (eds) (2017). *L'arte di fare (e disfare) i governi. Da De Gasperi a Renzi, 70 anni di politica italiana*. Milano: Egea Bocconi.

Dalton, R., and Wattenberg, M. P. (eds) (2000). *Parties without Partisans: Political Change in Advanced Industrial Democracies*. New York: Oxford University Press.

Dassonneville, R., and Lewis-Beck, M. S. (2020). Inequality and party support: Positional economic voting or a new dimension of valence? *Regional Studies*, *54*(7), 897–906.

De Boef, S., and Kellstedt, P. M. (2004). The political (and economic) origins of consumer confidence. *American Journal of Political Science*, *48*(4), 633–49.

Diamond, L. J., and Morlino, L. (*2005*). *Assessing the Quality of Democracy*. Baltimore, MD: Johns Hopkins University Press.

Duch, R., and Stevenson, R. T. (2008). *The Economic Vote: How Political and Economic Institutions Conditions Election Results*. Cambridge: Cambridge University Press.

Durante, R., and Knight, B. (2012). Partisan control, media bias, and viewer responses: Evidence from Berlusconi's Italy. *Journal of the European Economic Association*, *10*(3), 451–81.

Enns, P. K., Kellstedt, P. M., and McAvoy, G. E. (2012). The consequences of partisanship in economic perceptions. *Public Opinion Quarterly*, *76*(2), 287–310.

Farrell, D., and Webb, P. (2000). Political parties as campaign organizations. In *Parties without Partisans: Political Change in Advanced Industrial Democracies*, R. Dalton and M. Wattenberg, eds. New York: Oxford University Press. 102–28.

Garzia, D. (2019). The 2018 Italian parliamentary election and the first populist government in Western Europe. *West European Politics*, *42*(3), 670–80.

Garzia, D., and Viotti, F. (2012). Party identification, leader effects and vote choice in Italy, 1990–2008. *World Political Science Review*, *8*(1), 1–23.

Gavin, N. T., Sanders, D., and Farrall, N. (1996). The impact of television news on public perception of the economy and government, 1993–94. In *British Elections and Parties Yearbook*, D. M. Farrell, D. Broughton, D. Denver, and J. Fisher, eds. London: Frank Cass. 64–68.

Gunther, R., and Mughan, A. (eds) (2000). *Democracy and the Media. A Comparative Perspective*. Cambridge: Cambridge University Press.

Hallin, D. C., and Mancini, P. (eds) (2004). *Comparing Media Systems: Three Models of Media and Politics*. Cambridge: Cambridge University Press.

Hellwig, T. (2012). Constructing accountability: Party position taking and economic voting. *Comparative Political Studies*, *45*(1), 91–118.

Hernández, E., and Kriesi, H. (2016). The electoral consequences of the financial and economic crisis in Europe. *European Journal of Political Research*, *55*(2), 203–24.

Isernia, P. (2008). Present at creation: Italian mass support for European integration in the formative years. *European Journal of Political Research*, *47*(3), 383–410.

Itanes-Italian National Election Study (2008). *Il ritorno di Berlusconi*. Bologna: il Mulino.

Iyengar, S. (2018). A typology of media effects. In *The Oxford Handbook of Political Communication*, K. Kenski, and H. Jameison, eds. Oxford: Oxford University Press.

Iyengar, S., and Simon, A. (2000). New perspectives and evidence on political communication and campaign effects. *Annual Review of Psychology*, *51*(1), 149–69.

Kaufmann, D., Kraay, A., and Mastruzzi, M. (2010). The Worldwide Governance Indicators: Methodology and analytical issues. *Hague Journal on the Rule of Law*, *3*(2), 220–46.

Kayser, M. A., and Wlezien, C. (2011). Performance pressure: Patterns of partisanship and the economic vote. *European Journal of Political Research*, *50*(3), 365–94.

Key, V. O. (1966). *The Responsible Electorate: Rationality in Presidential Voting, 1936–1960*. New York: Vintage Books.

La Repubblica (2017). La possibile spinta al PD che può arrivare dall'essere al governo, P. Bellucci, 17 December. https://www.repubblica.it/politica/2017/12/14/news/stare_al_governo_fa_vincere_o_perdere_le_elezioni_-184075104/.

Larsen, M. V. (2021). Incumbent tenures crowds out economic voting. *British Journal of Political Science*, *51*(2), 646–65.

Legnante, G., and Baldassarri, D. (2010). Campagne elettorali e mediazione sociale: esposizione ai media e relazioni interpersonali. In P. Bellucci and P. Segatti, eds. *Votare in Italia: 1968–2008, Dall'appartenenza alla scelta*. Bologna: il Mulino. 249–88.

Lewis-Beck, M. S. (1988). *Economics and Elections: The Major Western Democracies*. Ann Arbor, MI: University of Michigan Press.

Lewis-Beck, M. S., and Nadeau, R. (2011). Economic voting theory: Testing new dimensions. *Electoral Studies*, *30*(2), 288–94.

Lewis-Beck, M. S., and Nadeau, R. (2012). Pigs or not? Economic voting in Southern Europe. *Electoral Studies*, *31*(3), 472–7.

Lewis-Beck, M. S., and Paldam, M. (2000). Economic voting: An introduction. *Electoral Studies*, *19*(2–3) 113–21.

Lewis-Beck, M. S., and Stegmaier, M. (2013). The VP-function revisited: A survey of the literature on vote and popularity functions after over 40 years. *Public Choice*, *157*, 367–85.

Lewis-Beck, M. S., Costa-Lobo, M., and Bellucci, P. (eds) (2012). Economic crisis and elections: The European periphery, *Electoral Studies*, *31*(3), 469–71.

Lewis-Beck, M. S. and Costa-Lobo, M. (2017). The Economic Vote: Ordinary vs. Extraordinary Times. In *The Sage Handbook of Electoral Behaviour*, K. Arzheimer, J. Evans and M. S. Lewis-Beck eds. London: Sage Publications. 606–29.

Magalhães, P. C. (2020). Public opinion and executive approval. In *The Oxford Handbook of Political Executives*, B. A. Rudy, R. Elgie, L. Helms, J. Kaarbo, and F. Müller-Rommel, eds. Oxford: Oxford University Press. 627–45.

Maier, J. (2011). The impact of political scandals on the political support: An experimental test of two theories, *International Political Science Review*, *32*(4), 283–302.

Mair, P. (2009). Representative versus responsible government. Working Paper 09/8, Cologne: Max Planck Institute for the Study of Societies.

Malet, G., and Kriesi, H. (2019). Economic shocks and the cost of ruling: Evidence from Italy, *Journal of Elections, Public Opinion and Parties*, *30*(1), 22–41.

Mancini, P. (2015). *Il Post-partito. La fine delle grandi narrazioni*. Bologna: il Mulino.

Memoli, V. (2011). Government, scandals and political support in Italy. *Interdisciplinary Political Studies*, *1*(2), 127–36.

Memoli, V. (2015). The support for and popularity of the government. In *The Challenge of Coalition Government: The Italian Case*, N. Conti and F. Marangoni, eds. London and New York: Routledge. 128–43.

Muller, J. E. (1973). *War, Presidents, and Public Opinion*. New York: John Wiley and Sons.

Nadeau, R., Niemi, R. G., Fan, D. P., and Timothy, A. (1999). Elite economic forecasts, economic news, mass economic judgments, and presidential approval. *The Journal of Politics*, *61*(1), 109–35.

Nannestad, P., and Paldam, M. (2002). The cost of ruling: A foundation stone for two theories. In *Economic Voting*, H. Dorussen and M. Taylor, eds. London and New York: Routledge. 17–44.

O'Connor, N. (2017). Three connections between rising economic inequality and the rise of populism. *Irish Studies in International Affairs*, *28*, 29–43.

Paldam, M., and Nannestad, P. (2000). What do voters know about the economy? A study of Danish data, 1990–1993. *Electoral Studies*, *19*(2–3), 363–91.

Passarelli, G., and Tuorto, D. (2018). *La Lega di Salvini. Estrema destra di governo*. Bologna: il Mulino.

Ricolfi, L. (1994). *Elezioni e mass media. Quanti voti ha spostato la TV?* Bologna: il Mulino.

Rottinghaus, B. (2015). *The Institutional Effects of Executive Scandals*. Cambridge: Cambridge University Press.

Sanders, D. (2000). The real economy and the perceived economy in popularity functions: How much do voters need to know? A study of British data, 1974–97. *Electoral Studies*, *19*(2–3), 275–94.

Sanders, D., and Gavin, N. (2004). Television news, economic perceptions and political preferences in Britain, 1997–2001. *The Journal of Politics*, *6*(4), 1245–06.

Sanders, D., Marsh, D., and Ward, H. (1993). The electoral impact of press coverage of the British economy, 1979–87. *British Journal of Political Science*, *23*(2), 175–210.

Santagata, W. (1985). The demand side of politico-economic models and politicians' beliefs: The Italian case. *European Journal of Political Research*, *13*(2), 121–34.

Schadee, H., Segatti, P., and Vezzoni, C. (eds) (2019). *L'apocalisse della democrazia italiana. Alle origini di due terremoti elettorali*. Bologna: il Mulino.

Solt, F. (2020). Measuring income inequality across countries and over time: The standardized World Income Inequality Database. *Social Science Quarterly*, *101*(3), 1183–99. SWIID Version 9.2, December 2021.

Soroka, S. N., Stecula, D. A., and Wlezien, C. (2015). It's (change in) the (future) economy, stupid: Economic indicators, the media, and public opinion. *American Journal of Political Science*, *59*(2), 457–74.

Stevenson, R. and Duch, R. (2013). The meaning and use of subjective perceptions in studies of economic voting. *Electoral Studies*, 32, 305–20.

Talvig, L., and Braghiroli, S. (2017). Has economic voting changed? A comparative analysis of Italy and other Southern European countries. *Contemporary Italian Politics*, *9*(1), 84–107.

Tronconi, F. (2015). *Beppe Grillo's Five Star Movement*. London: Routledge.

Vannucci. A. (2009). The controversial legacy of '*mani pulite*': A critical analysis of Italian corruption and anti-corruption policies. *Bulletin of Italian Politics*, *1*(2), 62–8.

8

Moving beyond the Economy

Executive Approval in Spain

Xavier Romero-Vidal, Lluís Orriols, and Pedro Riera

Spanish politics are no longer what they used to be. In the last decade, the country left behind forty years of autocratic rule followed by other almost forty years of a two-party system, becoming a typical European multi-party democracy. More recently, the entrance of new parties into the political arena has not only fragmented the party system but also contributed to an increase of electoral volatility and considerable ideological and affective polarization. A growing literature identifies the Great Recession as largely responsible for this transformation in the Spanish political landscape (Orriols and Cordero, 2016; Vidal, 2018). In addition to these changes, the Basque terrorist group ETA (*Euskadi Ta Askatasuna* [Basque Country and Freedom]) ended its armed activity in 2011 after decades of recurrent attacks. How have these historical events and systemic transformations influenced public opinion? In this chapter, we examine government popularity dynamics in democratic Spain in the last four decades.

When explaining dynamics in executive approval rates, previous work has referred to the key role of the economy (Paldam, 1991). At the aggregate level, there is a tendency in many countries to approve the executive's performance when the economic situation is good and to register dissatisfaction when the economy fares poorly. Building on these comparative insights and using data from the Executive Approval Project, we find evidence that the economy (i.e. unemployment) helps explain government popularity in Spain between 1985 and 2019. We study the evolution of the economic determinants of approval over time, but do not find a clear linear trend. Instead, our results suggest a u-shaped evolution, in which the economy had an impact especially in the former (1985–2001) and latter (2008–2019) periods, but it turned out to be irrelevant in the years between them (2001–2008). In the Spanish case,

Xavier Romero-Vidal, Lluís Orriols, and Pedro Riera, *Moving beyond the Economy*. In: *Economics and Politics Revisited*. Edited by: Timothy Hellwig and Matthew Singer, Oxford University Press. © Xavier Romero-Vidal, Lluís Orriols, and Pedro Riera (2023). DOI: 10.1093/oso/9780192871664.003.0008

the economy mainly influences government approval in periods of economic difficulties.

Yet, the economy is not the only driver of approval in Spain. In this chapter, we also move beyond the economy to explore how political factors matter as well. We bring into the equation two different determinants: (a) the salience of non-economic issues (i.e. domestic and international terrorism), and (b) the evolution of policy preferences (i.e. the policy mood). First, we find that the approval ratings of government leaders increase when terrorism becomes a major problem among Spanish citizens. Therefore, our results indicate that terrorism generates a sort of 'rally-round-the-flag' effect in Spain. Second, executive approval deteriorates when public policy preferences shift in the opposite direction of the government's ideology. The literature on dynamic representation concludes that policies reflect public preferences due to two mechanisms: either the government adapts its policies to meet public demands (policy accommodation), or citizens use their vote to elect a new government more in line with their preferences (electoral turnover) (Bartle et al., 2019). The evidence of this chapter is consistent with the electoral turnover mechanism. Indeed, we find that when ideological congruence between the executive and the public is absent, government approval ratings drop, eventually leading to an electoral defeat for the party in power.

In sum, this chapter makes two contributions. On the one hand, we provide evidence that the economy generally remains an important determinant of executive approval in Spain. Previous studies have approached this issue mainly taking voting behaviour (rather than approval) as dependent variable (Bosch and Riba, 2005; Fraile and Lewis-Beck, 2010; 2014b). On the other hand, we show that the economy is not the only relevant factor to explain government popularity: executive approval in Spain is also influenced by non-economic factors such as terrorism and the congruence between citizens' issue preferences and government public policies.

We next briefly review previous research about popularity functions in Spain to then formulate our expectations about how economic and political factors drive the popularity of the Spanish governments between 1985 and 2019. We then describe the data, discuss the operationalization of our variables, and justify the choice of the method guiding the empirical analysis. After commenting on the results of the econometric models, the final section concludes with an assessment of the drivers of approval in the Spanish case and how they relate to those in other countries.

Economics and Executive Approval in Spain

The study of popularity functions is a relatively *rara avis* in Spain, and there are only few works on this topic (Bosch and Riba, 2005; Rico, 2009; Orriols and Rico, 2014). Previous studies have typically focused on vote choice rather than government popularity (e.g. Lancaster and Lewis-Beck, 1986). This neglect is quite surprising given the relative youth of Spain as a democracy, which leaves fewer elections as data points, and the wealth of information offered by the survey barometers of the *Centro de Investigaciones Sociológicas* (CIS, Centre for Sociological Research).

Extant research on the effect of the economy on the vote—that is, the vote-function rather than popularity function (Paldam, 1991)—produces mixed results. Studies using individual-level data provided evidence of an effect of the perceived state of the economy (Fraile and Lewis-Beck, 2010), of objective economic indicators (Fraile and Lewis-Beck, 2014a), or of a combination of both (Fraile and Lewis-Beck, 2012). Yet, Hamman (2000) casts doubts on the economic voting in Spain as she did not find a clear pattern between macroeconomic conditions and vote choice for the governing Socialist party in the context of the 1986, 1989, and 1993 general elections. The mixed findings regarding economic voting patterns have led scholars to develop alternative arguments to account for them. For example, Maravall and Przeworski (1999) claim that previous political predispositions decisively shape the effect of economic perceptions on vote choice in Spain. Likewise, Maravall and Fraile (2000) state that the potential negative effect of unemployment rates on vote for the incumbent Socialist Party during the 1980s and the 1990s was neutralized by both its welfare policies and citizens' mistrust of the main centre-right opposition party. Likewise, León (2012) shows with Spanish data that the type of decentralization adopted in a country blurs responsibility attribution across levels of government.

While the literature on voting behaviour has been prolific in Spain, executive approval dynamics have been largely ignored. However, there are some notable exceptions. In line with research on other democracies, Orriols and Rico (2014) find a significant negative relation between objective measures of the economy (and, in particular, unemployment rates) and the popularity of the Spanish prime minister during the 1983–2008 period. There also is evidence of the relevance of subjective economic perceptions at the individual level. For instance, Rico (2010) finds that, after controlling for political predispositions, perceptions of the national economy had an impact on Prime Minister José Luis Rodríguez-Zapatero's evaluations in 2008. Similarly, Bosch and Riba (2005) show that the economy, both objective (especially, unemployment and, to a lesser extent, inflation) and subjective, was the main factor behind the loss of popularity of the incumbent Socialist Party during the 1983–1993 period.[1] Finally, Bellucci and Lewis-Beck (2011) include Spain in their study of popularity functions in Western democracies (with France, Germany, Italy, the United Kingdom, and the United States) between 1994 and 2006. Pooling time series of these democracies, they conclude that government popularity tends to decline when the electorate perceives an economic crisis.

Moving beyond the Economy

While economics are often assumed to be a key driver of leader popularity, leaders can also be held accountable for non-economic outcomes. Research on the potential impact of non-economic issues on the popularity of Spanish governments is rather scarce. The exception is Rico (2010), who, using individual-level data, finds that non-economic issues such as terrorism or same-sex marriage explained Prime Minister Rodríguez-Zapatero's popularity in 2008. A larger set of work on vote choice finds that it is related to a wide set of non-economic issues such as health services (Fraile, 2002), corruption (Costas-Pérez et al., 2012; Riera et al., 2013), or public investments (de la Calle and Orriols, 2010).

Building on this research, we strive to move beyond the economy and explore to what extent executive approval depends on two different factors: the changing salience of non-economic issues (in particular, terrorism) and the evolution of public policy preferences (or 'policy mood'). The first non-economic factor we examine is issue salience. Since the publication of *The American Voter* (Campbell et al., 1960), scholars of public opinion have shown a great interest in the role of issue salience. Salience is a necessary (but not sufficient) condition for an issue to become influential for vote choice and, probably, executive approval (Edwards et al., 1995). The mechanism that accounts for this relation is that salient issues become more cognitively accessible for voters and, thus, more prone to come to mind when evaluating government performance. Issue salience also increases incentives to gather information about party positions and government performance on these topics (Krosnick, 1990; Krosnick et al., 1993).

[1] However, it is important to point out that they measure popularity using vote intention instead of a more direct measure of executive approval.

Although non-economic concerns such as corruption, health-related issues, and, especially, terrorism became extremely salient during a big portion of the 1990s and 2000s decades (Chaqués-Bonafont and Palau, 2011), overshadowing to a large extent the importance of the economy, the latter has been traditionally considered the most important problem by the Spanish electorate. This is particularly true during the last decade. According to the CIS survey series (1985–2021), the salience of economic-related problems substantially increased with the Great Recession, and it reached its peak of the whole series in the first quarter of 2012.

We still do not know much about the relation between issue salience and public opinion in Spain. Palau and Davesa (2013) find an association between newspapers' coverage and the perception of the most important issues in the country. For instance, increased coverage of corruption scandals is associated with an increase in the salience of corruption as an issue. Using the 'Most Important Problem' survey item, Chaqués-Bonafont and Palau (2011) also study the relation between citizens' priorities and policymakers' speeches and legislative activity. However, there is no research on the relation between issue importance and government popularity yet.

The second non-economic factor we want to analyse that has been largely ignored in the executive approval literature is the impact of policy mood. As developed by Stimson (1999), mood is a measure that summarizes the evolution of public opinion latent preferences in different policy domains. It mostly focuses on attitudes towards the desirable scope of government intervention (Bartle et al., 2011). The literature has largely explored the extent to which mood reacts to economic outcomes. Erikson et al. (2002) and Stevenson (2001), for instance, show that unemployment and good economic perspectives push the mood towards a more liberal (or left-wing) position, while high consumer prices or economic downturns move it towards a more conservative (or right-wing) position. Romero-Vidal (2020) finds a similar pattern in Catalonia, as the years that the policy mood reaches more conservative positions were preceded by the outbreak of economic turndowns.

Policy mood has also been used in the literature as an independent variable to explain different political phenomena. For instance, governmental and legislative activity is responsive to public mood in the United States (Erikson et al., 2002), but not in the United Kingdom and Spain (Bartle et al., 2019; 2020). In these latter countries, voters can only bring policies into line with public mood via cabinet turnover. Indeed, government replacement through elections is the only mechanism to induce political representation in Spain.

Likewise, the literature finds that changes in policy mood have electoral consequences in the expected direction: mood movements to the right lead to increases in vote intention for right-wing parties, whereas movements to the left are correlated with higher left-wing parties' success. Since there is a connection between mood and vote choice in many democracies, including Spain (Bartle et al., 2020), it is reasonable to expect an analogous effect on executive approval. If leaders are out of line with their nation's mood, then their approval will suffer.

Hypotheses

Building on the existing literature, we derive a set of expectations regarding the determinants of government popularity in Spain. More specifically, we highlight several economic and political features that may affect executive approval.

In line with previous research on economic voting, we start with the initial expectation that the economy influences government popularity. This literature is, however, surprisingly inconclusive about the exact impact of economic variables on incumbents' popularity. While a long tradition of research has shown that the popularity of the executive is related to macroeconomic results (Mueller, 1970; Fiorina, 1981), scholars have increasingly turned to subjective indicators (Sanders et al., 1987; Clarke and Stewart, 1995). We remain agnostic about this controversy. Although we measure the economy by using a classic objective indicator (the evolution of unemployment rates), we also discuss in the results section how our models perform when we use citizens' subjective perceptions as independent variables. All in all, the baseline hypothesis of this chapter is:

H1: When the economy improves, government popularity increases.

In Spain, there are also grounds to believe that the influence of the economy on executive approval has changed over time. The literature on Spanish elections shows that the economy was clearly a major factor in the 2011 general elections, but it was how voters evaluated government economic policies rather the objective economic conditions what mattered the most (Fraile and Lewis-Beck, 2014b). During the Great Recession, Lewis-Beck and Nadeau (2012) suggest that in Southern European countries like Spain the impact of the economy became stronger because they had one-party governments, making attribution of responsibility easier, and because their economic conditions were comparatively poorer. Similarly, Costa Lobo and Pannico (2020) show that in Spain economic perceptions became more correlated with voting for the incumbent party after the Great Recession. Bearing all these considerations in mind, we expect the economy to become more salient in times of crisis and, hence, to affect popularity dynamics more decisively in these contexts.

Moreover, there is a second possible reason for this 'asymmetric effect'. This phenomenon is also known as a 'grievance asymmetry' or 'negativity effect' (Nannestad and Paldam, 1997; Lau, 1985). According to this idea, citizens tend to attach greater weight to negative than to positive information in a variety of attitude-formation processes (Aragonés, 1997). The evidence for this asymmetry is still inconclusive (Lewis-Beck and Stegmaier, 2013): whereas some studies do not find support for this phenomenon (Kiewiet, 1983; Lewis-Beck, 1988), others do (Mueller, 1970; Holbrook et al., 2001). We build on this debate and expect the following conditioning effect:

> H2: The magnitude of the effect of the economy on government popularity increases as the overall state of the economy deteriorates.

As noted, we expect the relation between the economy and executive approval to be mediated by the clarity of responsibility. Accountability can only be guaranteed when voters have a clear idea of who is responsible for economic outcomes (Powell and Whitten, 1993; Anderson, 2000; León and Orriols, 2016). Where party-system fragmentation is high, we expect lower levels of clarity of responsibility and, thus, lower connection between the economy and executive approval.

In Spain, the two-party system collapsed in the aftermath of the 2015 general election with the appearance of two new state-wide parties, Podemos and Ciudadanos. The economy seemed to impact support for the two traditional mainstream parties, but it was less relevant for voting for the two newcomers (Orriols and Cordero, 2016). In the case of these latter parties, their emergence and electoral success were attributed to the crisis of representation and political disaffection (Vidal, 2018). Adding to an already complex environment, in 2019 a new third party, the radical right *Vox*, also obtained representation at the national level. This creates the possibility that the Spanish public will have a harder time holding incumbent governments accountable for economic outcomes in the present multi-party era than when the Spanish party system was dominated by two parties. In summary, we expect the following conditioning effect:

> H3: The magnitude of the effect of the economy on government popularity decreases as the size of the party system increases.

As the preceding chapter on Italy and other contributions to this volume have noted, executive approval may also be affected by non-economic factors. In this chapter, we focus on the role of two different considerations: (i) the salience of other types of issues or events and (ii) the evolution of public policy preferences. Regarding the former, we focus on the most salient non-economic issue over the last decades among Spanish citizens: terrorism. According to the survey data we use in this chapter, 23 per cent of the Spanish population has considered terrorism, especially ETA's terrorist activity, as one of the three most important problems during the last three decades. Since terrorist attacks can foster in-group solidarity (Van Hauwaert and Huber, 2020) and change attitudes towards incumbents (Campbell, 2005), we hypothesize that salience of terrorism generates the so-called rally-round-the flag effect (Godefroidt, 2023) and, therefore, it boosts executive's popularity in the short run. Mueller (1970) posited that if they are to produce a rally effect, events must be specific, dramatic, and sharply focused. These characteristics apply most directly to those related to foreign policy and, especially, military actions (Mueller, 1970; Lee, 1977). However, other type of events like terrorist attacks (Hetherington and Nelson, 2017) or even, more recently, COVID-19 (Kritzinger et al., 2021) have also been examined.

Issue salience is a good way to study the rally effect of terrorism since it captures one of the most important assumptions in the literature: in order to generate the rally-round-the-flag effect, events should 'assure public attention and interest' (Mueller 1970, 21). The Most Important Problem question therefore stands to be a better indicator of how terrorism affects public opinion than is the magnitude of the events themselves (e.g. the number of attacks or casualties). As a result, we expect the following hypothesis:

> H4: When the salience of terrorism increases, government popularity also increases.

Finally, we expect movements in the policy mood, a measure that summarizes preferences on a wide variety of policy domains, to lead to changes in government popularity conditioned by incumbent partisanship. Shifts in mood to the left, signalling higher preferences for government intervention, will increase popularity of left-wing governments but will have the opposite effect for conservative cabinets. In other words, we expect increases in *mood congruence* to be associated with increases in executive approval, while decreases—public shifts in the opposite direction of the incumbent's ideology—should result in less popularity. This line of reasoning leads us to our final hypothesis:

H5: Movements to the right (left) in the public's policy mood increase the popularity of right-wing (left-wing) governments.

Data and Methods

Our measure of executive approval comes from the Executive Approval Database (Carlin et al., 2019), which for the Spanish case combines poll marginals for the popularity of the national government and prime minister. To assess systematically the effect of some contextual factors on government popularity, our data set combines the approval series with a wide range of variables from different sources.

As regards our independent variables, we use quarterly unemployment rates from OECD as our main economic indicator.[2] To address the clarity-of-responsibility hypothesis, we build on the information provided by the election archive of the Spanish Ministry of Interior to calculate the effective number of parliamentary parties (ENPP) for each term. To account for the public salience of terrorism, we use survey data from CIS. Namely, we rely on an open-ended question in which respondents are asked to name the three most important problems (MIP) in Spain. These responses are combined in relatively narrow categories by CIS (e.g. unemployment, economic problems, terrorism, housing, corruption, etc.), so we aggregate the two categories of interest: ETA terrorist activity and international terrorism. As a result, our salience variable accounts for the percentage of respondents considering either domestic or international terrorism (or both) as one of the three main problems for the country at one moment in time.

Since economic and cultural issues highly correlate in Spain, our measure of policy mood is based on a minimal spatial approach derived from a single

[2] Additional analyses (not included here) show that unemployment is the strongest predictor among similarly available objective indicators of the state of the economy (such as GDP or inflation). Moreover, unlike public perceptions on the state of the economy, data for unemployment are available for the entire period under study.

left-right dimension. Our measure of the central tendency of public opinion in the left-right axis is the Spanish policy mood developed by Bartle et al. (2020). These authors combine a wide range of survey data series to construct an indicator of public opinion changes in the left-right dimension. We transform changes in the policy mood such that shifts towards the right take positive values under conservative governments (since they are assumed to increase congruence), but negative values under social democratic governments (as they indicate that the public is moving in the opposite direction of government ideology). Similarly, shifts to the left take positive values under left-wing governments and negative values under right-wing governments. We refer to the resulting variable as *mood congruence*.[3]

Finally, all models control for the effect of three additional factors that we expect to influence the dynamics of executive approval in Spain. First, we control for the potential existence of honeymoon effects by including a dichotomous variable in the models that takes value 1 in the two first quarters after a general election takes place and 0 otherwise. Second, we account for the potential cost of governing by including a continuous variable in the models that captures the number of months the current prime minister has been in power. Third, the models also consider the party of the government: party affiliation is a dichotomous variable that takes value 1 if the current prime minister belongs to the Popular Party and 0 if he belongs to the Socialist Party.

Since we are modelling longitudinal data, we need to consider both the series memory and the possibility that some historical events disrupt it. An Augmented Dickey-Fuller test indicates that the series on executive approval is stationary ($p < 0.10$). Since ACFs and PACFs functions reveal a first-order autoregressive process, we start our analysis with a general autoregressive distributed lag model (De Boef and Keele, 2008) with partial restrictions based on the assumptions that some variables have an immediate effect only (cyclical and incumbency variables, at t) while others have a delayed effect (economic context and public opinion, at t+1). Moreover, given our limited number of observations, we partially adjust interactive models restricting our lagged dependent variable coefficient to be zero.[4]

[3] Note that we rely on annual rather than quarterly estimates of approval to examine the extent to which it is influenced by mass policy preferences. Estimating the policy mood is a data-demanding effort. Data availability is relatively scarce for the Spanish case, which impedes the estimation of the policy mood on a quarterly basis.

[4] We also considered accounting for specific events in our models, including the March 2004 terrorist attack in Madrid, the July 2008 onset and public acknowledgement of the economic crisis by Prime Minister Rodríguez-Zapatero, the Indignados protests of March 2011, and the June 2018 vote of no

Trends in Government Approval in Spain

Figure 8.1 displays the series of quarterly approval rates from the first quarter of 1985 through the second quarter of 2019 alongside the evolution of contextual factors that might have influenced it. As regards the economic context, the top figure displays the evolution of executive approval and that of quarterly unemployment rates. The two series are negatively correlated ($r = -0.72$, $p < 0.01$). The second panel shows the co-evolution of executive approval and public concerns over terrorism. These series are positively correlated ($r = 0.75$, $p < 0.01$). The third panel contrasts the evolution of executive approval and that of mood congruence, our measure of annual public opinion shifts in the left-right axis in the direction of the incumbent ideology. Higher values indicate shifts in the direction of the incumbent, while negative values mean that the public moves in the opposite direction. The correlation of annual values is substantially lower and only statistically significant at a lower confidence level ($r = 0.31, p < 0.10$).

Our approval series covers eleven cabinets and five heads of government from the two main parties: the centre-left Partido Socialista Obrero Español (PSOE) and the centre-right Partido Popular (PP). It begins in the final months of Felipe González's (PSOE) first term as prime minister. The first peak in the series coincides with the first two quarters of his second term in office, suggesting the existence of a typical honeymoon period. However, approval monotonically decreases afterwards, as the economy started to deteriorate very quickly. With approval rates at one of the lowest values in our series, González lost the 1996 elections and a minority government headed by the conservative leader José María Aznar (PP) came into power. Approval increased continuously through his first term in office. Benefitting from these high levels, in 2000 Aznar was re-elected with a parliamentary majority. These results allowed Aznar to take more conservative stances and his second term in office was characterized by a steady decrease in popularity. Again, an electoral defeat followed the deterioration of executive approval, which brought PSOE back to power with Rodríguez-Zapatero as prime minister this time.

confidence that ousted Rajoy's government. While the residuals of a baseline model are higher for the quarters in which these events happened, dummy event variables fail to reach statistical significance and including them does not substantially improve model fit. As a result, we decided to exclude them from the models reported in this chapter. Main results remain substantially the same if we include them.

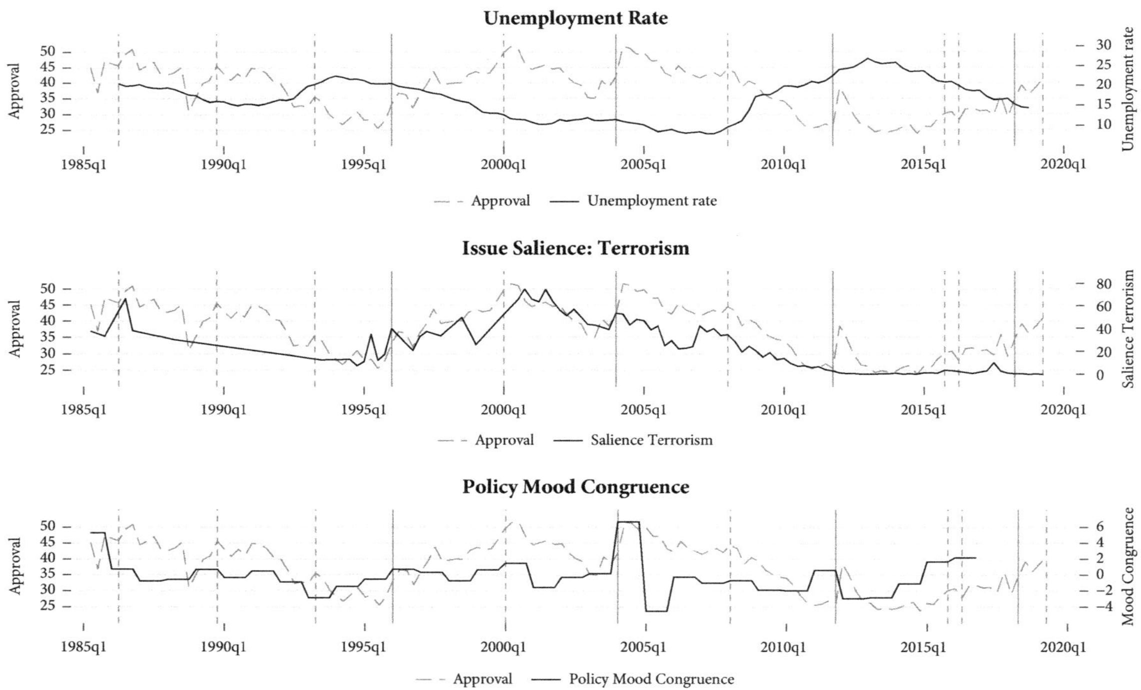

Figure 8.1 Quarterly approval of the government and the economy, terrorism salience, and policy mood congruence, Spain (1985–2019)

Source: Executive Approval Data V 2.0 from Carlin et al. (2019), terrorism salience based on CIS data, unemployment rates from OECD and policy mood from Bartle et.al (2020).
Note: Vertical dashed lines indicate general elections, whereas vertical solid lines indicate changes of head of government.

After an initial peak in popularity, the first term of Rodríguez-Zapatero in office eroded approval only to a moderate extent, allowing him to be re-elected in 2008. His second term coincided with the start of the Great Recession: approval dropped at a fast pace and Rodríguez-Zapatero called an early election in fall 2011. With popularity rates as low as those of González in his last months in power, the conservative PP won the elections again and Mariano Rajoy became the head of a majority government. After a sudden peak in popularity after the election, approval ratings went back to previous levels and even worsened, reaching the lowest values since 1985. Approval would only increase again as the economy recovered in the last part of the term (2014–2015). This partial recovery of Rajoy's popularity rates brought him into office in two consecutive elections (2015 and 2016), though without a majority government this time. In fact, in June 2018 PSOE won a vote of no confidence against Rajoy and Pedro Sánchez became the prime minister. Less than one year after his arrival in power, Sánchez called a snap election where he was re-elected due to his moderately good approval rates.

This first overview of the evolution of executive approval in Spain and its correlation with the variables displayed in Figure 8.1 suggests that approval is responsive to both political and economic stimuli.

The Effects of the Economy on Approval over Time

We begin our analysis by exploring the extent to which the economy—in this case, unemployment—influences executive approval in Spain and whether this effect has varied over time between 1986 and 2019. Building on the comparative analyses presented in the introductory chapter of this volume, we divide this time span into three periods: from the beginning of our series in 1986 until 11 September 2001. The terrorist attacks in the United States brought terrorism to the front of political debate, an issue that was already present in Spain. This first period also comprises an economic crisis that resulted in high unemployment rates between 1993 and 1997. The second period goes until the beginning of the 2008 Global Financial Crisis, which hit Southern European countries particularly hard. Given its notorious economic and political consequences, we take the start of the economic crisis (third quarter of 2008) as the breaking point of our third period which covers the Great Recession, a period of high unemployment.

The first model in Table 8.1 estimates the effect of unemployment rates on approval for the entire period. Results indicate that, as expected, unemployment is negatively associated with approval.[5] This finding is robust to alternative econometric specifications and seems to support our first expectation (H1). We then compare the influence of this variable over time in three separate models (2 to 4) and find that the economy influences executive approval ratings in the two periods that witnessed dramatic increases of unemployment rates: the first period including the 1990s recession, and the third one from the Great Recession onwards. The period in between these two crises, where unemployment rates remained relatively low, is a parenthesis in which the economy did not seem to have an impact on government's approval. In these models, we also control for cyclical effects and find evidence of both honeymoon effects and a sustained decline of approval as governments remain in power.

Table 8.1 The effect of the economy over time on quarterly approval in Spain (1986–2019)

	(1) 1986–2019	(2) 1986–2001	(3) 2001–2008	(4) 2008–2019
Unemployment rate$_{t-1}$	−0.794*	−1.269*	0.159	−1.495*
	(0.230)	(0.262)	(0.884)	(0.167)
Honeymoon$_t$	1.957*	3.246*	1.129	2.680*
	(0.792)	(1.185)	(2.096)	(0.991)
Months in power$_t$	−0.062*	−0.106*	−0.188*	−0.084*
	(0.0181)	(0.0231)	(0.0648)	(0.0151)
PP government $_{t-1}$	−0.263	−7.595*	5.007	1.880
	(1.427)	(2.417)	(4.615)	(1.261)
ENPP$_t$	−0.701	−10.99	−1.214	−1.840*
	(1.346)	(6.671)	(14.04)	(0.686)
Constant	56.73*	102.1*	51.59*	69.10*
	(9.89)	(5.24)	(1.35)	(14.56)
N	131	61	28	42
R^2	0.407	0.664	0.750	0.819

Source: Authors' own estimations based on data from the sources mentioned in the Data and Methods section.
Note: Cells report OLS coefficients with standard errors in parentheses, * p<0.05 (two-tailed test).

[5] Additional non-reported analyses suggest that subjective economic perceptions have an equivalent positive effect on approval through the whole period, although the coefficient for the last period fails to reach statistical significance.

Overall, we do not find a clear historical trend in the relation between the economy and approval ratings. Consistent with the introductory chapter of this volume and H2, we find a somewhat u-shaped trend, in which the economy had an impact in the first period (1986–2001), lost its relevance in the second one (2001–2008), and became more influential from the onset of the Great Recession (2008–2019). The two periods in which unemployment had a stronger effect on approval are the two in which economic crises destroyed jobs, while unemployment didn't play a significant role in the period of economic growth and low unemployment rates. These results suggest an asymmetric effect by which governments are more punished for high unemployment rates than rewarded for low ones.

We next turn to the role of party-system dynamics, with a particular focus on the moderating effect its size might have on the impact of unemployment on approval. Models in Table 8.1 include a measure of party-system fragmentation, whose coefficients are consistently negative but only reach statistical significance in one of the three periods. In particular, party-system fragmentation lowers approval ratings once the imperfect two-party system collapsed and new national challenger parties emerged. Thus, fragmentation had only a direct effect on approval ratings from 2008 onwards.

To analyse whether party-system fragmentation had an additional effect via the economy, Table 8.2 displays the results of a first regression model where we interact the effective number of parties and unemployment. We hypothesized that the magnitude of the effect of the economy on government popularity decreases as the party system becomes more fragmented. However, results do not support this assumption. First, the number of parties does not seem to have any direct effect on executive approval. Second, when we interact its effect with that of unemployment rates (Model 1), this interactive coefficient fails to reach statistical significance. Thus, party-system fragmentation does not seem to have blurred attribution of responsibility vis-à-vis executive approval.

Approval Dynamics beyond the Economy

As expected, we find that unemployment is negatively associated with approval ratings.[6] The three models of Table 8.2 include the salience of terrorism, which we measure as the percentage of respondents considering terrorism as one of the three most important problems facing Spain. In line with our expectation

[6] The results remain the same if we use public subjective perceptions of the state of the economy. When the public perceive good economic performance, approval tends to increase. This effect is not moderated by party-system fragmentation.

Table 8.2 The effect of party-system fragmentation and issue salience on quarterly approval in Spain (1986–2019)

	(1) Prais-Linear	(2) ADL	(3) Prais-Linear
$Approval_{t-1}$		0.571*	
		(0.0702)	
Unemployment rate $_{t-1}$	−0.812	−0.154	−0.617*
	(0.984)	(0.0806)	(0.181)
$Honeymoon_t$	1.398	1.290	1.404
	(0.827)	(0.719)	(0.824)
Months in $power_t$	−0.053*	−0.023*	−0.053*
	(0.016)	(0.008)	(0.016)
Issue salience—$terrorism_{t-1}$	0.133*	0.118*	0.136*
	(0.038)	(0.028)	(0.037)
PP $government_t$	−1.521	−1.654*	−1.525
	(1.291)	(0.712)	(1.260)
$ENPP_t$	−1.311	1.319*	0.128
	(7.193)	(0.615)	(1.199)
Unemployment $rate_{t-1}$ × $ENPP_t$	0.074		
	(0.370)		
Constant	51.82*	13.93*	47.89*
	(2.62)	(3.78)	(8.97)
N	131	131	131
R^2	0.522	0.862	0.526

Source: Authors' own estimations based on data from the sources mentioned in the Data and Methods section.
Note: Cells report parameter estimates with standard errors in parentheses, * p<0.05 (two-tailed test).

(H4), the positive and significant effect of terrorism on approval suggests that when terrorism becomes more salient, government popularity tends to increase. When public concern with terrorist attacks rises, it triggers a popularity boost consistent with the rally-round-the-flag-effect theory. Moreover, the effect of terrorism is not conditioned by the ideology of the incumbent party. Although previous work suggests that in times of terror public opinion tends to move towards conservative positions (Godefroidt, 2023), we fail to find significant differences in the rally effects of terrorism between left-wing (PSOE) and right-wing (PP) governments.[7]

[7] Although we do not include the model in this chapter, the interaction between issue salience—terrorism and government's ideology is not statistically significant.

ETA announced the definitive cessation of its armed activity in 2011. Until then, it was a constant threat that produced many yearly fatalities and inevitably affected Spanish political debate. Furthermore, the last years of ETA overlapped with a new wave of international terrorism, with one large-scale terrorist attack in Madrid in 2004. Within this context, public concerns have not always matched the number of attacks or victims. Additional analyses not reported in these pages suggest that, in contrast to the main results included in Table 8.2, the number of casualties from terrorist attacks does not predict approval as accurately as public concerns do. Issue salience is, thus, a better measure to capture public attention to a long-standing problem in Spanish history.

Finally, in order to scrutinize the association between the abovementioned *policy mood congruence* and executive approval, we estimate a series of models using annual time series, reported in Table 8.3.[8] Using annual data, we corroborate the influence of the two most crucial factors we have identified in our analyses of the quarterly data, namely unemployment and salience of terrorism. Models 1 and 2 indicate again the negative consequences of unemployment[9] for government popularity as well as the positive association between executive approval and the salience of terrorism.

Models 3 and 4 explore the role of mood congruence, both in a simple model with LDV and mood congruence, as well as in a full model. The coefficients for mood congruence in both models suggest that approval grows when the mood gets closer to government positions. By contrast, when the public moves in the opposite direction of the incumbent's ideology, approval declines. Thus, the dynamic relation between public opinion and government ideology is an important determinant of executive approval, as predicted by our Hypothesis 5. While the effect of congruence is typically analysed looking at how governments adapt to mass preferences, we show that the extent to which the public moves closer to government positions is equally important, as it is systematically linked to approval ratings.

[8] In our annual analysis we do not lag our independent variables, as we assume that the fluctuation within the same year is already incorporated in the approval ratings of that same year. We exclusively lag our dependent variable to account for the series memory.

[9] In alternative annual models, we find that other economic indicators like GDP growth or public perceptions of the state of the economy do not exhibit any statistically significant association with approval ratings.

Table 8.3 The effect of policy mood congruence on annual approval in Spain (1985–2016)

	(1)	(2)	(3)	(4)
Approval$_{t-1}$	0.398*	0.696*	0.838*	0.547*
	(0.167)	(0.093)	(0.082)	(0.212)
Unemployment rate$_{t-1}$	−0.541*			−0.171
	(0.181)			(0.214)
Issue salience—terrorism$_{t-1}$		0.086*		0.0741
		(0.029)		(0.036)
Mood congruence$_t$			0.994*	0.744*
			(0.259)	(0.345)
Constant	29.18*	8.496*	5.672	16.50
	(8.220)	(3.068)	(2.940)	(10.04)
N	29	35	32	26
R^2	0.720	0.769	0.805	0.826

Source: Authors' own estimations based on data from the sources mentioned in the Data and Methods section.
Note: Cells report OLS coefficients with standard errors in parentheses, * $p<0.05$ (two-tailed test).

Conclusion

The few studies available on popularity functions in Spain have reached the conclusion that the economy is an important factor to explain government approval. This chapter aims to advance our understanding of the role of the economy for approval over time as well as identifying non-economic factors that might be equally important for a comprehensive account of approval dynamics in Spain. More specifically, we scrutinize whether the predominance of the economy still holds once we consider the role of other factors such as clarity of responsibility, issue salience, or public preferences. To do so, we rely on the Executive Approval Database (Carlin et al., 2019), which combines poll marginals for both national government and prime minister popularity.

Our results support the notion that the economy indeed matters in the Spanish case. The influence of economic factors, however, fluctuates over time: while governments tend to be punished for high unemployment rates, we find that unemployment was less crucial between 2001 and 2008, a period in which the Spanish economy grew, and unemployment rates remained low. However, we do not find support for our hypothesis on the moderating effect of party-system fragmentation. The important changes that the Spanish party system have witnessed in the last decade have not blurred responsibility in a way that could reduce the negative consequences of poor economic performance for executive approval. Remarkably enough, these findings are very much in line with the evidence included in other chapters of this volume.

As regards non-economic factors, we find that issue salience can be equally important. Our study focuses on the salience of terrorism, one of the top concerns of Spaniards according to survey data. The results robustly show that when public concern about terrorism increases, so do approval ratings. We argue that such dynamic is consistent with a rally-round-the-flag effect.

Finally, the present study scrutinizes the link between policy mood and executive approval. In particular, we transform the Spanish policy mood (Bartle et al., 2020) into a *policy mood congruence* measure that captures public opinion shifts that increase (or decrease) the ideological congruence between the public and the incumbent. Our findings show that government popularity grows when policy mood moves in the direction of government's ideology. Hence, when mood moves to the left, approval increases if the incumbent is the Socialist Party, but the opposite takes place with PP governments. Our results are consistent with the hypothesis that executive approval partly depends on the congruence between public opinion and government policy and with some of the causal mechanisms studied by the literature on dynamic representation: when mass preferences deviate from government ideology, the popularity of the latter deteriorates, and this may provoke electoral turnover.

In sum, our findings imply that the economy continues to be a crucial factor behind government popularity in Spain, but also sheds light on non-economic issues that have received much less attention. Executive approval seems to be shaped by issue salience and ideological congruence as well, and we could expect such mechanisms to be present not only in Spain but also elsewhere.

This chapter has mainly focused on the role of unemployment to explain incumbents' popularity. Future research might examine the potential impact of other economic drivers of approval rates such as inflation. More relevantly, in further iterations of this piece it could be interesting to assess whether and how coalition government shapes popularity dynamics in Spanish politics from now onwards. Finally, it seems safe to expect that, with the end of domestic terrorism, the rally effect provoked by the salience of this issue among Spanish citizens will no longer determine approval levels in the future. Expanding this result to other issues constitutes a pending task for scholars interested in establishing the determinants of leaders' popularity in Spain.

References

Anderson, C. J. (2000). Economic voting and political context: A comparative perspective. *Electoral Studies, 19*(2–3), 151–70.

Aragonés, E. (1997). Negativity effect and the emergence of ideologies. *Journal of Theoretical Politics, 9*(2), 189–210.

Bartle, J., Bosch A., and Orriols, L. (2020). The policy mood in Spain: The thermostat in a warm climate, 1978–2017. *European Political Science Review, 12*(2), 133–53.

Bartle, J., Dellepiane Avellaneda, S. and McGann, A. (2019). Policy accommodation versus electoral turnover: Policy representation in Britain, 1945–2015. *Journal of Public Policy, 39*(2), 235–65.

Bartle, J., Dellepiane Avellaneda, S., and Stimson, J. A. (2011). The moving centre: Preferences for government activity in Britain, 1950–2005. *British Journal of Political* Science, *41*(2), 259–85.

Bellucci, P. and Lewis-Beck, M. (2011). A stable popularity function? Cross-national analysis. *European Journal of Political Research, 50*(2), 190–211.

Bosch, A., and Riba, C. (2005). Coyuntura económica y voto en España, 1985–1996. *Papers*, 75, 117–40.

Campbell, A., Converse, P. E., Miller, W. E., and Stokes, D. E. (1960). *The American Voter*. New York: John Wiley and Sons.

Campbell, J. E. (2005). Why Bush won the presidential election of 2004: Incumbency, ideology, terrorism, and turnout. *Political Science Quarterly, 120*(2), 219–41.

Carlin, R. E., Hartlyn, J., Hellwig, T., Love, G. J., Martinez-Gallardo, C., and Singer. M. M. (2019). Executive Approval Database 2.0. Available for download at www.executiveapproval.org.

Chaqués Bonafont, L., and Palau, A. M. (2011). Assessing the responsiveness of Spanish policymakers to the priorities of their citizens. *West European Politics, 34*(4), 706–30.

Clarke, H. D., and Stewart, M. (1995). Economic evaluations, prime ministerial approval and governing party support: Rival models reconsidered. *British Journal of Political Science 25*(2), 145–70.

Costas-Pérez, E., Solé-Ollé, A., and Sorribas-Navarro, P. (2012). Corruption scandals, voter information, and accountability. *European Journal of Political Economy, 28*(4), 469–84.

Costa Lobo, M. and Pannico, R. (2020). Increased economic salience or blurring of responsibility? Economic voting during the great recession. *Electoral Studies, 65*, 102141.

De Boef, S., and Keele, L. (2008). Taking time seriously. *American Journal of Political Science, 52*(1), 184–200.

De la Calle, L., and Orriols, L. (2010). Explaining the electoral effects of public investments: The case of the expansion of the underground in Madrid, 1995–2007. *European Journal of Political Research*, *49*(3), 393–417.

Edwards, G. C., Mitchell, W., and Welch., R. (1995). Explaining presidential approval: The significance of issue salience. *American Journal of Political Science*, *39*(1), 108–34.

Erikson, R. S., MacKuen, M. D., and Stimson, J. A. (2002). *The Macro Polity*. Cambridge: Cambridge University Press.

Fiorina, M. P. (1981). *Retrospective Voting in American National Elections*. New Haven, CT: Yale University Press.

Fraile, M. (2002). El voto económico en las elecciones de 1996 y 2000: Una comparación. *Revista Española de Ciencia Política*, *6*, 129–51.

Fraile, M., and Lewis-Beck, M. S. (2010). Economic voting in Spain: A 2000 panel test. *Electoral Studies*, *29*(2), 210–20.

Fraile, M. and Lewis-Beck, M. S. (2012). Economic and elections in Spain (1982–2008): Cross-measures, cross-time. *Electoral Studies*, *31*(3), 485–90.

Fraile, M. and Lewis-Beck, M. S. (2014a). Economic vote instability: Endogeneity or restricted variance? Spanish panel evidence from 2008 and 2011. *European Journal of Political Research*, *53*(1), 160–79.

Fraile, M. and Lewis-Beck, M. S. (2014b). Es la economía y es la austeridad, estúpido: las consecuencias electorales de las políticas de recesión en las elecciones 2011. In *Elecciones generales* 2011, E. Anduiza, A. Bosch, L. Orriols, and G. Rico eds. Madrid: Centro de Investigaciones Sociológicas. 127–42.

Godefroidt, A. (2023). How terrorism does (and does not) affect citizens' political attitudes: A meta-analysis. *American Journal of Political Science*, *67*(1), 22–38.

Hamann, K. (2000). Linking policies and economic voting: Explaining reelection in the case of the Spanish Socialist Party. *Comparative Political Studies*, *33*(8), 1018–48.

Hetherington, M. J., and Nelson, M. (2017). Anatomy of a rally effect: George W. Bush and the war on terrorism. *PS: Political Science and Politics*, *36*(1), 37–42.

Holbrook A. L., Krosnick, J. A., Visser, P. S., Gardner, W. L., and Cacioppo, J. T. (2001). Attitudes toward presidential candidates and political parties: Initial optimism, inertial first impressions, and a focus on flaws. *American Journal of Political Science*, *45*(4), 930–50.

Kiewiet, D. R. (1983). *Macroeconomic and Micropolitics: The Electoral Effects of Economic Issues*. Chicago, IL: University of Chicago Press.

Kritzinger, S., Foucault, M., Lachat, R., Partheymüller, J., Plescia, C., and Brouard, S. (2021). 'Rally round the flag': The COVID-19 crisis and trust in the national government. *West European Politics*, *44*(5–6), 1205–31.

Krosnick, J. A. (1990). Government policy and citizen passion: A study of issue publics in contemporary America. *Political Behavior*, *12*(1), 59–92.

Krosnick, J. A., Boninger, D. S., Chuang, Y. C., Berent, M. K., and C. G. Carnot (1993). Attitude strength: One construct or many related constructs? *Journal of Personality and Social Psychology*, *65*(6), 1132–51.

Lancaster, T. D. and Lewis-Beck, M. S. (1986). The Spanish voter: Tradition, economics, ideology. *Journal of Politics*, *48*(3), 648–74.

Lau, R. R. 1985. Two explanations for negativity effects in political behavior. *American Journal of Political Science*, *29*, 119–38.

Lee, J. R. (1977). Rallying around the flag: Foreign policy events and presidential popularity. *Presidential Studies Quarterly*, *7*(4), 252–6.

León, S. (2012). How do citizens attribute responsibility in multilevel states? Learning, biases and asymmetric federalism: Evidence from Spain. *Electoral Studies*, *31*(1), 120–30.

León, S., and Orriols, L. (2016). Asymmetric federalism and economic voting. *European Journal of Political Research*, *55*(4), 847–65.

Lewis-Beck, M. S. (1988). *Economics and Elections: The Major Western Democracies*. Ann Arbor, MI: University of Michigan Press.

Lewis-Beck, M., and Nadeau, R. (2012). PIGS or not? Economic voting in Southern Europe. *Electoral Studies*, *31*(3), 472–7.

Lewis-Beck, M. S., and Stegmaier, M. (2013). The VP-function revisited: A survey of the literature on vote and popularity functions after over 40 years. *Public Choice 157*, 367–85.

Maravall, J. M., and Fraile, M. (2000). Desempleo y política. *Revista Española de Ciencia Política*, *1*(2), 7–42.

Maravall, J. M., and Przeworski, A. (1999). Reacciones políticas a la economía. *Revista Española de Investigaciones Sociológicas*, 87, 11–52.

Mueller, J. E. (1970). Presidential popularity from Truman to Johnson. *American Political Science Review*, *64*(1), 18–34.

Nannestad, P., and Paldam, M. (1997). Grievance asymmetry revisited: A micro study of economic voting in Denmark, 1986–1992. *European Journal of Political Economy*, *13*, 81–99.

Orriols, L., and Cordero, G. (2016). The breakdown of the Spanish two-party system: The upsurge of Podemos and Ciudadanos in the 2015 general election. *South European Society and Politics*, *21*(4), 469–92.

Orriols, L. and Rico, G. (2014). El clima de opinión. In *Elecciones generales* 2011, E. Anduiza, A. Bosch, L. Orriols, and G. Rico, eds. Madrid: Centro de Investigaciones Sociológicas. 63–82.

Palau, A. M., and Davesa, F. (2013). The impact of media coverage of corruption on Spanish public opinion. *Revista Española de Investigaciones Sociológicas*, *144*, 97–124.

Paldam, M. (1991). How robust is the vote function? A study of seventeen nations over four decades. In *Economics and Politics: The Calculus of Support*,

H. Norpoth and M. Lewis-Beck, eds. Ann Arbor, MI: University of Michigan Press. 9–31.

Powell, G. B., and Whitten, G. D. (1993). A cross-national analysis of economic voting: Taking account of political context. *American Journal of Political Science*, *37*(2), 391–414.

Rico, G. (2009). *Líderes políticos, opinión pública y comportamiento electoral en España*. Madrid: Centro de Investigaciones Sociológicas.

Rico, G. (2010). El impacto de los líderes en las elecciones de 2008 y más allá. In *Elecciones Generales* 2008, J. R. Montero and I. Lago, eds. Madrid: Centro de Investigaciones Sociológicas. 303–30.

Riera, P., Barberá, P., Gómez, R., Mayoral, J. A., and Montero, J. R. (2013). The electoral consequences of corruption scandals in Spain. *Crime, Law and Social Change*, *60*(5), 515–34.

Romero-Vidal, X. (2020). Two temperatures for one thermostat: The evolution of policy attitudes and support for independence in Catalonia (1991–2018). *Nations and Nationalism*, *26*(4), 960–78.

Sanders, D., Ward, H., and Marsh, D. (1987). Government popularity and the Falklands War: A reassessment. *British Journal of Political Science*, *17*(3), 281–313.

Stevenson, R. T. (2001). The economy and policy mood: A fundamental dynamic of democratic politics? *American Journal of Political Science*, *45*(3), 620–33.

Stimson, J. A. (1999). *Public Opinion in America: Moods, Cycles and Sings*. Boulder, CO: Westview Press.

Van Hauwaert, S. M., and Huber, R. A. (2020). In-group solidarity or out-group hostility in response to terrorism in France? Evidence from a regression discontinuity design. *European Journal of Political Research*, *59*(4), 936–53.

Vidal, G. (2018). Challenging business as usual? The rise of new parties in Spain in times of crisis. *West European Politics*, *41*(2), 261–86.

9

Federal Government Approval in Canada

Economics, Politics, and Fiscal Policy in Changing Times

Éric Bélanger and Olivier Jacques

As in most Western democracies, the link between economics, politics, and executive popularity has been found to be prevalent in Canada. However, the study of the popularity function in Canada has been relatively slow to emerge, with the first studies published in the mid-1980s reporting only a weak relationship between economics and popularity (Monroe and Erickson, 1986; Clarke and Zuk, 1987). But as Johnston (1999, 504) later argued, these early weak results may have been due to the fact that the time period these studies covered preceded Canada's 'quickening of the economic agenda' with the federal government working to address the inflation crisis of the 1970s and establish free-trade relations with the United States, then Mexico, starting in the 1980s.

Further popularity functions showed a significant relationship between macroeconomic indicators and the popularity of the Canadian government, yet they also hinted at a possible break starting in the early 1990s. The weakening impact of the economy on government support has been attributed by some to a fragmented opposition in the Canadian House of Commons following the rise of a new multi-party system in the 1993 federal election (Johnston, 1999; Pickup, 2004). In this chapter, we contend that the decline of the effect of the economy may also be related to the Canadian government's macroeconomic agenda shifting to budget deficit reduction around that same period (Haffert, 2019). We believe the possible impact of fiscal performance on the dynamics of executive popularity in Canada needs to be investigated, as it constitutes a recent key development in the political and economic landscape of the country.

We explore this question by constructing a popularity function for Canada that covers the period 1978–2018. Canada being a federation, we note at the outset that we only investigate popularity at the *federal* level and, for clarity

Éric Bélanger and Olivier Jacques, *Federal Government Approval in Canada*. In: *Economics and Politics Revisited*. Edited by: Timothy Hellwig and Matthew Singer, Oxford University Press. © Éric Bélanger and Olivier Jacques (2023). DOI: 10.1093/oso/9780192871664.003.0009

reasons, in this chapter we thus refer to federal government approval instead of executive approval. We aim to answer this volume's two core research questions: what moves government approval in Canada, and how has this changed over time? Our popularity function includes several macroeconomic, political, and fiscal policy variables as predictors of federal government approval. This chapter makes two additional contributions. First, it considers the impact of *fiscal policy performance* on executive approval, a factor that has not received enough attention in the popularity function literature more generally. Second, for the first time in Canada we make use of a direct measure of government approval. Extant studies of the Canadian popularity function have all relied, so far, on vote intention data as a measure of executive popularity, but thanks to the data collection efforts of the Executive Approval Project (EAP) we now have for Canada an indicator of *actual approval*. This brings our Canadian popularity function work more in line with the relevant comparative literature than was possible before.

Our analysis of the determinants of federal government approval in Canada indicates that, among macroeconomic factors, inflation has a robust negative effect on approval. Results further show that economic effects are weakening over time during the period under study. We finally show that individual and corporate income taxes, as well as budget balance, influence federal government approval. These fiscal effects, moreover, clearly indicate that the effect of budget balance has changed over time. Around the early 1990s, Canadians started to reward the federal government for their budget control efforts, whereas they were rewarding it for running deficits in the previous era.

Chapter findings provide additional perspective for our understanding of the dynamics and sources of government approval in Canada. They point to the general role of economic performance, but also to the weakening of its influence. They also suggest that the government's austerity discourse and actions, put forward since the 1990s, have convinced a significant proportion of Canadians of the purported benefits of a balanced federal budget. In that respect, our findings provide support to one of the theoretical perspectives laid out in this volume's introduction, according to which the salience of certain issues has changed over time. In our case, the salience of the economy has declined, in part because the transformation of the fiscal policy regime has put budget deficit reduction at the forefront of governments' objectives. The other two factors that this volume argues may be driving the decline of the economy's influence do not seem to apply to the Canadian case. For one, Canada has Westminster-style institutional features where clarity of responsibility is strong (Anderson, 2000), thus facilitating the mechanism of economic accountability despite the presence of multilevel governance (Anderson, 2008). For another, Canada has relatively weak partisan identification and polarization, especially when compared to its American neighbour (Clarke et al., 2009; see also Chapter 13 on the United States). This suggests that the driving factors reducing the economy's importance are due to its salience and not these other factors.

Economics and Politics in Canada: Bringing Fiscal Policy into the Picture

In the comparative political behaviour literature, popularity functions have a long history (for a useful review, see Lewis-Beck and Stegmaier, 2013). This body of work has helped inform the field of economic voting, which shows that the citizens of Western democracies generally hold their governments accountable for the state of the economy (see, e.g. Duch and Stevenson, 2008; Nadeau et al., 2013). Beyond economics, studies of the popularity function demonstrate that government approval is driven by several other factors that are more political in nature, such as the cost of ruling or rally-round-the-flag effects following the onset of a national political crisis.

In Canada, at the federal level, several studies of economic voting confirm a link between economic conditions and incumbency voting (e.g. Carmichael, 1990; Nadeau and Blais, 1993; Gélineau and Bélanger, 2005; Anderson, 2008). Popularity function work has also uncovered a relationship between government popularity and a host of macroeconomic and/or political factors (Monroe and Erickson, 1986; Clarke and Zuk, 1987; Pétry and Harmatz, 1995; Johnston, 1999; Pickup, 2004). However, data constraints mean these popularity functions have had to rely on voting intentions over time rather than approval ratings per se. Yet, we know that vote intention and approval are not exactly the same, and that models relying on the former tend to underestimate the impact of the economy on government support (see Pickup, 2010) because vote intentions depend on the behaviour of other parties, or on citizens' identification with specific parties (Jacques and Haffert, 2021).[1]

What do these previous studies highlight as the determinants of federal government approval in Canada? First, economics matter, but it does so in a rather inconsistent way. Some studies have reported a link between unemployment and government popularity (Pétry and Harmatz, 1995; Pickup, 2004) while

[1] See Chapter 2 in this volume for more discussion of vote functions versus popularity functions.

others found no such relationship (Monroe and Erickson, 1986; Clarke and Zuk, 1987; Johnston, 1999). Similarly, inflation matters to the popularity function in some studies (Johnston, 1999; Pickup, 2004) but not in others (Monroe and Erickson, 1986; Clarke and Zuk, 1987; Pétry and Harmatz, 1995). As for economic growth, some scholars show a significant relationship with government support (Pétry and Harmatz, 1995; Johnston, 1999) while others report null findings (Monroe and Erickson, 1986). The work on provincial government popularity has tended to confirm an effect for unemployment, but not for inflation nor economic growth (Tellier, 2006). These contradictory economic findings thus call for further investigation on our part.

Second, politics matter as well. Congruent with results from several popularity functions developed elsewhere, extant studies indicate that federal government support in Canada is affected positively by post-election honeymoons and negatively by the cost of ruling (Clarke and Zuk, 1987; Pétry and Harmatz, 1995). The provincial-level work of Tellier (2006) confirms both effects. In addition, some popularity functions have shown a growth in the support of the federal government in the wake of various Quebec-related constitutional crises that threatened the national community over the years (Monroe and Erickson, 1986; Clarke and Zuk, 1987). These various political factors certainly ought to be considered when developing and testing our own popularity function.[2]

Third and last, while the contradictory economic results found for Canada can certainly be attributable to the adoption of different methodologies, they may also be due to variability of economic effects over time. More precisely, both Johnston (1999) and Pickup (2004) have suggested that the new multiparty system that emerged in 1993 may have altered the relationship between economics and government popularity in Canada. Indeed, the October 1993 federal election is a landmark in Canadian politics. The government led by the Progressive Conservative Party of Canada suffered the worst defeat of an incumbent in Canadian history, holding 156 seats before the election and keeping only two after it. This decline is clearly reflected in our popularity data, as the Progressive Conservative government had the worst approval rating of the period covered, with an average net approval of −33.65 from 1991 up till the 1993 election. This defeat marked the end of the 'two and a half' federal party system and led to a multi-party system divided along regional lines

[2] Leadership conventions and change, and the provincial origin of leaders, have also been considered in some studies (Clarke and Zuk, 1987; Pétry and Harmatz, 1995; Johnston, 1999) but their effect is likely to be captured, at least partially, by some of the other political factors reviewed here and are not considered in our analysis.

(Johnston, 2017). Thus, the post-1993 fragmentation of the opposition may have blurred the lines of economic accountability. By diluting the clarity of available alternatives (Anderson, 2000), it may have weakened the relationship between economics and government support in Canada.

That said, there may be an additional reason explaining a possible decline of economic effects on executive approval in Canada. In particular, a shift in the fiscal policy regime[3] may have triggered change in how citizens assess government performance. Popularity function work conducted in the United Kingdom (Pissarides, 1980; Sanders et al., 1987; Clarke and Stewart, 1995; Clarke et al., 2000) and the United States (Geys and Vermeir, 2008a) has shown a negative relationship between taxation and executive approval. Such a relationship has also been reported for Denmark (Paldam and Schneider, 1980) and Germany (Geys and Vermeir, 2008b). A similar negative link between budgetary deficits and government approval has also been found in some US popularity functions (Cebula, 2005; Geys and Vermeir, 2008a; Berlemann and Enkelmann, 2014). These various findings suggest that citizens react to governments' fiscal decisions. In general, the same reward-punishment mechanism as the one found in economic voting studies seems to be at work: citizens support governments more (less) when taxation is low (high) and when the budget balance is positive (negative). This aversion of voters to taxes and deficits is not only a matter of them reacting as egotropic consumers; it is also related to a sociotropic concern on their part about government efficiency (Pissarides, 1980; Rose, 1985; Happy, 1992; Bansak et al., 2021).

Yet while public opinion studies show that voters punish governments for budget deficits, classical political economy models generally posit that voters exhibit a deficit bias, as they are unconcerned about budget deficits. In these models, voters reward governments for spending more and/or reducing taxes, while discounting the negative consequences of additional deficits in the future. This encourages government to engage in political budget cycles during which taxes are lowered and spending is increased before elections (Buchanan and Wagner, 1977). The empirical section below allows us to disentangle these two claims.

Fiscal policy factors have been largely ignored in previous Canadian studies of government popularity. Tellier's (2006) research on provincial-level vote intentions has looked at income tax and budgetary balance, finding that only the latter had a statistically significant effect. At the federal level, the available

[3] By fiscal policy regime, we mean 'the configuration of political interests, institutions and policy arrangements that structure conflicts over taxes and spending' (Pierson, 2001, 56).

evidence is even more scant. In a footnote, Johnston (1999, 505n10) reports inconclusive results associated with budget balance, while Happy's (1992) vote function model reveals a negative effect of income taxation on aggregate-level incumbency voting from 1953 to 1988. In short, much remains to be investigated when it comes to the impact of fiscal policy performance on federal government approval in Canada.

The question of the control of the public deficit and debt has proven to be a prominent economic issue in Canada during the period covered in our study. After the 1993 election, the Canadian government entered a new fiscal era. In the 1970s and 1980s, the government sustained large deficits in every budget. The early 1990s recession hit the Canadian economy particularly hard, contributing to even larger budget deficits and to unsustainable interest-rate payments of the public debt. By the early 1990s, interest payments on the federal government's public debt reached 6 per cent of the GDP, which represented almost 30 per cent of its expenditures. The 1994 Mexican peso crisis was the straw that broke the camel's back, as it prompted fears of a devaluation of the Canadian dollar and an ensuing sovereign debt crisis. The International Monetary Fund was knocking at the door with a painful structural adjustment plan (Lewis, 2003). Around that time, the deficit rose in salience among the Canadian citizenry, as shown in public opinion data displayed in Figure 9.1.

Such a crisis represented a critical juncture that led to a paradigm shift, as the policy priorities and the main tools to achieve them changed (Hall, 1993). It provided an opportunity for the newly appointed Chrétien government of the Liberal Party of Canada to implement significant reforms that would change

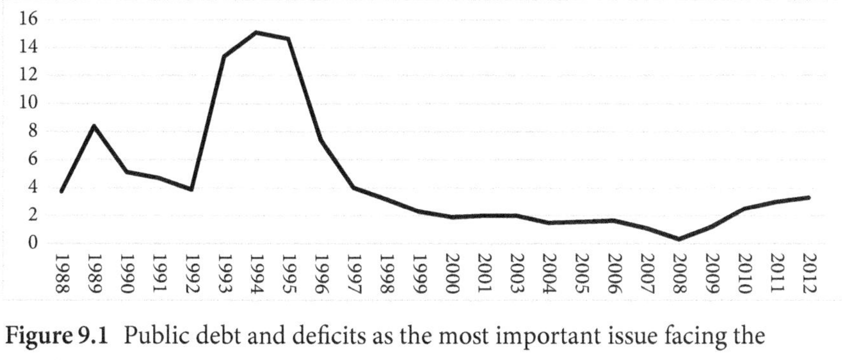

Figure 9.1 Public debt and deficits as the most important issue facing the country

Source: Environics Focus Canada.

Note: Percentage of Canadians saying public debt or deficits are the most important issue facing the country, yearly averages based on quarterly closed-ended questions.

fiscal policymaking for decades (Haffert, 2019). The government implemented two major reforms of the budget process. Firstly, it instituted a permanent programme review to evaluate the relevance of each public programme. More importantly, the concentration of power towards the prime minister and the minister of finance induced fiscal discipline by reinforcing the power of central agencies—the guardians of the public purse—over line departments (Savoie, 1999). The Chrétien government also implemented a 30 per cent cut to transfers towards the provinces to balance the budget, a move that forced provinces to implement fiscal consolidation measures.

To balance budgets, the government had to permanently transform the ideas, institutions, and the balance of power around fiscal policy. This required a transformation of Canada's fiscal regime from a 'deficit regime', unable to balance budgets, to a 'surplus regime' in which balancing budget and even creating permanent surpluses became the primary objective pursued by fiscal policy (Haffert, 2019). The fiscal consolidation of the early 1990s was almost entirely composed of expenditure cuts rather than tax increases, which contributed to the instalment of a surplus regime. Expenditure-focused consolidations weakened political coalitions that are in favour of additional public spending, notably by reducing the number of public-sector workers by 14 per cent (forty-five thousand employees) (Lewis, 2003). Moreover, a retrenchment of public services changes citizens' expectations, as they expect further cuts to public services and, therefore, anticipate relying less on the state (Haffert, 2019).

What is more, these consolidation measures were supported by most federal parties—with some, like the Reform Party, advocating for even harsher measures—while cuts to federal transfers forced provincial governments of all stripes to implement consolidations. The discourse about the importance of balancing budgets and implementing 'austerity' measures became dominant in Canada and worldwide (Blyth, 2013). However, consolidation measures and the entrenchment of surplus regimes were successful only in certain countries, like Canada (Haffert, 2019), which makes the study of the Canadian case particularly relevant. The surplus regime lasted at least until the 2015 election during which the Liberal Party broke with fiscal orthodoxy by promising to run deficits to increase public spending.

We thus expect that the entrenchment of the austerity discourse and the change of fiscal policy regime altered how citizens react to budget deficits. The period before 1993 was characterized by fiscal profligacy, whereas sustaining budget balance became a central objective of the government in the era after 1993. Fiscal policies were thus significantly different between the two periods. Before 1993, we expect citizens to follow classical models of preferences regarding fiscal policies and exhibit a deficit bias. In contrast, after 1993, we expect citizens to punish governments for a deterioration of the budget balance and to reward them for a reduction in deficits.

Several opinion polls support these expectations. In 1993, concern for the deficit surpassed unemployment as the most important policy issue for Canadians. Our systematic review of opinion polls[4] reveals that the proportion of Canadians saying it is very important for the federal government to reduce the deficit increased from only 50 per cent in the 1980s to around 75 per cent in the early to mid-1990s, before going down afterwards, as shown in Figure 9.2. At the same time, the proportion approving the way the federal government is handling debt and deficit reduction increased significantly from the late 1980s until the 2008 financial crisis. Clearly, citizens' views of the deficit changed after the early 1990s as they became more deficit averse. With budget deficits becoming a more important problem than other economic issues like unemployment or inflation, we can expect traditional macroeconomic indicators to have a lesser impact on executive approval after 1993.

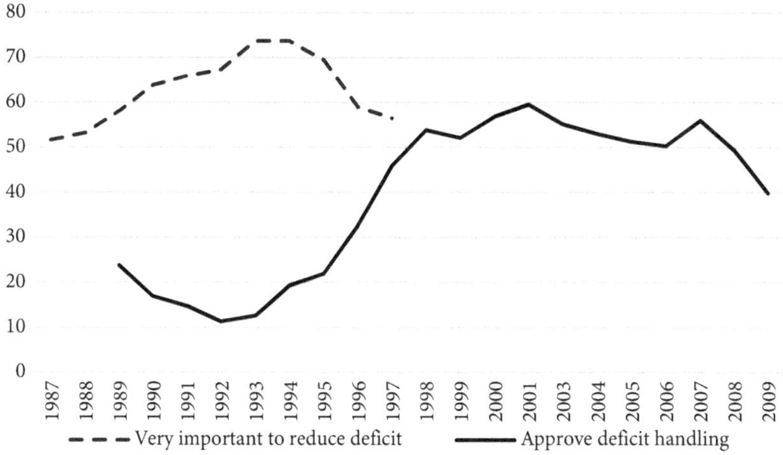

Figure 9.2 Approval and importance of deficit reduction

Source: Environics Focus Canada.

Note: Percentage of Canadians saying it is very important that the federal government try to reduce the deficit (dashed line) and those who approve the way the federal government is handling deficit and debt reduction, yearly data.

[4] Unfortunately, few surveys allow us to compare the evolution of Canadians' opinions since the late 1970s, since most surveys on the issue started in the late 1980s when the issue became salient in the public debate.

These various considerations lead us to express the following three hypotheses regarding the impact of economics and politics on federal government approval in Canada:

H1a: Government approval is responsive to changes to economic conditions, as voters reward governments for good economic conditions and punish them for bad economic conditions.
H1b: Government approval is positively affected by honeymoons and constitutional crises and negatively affected by the cost of ruling.
H1c: The effect of economic conditions on government approval weakens after 1993.

If our argument about the public's changing issue priorities is right, then we should observe not only a decline in the effect of the economy, but we also expect that the impact of fiscal policy on approval changes overtime:

H2: Citizens reward governments for higher deficits before 1993, while they punish governments for higher deficits after 1993.

We explore in more detail the effect of fiscal policies on government approval by analysing the effect of changes to taxes and expenditures. We expect that citizens will react particularly strongly to changes in visible taxes and expenditures, but not to changes in less visible ones. As such, citizens should respond negatively to higher income taxes, since these taxes are visible and directly reduce citizens' disposable income. In contrast, we expect that citizens do not react negatively to increases in other types of taxes since they are not particularly visible (Wildavsky, 1986). Furthermore, since voters prefer a higher tax burden on the rich (Barnes, 2015) and may perceive that corporate tax burden falls on wealthy corporations, we expect governments to be rewarded by higher corporate taxes.

H3a: Government approval decreases (increases) when individual income taxes increase (decrease).
H3b: Government approval increases (decreases) when corporate income taxes increase (decrease).

Lastly, regarding expenditures, we model the effect of changes to transfers to individuals, of transfers to provinces, and of programme expenditures, each expressed as a proportion of GDP. Only transfers to individuals should influence government approval since they are more visible than the other two categories. Several federal programmes are not particularly visible, and citizens may not be able to blame the federal government for a reduction of transfers to other levels of government.

H4: Government approval increases (decreases) when transfers to individuals increase (decrease).

Data and Models

We test these hypotheses using the government approval series collected for Canada by the EAP. The quarterly series covers the period 1978–2018 and is comprised of answers to questions asking samples of Canadians whether they approve or disapprove of the job the federal government is doing. Figure 9.3 illustrates the evolution of our dependent variable, net (positive minus negative) quarterly federal government approval during this period.[5] We can identify specific lows associated with the end of mandates (Liberal Party in the early 1980s and mid-2000s, Conservative Party in the early 1990s and mid-2010s). The two extreme points correspond to the economic recession and the constitutional crisis that both occurred at the beginning of the 1990s and to the arrival of Justin Trudeau as prime minister in 2015 (the largest honeymoon enjoyed by a new government during the period under study).

Our baseline model of net approval includes three macroeconomic variables common in studies of economic voting and popularity functions: inflation, unemployment, and GDP growth, measured as changes from one quarter to the next.[6] Since these three variables are only weakly correlated, we do not combine them into a single index. We expect that greater economic growth will correlate positively with approval, while both unemployment and inflation should decrease approval.

Models also include several political variables.[7] We introduce a honeymoon dummy variable coded 1 in the quarter of the election and the one after it, and zero otherwise. To account for the cost of ruling (Paldam, 1986), we include a variable counting the number of months in office since a government was

[5] We use net government approval because we believe that it is a more precise measure of the government's popularity than positive approval, which doesn't instruct us on the proportion of citizens having a neutral view of the government. The media usually presents both positive and negative approval of the government.

[6] Unfortunately, we cannot measure the effect of citizens' perceptions of the economy since historical series of consumer confidence data are not available for Canada.

[7] Adding a control for the effective number of parties, or interacting it with the economic variables, does not alter our results.

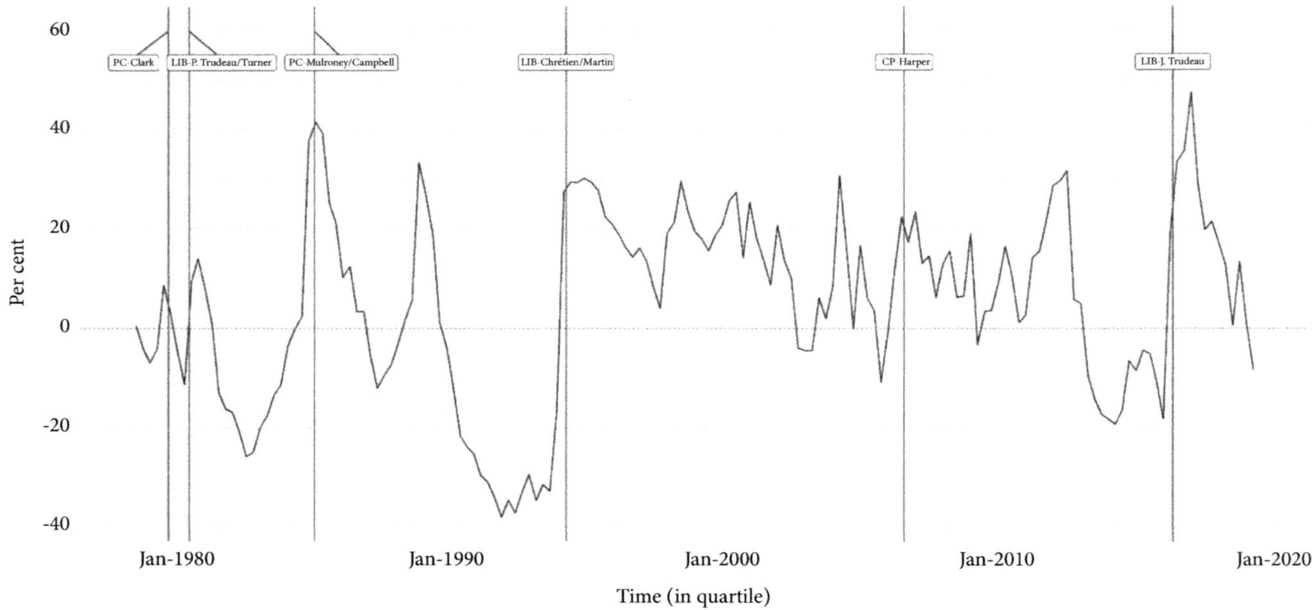

Figure 9.3 Federal government approval in Canada, 1978–2018

Source: Net approval ratings from Executive Approval Project.

elected. We add a dummy coded 1 for major constitutional crises and zero otherwise. We include a dummy for minority governments (Clark, Martin, and Harper I and II) since they may blur responsibility for various economic and political outcomes (Anderson, 2000); this may have as much a positive or a negative effect on approval depending on whether the minority government is successful at passing the buck to the opposition parties.[8] Finally, we include fixed effects for prime ministers to control for their personality and other unobserved factors.

To model the effect of fiscal policies on government approval, we analyse changes to governments' net lending expressed quarterly as a proportion of GDP, which is the difference between public expenditures and revenues. Our baseline fiscal policy model follows Tellier's (2006) model by including economic and political variables, net lending, and individual income taxes, expressed as a proportion of GDP.

We then present models with detailed measures of taxation and expenditures, following the broad categories provided by the Fiscal Reference Tables of the Government of Canada. We divide revenues into four categories: individual income taxes, corporate income taxes, other taxes (which include consumption taxes), and non-fiscal revenues (such as natural resource revenues). Concerning expenditures, we model the effect of changes to transfers to individuals, to provinces, and to other programme expenditures.[9]

We use autoregressive distributed lag models. There are few established theories regarding the appropriate number of lags to use, and we do not know how long it should take for the fiscal and economic variables to influence approval (Box-Steffensmeier et al., 2014). We thus use a general-to-specific modelling strategy to find the appropriate number of lags (De Boef and Keele, 2008). To do so, we start by including four lags for each variable, then remove one lag from each variable, one model at the time, starting with the lags with the lowest T statistic, and we keep the models with the lowest AIC/BIC possible (see Mishler and Sheehan, 1996; De Boef and Keele, 2008; Webb, 2018). This procedure leads to partial adjustment models with varying lag structures that are unbiased. Portmanteau, Breusch-Godfrey, and Cumby-Huizinga tests show that there is no serial correlation in the residuals of our models (Beck and

[8] Note that interactions between economic variables and minority governments do not have a significant effect on approval, possibly because of the small number of cases of minority governments in our series.

[9] In contrast to the macroeconomic and net lending measures available on a quarterly basis, these tax and expenditures measures are only available annually. We transform them into quarterly variables by doing a linear interpolation for the quarters in between the second quarter of each year, during which the budget is usually presented.

Katz, 2011). This modelling strategy leaves us with a lagged dependent variable. From these models, we also calculate long-run multipliers and use the Bewley transformation to estimate their standard error (De Boef and Keele, 2008).

Stationarity tests indicate that the economic and fiscal variables have a unit root.[10] To ensure stationarity, we first difference them. Our independent variable thus represents quarterly changes to economic conditions and to net lending. Government approval, however, is stationary and is thus presented in levels.

Results

Table 9.1 presents the results of the models for the full sample ranging from 1978 to 2018.[11] Model 1 includes only macroeconomic and political variables. In this model, inflation is the only economic variable with a significant effect on approval, thus partially confirming H1a. Note that our general-to-specific modelling strategy suggests that the impact of inflation takes about a year to influence government's popularity, suggesting that the public's reaction to inflation is relatively slow. After four quarters, a one standard deviation increase of inflation (0.81) reduces approval by 2.64 per cent, but its effect accumulates in the long term to reach 11.26 per cent. As for political factors, constitutional crises tend to produce a rally-round-the-flag effect, but the coefficient is not statistically significant. We observe strong honeymoon effects (they would increase approval by almost 15 per cent), but no obvious cost-of-ruling effect. Hence, H1b is partially confirmed.

Model 2 adds individual income taxes and net lending. Inflation maintains its strong negative effect. Net lending does not have a significant impact on approval, while an increase in income taxes reduces approval. Based on Table 9.1, we can conclude that inflation is the only economic variable with a clear effect on approval, although growth's positive coefficient almost reaches statistical significance. Again, this partially supports H1a—that federal government approval on average in Canada is a function of the economy.

Models 3 and 4 include different types of spending (Model 3) or taxes (Model 4) but keep net lending as a control. Model 4 confirms that increases in personal income taxes reduce approval (consistent with H3a). A one standard

[10] We perform Dickey-Fuller, Phillips-Perron, and KPSS tests.

[11] Note that the interaction of the economic or fiscal variables with the ideology of the government in power (liberal or conservative) is not statistically significant.

Table 9.1 Effect of fiscal and economic variables on net government approval, Canada 1978–2018

	(1) Economy	(2) Fiscal	(3) Spending	(4) Taxes
Net approval$_{t-1}$	0.765*	0.750*	0.743*	0.744*
	(0.0578)	(0.0575)	(0.0580)	(0.0575)
Δ GDP growth$_{t-2}$	1.990	1.918	2.308°	1.722
	(1.215)	(1.230)	(1.235)	(1.228)
Δ Inflation$_{t-4}$	−3.267*	−3.120*	−3.060*	−2.674*
	(1.293)	(1.290)	(1.334)	(1.319)
Δ Unemployment rate$_{t-1}$	0.951	0.560	1.418	0.736
	(2.673)	(2.668)	(2.752)	(2.671)
Δ Net lending$_{t-1}$		−0.797	−1.057	−0.920
		(0.812)	(0.824)	(0.820)
Δ Individual income tax$_{t-2}$		−22.01*		−24.27*
		(10.10)		(10.51)
Δ Individual transfers$_t$			−21.72*	
			(10.22)	
Δ Provincial transfers$_{t-4}$			−17.88	
			(11.81)	
Δ Program exp.$_{t-3}$			2.815	
			(5.006)	
Δ Corporate income tax$_{t-2}$				23.80*
				(11.52)
Δ Non-tax rev.$_{t-4}$				−1.334
				(8.956)
Δ Sales taxes$_{t-4}$				7.337
				(13.75)
Honeymoon$_t$	16.73*	16.72*	15.53*	15.92*
	(2.918)	(2.887)	(3.121)	(3.089)
Constitutional crisis$_{t-4}$	8.673	7.817	8.076	7.927
	(5.317)	(5.294)	(5.668)	(5.427)
Months since entering office$_t$	−0.0191	−0.0513	−0.00847	−0.0516
	(0.0323)	(0.0346)	(0.0330)	(0.0348)
Minority government$_t$	1.417	−1.464	1.780	−0.627
	(3.178)	(3.353)	(3.292)	(3.376)
Constant	2.764	9.822	−12.67°	−11.10
	(7.567)	(8.037)	(7.229)	(7.277)
Observations	158	158	156	157
R^2	0.819	0.827	0.831	0.833

Source: Authors' statistical modelling and calculations.
Notes: Cells report coefficients with standard errors in parentheses, * p<0.05, ° p<0.1 (two-tailed test). PM dummies included but coefficients not shown to save space.

deviation increase in individual income taxes (0.076) reduces approval by 1.84 per cent after two quarters and by 7.2 per cent in the long term. In contrast, an increase in corporate taxes tends to increase government popularity (confirming H3b). Finally, Model 4 shows that the effect of sales taxes and of non-fiscal revenues is not significant. As expected, Model 3 reveals that changes to programme expenditures and to provincial transfers do not influence approval. However, higher transfers to individuals are associated with lower popularity, which goes against the theoretical expectation presented in H4. We discuss this result further in the conclusion.

Periodization and Time-varying Models

A central objective of this volume is to assess whether the impact of the economy on governments' popularity changes over time. To answer this question, we divided the data set into two periods, between 1978 and the 1993 election (3rd quarter) (Model 1) and between the last quarter of 1993 and 2018 (Model 2), based on two theoretical arguments: the 1993 election signals a change in the party system and also marks the beginning of a period of fiscal consolidation during which, we argue, citizens' preferences regarding deficit spending change. Johnston (1999) and Pickup (2004) also did a similar division of their Canadian popularity series. We provide an alternative disaggregation of the sample by also limiting our analysis to the Chrétien/Martin era (1993–2006), the period most closely associated with successful fiscal consolidation (Savoie, 1999; Lewis, 2003; Haffert, 2019).

Table 9.2 presents the impact of the economic variables and of net lending, the variables for which we have theoretical expectations about over-time change. In Model 1, net lending has a statistically significant negative sign, while it has a positive sign in Model 2 and a statistically significant positive sign in Model 3. Before 1993, government popularity was increasing during budgetary expansions: a deterioration of one standard deviation in net lending (0.98) increased government approval by 2.4 per cent after four quarters, but the long-run multiplier is not significant. Since 1994 citizens have been rewarding governments for budgetary consolidations, especially during the Chrétien/Martin era during which a one standard deviation improvement to net lending (0.81) increased approval by 3.84 per cent after four quarters and significantly accumulates over the long run to reach 8 per cent. These results confirm H2 which stipulates a reversal over time in the impact of deficits on the approval rate. Note that in these models, the impact of net lending is lagged four quarters, suggesting that it takes a full budget cycle for citizens to react to the effects of budgetary expansions or contractions.

Table 9.2 Effect of fiscal and economic variables on net government approval, Canada 1978–1993(q3), 1993(q4)–2018, and Chrétien/Martin era

	(1) Pre-1993 election	(2) Post-1993 election	(3) Chrétien/Martin
Net approval$_{t-1}$	0.818*	0.665*	0.525*
	(0.0899)	(0.0865)	(0.158)
Δ Net lending$_{t-4}$	−2.472*	1.887	4.741*
	(1.178)	(1.196)	(1.518)
Δ GDP growth$_{t-2}$	3.591*	−0.168	1.245
	(1.296)	(1.531)	(2.386)
Δ Inflation$_{t-1}$	−5.094*	2.787°	−0.421
	(2.015)	(1.663)	(2.617)
Δ Unemployment rate$_{t-4}$	−7.926*	0.711	0.486
	(2.905)	(3.876)	(6.033)
Δ Honeymoon$_t$	11.55*	16.51*	
	(4.557)	(4.495)	
Constitutional crisis$_{t-4}$	20.620*		
	(5.112)		
Months since entering office$_t$	0.022	−0.041	−0.030
	(0.068)	(0.043)	(0.041)
Minority$_t$	−11.27	1.261	−2.788
	(10.61)	(3.768)	(4.263)
Constant	5.303	5.012	7.718
	(12.63)	(9.785)	(4.911)
Observations	58	97	45
R^2	0.891	0.655	0.584

Source: Authors' modelling and calculations.
Notes: Standard errors in parentheses, * $p<0.05$, ° $p<0.1$ (two-tailed test). PM dummies included but coefficient not shown to save space. All series are first differenced.

We use several robustness checks to confirm that the effect of net lending changes over time. Firstly, the result is robust to changes in the lag structure (such as using the same one as in Table 9.1) and to the inclusion of controls for taxes or spending. Secondly, we tested for structural breaks in the series by using a Wald test. When assigning the break to the 1993 election, the Wald test confirms a structural break for the net lending variable (at t−4). With an unspecified break determined by the test itself, the Wald test reveals a break in the third quarter of 1991 for net lending (at t−4). These findings reinforce our arguments: the effect of net lending on popularity changes around 1993. Thirdly, since our variables are first differences and are not using the same lag structure, it is possible that changes to the budget balance reflect changes to the economy. As a robustness check, we estimated models that force the number of lags to be identical between the economic and fiscal variables; these do not alter the results.

Table 9.2 also reveals that the effect of the economy decreases over time, thus confirming H1c. The coefficients for inflation and unemployment change signs between the two periods: both had significant and negative coefficients before 1993, while their coefficient becomes positive after the 1993 election. Similarly, the effect of GDP growth becomes insignificant post-1993, whereas it has a very significant positive effect pre-1993. Hence, the null effects of growth and unemployment in Table 9.1 can be explained by the weakening of the impact of the economy on governments' popularity since the early 1990s.

Wald tests for the economic variables also reveal structural breaks. When regressing net approval by GDP growth or inflation we find a break in the third quarter of 1993 or 1994, respectively, but the break for inflation disappears when using control variables. We also find a break for the unemployment rate in the fourth quarter of 2003. The breaks for these economic variables essentially confirm what we find in Table 9.2: the effects of the economy are significantly weaker since 1993.

We use rolling regressions to verify if the coefficients of our main variables change over time. Figure 9.4 presents rolling regressions using the same equation as in Table 9.1 (Model 1). The coefficients represent the estimate of the regression in a moving window of fifty time periods with 95 per cent confidence intervals.[12] For example, the estimate shown at 1990q1 represents the coefficient of net lending on approval from the first quarter of 1990 to the third quarter of 2002, a span of fifty quarters. These models must be interpreted with caution as they are more useful to detect a change in the coefficient over time than to obtain precise estimates. Even if the true coefficients are constant, the estimated coefficients may display random fluctuations (Lebo and Box-Steffensmeier, 2008). Moreover, sample errors can be large due to a rather short series (t=50).

Caveats aside, Figure 9.4 reveals a clear change in the coefficient of net lending: it is negative in the 1970s and 1980s, becomes positive around the moving window starting around 1990 (which goes up to the early 2000s), significant around the moving window starting in 1993, and stays positive in the moving window starting in 2003 and ending in 2015. This confirms the results of Table 9.2: from 1993, the government was rewarded for tightening the fiscal balance, especially during the Chrétien and Martin era. Afterwards, the size and significance of the net lending coefficient decrease. The drop in the

[12] Moving windows of thirty lead to similar results, except for economic growth.

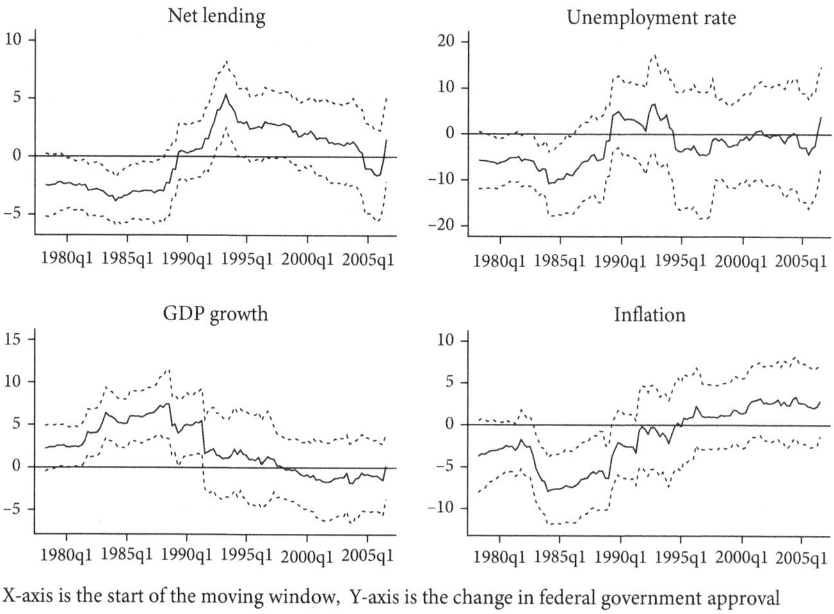

Figure 9.4 Rolling regression, moving window of fifty, with 95 per cent CI
Source: Authors' modelling and calculations.

coefficient in the last moving window reflects the fact that the popularity of the Trudeau government did not decline despite the return of budget deficits. The rolling regressions also support our findings indicating that the effect of three economic variables was significant and in the expected direction in the 1970s and 1980s and tends to become insignificant when the moving window only includes data in the 1990s and 2000s.

Conclusion

Our analysis finds that the economy significantly influences the federal government's approval in Canada. We find that inflation was particularly detrimental to governments' popularity, which points to political turmoil for the Trudeau government in the post-pandemic high-inflation environment. That said, our results also support the main claim of this volume: the effect of the economy on government's popularity is declining over time and was much stronger in the 1970s and 1980s than after the early 1990s. As for political variables, we find that constitutional crises are producing a rally-round-the-flag effect and that government approval significantly increases during honeymoon periods. Therefore, while we see a decline in the 'e-fraction' of popularity, the impact of the 'p-fraction' is steady (Paldam, 1991).

One of the main innovations of this chapter was to include fiscal policy variables in a popularity function. We find that citizens react negatively to personal income tax increases and reward governments for personal income tax cuts. Interestingly, corporate tax increases are positively related to the government's popularity. This result suggests that parties may wish to shift the tax burden towards corporations if they are looking for politically painless solutions to tax revenue shortages. We also find that citizens tend to punish governments for increases in personal transfers. However, these counterintuitive results may be explained by an endogenous relationship with the economic variables since a deterioration of the economy can lead to higher transfers and to lower corporate income taxes.

This chapter has also argued that public opinion towards the budget deficit has shifted along with the change in the fiscal policy paradigm achieved in Canada during the 1990s. Both public opinion and fiscal policy exhibited a deficit bias during the 1970s and 1980s: while the government was unable to balance budgets, the public was rewarding governments for higher deficits which could sustain additional public spending and lower taxes. As deficits became unsustainable during the economic crisis of the early 1990s, the federal government shifted its policy paradigm and implemented a severe fiscal consolidation, while citizens became eagerly concerned about the public debt. Since then, sustaining budgetary balance has been the primary fiscal objective of the state. At the same time, Canadians began to reward governments for tightening the budgetary balance and to support fiscal discipline. Citizens' 'deficit bias' morphed into an 'austerity bias'.

It is possible that the salience of the economy declined during the period under study because reducing budget deficits became a more important priority for Canadians. The dominance of the issue of budget deficit reduction, entrenched with the transformation of the fiscal policy regime, may have made the public less attentive to, or less concerned with, changes in economic conditions. In fact, it should be noted that some authors have argued that economic voting is relatively weak in Canada when compared to the impact of other policy issues on election outcomes during the 1990s and 2000s (see Blais et al., 2004; Gidengil et al., 2012). These studies have posited that the influence of the economy on Canadian government support may only be felt during times of crisis when the economy becomes highly salient. Overall, our results support this volume's main conclusion that the popularity function is shaped more by issue salience and political dispositions than by macro political and economic contexts. It remains difficult with the data at hand to determine precisely whether the phenomenon observed is due to the changing fiscal policy regime or the changing party system since they are contemporaneous. That said, we can note that the party system has not changed significantly since 1993, whereas the public discourse over fiscal policy has continued to shift since then, in a manner that corresponds relatively closely with the observed dynamics in government popularity.

This chapter's objective was not to disentangle whether public opinion drives policy changes or if policy changes influence public opinion, as the relationship is certainly endogenous. Still, we were able to identify a structural break in how public opinion reacts to budget deficits, a finding that supports the idea that public opinion and policy paradigms reinforce each other. In some ways, such a finding is congruent with the link between policy mood and government approval in Spain reported in this volume (see Chapter 8).

To conclude, we can note that Canadians' austerity bias may be fading. Table 9.2 and the rolling regressions revealed that the positive effect of an improvement to the budget balance was much stronger during the Chrétien/Martin era than during the full 1993–2018 period. This suggests that the popularity ratings of the governments of Stephen Harper and Justin Trudeau were less influenced by budget deficits. Indeed, in 2015 by breaking with the fiscal orthodoxy and proposing higher deficits to finance additional public spending, Trudeau's Liberal Party positioned itself as the main centre-left alternative to the governing Conservatives. The COVID-19 pandemic may be the event that triggers another shift in fiscal policy paradigm, as many mainstream international economic institutions have called on governments to further increase spending to sustain economic recovery. If the government of Canada continues to promote expansionist fiscal policies and decides to forego budget discipline, we may well observe public opinion reverting to a deficit bias in the next few years.

References

Anderson, C. D. (2008). Economic voting, multilevel governance and information in Canada. *Canadian Journal of Political Science*, *41*(2), 329–54.

Anderson, C. J. (2000). Economic voting and political context: A comparative perspective. *Electoral Studies*, *19*(2–3), 151–70.

Bansak, K., Bechtel, M., and Margalit, Y. (2021). Why austerity? The mass politics of a contested policy. *American Political Science Review*, *115*(2), 486–505.

Barnes, L. (2015). The size and shape of government: Preferences over redistributive tax policy. *Socio-Economic Review*, *13*(1), 55–78.

Beck, N., and Katz, J. N. (2011). Modeling dynamics in time-series–cross-section political economy data. *Annual Review of Political Science, 14*, 331–52.

Berlemann, M., and Enkelmann, S. (2014). The economic determinants of U.S. presidential approval: A survey. *European Journal of Political Economy, 36*, 41–54.

Blais, A., Turgeon, M., Gidengil, E., Nevitte, N., and Nadeau, R. (2004). Which matters most? Comparing the impact of issues and the economy in American, British and Canadian Elections. *British Journal of Political Science, 34*(3), 555–63.

Blyth, M. (2013). *Austerity: The History of a Dangerous Idea*. Oxford: Oxford University Press.

Box-Steffensmeier, J. M., Freeman, J. R., Hitt, M. P., and Pevehouse, J. C. (2014). *Time Series Analysis for the Social Sciences*. Cambridge: Cambridge University Press.

Buchanan, J. M., and Wagner, R. E. (1977). *Democracy in Deficit: The Political Legacy of Lord Keynes*. New York: Academic Press.

Carmichael, C. (1990). Economic conditions and the popularity of the incumbent party in Canada. *Canadian Journal of Political Science, 23*(4), 713–26.

Cebula, R. (2005). Presidential approval determinants. *Review of Business Research, 5*(3), 32–8.

Clarke, H., Ho, K., and Stewart, M. (2000). Major's lesser (not minor) effects: Prime ministerial approval and governing party support in Britain since 1979. *Electoral Studies, 19*(2), 255–73.

Clarke, H., Kornberg, A., and Scotto, T. (2009). *Making Political Choices: Canada and the United States*. Toronto: University of Toronto Press.

Clarke, H., and Stewart, M. (1995). Economic evaluations, prime ministerial approval and governing party support: Rival models reconsidered. *British Journal of Political Science, 25*(2), 145–70.

Clarke, H., and Zuk, G. (1987). The politics of party popularity: Canada 1974–1979. *Comparative Politics, 19*(3), 299–315.

De Boef, S., and Keele, L. (2008). Taking time seriously. *American Journal of Political Science, 52*(1), 184–200.

Duch, R., and Stevenson, R. (2008). *The Economic Vote: How Political and Economic Institutions Condition Election Results*. Cambridge: Cambridge University Press.

Gélineau, F., and Bélanger, É. (2005). Electoral accountability in a federal system: National and provincial economic voting in Canada. *Publius: The Journal of Federalism, 35*(3), 407–24.

Geys, B., and Vermeir, J. (2008a). Taxation and presidential approval: Separate effects from tax burden and tax structure turbulence? *Public Choice, 135*(3–4), 301–17.

Geys, B., and Vermeir, J. (2008b). The political cost of taxation: New evidence from German popularity ratings. *Electoral Studies, 27*(4), 633–48.
Gidengil, E., Nevitte, N., Blais, A., Everitt, J., and Fournier, P. (2012). *Dominance and Decline: Making Sense of Recent Canadian Elections.* Toronto: University of Toronto Press.
Haffert, L. (2019). Permanent budget surpluses as a fiscal regime. *Socio-Economic Review, 17*(4), 1043–63.
Hall, P. (1993). Policy paradigms, social learning and the state: The case of economic policymaking in Britain. *Comparative Politics, 26*(3), 275–96.
Happy, J. R. (1992). The effect of economic and fiscal performance on incumbency voting: The Canadian case. *British Journal of Political Science, 22*(1), 117–30.
Jacques, O., and Haffert, L. (2021). Are governments paying a price for austerity? Fiscal consolidations reduce government approval. *European Political Science Review, 13*(2), 189–207.
Johnston, R. (1999). Business cycles, political cycles and the popularity of Canadian governments, 1974–1998. *Canadian Journal of Political Science, 32*(3), 499–520.
Johnston, R. (2017). *The Canadian Party System: An Analytic History.* Vancouver: UBC Press.
Lebo, M., and Box-Steffensmeier, J. (2008). Dynamic conditional correlations in political science. *American Journal of Political Science, 52*(3), 688–704.
Lewis, T. (2003). *In the Long Run We're All Dead: The Canadian Turn to Fiscal Restraint.* Vancouver: UBC Press.
Lewis-Beck, M., and Stegmaier, M. (2013). The VP-function revisited: A survey of the literature on vote and popularity functions after over 40 years. *Public Choice, 157*(3–4), 367–85.
Mishler, W., and Sheehan, R. S. (1996). Public opinion, the attitudinal model, and supreme court decision making: A micro-analytic perspective. *Journal of Politics, 58*(1), 169–200.
Monroe, K., and Erickson, L. (1986). The economy and political support: The Canadian case. *Journal of Politics, 48*(3), 616–47.
Nadeau, R., and Blais, A. (1993). Explaining election outcomes in Canada: Economy and politics. *Canadian Journal of Political Science, 26*(4), 775–90.
Nadeau, R., Lewis-Beck, M. S., and Bélanger, É. (2013). Economics and elections revisited. *Comparative Political Studies, 46*(5), 551–73.
Paldam, M. (1986). The distribution of election results and the two explanations of the cost of ruling. *European Journal of Political Economy, 2*(1), 5–24.
Paldam, M. (1991). How robust is the vote function? A study of seventeen nations over four decades. In *Economics and Politics: The Calculus of Support*, H. Norpoth, M. Lewis-Beck, and J.-D. Lafay, eds. Ann Arbor, MI: University of Michigan Press. 9–31.

Paldam, M., and Schneider, F. (1980). The macro-economic aspects of government and opposition popularity in Denmark 1957–78. *Nationaløkonomisk Tidsskrift, 118*(2), 149–70.

Pétry, F., and Harmatz, H. (1995). Politico-economic interactions in Canada: An empirical assessment. *Public Finance Quarterly, 23*(3), 305–35.

Pickup, M. (2004). Economic performance and electoral accountability: The economy and party popularity in Canada 1975–2000. Paper presented at the Canadian Political Science Association Conference.

Pickup, M. (2010). Better know your dependent variable: A multination analysis of government support measures in economic popularity models. *British Journal of Political Science, 40*(2), 449–68.

Pierson, P. (2001). From expansion to austerity: The new politics of taxing and spending. In M. Levin, M. Landy, and M. Shapiro, eds. *Seeking the Center: Politics and Policymaking in the New Century*. Washington, DC: Georgetown University Press. 54–80.

Pissarides, C. A. (1980). British government popularity and economic performance. *Economic Journal, 90*(359), 569–81.

Rose, R. (1985). Maximizing tax revenue while minimizing political costs. *Journal of Public Policy, 5*(3), 289–320.

Sanders, D., Ward, H., Marsh, D., and Fletcher, T. (1987). Government popularity and the Falklands War: A reassessment. *British Journal of Political Science, 17*(3), 281–313.

Savoie, D. J. (1999). *Governing from the Centre: The Concentration of Power in Canadian Politics*. Toronto: University of Toronto Press.

Tellier, G. (2006). Effect of economic conditions on government popularity: The Canadian provincial case. *Canadian Journal of Political Science, 39*(1), 27–51.

Webb, C. (2018). Power politics or public pandering? An empirical investigation of economic sanctions and presidential approval. *International Interactions, 44*(3), 491–509.

Wildavsky, A. B. (1986). *Budgeting: A Comparative Theory of the Budgeting Process*. London: Transaction Books.

10

The Economy and Chancellor Approval in Germany

A Cautionary Tale about Data Vintages and Measures

Mark A. Kayser and Arndt Leininger

There is little question about the importance of the economy to voters in Germany, even though its importance, as shown in this chapter, seems to have receded over time.[1] While voters may care about many things, only retrospective assessments enable accountability. Retrospective accountability and its most common form, governmental accountability for the economy, is a cornerstone of democratic governance (Ashworth, 2012). Despite the importance of electoral accountability, however, we know little about the mechanism of how the economy influences government popularity, how voters learn about the economy, and how stable this relationship is over time. This chapter focuses on government popularity and the economy in Germany, a country in which parliamentary seats are allocated to parties proportional to their vote shares and coalition governments are the norm, factors thought to blur clarity of responsibility (Powell and Whitten, 1993). Nevertheless, with two big centrist parties competing for the chancellorship, for most of its history the Federal Republic seems to have enjoyed a strong link between the economy and government approval. The country experienced strong economic growth during its '*Wirtschaftswunder*' years from the 1950s through the early 1970s. Unemployment declined to almost full employment so that, perhaps, voters came to expect continuous improvements in material well-being. Underscoring the economy's salience, the interwar experience instilled a particular sensitivity of the public and elites to inflation.

Most early studies on Germany focused on the relationship between the popularity of the governing parties and aggregate indicators of the state of the economy, as measured by unemployment or inflation rates (e.g. Frey

[1] The authors thank Tom Arend for excellent research assistance.

Mark A. Kayser and Arndt Leininger, *The Economy and Chancellor Approval in Germany*. In: *Economics and Politics Revisited*. Edited by: Timothy Hellwig and Matthew Singer, Oxford University Press. © Mark A. Kayser and Arndt Leininger (2023). DOI: 10.1093/oso/9780192871664.003.0010

and Garbers, 1972; Kirchgässner, 1985b). However, as with other countries, aggregate-level studies using objective economic indicators collected by statistical agencies eventually gave way to individual-level studies using subjective economic evaluations, possibly because it proved to be more difficult to obtain evidence for an economic vote in Germany as time passed (Kirchgässner, 2009). The frequency of grand coalitions, especially in more recent times, undermined the clarity of responsibility (Debus, Stegmaier, and Tosun, 2014; Plescia, Kritzinger, and Spoon, 2022); Germany's increasing integration into world markets and politically into the European Union weakened the government's room to manoeuvre (Hellwig, 2001); and rising standards of living contributed to post-material issues challenging the primacy of the economy (Kitschelt, 1994).

In this chapter, beyond providing an update on economic voting in Germany, we make three substantive contributions. First, we indirectly investigate the role of the media in forming economic perceptions by addressing the question of whether real-time (i.e. media-reported) or revised (i.e. more accurate) macroeconomic estimates best predict executive approval (*which economy?*). This builds on previous research on US data that suggests that real-time economic vintages best predict voting behaviour (Kayser and Leininger, 2015). Second, we test the effect of different durations of measurement in our quarterly data, economic growth since the previous quarter (qoq) and since the same quarter in the previous year (yoy). Third, we estimate the size of effects over time (*does the economy still matter?*).

We use quarterly data for the first (i.e. real-time) and latest (i.e. revised) estimates of economic growth in Germany between 1978 and 2019. Because the media frequently report on (less-accurate) initial economic estimates but rarely report on (more-accurate) later revisions, we can exploit this difference to infer the media's influence in the effect of the economy on chancellor approval. The less-accurate but more-reported real-time economic measures outperform the more-accurate revised measures when they represent short-run changes (qoq) but this difference disappears when economic growth is measured over a longer period (yoy). This may suggest that media reporting on the economy influences individuals' approval of the chancellor in the short run but that the actual performance of the economy matters with longer assessments.

These findings also bear implications for research practice. The aggregate economic data downloaded by social scientists to predict attitudes and behaviour are not the same data that the individuals they are studying were exposed to at the time. If they download quarter-on-quarter revised economic estimates, they will find no effect but if they take the trouble to collect real-time economic estimates that match what was reported for each time period, also on a qoq basis, they will find effects. Alternatively, if they opt for year-on-year quarterly data, they will find similar effects, regardless of whether real-time or revised. These results, as we will show, will also differ depending on the period covered by the time series. It is possible that the results that one estimates may be an unwitting result of the type of economic measure that one collects. This observation may offer a solution to a puzzle in the literature in which objective economic measures have repeatedly been shown to be poor predictors of the vote and vote intentions (e.g. Paldam, 1991; Anderson, 2007; Kayser, 2014). Scholars partly responded by showing a conditional relationship relying on factors such as clarity of responsibility or benchmarking. We add an additional explanation: data vintage and duration of measurement.

We next ask whether the relationship between economic performance and chancellor approval has changed over time. This could occur due to changes in clarity of responsibility, changes in the salience of economic performance as wealth levels change, international economic integration, or changing media consumption patterns. Responsibility attributions have become murkier as grand coalitions and complex coalitions have become more frequent; second-dimension non-economic issues have grown in importance; comparisons to economic performance in neighbouring states have become less informative with economic convergence; and voters receive increasingly less news about the economy from relatively unbiased mainstream media and more from social media. Our purpose here, however, is not to identify why the strength of the economic vote has changed in Germany but simply to establish whether this is the case.

We find that the effect of economic growth on chancellor approval has not only receded over recent decades but, consistent with findings for other countries in this volume, has reversed its sign. We speculate about the reasons for this.

Theory and Literature

Voter Responses to the Economy

The first studies on vote and popularity functions focused on the objective economic situation, measured by the unemployment or inflation rate, and were located at the aggregate level. Although the literature was and is dominated by studies from the United States, several contributions tested the link between the economy and government popularity in other countries, including Germany. Contradictory findings emerged early on: evidence for economic voting at the aggregate level was found for some countries and time periods, but not for others, and no country showed as strong and consistent a relationship as the United States (e.g. Paldam, 1991).

The first study to be conducted on Germany found no link between economic conditions, specifically inflation and unemployment, and the popularity and electoral success of the governing Christian Democrats (CDU/CSU) (Frey and Garbers, 1972). Although subsequent studies did report a relationship between the popularity of the governing parties and the state of the economy measured by the unemployment and inflation rates (Kirchgässner, 1974; Ronning and Schneider, 1976; Kirchgäßner, 1977; Frey and Schneider, 1979), they were subsequently criticized for lacking methodological rigour (Norpoth and Yantek, 1983; Kirchgässner, 1986). Analysing chancellor approval, Norpoth and Yantek (1983) find no relationship between West German parties' popularity and either unemployment or inflation. In contrast, Kirchgässner (1983) found a robust link between polling aggregates and aggregated economic evaluations, but results for unemployment and inflation are weaker and inconsistent (see also Kirchgässner, 1985a; 1985b), pointing to a discrepancy between what is measured by official statistics and what voters perceive.

Only in 2000 did Feld and Kirchgässner (2000) confirm the continued existence of the economic vote in Germany, again measured through the governing parties' popularity and unemployment and inflation. However, Kirchgässner (2009) reported that Germany might have lost its economic accountability mechanism as he found no relationship between unemployment or inflation and the government's popularity during Gerhard Schröder's chancellorship 1998–2005. In a more recent analysis at the aggregate level, Williams, Stegmaier, and Debus (2017) link the popularity of German governing parties to aggregate subjective evaluations of the state of the economy. Finally, recent evidence also comes from election-forecasting models. Economic growth is predictive of the coalition's vote share overall (Kayser and Leininger, 2016) and, therein, of the chancellor's party, but not of other parties' vote shares (Kayser and Leininger, 2017). In sum, the evidence has been mixed—partly due, as we argue, to the fact that both subjective evaluations of the economy (endogeneity bias) and revised economic time-series (which deviate from what the media reported at the time) are imperfect measures that neglect the process of how voters learn about and assess the economy.

The Economic Vote across Contexts and over Time

Of great interest for our purposes is the puzzle of unstable estimates of the economy's influence on support for the government, the prime minister, or the prime minister's party when researchers use objective economic measures. Scholars have attributed this instability and frequent null results in smaller samples to a need for context and more statistical power. In response, several authors have made theoretical and empirical progress by showing how clarity of responsibility (Powell and Whitten, 1993), constraints of globalization (Hellwig and Samuels, 2007), and benchmarking (Kayser and Peress, 2012) improve the magnitude and efficiency of estimates.

Perhaps the most significant shift in the field was towards using subjective individual-level assessments of the economy in place of objective economic measures (cf. Duch and Stevenson, 2008). In Germany, the first individual-level studies appeared in the mid-1980s (Rattinger, 1986; Lewis-Beck, 1986) and produced findings in line with what others had found for other countries: sociotropic evaluations of the national economy were more predictive of voting than egotropic evaluations of voters' personal economic situation. Subsequent individual-level studies confirmed the existence of an economic vote in Germany from 1994 to 2002 (Maier and Rattinger, 1999; 2004). The economy–vote link continued to hold in 2009 despite the ongoing financial crisis (Rattinger and Steinbrecher, 2011). In Germany, it is mainly the chancellor's party that takes the blame or credit for a bad or good economy as recent research suggests (Debus, Stegmaier, and Tosun, 2014). While these studies confirm the importance of the economy for individual voters when casting their votes, they remain mute about how voters form their evaluations of the economy.

The Media and How Voters Learn about the Economy

Three mechanisms can explain the economic vote. First, voters may infer government competence from economic performance (Alesina and Rosenthal, 1995). Second, they might sanction all governments for poor economic performance (Ferejohn, 1986). Or, third, voting against the government during downturns might simply be a behavioural response. However, all three mechanisms rely on voters being able to assess the economy.

Despite its implications for scholarly debates, how voters learn about and assess the economy is mostly neglected in the literature. Economic perceptions are influenced by partisan preferences, making them an endogenous predictor of government approval and voting (e.g. Evans and Anderson, 2006; Stanig, 2013). Objective macroeconomic indicators, on the other hand, are, of course exogenous, to citizens' partisan predisposition but voters need to experience it—awareness of unemployment can arise from information about neighbours or acquaintances losing their jobs and citizens can directly experience inflation while shopping—or learn about it—through news about growth in economic production in the media. Despite its implications for scholarly debates, how voters learn about the economy is largely ignored in the literature. Some forms of direct experience of economic change—such as job loss—are readily measured. Krieger (1985), for example, reports that workers who experience unemployment reduce their support for the governing party in Germany. Other directly experienced measures, such as changes in personal income, require a rare combination of publicly available political and personal income data that are rarely found outside of Scandinavian registries.[2] Direct individual experience, however, is not the only means by which voters learn about the economy. The prime suspect for at least a supporting role is the media.[3] An increasing number of scholars have used text analysis to analyse the relationship between the economy and media reports on the economy, often searching for partisan bias in reporting. For example, Larcinese, Puglisi, and Snyder (2011) and, to a lesser degree, Kayser and Peress (2021) report that opposition newspapers print (mostly accurate) stories about the economy more frequently than newspapers ideologically aligned with the government during economic downturns. Of course, it is not obvious that voters absorb these reports while there is also evidence that coverage in the economic news responds most to developments relevant to a wealthy subset of the population (Jacobs et al., 2021) and that individual risk profiles influence the source of economic information (Hellwig and Marinova, 2023).

Our approach captures media effects by employing the initial economic estimates that are reported in the press. It does not directly estimate the effects of separate components of economic information (direct experience and via the media). However, it is also more encompassing than content-based studies using text analysis since it captures not only mainstream newspaper effects but all media effects. By estimating both the effects of real-time (i.e. initial) data

[2] Healy, Persson, and Snowberg (2017), for example, combine a survey and Swedish registry data to show that some of what looks like voter responses to national-level economic change is actually caused by personal income change.

[3] About 30 per cent of the effect of growth is mediated by newspaper reports (Kayser and Peress, 2022), which is likely a lower-bound estimate.

releases, which are covered by the media, and of the latest revised releases for the same periods, which are largely ignored by the media, we estimate how *all* media reporting on the economy influences the relationship between economic performance and executive approval. Should real-time data prove to be a stronger predictor, we will not only have uncovered evidence about the role of the media in the economic vote, but we will have a useful tool with which to understand the effect of the economy on chancellor approval in general but also over time.

An Introduction to Data Vintages

Revisions to Economic Data

Economic measures, such as GDP growth or the inflation rate, are estimates produced by national statistical agencies and frequently revised after initial publication. In Germany, the federal statistical office publishes the first estimate of quarterly growth in GDP (formerly GNP) forty-five days into the subsequent quarter. It then conducts ongoing revisions of an estimate with every new quarter for up to four years after the initial estimate was published. Such revisions are due to new data that have come in or to the data having been revised. The German federal statistical office also undertakes benchmark revisions every five years, implementing improved methodologies, definitions, or both. Since the federal statistical office began reporting quarterly growth rates in 1978, two major changes occurred in how it calculated economic growth. In 1992, Germany switched from reporting GNP to GDP, and in the early 2000s, qoq instead of yoy quarterly growth rates became the dominant economic figure.

These revisions and changes in methodology sometimes lead to substantial differences between initial and latest estimates. Figure 10.1 illustrates how estimates of quarterly growth rates in the quarter preceding national elections, one of the so-called *fundamentals* often used in election forecasting (e.g. Erikson and Wlezien, 2014), changed after initial estimates were published. As the revision histories for these and other estimates show, there is also quite some fluctuation over time in addition to systematic deviations between the first and latest estimate. This implies that researchers are using different economic data depending on when they obtain their data.

Growth rates are denoted in percentages and up until 1992 reflect yoy growth in GNP, after which Germany, as did many other countries at that

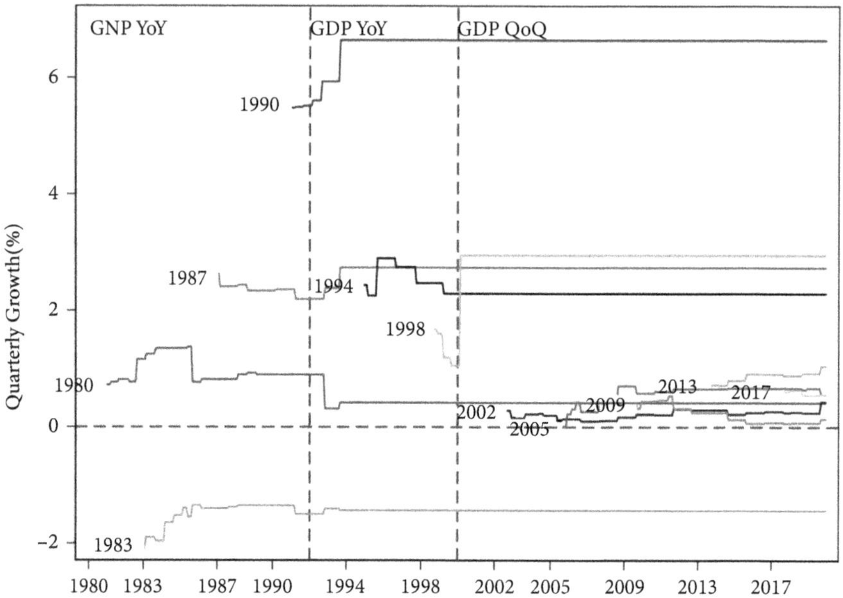

Figure 10.1 Estimates of quarterly growth in Germany for pre-election quarters
Source: Authors.

time, switched to reporting GDP as the main measure of economic output. In 2002, the federal statistical office switched to reporting qoq growth as the primary measure of change in economic output.

As Figure 10.2 demonstrates, the first and latest estimates of growth in any given quarter are only weakly correlated. Revisions can lead to upward or downward corrections in estimates and thereby introduce substantial noise to the initial estimate. Also, revised growth estimates tend to be more moderate in size than the first estimates, as evidenced by the slope of the linear fit line, which is less than 1.

Economists are well aware that revisions of economic data occur frequently, can sometimes be substantial, and therefore have important implications for economic forecasts (Runkle, 1998; Croushore and Stark, 2003). These lessons, however, have been largely overlooked by political scientists.[4] Whereas economic research has found that real-time data performs worse than revised data in forecasting economic quantities (Diebold and Rudebusch, 1991; Ghysels, Horan, and Moench, 2018), it might well be the other way round in political science applications, especially those where voters or the public respond at least partly to reporting on the economy, not just the economy itself. If

[4] An exception is Kayser and Leininger (2015) who focus on out-of-sample election forecasts in the United States. This chapter, to the best of our knowledge, is the first application to government or prime ministerial approval, as well as the first political science application outside of the United States.

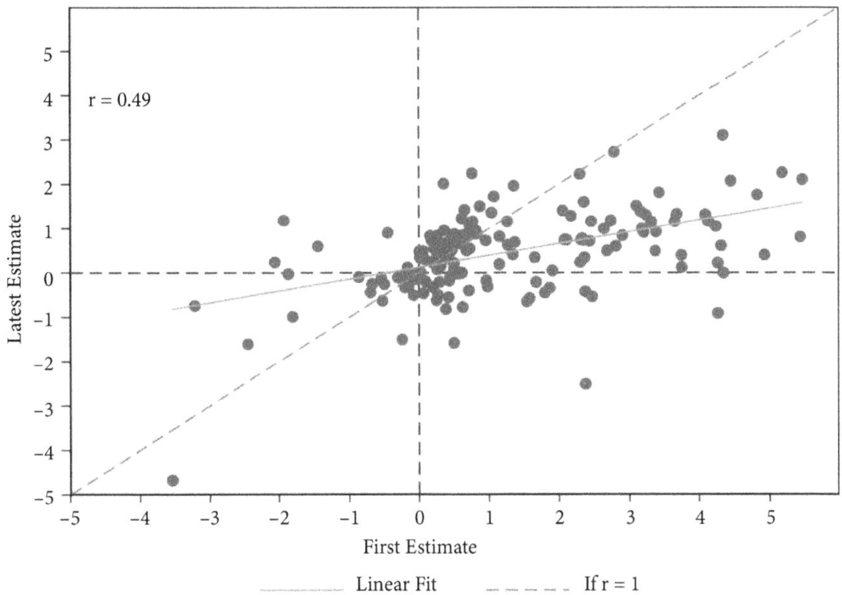

Figure 10.2 First versus latest estimate of the quarterly growth rate for all quarters 1978–2019
Source: Authors.

researchers today use current estimates of GDP growth for a period before 1992, for example, they might be capturing the most accurate estimate of actual economic output. However, this does reflect the information available at that time. There is a discrepancy not just because they are using revised data but also because they are using qoq GDP growth for a time period when yoy quarterly GNP growth was the key measure reported in the news. Not only did the definition of gross economic output change—from national to domestic product—but also the definition of growth—from yearly to quarterly, as well as other minor technical details—changed. However, these technicalities define what is reported by statistical agencies and picked up by the media, which ultimately influence voting behaviour with their reporting.

A Brief History of GDP in Germany

Germany is typical of many industrialized economies in that economic growth gained only slowly in public attention and importance, and that the methodology and frequency of measurement changed (Lepenies, 2016). It was not until the mid-1960s that the German media began to process the economic figures published by the federal statistical office and turn them into news about the nation's economic situation. The federal statistical office began publishing quarterly estimates of GNP growth only in 1978. These estimates were based on a comparison of production in the preceding quarter against the same quarter of the previous year, i.e. yoy growth. In the early 1990s, Germany switched to GDP, as did other nations like the United States. The federal statistical office continued to report quarterly yoy growth rates. From 2000 onward, the federal statistical office began to report qoq growth rates, which continue to be the most prominent growth estimates being mentioned first in press releases. In 2005, the method for adjusting for inflation was changed from using fixed prices to using the previous year's prices. Further minor changes to methodology occurred with the introduction of the European System of Current Accounts in 2010. All of these changes contribute to a discrepancy between first and latest estimate of economic growth that is evident in Figure 10.2.

With some delay, the media adjusted its reporting to the current reporting standard by Germany's statistical agency. Figure 10.3 shows the yearly number of articles that contained either one of the key terms associated with GNP or GDP published in Germany's major quality newspapers.[5] Up until 1993/94, it

Figure 10.3 Reporting on growth in GDP versus GNP in Germany's two major newspapers, the (Conservative) *Frankfurter Allgemeine Zeitung* (FAZ) and the (Liberal) *Süddeutsche Zeitung*
Source: Authors.

[5] For GNP, these terms are '*Bruttosozialprodukt*' or '*Sozialprodukt*', '*BSP*', '*Bruttonationaleinkommen*', or '*BNE*'. The key terms associated with GDP are '*Bruttoinlandsprodukt*' or '*BIP*'.

appears as if GNP was still preferred by the press. In the Frankfurter Allgemeine Zeitung, the switch to GDP appears to have happened in 1994, and in the Süddeutsche Zeitung, a year earlier.

Vertical dashed lined indicates the time point (1992) when official reporting switched from GNP to GDP.

Data and Research Design

Data on the popularity of the head of government, the chancellor in Germany, comes from the Executive Approval Project, which collects poll margins for the popularity of national heads of government and state (Carlin et al., 2019). Figure 10.4, top panel, shows how our dependent variable varies over time. We capture the development of the popularity of four different heads of government. Two chancellors hail from Germany's centre-right catch-all party, the CDU, the Christian Democratic Union, and two chancellors hail from Germany's centre-left catch-all party, the SPD, the Social-Democratic Party of Germany. We focus on the chancellor's popularity because economic responsibility is mainly attributed to the chancellor and their party (Debus, Stegmaier,

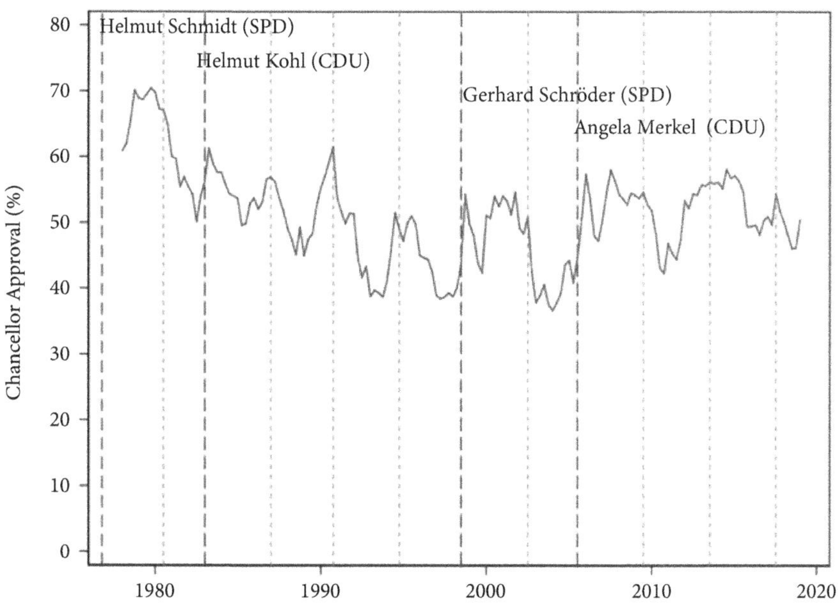

Figure 10.4 Chancellor approval (smoothed version), 1978, Q1–2019, Q1

Source: Executive Approval Database version 2.0.

Note: Percentage of respondents approving of the chancellor, over time, Lighter short-dashed lines indicate national parliamentary elections and darker dashed lines indicate transitions to a new chancellor.

and Tosun, 2014; Williams, Stegmaier, and Debus, 2017). Also, the chancellor's popularity is highly predictive of the ruling coalition's electoral prospects, as Norpoth and Gschwend (e.g. 2013) have repeatedly shown.

Our data set includes quarterly growth rates, adjusted for inflation, for Germany from 1978 (Q1), when quarterly reporting of economic growth by the federal statistical office began, to the first quarter of 2019. For any given quarter in this period, we have collected the initial estimate and any following revised estimate until the most recent estimate available at the end of 2019. We contrast the first and latest available estimates in the analyses to follow. Figure 10.5 plots the development of both variables over time. It demonstrates that one can get a very different picture of past economic performance depending on whether one looks at real-time estimates available back at that time or the latest revised estimate. This pattern likely reflects more inaccurate methodology in the early days of Germany's national accounts system, further compounded by data revisions and methodology changes that have happened since then.

First estimate represents the first official estimate of GDP growth, usually published in the first weeks of the following quarter: from 1978–1992 this was quarterly yoy growth in GNP, from 1992–1999 quarterly yoy growth in GDP and from 2000 onwards quarterly qoq growth in GDP. Latest estimate contains

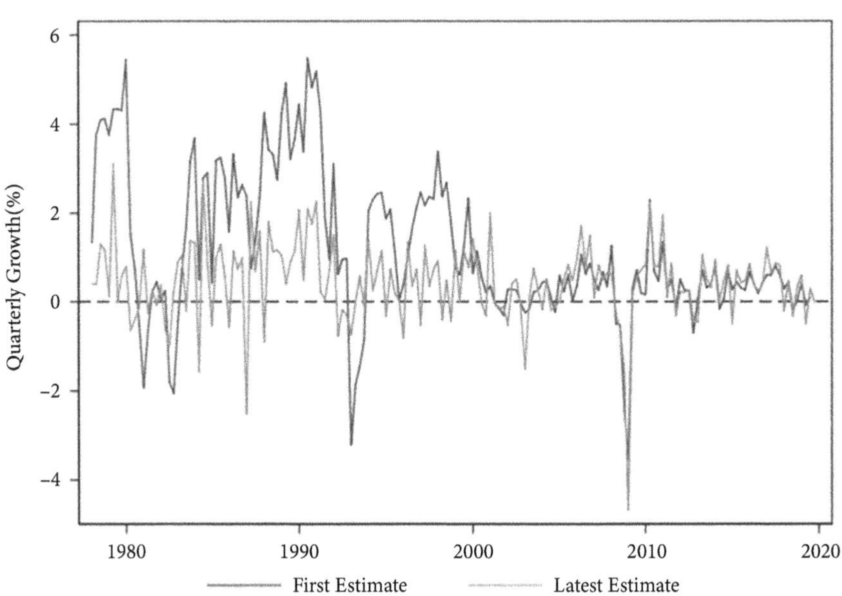

Figure 10.5 First—that is, real-time—estimate and latest estimate of GDP growth for all quarters 1978, Q1–2019, Q4

Source: Authors.

the most up-to-date estimates available at the time of data collection. Therefore the full time series represents quarterly qoq growth in GDP.

The variable 'first estimate' captures yoy quarterly growth in GNP from the beginning of the series until 1991, yoy quarterly growth in GDP between 1992 and 1999, and qoq growth in GDP from 2000 onward. The variable captures what the media reported at the time. In contrast, the variable 'latest estimate' captures estimated (as of 2019) qoq quarterly growth in GDP for all quarters from 1978 to 2019. The 'latest estimate' represents the most recently available data from the federal statistical office as of 2019. All time series, of course, are subject to potential further revisions in the future.

To relate changes in chancellor approval to economic growth, we estimate several models. We begin by estimating simple OLS models regressing our dependent variable, chancellor approval, on our key explanatory variables, first and latest estimate of quarterly economic growth, and a set of control variables. We lag our key independent variable to reflect the fact that the most recently available information available to the public when the survey was in the field is the first estimate of growth in the preceding quarter. The first estimate of growth in the past quarter is usually published by the statistical agency a few weeks into the following quarter.[6] Finally, note that when using a lagged dependent variable (LDV) model we effectively account for all lags of our independent variables. All models include dummies for the last three chancellors, omitting Helmut Schmidt as the baseline. We also include a counter for a chancellor's time in office to capture cost-of-ruling effects (Thesen, Mortensen, and Green-Pedersen, 2020), which together with the chancellorship dummies is perfectly collinear with an overall time counter, thus adjusting for any trend non-stationarity. However, as the time-series could be persistent, we also estimate lagged-dependent variable models.[7] We further adjust for the electoral cycle, the official unemployment and inflation rates, victories in international football tournaments as exogenous shocks to the national mood, and quarter fixed-effects. Lastly, a pair of variables for the observation's position in the electoral cycle and for its squared term accounts for the empirical regularity that governments tend to lose popularity over time, reaching a low point towards the middle of the electoral period and not recovering until the next

[6] Note that we do not lag the unemployment and inflation rates. This is because these two estimates are published almost immediately by the government agencies responsible—i.e. they are reported on a monthly basis and usually within the first week of the following month if not the last week of the same month. Hence, unlike growth, unemployment and inflation rates are almost instantaneously made known to citizens and can also be experienced by them more directly through unemployment among neighbours and relatives or prices at the local shops.

[7] Augmented Dickey-Fuller tests, with and without trend term, reject the null at the 1 per cent level of a unit root within for the chancellor approval, first estimate, and latest estimate time series.

Table 10.1 Summary statistics for variables included in regression models

	Mean	SD	Min	Max	N
Chancellor approval	51.2	7.33	36.6	70.5	165
First estimate	1.18	1.67	−3.54	5.48	167
First estimate (yoy)	1.62	1.91	−6.72	5.48	167
Latest estimate	0.439	0.911	−4.67	3.11	168
Latest estimate (yoy)	1.81	2.09	−7.03	6.78	168
Helmut Schmidt	0.071	0.258	0	1	168
Helmut Kohl	0.423	0.495	0	1	168
Gerhard Schröder	0.167	0.374	0	1	168
Angela Merkel	0.339	0.475	0	1	168
Time in office	29.4	18.4	1	71	168
Electoral cycle	0.434	0.283	0	0.944	168
Political interest	2.9	1.04	2.25	9	117
Unemployment rate	7.9	2.2	2.93	12.6	165
Inflation rate	0.529	0.563	−0.61	2.55	167
WC/EC Win	0.024	0.153	0	1	168
Year	1998.5	12.2	1978	2019	168
Grand coalition	0.244	0.431	0	1	168
Chancellor and finance minister	0.807	0.396	0	1	166
SPD chancellor	0.238	0.427	0	1	168
CDU chancellor	0.762	0.427	0	1	168

Source: Authors.

election (Müller and Louwerse, 2020). Table 10.1 reports summary stats for all variables included in the statistical models presented in the next section.

Results

First versus Latest Estimate

Our analyses first investigate differences in the effects of first and latest growth estimates on chancellor approval in order to infer the effect of media reporting on the economy. We then move on to estimate the strength of the relationship between the economy and chancellor approval across four decades and the conditional effect of the economy on approval in varying contexts of responsibility of the chancellor's party for outcomes.

So, do first and latest estimates of economic growth have different effects on chancellor approval? To test this, we begin with the simplest of tests, plotting approval against first (left panel) and latest (right panel) growth vintages in

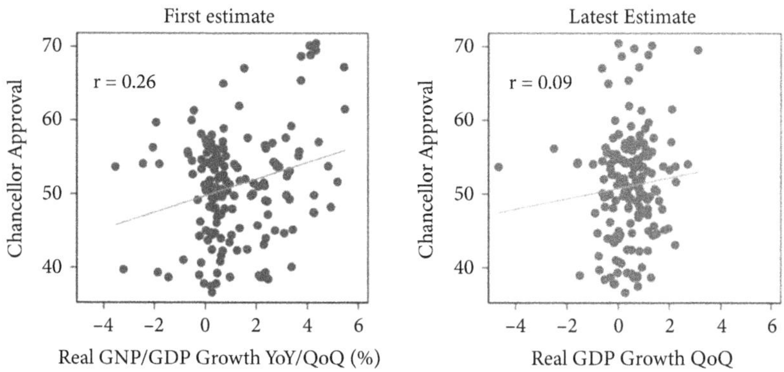

Figure 10.6 Scatter graph plotting chancellor approval against the real-time (first) and current (latest) estimate of economic growth
Source: Authors.

bivariate scatterplots (Figure 10.6). A few things quickly emerge. The variance in real-time (i.e. first) growth estimates is considerably larger than for revised (latest) estimates. Neither plot shows a strong relationship (r = 0.26 and r = 0.09, respectively), but there is a discernible positive relationship when real-time growth estimates are the explanatory variable, which is not the case for revised estimates.

Of course, these plots are only suggestive, so we investigate further with a series of OLS models in Table 10.2 that can better address concerns about omitted confounders, non-stationarity, and persistence. The models in columns (1) to (3) estimate the effects of first and latest growth vintages as well as the difference between the two, respectively, on chancellor approval in a static model. Despite being a less accurate measure of economic growth, initial growth estimates show a positive and statistically significant relationship with approval. A one-point increase in the real-time growth estimate corresponds to a 0.5 percentage point increase in approval. The latest revised estimates show a smaller coefficient that cannot be distinguished from zero at standard significance levels. Not only is it counter-intuitive that the less-accurate measure proves to be the better predictor, but it also raises the question of why. The mechanism could be media reporting on the economy, which provides high coverage of real-time data releases (and even forecasts) but rarely reports on revisions. Moreover, even if they reported on revisions as frequently, by the time many revisions are estimated, they are no longer politically relevant.

The models in columns (4) to (6) add a lagged dependent variable to address possible persistence in the data. The memory processes in the approval time

Table 10.2 OLS models regressing chancellor approval on first and latest estimate of quarterly growth rates, a set of control variables, and quarter dummies

		Static			LDV	
	[1]	[2]	[3]	[4]	[5]	[6]
Chancellor approval$_{t-1}$				0.68*	0.68*	0.68*
				(0.06)	(0.06)	(0.06)
First estimate$_{t-1}$	0.49*		0.47	0.29°		0.28
	(0.22)		(0.34)	(0.16)		(0.24)
Latest estimate$_{t-1}$		0.38			0.22	
		(0.34)			(0.24)	
Diff (latest-first)$_{t-1}$			−0.02			−0.02
			(0.40)			(0.28)
Electoral cycle	−19.92*	−20.15*	−19.90*	−8.59*	−8.59*	−8.57*
	(3.89)	(3.94)	(3.91)	(2.92)	(2.95)	(2.94)
Electoral cycle^2	21.25*	21.52*	21.23*	10.23*	10.25*	10.20*
	(4.27)	(4.35)	(4.31)	(3.17)	(3.22)	(3.20)
Unemployment rate	−1.35*	−1.39*	−1.35*	−0.33°	−0.33°	−0.33°
	(0.21)	(0.21)	(0.21)	(0.17)	(0.18)	(0.17)
Inflation rate	−0.75	−0.96	−0.75	−0.59	−0.71	−0.59
	(0.66)	(0.66)	(0.66)	(0.47)	(0.47)	(0.47)
World/European Cup win	4.17*	3.96°	4.17*	1.94	1.79	1.94
	(2.05)	(2.07)	(2.06)	(1.47)	(1.48)	(1.48)
Helmut Kohl	−8.88*	−9.63*	−8.87*	−3.42*	−3.79*	−3.41*
	(1.63)	(1.61)	(1.64)	(1.24)	(1.24)	(1.25)
Gerhard Schröder	−13.32*	−14.49*	−13.31*	−5.00*	−5.60*	−4.99*
	(2.10)	(2.05)	(2.12)	(1.65)	(1.63)	(1.66)
Angela Merkel	−9.26*	−10.75*	−9.24*	−3.18*	−3.99*	−3.16*
	(1.70)	(1.56)	(1.74)	(1.31)	(1.24)	(1.33)
Time in office	−0.19*	−0.18*	−0.19*	−0.07*	−0.06*	−0.07*
	(0.02)	(0.02)	(0.02)	(0.02)	(0.02)	(0.02)
Q2	−1.79*	−1.70°	−1.79*	−0.86	−0.80	−0.86
	(0.87)	(0.88)	(0.88)	(0.62)	(0.63)	(0.63)
Q3	−2.32*	−2.35*	−2.32*	−0.75	−0.75	−0.75
	(0.91)	(0.92)	(0.92)	(0.66)	(0.67)	(0.67)
Q4	−1.83°	−1.91*	−1.83°	−0.26	−0.28	−0.25
	(0.94)	(0.95)	(0.94)	(0.68)	(0.69)	(0.68)
Intercept	80.50*	82.20*	80.48*	25.79*	26.15*	25.78*
	(2.24)	(2.10)	(2.27)	(4.80)	(4.84)	(4.82)
N	163	163	163	163	163	163
R2	0.75	0.75	0.75	0.88	0.87	0.88
RMSE	3.8	3.84	3.81	2.7	2.73	2.71

Source: Authors.
Note: Standard errors in parentheses, ° $p < 0.10$, * $p < 0.05$ (two-tailed test)

series are high, as shown by a coefficient of 0.7. Because the dependent variable is a function of the covariates, its lag also is a function of the lagged covariates, implying that a dynamically complete regression model should be similar to one with a lagged dependent variable. Though a good strategy for modelling serial correlation, this approach also poses certain problems. The lagged dependent variable is correlated with lagged economic growth—both first and latest vintages—inflating its standard errors. Furthermore, including a lagged dependent variable may bias the coefficients on the other explanatory variables downwards (Keele and Kelly, 2006). However, using a contemporaneous measure of the growth estimates is not a viable option, given that our theory assumes that the information is compiled, estimated, and reported before the public responds to it. Also, the potential downward bias is not so problematic in our application because it runs counter to the theoretically expected positive effect of growth on chancellor approval and should affect the first and latest estimate equally, thereby not biasing our comparison.

All models control for factors commonly known to move executive approval. Just as in many other countries (Carlin et al., 2018; Müller and Louwerse, 2020), Germany sees a cyclical pattern in government approval (Burkhart, 2005), whereby the government loses support soon after the election, reaching a low point towards the middle of an electoral cycle and increasing again in popularity as the next election approaches, which is also reflected in our data on chancellor approval. The unemployment and inflation rate are negatively correlated with chancellor approval, as one would expect. However, only the coefficient on the former variable attains statistical significance. Perhaps not surprisingly, for a football-crazy nation like Germany, wins by the male national team in international contests raise the public mood, which filters through to chancellor approval. Finally, while all chancellors started their time in office at different popularity levels, all experienced a secular decline in support over time, reflecting the well-known cost of ruling (Paldam, 1986).

Of course, we are not only interested in which economic growth vintages are unlikely to occur due to random error but whether the difference between the two is itself statistically significant. Table 10.2 also reports two models—(3) and (6)—that combine the first estimate with a covariate measuring the difference between latest and first estimate (latest minus first). The point estimates on the difference variable in models (3) and (4) report the effect of upward deviations in the latest estimates, holding first estimates constant. Changes in the latest revised vintage have no effect on the popularity of the chancellor's party. Revisions to economic estimates may provide a more accurate assessment of economic activity at the time but they deliver no improvement in modelling a very political variable, executive approval. The reason, one might suppose, is that only the real-time (first) estimate, despite greater measurement error, receives notable attention in the press, thereby influencing individuals' perceptions of the economy.

Less Myopic?

Scholars debate how much voters discount economic variation further in the past when assessing economic change. Do assessments rely on only very recent change (e.g. Achen and Bartels, 2016, Ch. 6) or does economic performance prior to the few months before the election continue to influence voters, albeit to a lesser degree (e.g. Healy and Lenz, 2014; Wlezien 2015)? Results reported in Table 10.2 all relied, partly or fully, on quarterly measures of GDP growth assessed relative to the previous quarter (qoq). What if individuals are not so myopic?

Table 10.3 re-estimates the same models above but alters first estimate and latest estimate variables as measured by economic growth since the same quarter in the previous *year* (yoy). Although only the duration of assessment has changed, the model estimates are markedly different. Whereas the coefficient on the latest estimate of growth in Table 10.2 was smaller than that on the first estimate and statistically insignificant in both the static and LDV models, we see no such pattern in Table 10.3. Once a longer assessment period is employed, the effect of real-time (i.e. first) estimates and revised (i.e. latest) estimates converge in both the static and LDV models, and all reach statistical significance. Expressed differently, there is no evidence that real-time economic measures perform better, which raises doubts about the magnitude of the effect of media reporting about the economy.

These results testify to the sensitivity of the economic vote and executive approval to different measures of the economy. That revised economic measures show no effect when measuring changes since the previous quarter but similar effects to real-time estimates when measuring growth since the same quarter in the previous year, speaks to the potential pitfalls of using objective economic measures in political research and the potential for drawing false inferences. No less worrying, qoq measures of economic growth have become the standard both in the reporting of statistical offices to the media and in quarterly time series. Qoq measures have become dominant even though citizens may be better able to grasp annual changes and could, in effect, be more

Table 10.3 OLS models regressing chancellor approval on first and latest estimate of quarterly growth rates (year-on-year), a set of control variables, and quarter dummies

		Static			LDV	
	[1]	[2]	[3]	[4]	[5]	[6]
Chancellor Approval$_{t-1}$				0.68*	0.68*	0.68*
				(0.06)	(0.06)	(0.06)
First Estimate (yoy)$_{t-1}$	0.37*		0.37*	0.28*		0.28*
	(0.17)		(0.17)	(0.12)		(0.12)
Latest Estimate (yoy)$_{t-1}$		0.33*			0.26*	
		(0.16)			(0.11)	
Diff(Latest-First)$_{t-1}$			0.10			0.17
			(0.45)			(0.31)
Electoral Cycle	−21.77*	−22.12*	−21.93*	−9.94*	−10.25*	−10.19*
	(3.98)	(4.03)	(4.05)	(2.98)	(3.00)	(3.02)
Electoral Cycle^2	23.15*	23.57*	23.33*	11.65*	12.03*	11.95*
	(4.38)	(4.44)	(4.47)	(3.24)	(3.27)	(3.29)
Unemployment Rate	−1.35*	−1.34*	−1.35*	−0.32°	−0.30°	−0.31°
	(0.21)	(0.21)	(0.21)	(0.17)	(0.17)	(0.17)
Inflation Rate	−0.85	−1.00	−0.89	−0.64	−0.75	−0.71
	(0.65)	(0.65)	(0.68)	(0.46)	(0.46)	(0.48)
World/European Cup Win	3.98°	3.87°	3.95°	1.83	1.75	1.78
	(2.05)	(2.05)	(2.06)	(1.46)	(1.46)	(1.46)
Helmut Kohl	−9.14*	−9.51*	−9.24*	−3.47*	−3.73*	−3.62*
	(1.61)	(1.59)	(1.67)	(1.23)	(1.22)	(1.26)
Gerhard Schröder	−14.00*	−14.32*	−14.08*	−5.27*	−5.49*	−5.40*
	(2.04)	(2.03)	(2.08)	(1.61)	(1.60)	(1.63)
Angela Merkel	−10.13*	−10.54*	−10.23*	−3.56*	−3.85*	−3.73*
	(1.57)	(1.55)	(1.65)	(1.24)	(1.22)	(1.28)
Time in Office	−0.19*	−0.18*	−0.19*	−0.07*	−0.07*	−0.07*
	(0.02)	(0.02)	(0.02)	(0.02)	(0.02)	(0.02)
Q2	−1.74*	−1.77*	−1.75*	−0.83	−0.84	−0.84
	(0.87)	(0.87)	(0.87)	(0.62)	(0.62)	(0.62)
Q3	−2.28*	−2.33*	−2.30*	−0.71	−0.75	−0.74
	(0.91)	(0.91)	(0.92)	(0.66)	(0.66)	(0.66)
Q4	−1.84°	−1.92*	−1.87°	−0.25	−0.31	−0.29
	(0.94)	(0.04)	(0.95)	(0.68)	(0.68)	(0.68)
Intercept	81.30*	81.64*	81.37*	25.88*	26.00*	25.95*
	(2.13)	(2.10)	(2.16)	(4.77)	(4.76)	(4.78)
N	163	163	163	163	163	163
R2	0.75	0.75	0.75	0.88	0.88	0.88
RMSE	3.8	3.8	3.81	2.68	2.68	2.69

Source: Authors.
Note: Standard errors in parentheses, ° $p < 0.10$, * $p < 0.05$ (two-tailed test).

interested in the medium-term trajectory of the economy, as captured by yoy growth.

Temporal Instability and Context

We now have estimates for the effect of economic growth in Germany. But might they vary over time and across contexts? One of the most striking results to emerge from this volume is the evidence of an attenuated economic vote in more recent decades. The introductory chapter of this volume lists Germany among those countries that have seen a weakening and, indeed, reversal of the economic vote. Table 10.4 reports the estimated effect of first and latest economic growth estimates on chancellor approval in four decades (as well as over the entire period) for a simple Pearson correlation and for the two models in Table 10.3. Estimates from models using year-on-year growth measures are noted with 'YoY' after the variable name. Two patterns emerge. First, in nearly all the regression models, but not in the bivariate correlations, the effect of growth on chancellor approval is positive and statistically significant in the first period (1978–1989) but no longer positive by the final period (2010–2019). This finding aligns with the pattern demonstrated for some of the other countries in this volume. The greater frequency of grand coalition governments that obscure clarity of responsibility may be partly responsible for this weakening of the economy's effect in later periods in Germany, as we consider below, but the common pattern across several of the countries remains puzzling.

Second, an interesting pattern that emerges in several countries in the introductory chapter also emerges here. The effect of economic growth on approval, regardless of whether real-time or revised, is often negative in the final period. This is theoretically puzzling and deserves more extensive analysis than we can undertake here. We do note, however, that the unexpected direction of the effect is consistent with the finding that right-wing parties often gained vote share during the Great Recession and Euro Crisis and were also more frequently heading governments (LeDuc and Pammett, 2013; Lindvall, 2014).

What might explain the drop in the effect of the economy over time? Although, several country chapters in this volume report a diminishing economic vote, might factors specific to Germany still play a role in this trend?

Table 10.4 Relationship over time of chancellor approval and economic growth, correlations and regression coefficients

Stat	Variable	1978–2019	1978–1989	1990–1999	2000–2009	2010–2019
r	First Estimate$_{t-1}$	0.26*	0.14	0.6*	−0.05	−0.39*
	First Estimate$_{t-1}$ (yoy)	0.19*	0.14	0.6*	0.07	−0.61*
	Latest Estimate	0.09	0.03	0.42*	0.03	−0.37*
	Latest Estimate$_{t-1}$ (yoy)	0.18*	0.08	0.67*	0.15	−0.54*
β_{static}	First Estimate$_{t-1}$	0.49* (0.22)	1.15* (0.31)	1.05* (0.44)	0.42 (0.89)	−3.36* (1.60)
	First Estimate$_{t-1}$ (yoy)	0.37* (0.17)	1.15* (0.31)	1.05* (0.44)	0.19 (0.44)	−1.52* (0.59)
	Latest Estimate$_{t-1}$	0.38 (0.34)	0.73° (0.40)	0.78 (0.84)	0.43 (0.81)	−3.04* (1.20)
	Latest Estimate$_{t-1}$ (yoy)	(0.16)	0.33* (0.35)	1.22* (0.54)	0.05 (0.41)	−0.94* (0.44)
β_{LDV}	First Estimate$_{t-1}$	0.29° (0.16)	0.68* (0.29)	0.31 (0.39)	0.43 (0.81)	−1.66° (0.95)
	First Estimate$_{t-1}$ (yoy)	0.28* (0.12)	0.68* (0.29)	0.31 (0.39)	0.12 (0.40)	−0.56* (0.38)
	Latest Estimate$_{t-1}$	0.22 (0.24)	0.65* (0.30)	−0.21 (0.65)	−0.08 (0.75)	−1.03 (0.78)
	Latest Estimate$_{t-1}$ (yoy)	0.26 (0.11)	0.79* (0.30)	0.51 (0.46)	−0.08 (0.38)	−0.25 (0.28)

Source: Authors.
Note: ° $p < 0.10$, * $p < 0.05$ (standard errors in parentheses). Estimates are obtained by calculating correlations (as presented in Figure 10.6) and rerunning models presented in Tables 10.2 and 10.3 on time period sub-samples. The first column of results (1978–2019) repeats key estimates from Figure 10.6 and Tables 10.2 and 10.3.

Two political alignments that have become more frequent over time in Germany, could potentially obscure clarity of responsibility for economic outcomes (Powell and Whitten, 1993). Grand coalitions in which the two largest parties, the CDU/CSU and the SPD, join together in government result in a more even division of power, making it more difficult to connect outcomes with the chancellor's party. While not a single year in the 1980s or 1990s was governed by a grand coalition, four of the ten years between 2000 and 2009 and seven years in the following decade were overseen by one.

Similarly, the assignment of the finance ministry to a party other than that of the chancellor, also obscures responsibility for economic outcomes. If one considers the CDU and CSU as a single party for governing purposes, Germany did not witness a finance minister from a different party from that of the chancellor between 1966 and 2005. The first decade of the 2000s, however, saw a finance minister and chancellor from different parties for four years and the second decade for nearly two years.

Table 10.5 interacts each of these political contexts with our economic measures. Models (1) and (2) interact first and latest growth estimates, respectively, with a grand coalition dummy in a static model; Models (3) and (4) replicate this in a model with a lagged dependent variable. We see that during grand coalitions, first growth estimates have a considerably smaller effect on chancellor approval, shrinking it from 0.55 and 0.32 in the static and LDV models to 0.33 and 0.22. The effect of real-time estimates cannot be distinguished from zero during grand coalitions in either model, whereas revised estimates simply never reach statistical significance regardless of model or grand coalition status. Grand coalitions, which are more frequent in later decades, do seem to be associated with a weaker relationship between the (real-time) economy and chancellor approval. As with the results in Tables 10.2 and 10.3, however, these differences in effects between real-time and revised measures erode when growth is measured over a longer period (yoy). With both growth measures, coalition governments weaken their effect and by a similar amount, as shown in the online appendix.

The final four models of the table interact, in static and LDV models, the two growth variables with a dummy indicating that the chancellor and finance minister are from the same party. When that is the case, we see a twelve-fold increase in the effect of the first estimate in the static model and nearly four-fold increase in the LDV model. When the chancellor and finance minister are from different parties, however, the coefficient on first estimate is small and statistically insignificant in both the static and LDV models. The effect of revised (latest) estimates, in contrast, only increases slightly when the two most important posts are filled by the same party in the static model and actually drops in the LDV model. Overall, as with grand coalitions, we see some evidence that obscured clarity of responsibility is associated with a weaker link between real-time estimates of the economy and approval. What if we use a

Table 10.5 Context interactions

	Static		LDV		Static		LDV	
	(1)	(2)	(3)	(4)	(5)	(6)	(7)	(8)
Chancellor approval$_{t-1}$			0.66*	0.67*			0.68*	0.68*
			(0.06)	(0.06)			(0.06)	(0.06)
First estimate$_{t-1}$	0.55*		0.32°		0.04		0.08	
	(0.23)		(0.17)		(0.72)		(0.52)	
Latest estimate$_{t-1}$		0.56		0.30		0.29		0.32
		(0.39)		(0.28)		(0.66)		(0.47)
Grand coalition	3.29*	3.33*	1.16	1.15				
	(1.13)	(1.17)	(0.84)	(0.87)				
Grand coalition × first estimate$_{t-1}$	−0.22		−0.10					
	(0.77)		(0.56)					
Grand coalition × latest estimate$_{t-1}$		−0.37		−0.20				
		(0.73)		(0.53)				
Chancellor/FM same party					0.39	0.62	0.28	0.49
					(0.99)	(1.02)	(0.71)	(0.73)
Chancellor/FM same party × first estimate$_{t-1}$					0.45		0.23	
					(0.78)		(0.56)	
Chancellor/FM same party × latest estimate$_{t-1}$						0.05		−0.18
						(0.77)		(0.55)
Intercept	80.09*	81.93*	27.04*	27.40*	80.36*	82.10*	25.33*	25.80*
	(2.23)	(2.07)	(4.90)	(4.94)	(2.51)	(2.35)	(4.97)	(5.01)
Control variables	Yes	Yes	Yes	Yes	Yes	Yes	Yes	Yes
Quarter dummies	Yes	Yes	Yes	Yes	Yes	Yes	Yes	Yes
N	163	163	163	163	162	162	162	162
R2	0.77	0.76	0.88	0.88	0.75	0.75	0.87	0.87
RMSE	3.72	3.76	2.70	2.73	3.82	3.86	2.73	2.75

Source: Authors.
Note: ° $p < 0.10$, * $p < 0.05$ (standard errors in parentheses). OLS models regressing chancellor approval on first and latest estimate of quarterly growth rates, each interacted with a grand coalition dummy and a dummy indicating a finance minister and chancellor from the same party. All models control for position in electoral cycle, unemployment and inflation rate, World and European Cup wins, chancellor dummies and time in office. For a version of this table with yoy quarterly data, see the online appendix.

longer period for growth measures (yoy)? As in earlier results, the difference in effect between the first and latest growth vintages largely disappears but the clarity effect of one party holding the two most important posts remains (see online appendix).

Clarity, however, might not be limited to the government. The economic variation reported by the aggregate national growth estimates might also be more or less reflective of actual economic conditions in different parts of Germany. This is especially the case for the region of the former East Germany (the German Democratic Republic), which experienced a shrinking economy after unification in 1990 and then higher growth in per capita terms than in the former West Germany because of large capital investment and out-migration. Because of its larger population and economy, the former West Germany, dominates the aggregate national economic statistics. Furthermore, eastern Germany's economic production was only included in national estimates of GDP in 1995, as it took the federal statistical agency some time to reliably capture economic production in eastern Germany's rapidly changing economy. If we do see a weaker relationship between the economy and approval in the East than in the West, this could also explain some of the weakening of the effect of growth on chancellor approval after reunification in 1990.

Table 10.5 explores the differences between the former West and East Germany in a series of static and LDV models. Real-time (first) estimates of economic growth are 86 per cent larger in the West than in the East in the static models and more than twice as large in the LDV models, although the only point estimate that is statistically significant among all the growth estimates, first and latest and West and East, is the real-time (first) estimate for the West in the static model. In the yoy models in the online appendix, the difference in effect between first and latest growth vintages erodes, and all growth coefficients are positive and significant, and effects are uniformly smaller in the East. Unification may have indeed weakened the relationship between growth and chancellor approval in the time-series for all of Germany by adding an economically dissimilar region that deviates from the aggregate economic estimates.

Discussion and Conclusion

Chancellor approval, we have seen, responds to real-time (first) growth estimates but not to economically more-accurate latest revisions when growth is measured over short periods (qoq). When measured over a full year (yoy), however, both vintages show similar and statistically significant effects.

Table 10.6 OLS models regressing chancellor approval separately in West and East Germany post-1990 on first and latest estimate of quarterly growth rates

	Static				LDV			
	(1) W1	(2) E1	(3) W2	(4) E2	(5) W3	(6) E3	(7) W4	(8) E4
Chancellor approval$_{t-1}$					1.14*	0.95*	1.18*	0.97*
					(0.18)	(0.16)	(0.18)	(0.16)
First estimate$_{t-1}$	1.66*	0.89			1.16	0.47		
	(0.82)	(0.71)			(0.70)	(0.62)		
Latest estimate$_{t-1}$			0.55	−0.25			0.27	−0.48
			(1.12)	(0.97)			(0.95)	(0.84)
Electoral cycle	−25.91*	−17.06°	−30.80*	−19.64°	−10.49	−4.23	−13.41	−5.30
	(11.70)	(10.21)	(11.67)	(10.07)	(10.27)	(9.13)	(10.26)	(9.01)
Electoral cycle^2	35.64*	20.77°	39.30*	22.18°	19.57°	7.41	21.52°	7.51
	(12.79)	(11.16)	(12.99)	(11.21)	(11.20)	(9.95)	(11.35)	(9.97)
Unemployment rate	−3.77*	−2.79*	−3.97*	−2.90*	−1.88*	−1.22*	−1.97*	−1.25*
	(0.66)	(0.58)	(0.67)	(0.58)	(0.64)	(0.57)	(0.65)	(0.57)
Inflation rate	−2.65	−2.90	−2.65	−2.80	−1.37	−1.83	−1.31	−1.70
	(2.21)	(1.93)	(2.26)	(1.95)	(1.89)	(1.68)	(1.92)	(1.69)
World/European Cup win	8.94	2.94	9.13	3.19	4.62	−0.66	4.66	−0.50
	(5.87)	(5.12)	(5.98)	(5.16)	(5.05)	(4.48)	(5.12)	(4.49)
Gerhard Schröder	2.65	2.84	0.49	1.59	8.10*	7.38*	6.75°	6.75*
	(4.28)	(3.73)	(4.21)	(3.63)	(3.75)	(3.33)	(3.70)	(3.25)
Angela Merkel	5.78	7.06°	2.68	5.37	7.69*	8.65*	5.61	7.78*
	(4.18)	(3.65)	(3.96)	(3.42)	(3.58)	(3.18)	(3.39)	(2.97)
Time in office	−0.11	−0.02	−0.12	−0.03	0.1	0.15*	0.1	0.15*

	(0.08)	(0.07)	(0.08)	(0.07)	(0.08)	(0.07)	(0.08)	(0.07)
Q2	−3.61	−3.08	−3.30	−2.89	−2.47	−2.13	−2.22	−2.00
	(2.58)	(2.25)	(2.62)	(2.26)	(2.20)	(1.96)	(2.23)	(1.95)
Q3	−3.84	−2.29	−3.77	−2.18	−1.45	−0.30	−1.32	−0.16
	(2.64)	(2.31)	(2.69)	(2.32)	(2.28)	(2.03)	(2.32)	(2.03)
Q4	−4.43	−5.04*	−4.33	−4.90°	−1.79	−2.84	−1.63	−2.66
	(2.84)	(2.48)	(2.90)	(2.50)	(2.46)	(2.18)	(2.49)	(2.19)
Intercept	84.89*	71.44*	91.01*	75.04*	0.06	0.89	1.97	1.61
	(10.69)	(9.33)	(10.42)	(8.99)	(16.35)	(14.52)	(16.52)	(14.50)
N	114	114	114	114	114	114	114	114
R^2	0.53	0.5	0.51	0.49	0.66	0.63	0.65	0.63
RMSE	9.37	8.18	9.55	8.24	7.99	7.1	8.09	7.11

Source: Authors.
Note: For a version of the table with yoy quarterly data, see the online appendix. ° $p < 0.10$, * $p < 0.05$ (standard errors in parentheses).

This suggests that media reporting on the economy may only have short-term effects on individuals' assessments of the economy and subsequent approval of the chancellor's party. Individuals learn about growth through the media in the short run but have more direct experience as time passes. The difference in results for first and latest economic estimates in the qoq time-series are non-negligible. They imply that chancellor approval would have been different, especially in earlier periods, if voters had had a better picture of the economic situation, as represented by revised estimates. Figure 10.7 shows what chancellor approval in Germany would have looked like had the initial real-time estimates equalled the latest improved estimates.[8] Differences between actual and what we call counterfactual approval are substantial and both positive and negative. Our model under- or overestimates chancellor approval depending on whether initial economic estimates overestimated or underestimated economic growth relative to revised estimates.

The media undoubtedly plays an essential role in these deviations, not because of partisan bias (cf. Kayser and Peress, 2021) but more likely because they report inaccurate initial estimates from the federal statistics agency.

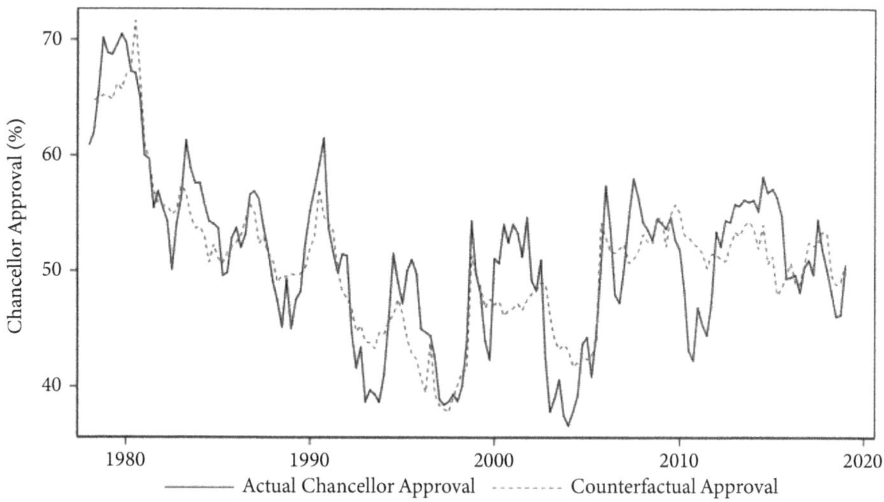

Figure 10.7 Actual chancellor approval (smoothed version) over time and counterfactual approval generated with predicted values from Model 1 in Table 10.2
Source: Authors.

[8] Based on Model 1 of Table 10.2.

In periods shortly before elections—but also in between elections, given governments are responsive to public opinion (Stimson, MacKuen, and Erikson, 1995)—these deviations suggest possible political effects. If governments' actions are influenced by their perceived popularity, which, in turn, is partly driven by inaccurate real-time economic estimates reported in the press, how responsive are they really?

This question becomes more pressing as we present further evidence that the economic vote has become considerably weaker if not altogether absent over the years, even with the more predictive real-time (first) economic measures and yoy measures. We have found some evidence that developments particular to Germany likely played at least a partial role in weakening the relationship between the economy and approval over time. The increasing frequency of grand coalitions and of different parties holding the chancellorship and finance ministry increased after 2000 and German reunification in 1990 added a region with economic growth figures that deviated from the west-dominated national average. Two important questions remain unanswered, however: why did multiple countries see a similar weakening of the economic vote as shown in the other chapters of this volume and why did economic growth become associated with a *decline* in chancellor approval in the decade from 2010?

We can only speculate, but we suspect two phenomena: globalization and inequality. Considerable evidence has emerged in recent years that relative growth rates between countries matter for how individuals evaluate and vote for incumbent governments (Kayser and Peress, 2012; Hansen, Olsen, and Bech, 2015; Park, 2019; Hart and Matthews, 2022). Increasing economic integration over the period of this analysis implies increasingly correlated business cycles, convergence of national growth rates with those of benchmark countries and a weaker economic vote (Kayser and Peress, 2016; Kosmidis, 2018). Such convergence of growth rates, however, would only explain an attenuation of the approval effect of growth over time, not the reversal of sign. Rising inequality, in contrast, might do so. By controlling for inflation and unemployment, our regression results suggest that growth effects result from expansions with no effect on jobs or wage growth, the means by which the less-affluent experience the economy. If more of the benefits of growth are captured by the wealthy than in the past, such growth corresponds to rising inequality that most voters might punish.

The final contribution of this chapter is methodological. Our research has implications for social science research on the behavioural and attitudinal effects of the economy. The currently most prevalent approach of using subjective economic perceptions as the key explanatory variable invites endogeneity bias. The alternative practice of employing objective macroeconomic aggregates, however, does not seem to be a simple panacea. When researchers simply download the latest vintage of revised estimates of economic aggregates from governmental or international organizations, which is almost always the case, they are often making an unwitting decision. If their downloaded data measure growth over a short period, they may well find no effect on approval or the vote, although the original real-time data releases might well show an effect. The increasing popularity of qoq measures of growth in official data reports in Germany and elsewhere underscores the acuity of this problem. If, on the other hand, they choose quarterly data measured over a longer period (e.g. relative to the same quarter in the previous year), the vintage of the data release probably does not matter. There are strong arguments in favour of using objective economic measures for some research designs, but this is only the first of several important data decisions that can profoundly affect results.

References

Achen, C. H., and Bartels, L. M. (2016). *Democracy for Realists.* Princeton, NJ: Princeton University Press.

Alesina, A., and H. Rosenthal. (1995). *Partisan Politics, Divided Government, and the Economy.* Cambridge: Cambridge University Press.

Anderson, C. J. (2007). The end of economic voting? Contingency dilemmas and the limits of democratic accountability. *Annual Review of Political Science, 10*(1), 271–96.

Ashworth, S. (2012). Electoral accountability: Recent theoretical and empirical work. *Annual Review of Political Science, 15*(1), 183–201.

Burkhart, Simone. (2005). Parteipolitikverflechtung. Über den Einfluss der Bundespolitik auf Landtagswahlentscheidungen von 1976 bis 2000. *Politische Vierteljahresschrift, 46*(1), 14–38.

Carlin, R. E., Hartlyn, J., Hellwig, T., Love, G. J., Martinez-Gallardo, C., and Singer, M. M. (2018). Public support for Latin American presidents: The cyclical model in comparative perspective. *Research & Politics, 5*(3).

Carlin, R. E., Hartlyn, J., Hellwig, T., Love, G. J., Martinez-Gallardo, C., and Singer, M. M. (2019). Executive approval database 2.0 (beta). www.executiveapproval.org.

Croushore, D., and Stark, T. (2003). A real-time set for macroeconomists: Does the data vintage matter? *The Review of Economics and Statistics, 85*(3), 605–17.

Debus, M., Stegmaier, M., and Tosun, J. (2014). Economic voting under coalition governments: Evidence from Germany. *Political Science Research and Methods, 2*(1), 49–67.

Diebold, F. X., and Rudebusch, G. D. (1991). Forecasting output with the composite leading index: A real-time analysis. *Journal of the American Statistical Association, 86*(415), 603–10.

Duch, R. M. and Stevenson, R. (2008). *The Economic Vote: How Political and Economic Institutions Condition Election Results.* Cambridge: Cambridge University Press.

Erikson, R. S., and Wlezien, C. (2014). Forecasting US presidential elections using economic and noneconomic fundamentals. *PS: Political Science and Politics, 47*(2), 313–16.

Evans, G., and Anderson, R. (2006). The political conditioning of economic perceptions. *Journal of Politics, 68*(1), 194–207.

Feld, L. P. and Kirchgässner, G. (2000). Official and hidden unemployment and the popularity of the government: An econometric analysis for the Kohl government. *Electoral Studies, 19*(2), 333–47.

Ferejohn, J. (1986). Incumbent performance and electoral control. *Public Choice,* 50(1–3), 5–25.

Frey, B. S. and Garbers, H. (1972). Der einfluss wirtschaftlicher variabler auf die popularität der regierung—eine empirische analyse. *Jahrbu ̈cher fu ̈r Nationalökonomie und Statistik 186*, 281–95.

Frey, B. S., and Schneider, F. (1979). An econometric model with an endogenous government sector. *Public Choice, 34*(1), 29–43.

Ghysels, E., Horan, C., and Moench, E. (2018). Forecasting through the rearview mirror: Data revisions and bond return predictability. *The Review of Financial Studies, 31*(2), 678–714.

Hansen, K. M., Olsen, A. L., and Bech, M. (2015). Cross-national yardstick comparisons: A choice experiment on a forgotten voter heuristic. *Political Behavior, 37*(4), 767–89.

Hart, A., and Matthews, J. S. (2022). Unmasking accountability: Judging performance in an interdependent world. *The Journal of Politics, 84*(3), 1607–22.

Healy, A., and Lenz, G. S. (2014). Substituting the end for the whole: Why voters respond primarily to the election-year economy. *American Journal of Political Science, 58*(1), 31–47.

Healy, A. J, Persson, M., and Snowberg, E. (2017). Digging into the pocketbook: Evidence on economic voting from income registry data matched to a voter survey. *American Political Science Review, 111*(4), 771–85.

Hellwig, T. (2001). Interdependence, government constraints, and economic voting. *Journal of Politics, 63*(4), 1141–62.

Hellwig, T. and Marinova, D. M. (2023). Evaluating the unequal economy: Poverty risk, economic indicators, and the perception gap. *Political Research Quarterly, 76*(1), 253-66.

Hellwig, T., and Samuels, D. (2007). Voting in open economies: The electoral consequences of globalization. *Comparative Political Studies, 40*(3), 283–306.

Jacobs, A. M., Matthews, J. S., Hicks, T., and Merkley, E. (2021). Whose news? Class-biased economic reporting in the United States. *American Political Science Review, 115*(3), 1016–33.

Kayser, M. A. (2014). The elusive economic vote. In *Comparing Democracies* (fourth edn), L. LeDuc, R. G. Niemi, and P. Norris, eds. Thousand Oaks, CA: Sage. 112–32.

Kayser, M. A., and Leininger, A. (2015). Vintage errors: Do real-time economic data improve election forecasts? *Research & Politics, 2*(3), 2053168015589624.

Kayser, M. A., and Leininger, A. (2016). A predictive test of voters' economic benchmarking: The 2013 German Bundestag election. *German Politics, 25*(1), 106–30.

Kayser, M. A., and Leininger, A. (2017). A Länder-based forecast of the 2017 German Bundestag election. *PS: Political Science and Politics* 50(3), 689–92.

Kayser, M. A., and Peress, M. (2012). Benchmarking across borders: Electoral accountability and the necessity of comparison. *American Political Science Review, 106*(3), 661–84.

Kayser, M. A., and Peress, M. (2016). The buck stops over there? Benchmarking elections in the open economy. In *Globalization and Domestic Politics: Parties, Elections, and Public Opinion*, CSES series, J. Vowles and G. Xezonakis, eds. Oxford: Oxford University Press. 89–112.

Kayser, M. A., and Peress, M. (2021). Does the media cover the economy accurately? Evidence from sixteen developed democracies. *Quarterly Journal of Political Science, 16*(1), 1–33.

Kayser, M. A., and Peress, M. 2022. Do voters respond to the economy or to news reporting on the economy? A mediation analysis. Working Paper: Hertie School and SUNY Stonybrook. http://mark-kayser.com/research.html.

Keele, L., and Kelly, N. J. (2006). Dynamic models for dynamic theories: The ins and outs of lagged dependent variables. *Political Analysis, 14*(2), 186–205.

Kirchgässner, G. (1974). Ökonometrische Untersuchungen des Einflusses der Wirtschaftslage auf die Popularität der Parteien. *Schweizerische Zeitschrift für Volkswirtschaft und Statistik, 110*, 409–44.

Kirchgäßner, G. (1977). Wirtschaftslage und wählerverhalten: Eine empirische studie für die Bundesrepublik Deutschland von 1971 bis 1976. *Politische Vierteljahresschrift, 18*(2/3), 510–36.

Kirchgässner, G. (1983). Welche Art der Beziehung herrscht zwischen der objektiven wirtschaftlichen Entwicklung, der Einschätzung der Wirtschaftslage und der Popularität der Parteien: Unabhängigkeit, Scheinunabhängigkeit,

Scheinkorrelation oder kausale Beziehung? In *Wahlen und politisches System: Analysen aus Anlaß der Bundestagswahl* 1980, M. Kaase and H. Klingemann, eds. Schriften des Zentralinstituts für sozialwissenschaftliche Forschung der Freien Universität Berlin Wiesbaden: VS Verlag für Sozialwissenschaften. 222–56.

Kirchgässner, G. (1985a). Causality testing of the popularity function: An empirical investigation for the Federal Republic of Germany, 1971–1982. *Public Choice*, *45*(2), 155–73.

Kirchgässner, G. (1985b). Rationality, causality, and the relation between economic conditions and the popularity of parties: An empirical investigation for the Federal Republic of Germany, 1971–1982. *European Economic Review*, *28*(1), 243–68.

Kirchgässner, G. (1986). Economic conditions and the popularity of West German parties: A survey. *European Journal of Political Research*, *14*(4), 421–39.

Kirchgässner, G. (2009). The lost popularity function: Are unemployment and inflation no longer relevant for the behaviour of German voters? CESifo Working Paper No. 2882:25.

Kitschelt, H. (1994). *The Transformation of European Social Democracy*. Cambridge: Cambridge University Press.

Kosmidis, S. (2018). International constraints and electoral decisions: Does the room to maneuver attenuate economic voting? *American Journal of Political Science*, *62*(3), 519–34.

Krieger, H. (1985). Anti-regierungs oder klientelthese? Wirkungen persönlicher betroffenheit von arbeitslosigkeit im rahmen des etablierten parteienspektrums (1980—1985). *Politische Vierteljahresschrift*, *26*(4), 357–80.

Larcinese, V., Puglisi, R., and Snyder, J. M. (2011). Partisan bias in economic news: Evidence on the agenda-setting behavior of U.S. newspapers. *Journal of Public Economics*, *95*(9), 1178–89.

LeDuc, L., and Pammett, J. H. (2013). The fate of governing parties in times of economic crisis. *Electoral Studies*, *32*(3), 494–9.

Lepenies, P. (2016). *The Power of a Single Number: A Political History of GDP*. New York: Columbia University Press.

Lewis-Beck, M. S. (1986). Comparative economic voting: Britain, France, Germany, Italy. *American Journal of Political Science*, *30*(2), 315–46.

Lindvall, J. (2014). The electoral consequences of two great crises. *European Journal of Political Research*, *53*(4), 747–65.

Maier, J., and Rattinger, H. (1999). Economic conditions and the 1994 and 1998 federal elections. *German Politics*, *8*(2), 33–47.

Maier, J., and Rattinger, H. (2004). Economic conditions and voting behaviour in German federal elections, 1994–2002. *German Politics*, *13*(2), 201–17.

Müller, S., and Louwerse, T. (2020). The electoral cycle effect in parliamentary democracies. *Political Science Research and Methods*, *8*(4), 795–802.

Norpoth, H. and Yantek, T. (1983). Von Adenauer bis Schmidt: Wirtschaftslage und Kanzlerpopularität. In *Wahlen und politisches System: Analysen aus Anlaß der Bundestagswahl* 1980, M. Kaase and H. Klingemann, eds. Schriften des Zentralinstituts für sozialwissenschaftliche Forschung der Freien Universität Berlin. Wiesbaden: VS Verlag für Sozialwissenschaften. 198–221.

Norpoth, H., and Gschwend, T. (2013). Chancellor model picks Merkel in 2013 German election. *PS: Political Science and Politics*, *46*(3), 481–2.

Paldam, M. A. 1986. The distribution of election results and the two explanations for the cost of ruling. *European Journal of Political Economy*, *2*(1), 5–24.

Paldam, M. A. (1991). How robust is the vote function? A study of seventeen nations over four decades. In *Economics and Politics: The Calculus of Support*, H. Norpoth, M. S. Lewis-Beck, and J.-D. Lafay, eds. Ann Arbor, MI: University of Michigan Press. 9–33.

Park, B. B. (2019). Compared to what? Media-guided reference points and relative economic voting. *Electoral Studies*, *62*, 102085.

Plescia, C., Kritzinger, C., and Spoon, J. 2022. Who's to blame? How performance evaluation and partisanship influence responsibility attribution in grand coalition governments. *European Journal of Political Research 61*(3), 660–77.

Powell, B. G., and Whitten, G. D. (1993). A cross-national analysis of economic voting: Taking account of the political context. *American Journal of Political Science*, *37*(2), 391–414.

Rattinger, H. (1986). Collective and individual economic judgments and voting in West Germany, 1961–1984. *European Journal of Political Research*, *14*(4), 393–419.

Rattinger, H., and Steinbrecher, M. (2011). Economic voting in times of economic crisis. *German Politics* 20(1), 128–45.

Ronning, G., and Schneider, F. (1976). Popularitätsfunktionen—eine empirische Zwei-Länder-Studie. *Jahrbuch für Sozialwissenschaft*, *27*(3), 370–90.

Runkle, D. E. (1998). Revisionist history: How data revisions distort economic policy research. *Federal Reserve Bank of Minneapolis Quarterly Review*, *22*(4), 3–12.

Simonsohn, U., Simmons, J. P., and Nelson, L. D. (2019). Specification curve: Descriptive and inferential statistics on all reasonable specifications. Available at SSRN 2694998.

Stanig, P. (2013). Political polarization in retrospective economic evaluations during recessions and recoveries? *Electoral Studies*, *32*(4), 729–45.

Stimson, J. A., MacKuen, M. B., and Erikson, R. S. (1995). Dynamic representation. *American Political Science Review*, *89*(3), 543–65.

Thesen, G., Mortensen, P. B., and Green-Pedersen, C. (2020. Cost of ruling as a game of tones: The accumulation of bad news and incumbents' vote loss. *European Journal of Political Research*, *59*(3), 555–77.

Williams, L. K., Stegmaier, M., and Debus, M. (2017). Relaxing the constant economic vote restriction: Economic evaluations and party support in Germany. *Party Politics*, *23*(3), 286–96.

Wlezien, C. (2015). The myopic voter? The economy and US presidential elections. *Electoral Studies*, *39*(3), 195–204.

11

Economic Crisis, Polarization, and Prime Ministerial Approval in Greece

Panos Koliastasis and John Yfantopoulos

In line with other countries in Southern Europe like Spain and Portugal, Greece restored its democracy in the mid-1970s. After the fall of the colonels' regime in 1974, the country established a parliamentary system in which two parties dominated the political scene, forming in most cases single-party governments: the centre-right New Democracy (ND) and the centre-left Panhellenic Socialist Movement (PASOK) (Nikolacopoulos, 2005; Teperoglou and Tsatsanis, 2014).[1] However, the outbreak of the Greek debt crisis in 2009–10—after the 2008 Global Financial Crisis—and the subsequent adoption of the bailout agreement (Memorandum) with the European Union (EU) and the International Monetary Fund (IMF) triggered the reconfiguration not only of the economic, but also of the political landscape. From 2009 until 2019, the recession deepened and unemployment soared. Economic malaise contributed to a further increase in party polarization, electoral volatility, partisan fragmentation, the decline of the old two-partyism and rise of a new one consisting of ND and the radical left SYRIZA, and the dominance of multi-party governments (Koliastasis, 2015; Tsatsanis et al., 2020).

Against this backdrop, it seems evident that the economy has affected the political fates of the Greek governments. So far, in line with the vast amount of the relevant literature (see Introduction), most empirical studies on Greek economic voting have concentrated on the vote function (e.g. Freire and Lobo, 2005; Lewis-Beck and Nadeau, 2012; Nezi, 2012; Nezi and Katsanidou, 2014; Teperoglou and Tsatsanis, 2014; Karyotis and Rudig, 2015; Teperoglou et al., 2015). Popularity functions, in contrast, have received little attention.

[1] An exception to this trend is the period 1989–1990, in which the 'pure' proportional-representation electoral system was applied, resulting in the emergence of short-lived coalition governments and the holding of three consecutive elections: in June 1989, November 1989, and April 1990. In the last election, the ND party under the leadership of Konstantinos Mitsotakis managed to win a marginal parliamentary majority of 151 seats (in a 300-seat parliament) and form a single-party government (Nikolacopoulos, 2005).

Panos Koliastasis and John Yfantopoulos, *Economic Crisis, Polarization, and Prime Ministerial Approval in Greece.* In: *Economics and Politics Revisited.* Edited by: Timothy Hellwig and Matthew Singer, Oxford University Press.
 DOI: 10.1093/oso/9780192871664.003.0011

Kosmidis (2013), for example, examines the link between the economy and government popularity from 2000 to 2012 by using aggregated data and time-series analysis while Koliastasis (2020a) evaluated the impact of campaign activities on the popularity of Greek incumbent leaders, finding a weak relationship. The latter suggests that larger forces, both economic and non-economic, may exert influence on premiers' popularity. However, exploring the factors shaping Greek executive approval has been largely neglected to date. Two questions naturally emerge: what drives prime ministerial approval in Greece and to what extent have these factors changed in importance over time.

This study aims to fill the research gap exploring, for the first time, the economic and political factors shaping prime ministerial popularity in Greece. Based on quarterly data provided by the Executive Approval Project, it examines the effect of economic and political variables over the period 1998 to 2019. Given the impact of the economic crisis and the Memorandum on Greek politics during this period, the study distinguishes between the pre- and post-crisis or, in other words, the pre-bailout (1998–2009) and post-bailout periods (2010–2019).

Our findings suggest that subjective economic evaluations had a moderate effect on prime ministerial approval, while party polarization on economic issues, such as the Memorandum, had a strong negative effect. Moreover, it appears that economic polarization weakens the strength of the economic evaluations effect. Thus, it seems that in Greece the 'p-fraction' emerges as larger than the 'e-fraction', suggesting that even in an era of deep economic crisis the effect of the economy on popularity is influenced by the party polarization that traditionally prevails in the country. However, polarization focuses on economic issues like the three memoranda the country implemented between May 2010 and August 2018. Similar to other countries (see Chapters 1 and 15), there is an interplay between economic and political factors which indicates that multiple mechanisms are at work shaping prime ministerial popularity in Greece.

The structure of the chapter is as follows. The first section reviews the relevant literature including the literature on Greek economic voting and discusses the economic and political context in Greece before and after the outbreak of the financial crisis. The second section outlines the research hypotheses, while the next section describes the methods and data. The final section analyses the results and last section summarizes the main conclusions.

Literature Review

General Theoretical Background

Most authors share the assumption that the economy plays the most significant role in defining the political fate of political executives. According to the reward-punishment model (Key, 1966), when the economy prospers, premiers' popularity prospers as well, while when the economy falls, then approval ratings plummet. The economy—either in the form of objective economic indicators like mainly unemployment and GDP (Lewis-Beck and Stegmaier, 2013, 376) or in the form of subjective ones including mainly retrospective and sociotropic factors (Lewis-Beck, 1988; Nadeau et al., 2013)—appears to have a heavy influence on executive approval.

However, the relationship between the economy and support for the incumbent leaders is not straightforward since it is mediated, to a greater or a lesser extent, by a number of political factors. One of the most important factors is clarity of responsibility for the state of the economy. Outcomes are more easily attributed to single-party governments compared to multi-party ones (e.g. Anderson, 2000). Other non-economic factors include partisanship (e.g. Nannestad and Paldam, 1994), policy competence (Green and Jennings, 2011), the media (Boydstun et al., 2018), extreme polarization (Donovan et al., 2020), intense populism (Carlin and Love, 2020), and cultural cleavages (Inglehart and Norris, 2016). Yet, there are also economic factors like globalization that appear to trump government accountability for the economic state and thus the role of economic performance (Hellwig, 2015).

Economic Voting in Greece

In this context, this work focuses on Greece. Studies on Greek economic voting are far from extensive. Most have concentrated on the vote function rather than the popularity one. However, their empirical findings inform our theoretical approach in exploring the forces influencing Greek premiers' approval.

The existing literature on economic voting suggests that there should be a high degree of accountability in Greece. This is most clearly evident in the pre-crisis era; prior to the Memorandum, single-party governments had dominated the political scene in Greece, a scenario that facilitates accountability and allows economic factors to take effect (Anderson, 1995; 2000). Rising party-system fragmentation and the big role played by multinational institutions in economic policy may have been expected to change this dynamic (Alcañiz and Hellwig, 2011; Lobo and Lewis-Beck, 2012). Yet, the clarity of responsibility seems to have remained high in the post-Memorandum period as well. As Kosmidis has found, despite the strict supervision of the bailout programme by the EU and the IMF, most voters blamed the Greek government for the rapid deterioration of the state of the economy 'which in turn heightened the impact of objective economic conditions on governing party support' (2013, iii). Possibly most of them shared the view that the government should be held responsible for permitting international lenders to impose a harsh austerity package that, although averted disorderly default and a 'Grexit' (exit of Greece from the eurozone), contributed to the sharp deepening of the recession and the rise in unemployment (Kosmidis, 2013, 34).

In addition, clarity of responsibility was hardly diffused by the emergence of multi-party governments. In November 2011, PASOK Prime Minister George Papandreou was forced to resign from the post, amid public discontent and long protests, allowing for the formation of a coalition of PASOK, ND, and the right-wing Popular Orthodox Movement (LAOS) led by the non-partisan technocrat Lucas Papademos (Gemenis and Nezi, 2015). Yet, as Kosmidis (2013) reports, the effect of objective economic conditions upon government support from 2000 until the first quarter of 2012, including the Papademos-led coalition, remained statistically significant and strong. It seems that most voters associated the state of the economy with PASOK as the main coalition partner (Nezi and Katsanidou, 2014, 426).

In light of these contextual factors, it is not surprising that many of the studies of economic voting in Greece find that the effect of economic factors upon vote choice is evident and statistically significant. Yet these studies also find that the economy's effect co-exists and, to some extent, is mediated by the role of political factors. Examining Eurobarometer data in a set of Southern European countries (including Greece) from 1985 to 1999, Freire and Lobo (2005) find that both objective and subjective economic factors exert a similarly strong influence on vote choice, yet ideology emerges as the most significant single indicator shaping the vote. Lewis-Beck and Nadeau (2012), examining European Election Studies data from 1988 to 2004 across ten European countries of both Northern and Southern Europe, show that economic voting was stronger in the latter, including Greece, but ideology remains one of the most important predictors. In addition, Nezi (2012) suggests that sociotropic economic evaluations are linked to the support for the Greek governing party in the 2004 national election and the 2009 European poll, though the association is mediated by partisanship. It is indicative that until 2009, both PASOK and ND enjoyed comparatively high levels of party identification in the Greek electorate (Teperoglou and Tsatsanis, 2014, 224).

Yet while many studies have identified the economy as an important driver of vote intentions in Greece, recent studies call this association into question. Studying individual-level data gathered in the early months after the adoption of the first Memorandum in May 2010, Karyotis and Rudig (2015) find that although subjective economic indicators exerted some influence on vote intentions, the most important variable proved to be the extent to which the public accepted the government's rhetoric regarding the need to implement the bailout agreement and thus 'saving the country' from a disorderly default. In addition, Teperoglou and Tsatsanis (2014, 237), examining the result of the first post-bailout national election of May 2012, point out that 'voters were discriminating among parties based on a range of issues and not simply on economic performance grounds. Public support for the bailout deal mattered for voters for all parties and followed the expected direction', with pro-bailout voters supporting the pro-bailout PASOK and ND and anti-bailout voters backing the anti-bailout parties like SYRIZA and the right-wing Independent Greeks (ANEL). Furthermore, Teperoglou et al.'s (2015) analysis of vote choice in the 2014 European elections finds that ideology, as traditionally has been the case in Greece (Dinas, 2008), mattered more than retrospective evaluations and one's personal economic situation. The same finding emerges from an early popularity function; Kosmidis finds that in the post-Memorandum era, the influence of objective economic indicators influenced government support (2013, 21–2). Yet, the effect of the bailout agreement was much more powerful. This suggests that the Memorandum, as Nezi and Katsanidou (2014) have indicated, has emerged as an influential factor of positional economic voting that is more important for political choices than traditional economic fluctuations are.

The existing literature thus suggests that the Greek economy may have a strong impact on the support of leaders. But past work also suggests that other considerations may be more important and may be displacing the economy as a driver of leader approval. The effect of the Memorandum and the accompanying political shifts is also unclear. We intend to explore these questions here.

Before formulating hypotheses on the factors shaping the popularity of Greek prime ministers, it is worth outlining the political and economic developments in the country during the period under consideration, with emphasis on that of the economic crisis.

The Greek Political and Economic Context Before and After the Crisis

The political culture of Greece is characterized by political polarization, intense partisanship, extreme populism, and a tradition of clientelism together with constant accusations over scandals and a relatively large proportion of underground economy.[2] It is deeply rooted to historical divisions including the post-World War II civil war between the left and right as well as the colonels' regime from 1967 to 1974 (Featherstone, 2005) Thus, according to Teperoglou and Tsatsanis, the political culture has led to the formation of a 'highly durable parallel networks of "left" and "right" political blocs' (2014, 224). In parallel, the prime minister in the Greek context emerges as the dominant political actor exercising both the executive power as the head of the government (either one-party or multi-party) and the legislative power as the head of the largest parliamentary party (Lijphart, 1999; Gallagher et al., 2006). Thus, in such contexts prime ministerial approval is seen as a key measure of political success allowing executive leaders to sustain or even strengthen their political authority and thus achieving their policy goals (Foley, 2000; Heffernan, 2003).

In this context, from the restoration of democracy in 1974 until 2009, PASOK and ND dominated the political scene, creating one-party governments, enjoying high levels of party identification and acting in a polarized political environment reflected in the left–right axis. However, this stable situation changed in the wake of the Global Financial Crisis of 2008. The ensuing Greek debt crisis in 2009–2010 altered radically both the economic and political landscape. Unable to borrow funds from the international markets, Greece and the then PASOK government led by Papandreou turned for assistance to the EU and the IMF to avert a disorderly default. In exchange for refinancing its debt, Greece had to implement, under the supervision of its lenders, a Memorandum consisting of austerity measures and market-oriented reforms (Gemenis, 2010). Although it averted a catastrophic collapse, the Memorandum initially exacerbated the recession leading to massive unemployment (Kazakos, 2011). Hence, the bailout emerged as the dominant position issue

[2] The share of the underground economy as a percentage of GDP in Greece is one of largest in the EU, accounting for around 30 per cent of GDP (Yfantopoulos, 2013).

transcending the left–right cleavage, dividing parties between pro- and anti-bailout and strengthening polarization on economic issues (Gemenis and Triga, 2013; Voulgaris and Nikolacopoulos, 2014; Tsatsanis et al., 2020).

The first Memorandum of May 2010 was backed only by the PASOK government, while the main opposition party of ND led by Antonis Samaras adopted an anti-bailout position. In November 2011, however, after the resignation of Papandreou from the premiership, ND joined a pro-bailout coalition that included PASOK and (initially) LAOS. The coalition aimed to agree to a second bailout agreement with the EU-IMF and avert a Grexit.[3]

In the first post-bailout election held in May 2012, most voters turned against the Memorandum punishing the parties of the pro-bailout coalition PASOK-ND. As the main governmental actor, PASOK ranked third, seeing its vote share fall from 43.9 per cent in 2009 to 13.2 per cent—a record low (Nezi and Katsanidou, 2014). ND also fell from 33.5 per cent to 18.9 per cent, though it moved to first position. In contrast, parties of the anti-bailout camp benefited with the radical left SYRIZA rising from 4.7 per cent in 2009 to 16.3 per cent to rank second.

Yet, the inconclusive result of the May poll led to a second election in June 2012. The political uncertainty, combined with the rise of the anti-bailout SYRIZA, raised concerns over the willingness of Greece not only to implement the Memorandum, but also to remain in the eurozone (Vasilopoulou and Halikiopoulou, 2013, 529). Benefiting from its credible pro-euro, pro-bailout stance, ND received a plurality of 29.7 per cent of the vote, a total that translated into 129 seats, shy of the 151 needed for a majority. The anti-bailout SYRIZA came in second with 26.9 per cent of the vote and 71 seats. ND formed a coalition with PASOK ranking third (12.3 per cent and thirty-three seats) and the moderate Democratic Left (DIMAR) under the premiership of the ND leader Samaras.

The new coalition prioritized the implementation of the second Memorandum including unpopular austerity measures and structural reforms generating social unrest. Against this backdrop, in June 2013 DIMAR withdrew its support from the coalition due to its dispute with the government's decision to restructure the Greek Public Broadcasting Network by reducing its workforce (Iosifidis and Papathanassopoulos, 2019). The coalition of ND and PASOK was left with a narrow majority of 153 in a 300-seat Parliament. Yet, it continued to apply the economic consolidation programme, improving slightly the

[3] LAOS left the coalition before the parliamentary vote on the second Memorandum in February 2012.

state of the economy as Greece had returned to marginally positive growth rates by the end of 2014 (Koliastasis, 2015).

By December 2014, however, the failure of the Hellenic parliament to elect a new head of government led to a snap poll, as stipulated by the Greek constitution. Public frustration with the austerity package and the economic state led to the electoral defeat of ND. On 25 January 2015, SYRIZA came into office receiving 36.4 per cent of the vote and 149 seats. Having fallen short of an outright majority, it collaborated with the anti-bailout right-wing ANEL party to form the first anti-bailout coalition of Greece, led by the SYRIZA leader Alexis Tsipras (Koliastasis, 2015).

Once in office, the newly elected government engaged in negotiations with the EU-IMF aiming to formulate a new bailout agreement based on SYRIZA's pre-electoral platform consisting of debt relief, a fresh loan on favourable terms, and an expansionary policy mix (Tsebelis, 2016). After protracted yet fruitless negotiations, Tsipras announced on 5 July that the latest draft of the third Memorandum proposed by the EU-IMF, would be brought to a referendum and the government would recommend Greek people vote 'No'. The campaign, though it lasted only seven days, was highly polarized. The No vote was backed by SYRIZA, ANEL, and the anti-bailout neo-fascist Golden Dawn, while the 'Yes' camp included the parties of ND, PASOK, and the centrist Potami (the communist KKE party abstained).

Despite the economic deterioration and a possible Grexit, the No position won by a landslide taking 61.3 per cent of the vote over 38.7 per cent for the Yes camp. However, a few days later, in an unprecedented U-turn, Tsipras agreed on a third Memorandum abandoning his anti-bailout platform (Tsatsanis and Teperoglou, 2016). Although the U-turn caused the split of his party, the third bailout was approved by the parliament backed by the pro-bailout pro-euro opposition. Having lost the parliamentary majority though, Tsipras called for early elections on 20 September. Given that the division between pro-bailout and anti-bailout had been cancelled, Tsipras aimed at realigning his disillusioned voters by formulating a new dividing line. He projected himself as representing the 'new' politics against the 'old' political establishment of ND and PASOK meaning that he would be more capable than his predecessors of implementing the Memorandum, while protecting effectively the most vulnerable (Tsatsanis and Teperoglou, 2016; Koliastasis, 2019a). SYRIZA managed to be re-elected, taking 35.5 per cent of the vote and forming a new coalition with ANEL.

Nonetheless, the third Memorandum entailed a high political cost for the governing coalition. In particular, SYRIZA's U-turn to the Memorandum together with the austerity measures of heavy taxation fuelled a new division between the pro-SYRIZA and the anti-SYRIZA camp (Tsatsanis et al., 2020). The former was represented by SYRIZA and its right-wing allies. The latter consisted of right, centre-right, and centrist voters and was represented primarily by ND. In the European elections of May 2019, SYRIZA suffered heavy electoral losses taking only 23 per cent of the vote (Koliastasis, 2019b). As a result, Tsipras called for a snap election in July 2019. He was defeated again by ND led by Kyriakos Mitsotakis, that received 39.9 per cent of the vote and 158 seats forming a single-party government for the first time since 2009.

Research Hypotheses

In this context, the study aims to address two research questions: what drives prime ministerial approval in Greece and to what extent these drivers have changed over time. It focuses on the investigation of the impact of economic and political factors on prime ministerial approval. Following the limited previous studies on the popularity function (Kosmidis, 2013), we examine both objective economic indicators and more specifically unemployment as well as and subjective evaluations. It is expected that accountability has remained high in the post-Memorandum period during which coalition governments dominated. One of the reasons is the electoral law of 'reinforced' proportional representation according to which the winning party is granted a fifty-seat bonus (Gallagher et al., 2006) and thus having many more seats than the minor partners. In the June 2012 elections, ND received 129 seats compared to thirty-three and seventeen for its coalition partners PASOK and DIMAR respectively. Also, in the January and September 2015 polls, SYRIZA received 149 and 145 seats respectively, compared to thirteen and ten seats for its coalition partner ANEL. Another reason is that this study focuses on the factors shaping prime ministerial popularity. From 2012 to 2019, the leaders of the largest parties, namely Samaras (2012–2015) and Tsipras (2015–2019), emerged as prime ministers and it stands to reason that allocating blame for the state of the economy would have been an easy task for voters. Therefore, the study expects that the objective factor of the unemployment rate will have a significant and negative impact on the premiers' popularity, while subjective factors of sociotropic retrospective economic evaluations will improve executive approval. Thus, the first two working hypotheses are as follows:

H1: The rise in unemployment contributes to a decline in prime ministerial approval.

H2: The improvement of sociotropic retrospective economic evaluations contributes to an increase in prime ministerial approval.

Moreover, previous studies indicate that the effect of the Memorandum on voting behaviour in the first post-bailout elections was also strong (Nezi and Katsanidou, 2014; Teperoglou and Tsatsanis, 2014). Similarly, as Kosmidis (2013, 22) has found, the adoption of the first bailout reduced support for the then PASOK government, and this effect was comparatively stronger than that of the objective economy. One of the reasons seems to be that the content of the bailout plan consisted of austerity measures and liberal reforms contradicted the pre-election programme of PASOK that included expansionary policies and thus alienating its voters (Kazakos, 2011). Where countries like Ireland, Portugal, Cyprus and Spain that did not require a second bailout, Greece implemented a total of three memoranda lasting almost eight years (May 2010-August 2018), and it is likely that their effect on the government support was constantly strong (Tsatsanis and Teperoglou, 2016; Tsatsanis et al., 2020). Besides, as Koliastasis (2020b) has suggested, not only Papandreou, but also his successors in the premiership (Samaras and Tsipras) promoted austerity measures contradicting with their electoral pledges. In addition, the Memorandum emerged as a dominant economic position issue between 2010 and 2015 (Nezi and Katsanidou, 2014). After the 2012 elections, the centre-right ND emerged as the dominant pro-bailout force, while the radical left SYRIZA as the major anti-bailout one. Although the latter's U-turn in favour of the third Memorandum along with the subsequent cancellation of the pro versus anti-bailout division was expected to reduce economic polarization, the context hardly changed. While polarization on both economic and non-economic issues declined, economic polarization remained strong among particularly ND and SYRIZA voters (Tsatsanis et al., 2020, 514). The former supported policies of economic liberalism, while the latter backed policies of big government. It seems that the root-cause of the polarization of the period September 2015–July 2019 is traced to the heavy taxation policy imposed by the SYRIZA-led government after the adoption of the third Memorandum (Koliastasis, 2019b). Thus, the intensity of polarization on economic issues is expected to exert a strong negative effect on premiers' approval in the opposite direction. As a result, the third hypothesis is:

H3: The stronger the polarization on economic issues, the more prime ministerial approval decreases.

Methods and Data

To test the above research hypotheses, the study explores time-series quarterly data covering the period 1998–2019. Prime ministerial popularity in Greece is used as the dependent variable gathered by multiple well-known Greek polling organizations[4] and compiled as well as estimated by the Executive Approval Project into a single measure (Carlin et al., 2019). Conclusions about the premiers' approval in Greece are drawn from the positive views of respondents to the polling question: 'Do you have a positive or negative opinion regarding prime minister [name]?'

The examined period of the executive popularity covers twenty-one years from January 1998 to July 2019 and particularly six premiers including: the centre-left prime minister Kostas Simitis heading the PASOK government for two terms (January 1996–March 2004); the centre-right Kostas Karamanlis leading the ND government for two terms (March 2004–October 2009); the centre-left George Papandreou (October 2009–November 2011); the technocrat Lucas Papademos who led a coalition of PASOK, ND (and LAOS) November 2011–May 2012; the centre-right Antonis Samaras heading a coalition of ND, PASOK (and DIMAR) (June 2012–January 2015) and finally the radical left Alexis Tsipras leading a coalition with ANEL (January 2015–July 2019).[5]

Even though Simitis' tenure began in January 1996, the study examines the period from the first quarter of 1998 onwards due to the availability of the Greek economic data. Data on the unemployment rate, collected by the national statistical service of Greece, are quarterly data covering the period of the first quarter of 1998 until the second quarter of 2019 before the July 2019 national election.

The empirical part of our analysis focus on investigating the factors, both quantitative and qualitative, that influence prime ministerial approval before as well as during the economic crisis in Greece. To this end and due to the central role of the Memorandum in shaping approval, we specify three statistical models. The first is a *full model*: covering the entire period 1998–2019. The second is the *pre-bailout period*, covering the time trend from the first quarter

[4] These organizations include Metron Analysis, Alco, Rass, Public Issue, Kapa Research, and the Research Unit of the University of Macedonia.

[5] In January 2019, ANEL left the coalition because of its dispute over the government's decision to promote the Prespa Agreement, according to which the former Yugoslav Republic of Macedonia (FYROM) was renamed 'North Macedonia'. Yet, most of its MPs defected from the party and joined SYRIZA.

of 1998 until the second quarter of 2010. The third model looks at the *post-bailout period*, covering the time trend from the third quarter of 2010 until the second quarter of 2019.

All the above models include a set of both quantitative and qualitative variables associated with economic and political factors. As an objective economic indicator, the study model uses the unemployment rate. The latter is used for four reasons. First, as Lewis-Beck and Stegmaier (2013, 376) have suggested, unemployment and growth are considered the two important economic factors. Second, it stands to reason that they are highly correlated, especially at a time of economic crisis. The correlation coefficient between the two variables is very high, generating significant multicollinearity problems. Third, we argue that the relevant data on the unemployment rate, because of its large variability, before and during the economic crisis, captures more clearly the deterioration of the Greek economy than that of growth. Fourth, the variables of growth and unemployment are influenced in Greece by the large segment of underground economy.[6] We have explored several econometric models by including both variables of growth and unemployment as well as separate estimates by incorporating one each at a time. We found that unemployment is a more 'representative' indicator of the period under investigation, providing estimates consistent with economic theory. In addition to unemployment variable, we use a set of subjective indicators capturing sociotropic retrospective economic evaluations. Sociotropic and retrospective economic factors are considered more influential than the egocentric and the prospective ones respectively (Lewis-Beck and Stegmaier, 2013, 369). The relevant data are taken from the European Commission.[7] In terms of political factors, we use one variable measuring the strength of polarization on economic issues gathered by the MARPOR Manifesto Data (see Hellwig and Singer, this volume). Unfortunately, for Greece systematic time-series data on other non-economic factors like party identification, policy salience, and policy competence are unavailable.

To control for the electoral cycle, models include election dummy variables taking the score of 1 in an election quarter and 0 otherwise. Capturing the

[6] According to Yfantopoulos (2013) and the OECD estimates, Greece has the largest underground economy (30 per cent) in comparison to the rest of Southern European Countries (25 per cent). Empirical analysis has indicated the negative relationship between economic growth and underground economy. One per cent increase in economic growth would reduce the underground economy by 0.13 ($p < 0.012$) in the short run and by 1.26 in the long run ($p < 0.001$)

[7] Downloaded from https://ec.europa.eu/info/business-economy-euro/indicators-statistics/economic-databases/business-and-consumer-surveys/download-business-and-consumer-survey-dataset.

honeymoon effect for newly elected prime ministers, since relevant literature suggests it erodes twelve months after the election (Dinkel, 1978), requires the construct of a dummy variable that is coded 1 for the first four quarters of a premier's tenure and 0 for the rest. To control for the effect of clarity of responsibility we employ a dummy variable distinguishing single-party from multi-party governments. Quarters in which coalition governments do not rule take a score of 0, while quarters in which coalitions rule take a score of 1. Finally, models include separate dummy variables for each of the six different premiers' time in office, so that 0 means the given prime minister was not in power and 1 means he was.

We investigate series stationarity in two ways. We initially adopt a graphical analysis to test autocorrelation with the use of sample correlograms. We then use Augmented Dickey-Fuller (ADF) analysis to assess stationarity. ADF tests indicate that unemployment and subjective economic assessments are non-stationary (fail to reject the null of a unit root). Accordingly, we first difference these two series prior to including them in the model.

Results

The evolution of prime ministerial popularity during the Third Hellenic Republic over the period 1998–2019 is portrayed in Figure 11.1. The political cycle of six prime ministers is depicted in vertical lines in relation to their approval. As the figure indicates, all premiers enjoy high approval ratings in the early period of their term due to the honeymoon effect, though in the post-Memorandum era (May 2010 onwards) it eroded sooner than expected (Dinkel, 1978). Simitis saw his popularity increase after his re-election, Karamanlis also saw his popularity grow after his election and re-election. Similarly, Papandreou, Papademos, Samaras, and Tsipras enjoyed high popularity ratings when they came into office. Moreover, the evolution of the premiers' approval ratings varies. Those ruling the country in the pre-bailout era (Simitis and Karamanlis) enjoyed relatively higher approval ratings compared to their successors in the post-Memorandum period. Probably the economic state together with the memoranda have played a role. However, it should be noted that the completion of the third Memorandum in August 2018 and the gradual decline of unemployment hardly improved Tsipras' popularity levels. The latter is consistent with the findings of Carlin and Love (2020), showing that populist leaders are persistently disapproved of by the greatest part of the public.

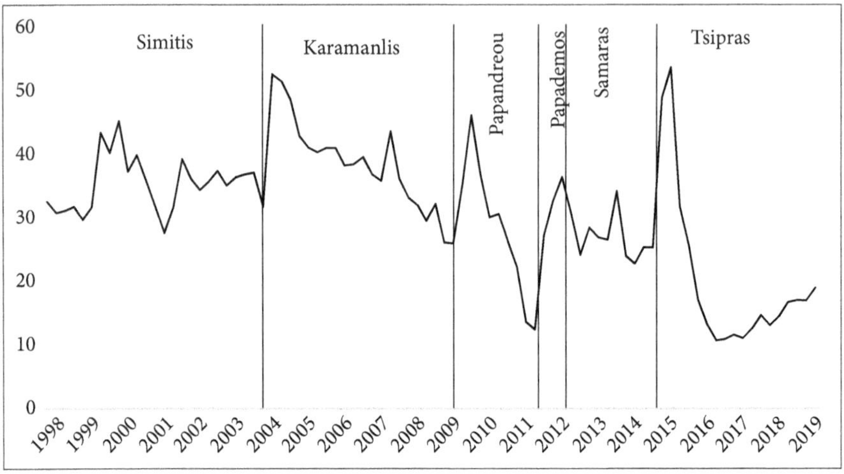

Figure 11.1 Evolution of prime ministerial approval, 1998–2019
Source: Executive Approval Database V 2.0.
Note: Vertical axis reflects prime ministerial approval ratings.

The results of our statistical analysis are presented in Table 11.1. The first three models model approval for three different time periods, as described above: the entire sample, the period before the first bailout agreement, and the period after the Memorandum. Interestingly, coefficients on the coalition, honeymoon, and election-period variables do not register consistent effects. In all three models under investigation the parameter on unemployment is not statistically significant, but it has the expected negative sign. The effects of unemployment on approval are likely to be muted because of the large underground economy. In Model 1 (full sample) and Model 2 (pre-bailout), subjective economic evaluations positively affect approval (political evaluations), while in the post-bailout Model 3, it has zero effect. In the pre-bailout sample of Model 2, the economy as measured subjectively seems to matter more than over the full sample. In contrast, in the post-bailout sample of Model 3, economic performance does not matter since neither unemployment nor subjective evaluations exert any influence on prime ministerial popularity. This suggests that the economy, as conceived by the public, became de-linked from their assessment of prime ministerial performance during the post-Memorandum period.

Taken together, the parameter estimates reported in the first three models of the table provide mixed support for Hypothesis 1, on the impact of unemployment, and on Hypothesis 2, on subjective economic perceptions. In the

Table 11.1 Modelling prime ministerial approval in Greece

	(1) Full sample	(2) Pre-bailout	(3) Post-bailout	(4) Full sample	(5) Pre-bailout	(6) Post-bailout
$Approval_{t-1}$	0.621*	0.466*	0.626*	0.514*	0.237	0.525*
	(0.090)	(0.129)	(0.163)	(0.093)	(0.148)	(0.156)
$\Delta Unemployment_t$	−0.201	−0.964	−0.070	−0.206	−0.416	−0.364
	(0.772)	(1.059)	(1.237)	(0.735)	(1.007)	(1.140)
ΔEconomic $evaluations_t$	0.287*	0.268*	0.515	0.207	0.203	0.427
	(0.119)	(0.119)	(0.277)	(0.116)	(0.114)	(0.301)
Economic $polarization_t$				−2.066*	−2.278*	−3.274*
				(0.709)	(0.854)	(1.342)
$Coalition_t$	−5.587		−5.222	−4.209		−4.364
	(4.319)		(5.455)	(4.138)		(5.012)
$Election_t$	3.647	1.078	5.767	5.601*	1.111	10.881*
	(2.550)	(2.908)	(5.148)	(2.518)	(2.708)	(5.163)
$Honeymoon_t$	2.293	1.347	4.971	2.777	3.287	4.245
	(1.671)	(1.895)	(3.426)	(1.599)	(1.909)	(3.154)
Prime ministers (Simitis reference category)						
$Karamanlis_t$	1.180	1.554		3.234	3.928*	
	(1.685)	(1.453)		(1.752)	(1.620)	
$Papandreou_t$	−4.170	3.629		3.939	12.629*	
	(2.568)	(4.005)		(3.705)	(5.031)	
$Papademos_t$	−5.249		−2.141	10.021		7.716
	(5.991)		(7.214)	(7.746)		(7.748)
$Samaras_t$	−10.594*		−6.042	13.111		16.666
	(4.756)		(6.721)	(9.313)		(11.160)
$Tsipras_t$	−12.478*		−7.752	−1.790		−5.221
	(4.433)		(5.929)	(5.592)		(5.532)
Constant	18.320*	18.610*	11.953	24.611*	30.890*	35.208*
	(4.909)	(4.583)	(6.098)	(5.148)	(6.280)	(11.048)
Observations	84	48	36	84	48	36
R-squared	0.752	0.463	0.687	0.779	0.546	0.747

Source: Executive Approval Database
Notes: Cells report OLS coefficients with standard errors in parentheses, * $p < 0.05$ (two-tailed test).

case of the former, jobless levels, as expected, carry a negatively signed coefficient but are not precisely estimated. In the case of the latter, the subjective economy does move approval ratings during the pre-bailout period, but that effect weakens during the post-Memorandum period.

To test the third hypothesis, in Models 4–6 we re-estimate the three models but include the economic polarization measure in the specification. Consistent with expectations, higher levels of party polarization on the economy contribute to lower prime ministerial approval levels. All else being equal, party polarization on the economy reduces approval, especially in the post-bailout era. The least popular prime ministers were Samaras and, especially, Tsipras, probably due to the intensity of the division regarding the Memorandum especially from 2012 onwards as well as the division between SYRIZA and the anti-SYRIZA camp from September 2015 onwards. In addition, note that the polarization effect masks any influence of subjective economic perceptions; and the former's influence is strongest. Our results suggest that one explanation for why the economy did not appear to matter as much during the post-bailout period is that economic polarization weakened the strength of the economic performance effect.

Conclusion

This work examines, for the first time, the factors shaping prime ministerial approval in Greece. It has assessed the explanatory power of economic and political variables over a period of twenty-one years from 1998 to 2019 covering both the pre-bailout era and the post-bailout era as well as six prime ministers during the Third Hellenic Republic. It finds that unemployment has hardly affected prime ministerial popularity in Greece. In addition, although subjective economic evaluations have exerted influence on executive approval, the effect is unstable over time. In particular, the economic effect matters more in the pre-crisis era rather than in the post-crisis one. This finding is consistent with the literature and the general message of this volume that the effect of the economy on government approval is far from systematic (e.g. Paldam, 1991; Anderson, 2007; see also Chapter 1 to this volume).

In parallel, economic polarization has had a much stronger effect on prime ministerial popularity in a negative direction, especially in the post-bailout era. The perception of the public majority from 2010 to 2015 that an anti-bailout economic platform would be feasibly implemented to deal effectively with the crisis contributed to the decrease of the pro-bailout premiers' approval. Moreover, even after Greece's exit from the memoranda in August 2018, economic polarization remained strong and reflected divergent economic visions of the two major parties of ND and SYRIZA. The reason for the anti-SYRIZA sentiment was fuelled by the policy of heavy taxation and the majoritarian preference for a divergent liberal policy mix (Tsatsanis et al., 2020).

The source of instability on the role of the economy lies in political factors and particularly in party polarization. Relevant literature has suggested that polarization is one of the potential mediating factors (e.g. Donovan et al., 2020 and Chapter 13 of this volume). In the case of Greece, the interaction of economic evaluations with economic polarization has revealed how much the latter has weakened the effect of the former. However, we must be cautious about the apparent weak influence of the economy. The strong influence of the factor of party polarization on economic issues was not so much fuelled by the issue of the Memorandum and austerity per se as by their economic consequences: further deepening recession and further rising unemployment. Had the economy been in good shape, the negative impact of economic polarization on the premiers' popularity would probably not have been evident. Nonetheless, the factors shaping the political framework in Greece seem to limit the direct influence of the economy on the popularity of prime ministers. In this sense, future research in Greece needs to focus more on the role of political factors in order to see whether they continue to weaken economic factors in an era, like the current one, characterized by high inflation.

References

Alcañiz, I., and Hellwig, T. (2011). Who's to blame? The distribution of responsibility in developing democracies. *British Journal of Political Science*, *41*(2), 389–411.

Afonso, A., Zartaloudis, S., & Papadopoulos, Y. (2015). How party linkages shape austerity politics: Clientelism and fiscal adjustment in Greece and Portugal during the Eurozone crisis. *Journal of European Public Policy*, *22*(3), 315–334. https://doi.org/10.1080/13501763.2014.964644

Anderson, C. (1995). *Blaming the Government: Citizens and the Economy in Five European Democracies*. Armonk: M. E. Sharpe.

Anderson, C. (2007). The end of economic voting? Contingency dilemmas and the limits of democratic accountability. *Annual Review of Political Science*, *10*, 271–96.

Anderson, C. J. (2000). Economic voting and political context: A comparative perspective. *Electoral Studies*, *19*(2–3), 151–70.

Boydstun, A. E., Highton, B., and Linn, S. (2018). Assessing the relationship between economic news coverage and mass economic attitudes. *Political Research Quarterly*, *71*(4), 989–1000.

Carlin, R. E., and Love, G. J. (2020). Populist popularity: Plebiscitarian vs. polarizing 73rd Perspectives. Paper delivered at the Annual Conference of the World Association for Public Opinion Research, Salamanca.

Carlin, R. E., Hartlyn, J., Hellwig, T., Love, G. J., Martinez-Gallardo, C., and Singer, M. M. (2019). Executive Approval Database 2.0. Available for download at www.executiveapproval.org.

Dinas, E. (2008). Big expectations, small outcomes: The impact of leaders' personal appeal in the 2004 Greek election. *Electoral Studies*, *27*(3), 505–17.

Dinkel, R. (1978). The relationship between federal and state elections in West Germany. In *Elections and Parties*, M. Kaase and K. Beyme, eds. London and Beverly Hills: Sage. 53–65.

Donovan, K., Kellstedt, P. M., Key, E. M. and Lebo, M. (2020). Motivated reasoning, public opinion, and presidential approval. *Political Behavior*, *42*(1), 1201–21.

Featherstone, K. (2005). Introduction: 'Modernization' and the structural constraints of Greek politics. *West European Politics*, *28*(2), 223–41.

Freire, A., and Lobo, C. M. (2005). Economics, ideology and vote: Southern Europe, 1985–2000. *European Journal of Political Research*, *44*(4): 493–518.

Foley, M. (2000) *The British Presidency: Tony Blair and the Politics of Public Leadership*, Manchester: Manchester University Press.

Gallagher M., Laver M., and Mair P. (2006) *Representative Government in Modern Europe*, fourth edition. Boston: McGraw-Hill.

Gemenis, K., and Nezi, R. (2015). Government–Opposition dynamics during the economic crisis in Greece. *The Journal of Legislative Studies*, *21*(1), 14–34.

Gemenis, K., & Triga, V. (2013). Party positions for the May and June 2012 parliamentary elections in Greece [data file and codebook], Data Archiving and Networked Services (DANS) [distributor].

Gemenis, K. (2010). Wining votes and weathering storms: The 2009 European and parliamentary elections in Greece. *Representation*, *46*(3), 353–362. https://doi.org/10.1080/00344893.2010.499704

Green, J., and Jennings, W. (2011). The dynamics of issue competence and vote for parties in and out of power: An analysis of valence in Britain, 1979–1997. *European Journal of Political Research*, *51*(4), 469–503.

Heffernan, R. (2003). Prime ministerial predominance? Core executive politics in the UK. *British Journal of Politics and International Relations*, *5*(3), 347–72.

Hellwig, T., (2015) *Globalization and Mass politics: Retaining the Room to Maneuver*. Cambridge: Cambridge University Press.

Inglehart, R., and Norris, P. (2016). Trump, Brexit, and the rise of populism: Economic have-nots and cultural backlash. HKS Faculty Research Working Paper Series RWP16-026, August.

Iosifidis, P., and Papathanassopoulos, S. (2019). Greek ERT: State or public service broadcaster? In *Public Service Broadcasting and Media Systems in Troubled*

European Democracies, E. Połońska and C. Beckett, eds. New York: Palgrave Macmillan. 129–53.

Karyotis, G., and Rudig, W. (2015). Blame and punishment? The electoral politics of extreme austerity in Greece. *Political Studies*, *63*(1), 2–24.

Kazakos, P. (2011) *After the 'Memorandum': Economic Policy under International Supervision*. Athens: Papazisis Publications.

Key, V.O. (1966). *The Responsible Electorate*. New York: Vintage.

Koliastasis, P. (2015). The Greek parliamentary elections of 25 January 2015. *Representation*, *51*(3), 359–72.

Koliastasis, P. (2019a). How to sell a U-turn to get re-elected: The case of SYRIZA from a political branding perspective. In *Political Marketing: Principles and Applications*, third edition, J. Lees-Marshment, B. Conley, E. Elder, R. Pettitt, V. Raynauld, A. Turcotte, eds. London: Routledge.

Koliastasis, P. (2019b). The first defeat of populists: The case of Greece. In *Euroflections: Leading Academics on the European Elections 2019*, N. Bolin, K. Falasca, M. Grusell, and L. Nord, eds. Sundsvall: Mid Sweden University, Demicom. 70.

Koliastasis, P. (2020a) The permanent campaign strategy of prime ministers in parliamentary systems: The case of Greece. *Journal of Political Marketing*, *19*(3), 233–57.

Koliastasis, P. (2020b). The brand has left the building: The cases of governing PASOK, ND, and SYRIZA at a time of economic crisis (2009–2019). In *The Emerald Handbook of Digital Media in Greece (Digital Activism and Society: Politics, Economy and Culture in Network Communication)*, A. Veneti and A. Karatzogianni, eds. Bingley, UK: Emerald Publishing Limited. 245–58.

Kosmidis, S. (2013). Government constraints and economic voting in Greece. GreeSE –Hellenic Observatory Papers on Greece and Southeast Europe 70. LSE: Hellenic Observatory. 1–48.

Lewis-Beck, M. S. (1988) *Economics and Elections: The Major Western Democracies*. Ann Arbor, MI: University of Michigan Press.

Lewis-Beck, M. S., and Nadeau, R. (2012) PIGS or not? Economic voting in Southern Europe. *Electoral Studies*, *13*(3), 472–7.

Lewis-Beck, M. S., and Stegmaier, M. (2013). The VP-function revisited: A survey of the literature on vote and popularity functions after over 40 years. *Public Choice*, *157*(3/4), 367–85.

Lijphart, A. (1999). *Patterns of Democracy: Government Forms and Performance in Thirty-Six Countries*, New Haven, CT: Yale University Press.

Lobo, M. C. and Lewis-Beck, M. S. (2012). The integration hypothesis: How the European Union shapes economic voting. *Electoral Studies*, *31*(3), 522–8.

Nadeau, R., Lewis-Beck, M. S. and Belanger, E. (2013). Economics and elections revisited. *Comparative Political Studies*, *46*(5), 551–73.

Nannestad, P., and Paldam, M. (1994). The VP function: A survey of the literature on vote and popularity functions after 25 years. *Public Choice*, *79*(3/4), 213–45.

Nezi, R., and Katsanidou, A. (2014). From valence to position: Economic voting in extraordinary conditions. *Acta Politica*, *49*(4), 413–30.

Nezi, R. (2012). Economic voting under the economic crisis: Evidence from Greece, *Electoral Studies*, *31*, 498–505.

Nikolacopoulos, I. (2005). Elections and voters, 1974–2004: Old cleavages and new issues. *West European Politics*, *28*(2), 260–78.

Paldam, M. (1991). How robust is the vote function? A study of seventeen nations over four decades. In *Economics and Politics: The Calculus of Support*, H. Norpoth, M. Lewis-Beck, and J.-D. Lafay, eds. Ann Arbor, MI: University of Michigan Press. 9–31.

Teperoglou, E., and Tsatsanis, E. (2014). Dealignment, de-legitimation and the implosion of the two-party system in Greece: The earthquake election of 6 May 2012. *Journal of Elections, Public Opinion and Parties*, *24*(2), 222–42.

Teperoglou, E., Tsatsanis, E., and Nicolacopoulos, E. (2015). Habituating to the new normal in a post-earthquake party system: The 2014 European election in Greece. *South European Society and Politics*, *20*(3), 333–55.

Tsatsanis, E., and Teperoglou, E. (2016) Realignment under stress: The July 2015 referendum and the September parliamentary election in Greece. *South European Society and Politics*, *21*(4), 427–50.

Tsatsanis, E., Teperoglou, E., and Seriatos, A. (2020). Two-partyism reloaded: Polarisation, negative partisanship, and the return of the left–right divide in the Greek elections of 2019. *South European Society and Politics*, *25*(3–4), 503–32.

Tsebelis, G. (2016). Lessons from the Greek crisis. *Journal of European Public Policy*, *23*(1), 25–41, DOI: https://doi.org/10.1080/13501763.2015.1087215.

Vasilopoulou, S., and Halikiopoulou, D. (2013). In the shadow of Grexit: The Greek election of 17 June 2012. *South European Society and Politics*, *18*(4), 523–42.

Voulgaris, J., and Nikolakopoulos, I. (2014). Introduction: The electoral earthquake of 2012. In *2012: The Double Electoral Earthquake*, J. Voulgaris and I. Nicolakopoulos, eds. Themelio Publications: Athens [in Greek]. 9–31.

Yfantopoulos, J. (2013). Dynamic aspects of the underground economy in Greece. *Journal of Economic and Social Measurement*, *38*(1), 97–112.

12
Diminishing Class Voting and the Increasing Influence of the Economy on Executive Approval in Denmark, 1974–2016

Henrik Bech Seeberg

The study of the economy and approval of the executive—the government and in particular the prime minister—has been a prominent part of political science research in Denmark. Nannestad and Paldam, two Danish scholars, were internationally renowned pioneers in this field in the early 1990s (Paldam, 1991; Nannestad and Paldam, 1994; 1995; 1997a; 1997b) and inspired a series of studies on Denmark (Borre, 1997; Lewis-Beck et al., 2013; Stubager et al., 2013; Stubager et al., 2014; Bisgaard et al., 2015; Larsen, 2016; Larsen et al., 2019) 'The Danish voter' remains of substantial international scholarly interest (Stubager et al., 2021).

One of the main developments in Denmark since World War II has been the diminishment of class politics and the rise of non-class-based issues, issue voting, and issue competition between the political parties (Mair et al., 2004; Green-Pedersen, 2011; 2019). This encompassed a transition from very stable socio-economic voting patterns and an almost complete dominance of the issue of the economy on the political agenda to a much more fluid and dynamic political landscape in which new issues appear on the political agenda and voters no longer have strong allegiances to a particular party. In this latter landscape, the economy is just one among other issues on the agenda, and voters increasingly assess the competence and performance of the executive critically. This has had major implications for the impact of the economy on how voters evaluate the executive.

The main aim of this chapter is to disentangle this development—(1) decreasing saliency of the economy and (2) less class voting—and its implications for government approval. By shedding light on the salience of

Henrik Bech Seeberg, *Diminishing Class Voting and the Increasing Influence of the Economy on Executive Approval in Denmark, 1974–2016.* In: *Economics and Politics Revisited.* Edited by: Timothy Hellwig and Matthew Singer, Oxford University Press. © Henrik Bech Seeberg (2023). DOI: 10.1093/oso/9780192871664.003.0012

the economy, this chapter aims to elaborate on one of the three main dimensions of the economy–approval mechanism highlighted in Chapter 1. This argument, that the impact of the economy on executive approval has changed, squares well with previous influential work in the field. In reviews of the literature, Paldam (1991), Lewis-Beck and Paldam (2000), and Anderson (2007) all make the case that the scale and nature of economic voting (or executive approval) is not constant over time. Rather, it is highly contingent.

The choice of focus in this chapter on the saliency of the economy is not entirely new. Previous scholarship has provided evidence that the economy predominantly matters to executive approval when the economy is salient to the voters who exercise the approval assessment (Edwards et al., 1995; Singer, 2011; 2013; de Vries and Giger, 2014; Dassonneville and Lewis-Beck, 2019). This chapter adds to this important scholarship with a fresh perspective based on new evidence on long-term developments in Denmark.

This chapter contributes to the literature by integrating the rise of issue voting and political parties' issue competition with economic considerations. Restated in Paldam's (1991) language with respect to vote-popularity functions, we compare the weight of the 'p-fraction' with that of the 'e-fraction'. Another contribution is that this chapter explicitly embraces how a multitude of issues move up and down the political agenda and models how changing political attention to the economy—elite communication and behaviour more than just voter saliency—affects voters' reliance on the economy in evaluating the executive.

The chapter analyses consumer confidence as an indicator of the economy and executive approval in Denmark, 1974–2016. The executive approval data were collected by the author for the Executive Approval Database (EAD; details in Chapter 2). These data were combined with data on the Danish political agenda and the level of class voting over time in Denmark. Using these data, the chapter finds that the impact of the economy on executive approval is not constant. Rather, it has moved from little impact to visible impact over time from 1974 to 2016 in Denmark. After the transition from a class-based political landscape to an issue-based one, consumer confidence has a marked influence on executive approval.

Integrating Economic Voting with Broader Trends

The economy figures prominently as a factor shaping leader evaluations, both in studies on the Danish case and beyond. Earlier research on economic voting in Denmark was mostly concerned with clarifying to what extent Danish voters are primarily sociotropic or egotropic in evaluating the incumbents' performance on the economy (Nannestad and Paldam, 1994; 1995; 1997a; 1997b; Borre, 1997; Lewis-Beck et al., 2013; Stubager, Lewis-Beck et al. 2013; Stubager et al. 2014; Larsen 2016). Studies out of this 'economy matters' tradition continues to be mainly concerned with ever-further conceptual clarification and ever-more sophistication in terms of understanding how exactly voters perceive the unemployment rate and the economy (Bisgaard et al., 2015; Larsen et al., 2019), the heterogeneity in how voters hold the executive to account (de Vries and Giger, 2014; Bisgaard, 2015), and which coalition partner is more responsible (Duch and Falcó-Gimeno, 2022). Rather than going into ever-more detail, I suggest the time is right to take a step back and consider the broader social context in which economic voting occurs.

Furthermore, the focus on the saliency of the economy and other issues on the political agenda is a fresh and novel contribution to the impressive line of research on the impact of the economy on executive approval. Studies of government approval have traditionally paid little attention to the role of parties and party communication. This is changing, however, and scholars are starting to show interest in the influence of party communication and media communication (Edwards et al., 1995; Soroka et al., 2015; Damstra and Boukes, 2019). Whereas Hellwig (2012) provides compelling evidence on what incumbents can do in terms of changing positions, Hart (2013), Pardos-Prado and Sagarzazu (2014), and Seeberg (2018) are among the first to look at how party communication affects voters' government evaluations.

The Impact of the Economy on Executive Approval during Tectonic Shifts

Plenty of research suggests that the economy is crucial to voters' evaluations of the government. Personal experience with unemployment and the housing market, for instance, are major ingredients in voters' evaluations (Bisgaard et al., 2015; Ansell, 2019; Larsen et al., 2019). This evaluation tends to be asymmetrical in the sense that voters punish the government more during economic downturns than they reward them during economic upswings (Nannestad and Paldam, 1997a; Larsen, 2021). The first key question in this chapter is whether an overall relationship exists throughout the extended period of analysis from the early 1970s until the present day. Previous studies of Denmark find an effect (Nannestad and Paldam, 1994; Larsen, 2016), although the institutional setup in Denmark might make it harder for voters to ascribe blame clearly to the incumbents (Hobolt et al., 2012). Danish governments are typically minority coalitions of multiple parties and large reforms are typically adopted by a broad coalition of parties in parliament (Seeberg and Christiansen, 2016). Moreover, most labour-market policy, including salaries and social assistance schemes, are negotiated collectively between employers, trade unions, and the government in Denmark's strong and persistent version of corporatism (Rommetvedt et al., 2013). Together, this blurs the political responsibility for the economy. Based on the literature, we test if an overall continuous effect in Denmark exists of the economy on government approval. This effect is probably weak due to the weak clarity of responsibility:

H1: When the economic conditions worsen, executive approval declines.

However, the political landscape in Denmark has changed monumentally in the past half-century, and we should therefore expect a change in the effect of the economy on executive approval. Hence, a main aim of this chapter is to determine if the influence of the economy on executive approval in Denmark has changed—receded, disappeared, or magnified—over time.

Like in most other Western countries, post-World War II politics in Denmark was heavily class-based, with workers voting for the Social Democrats and Socialists, and merchants and capital-owners voting for the bourgeois parties (Thau, 2019; Dalton, 2002; Mair et al., 2004). During the massive expansion of the welfare state, the post-war economic boom, and later the oil crisis, the dominant political controversy in Denmark was the economy (Green-Pedersen, 2011; 2019; Bille and Pedersen, 2004). How far should the state intervene in the market to ensure employment, price stability, and growth? This dominance of the economy in political conflict is visible from Figure 12.1, which plots political attention to the economy and to multiple non-economic issues (the environment, immigration, etc.).[1] Attention to the economy (the black line) hovers far above all other issues in the post-World War II period.

In such a political landscape, at first sight, we should expect a strong overall correspondence between the economy and executive approval. Since politics was all about the economy, the economy would be the natural and, perhaps, *only* basis for the voters to judge the government (as opposed to the influence of peripheral non-economic issues). This is what saliency theory of economic voting predicts (Singer, 2011; 2013). However, the class-based,

[1] As described below, political attention is measured as the percentage of all annual bill/law debates, interpellations, accounts, questions to the minister, and the annual executive speech in the Danish parliament devoted to the issue in question.

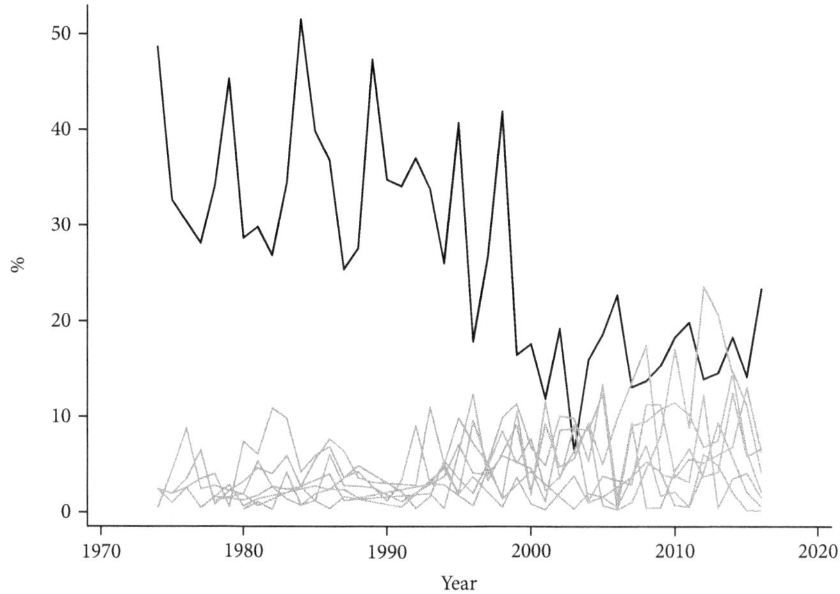

Figure 12.1 Political attention to the economy and other issues in Denmark, 1974–2016

Source: Comparative Agendas Project (CAP; Baumgartner et al., 2019).
Note: The black line is political attention to the economy. The grey lines are political attention to various non-economic issues including but not limited to education, health, crime, welfare, and the environment.

ideology-dominated landscape suggests a rather weak correspondence. After all, workers seeking de-commodification would have no reason to abandon the Social Democrats because, realistically, there is nowhere else to go. Hence, if the economy is in bad shape, voters' party loyalty, party identification, and ideological beliefs will be pervasive and government supporters will blame everything other than the executive (Bisgaard, 2015) or, even if they blame the incumbent, will support the executive despite those failings. Voters supporting the opposition will vote against the government regardless of the economy. The strength of class-based attachments should thus result in a weak relationship between the economy and executive approval in this early period.

In the early 1990s, a gradual erosion in class stratification and class-based voting became apparent and the Social Democrats loosened their ties to the trade unions (Bille and Pedersen, 2004). Large societal changes such as de-industrialization, prolonged austerity, and an influx of immigrant workers eroded traditional workers' position in the labour market. The Social Democrats were unable to shelter the workers from the threats of globalization (Kriesi et al., 2008) and pursued instead the 'third way' to modernize and adjust the welfare state (Kitschelt, 1994; 2001). Meanwhile, workers' memberships in labour unions and attachments to the Social Democrats started to decline (Kölln, 2016). Furthermore, they became concerned with the immigrants taking their jobs and from 1998 onwards workers increasingly vouched for newly established radical right party, the Danish People's Party, and electoral volatility went up (Andersen et al., 1999; 2003; 2007; Stubager, Hansen et al., 2013; Hansen and Stubager, 2017; 2021; see also Dassonneville and Lewis-Beck, 2019). Thus, workers became less incline to vote for the Social Democrats or the Socialists, according to their class, and more concerned with new, non-class issues such as immigration. The declining level of class-based voting is clearly visible in Figure 12.2, which reports how well voters' class membership predicts individual party choice in the election using R^2.

The Social Democrats' shift in views towards the welfare state is visible in Figure 12.3, which shows the ideological positions of the Social Democrats and the Liberals/Conservatives in Denmark since 1973 and the distance between them. The Social Democrats' reforms of social security and labour protection is visible as a move towards the centre ground. This move was a reinforcing loop since its reform agenda was intended to make the welfare state sustainable but instead it alienated its core constituency, the workers. This loss of the voter base forced the Social Democrats to moderate further to attract new voters

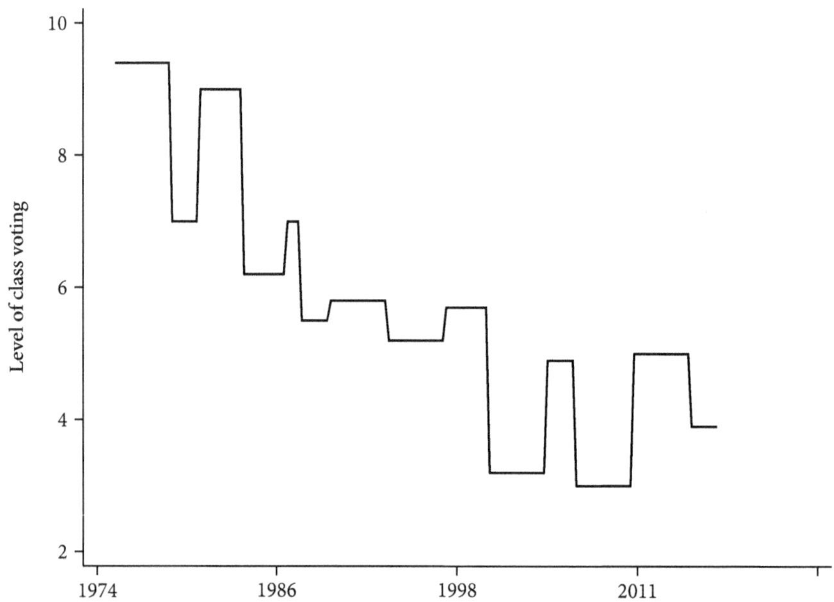

Figure 12.2 The level of class voting in Denmark, 1974–2016
Source: Stubager et al. (2021).
Note: The level of class voting is calculated as the R^2 in a regression of voters' party choice on their class belonging in each election.

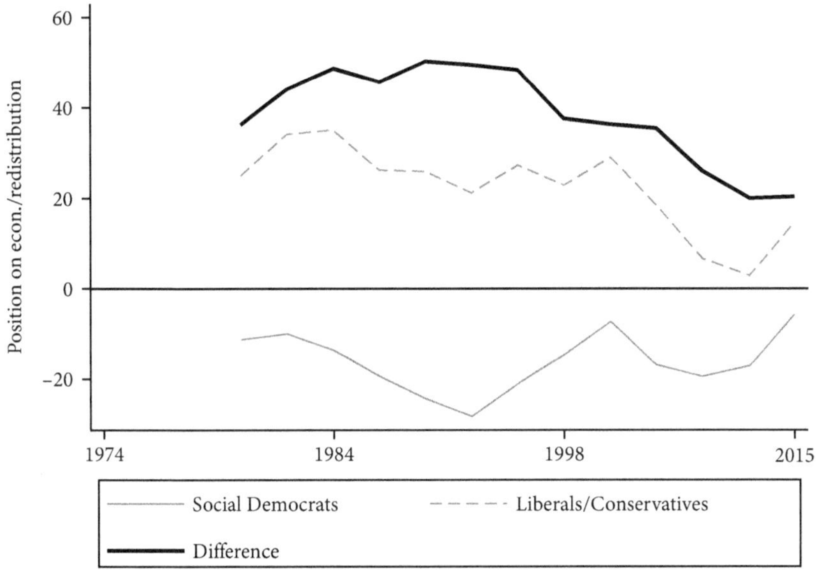

Figure 12.3 The position on the economy/redistribution ('rile') of Danish parties, 1979–2015

Source: Comparative Manifesto Project (Volkens et al., 2021).
Note: The position on the economy/redistribution runs from −100 (completely left-wing position) to +100 (completely right-wing position/no state intervention in economy or redistribution through taxes and welfare). This position is based on the battery of issue coding compiled in the 'rile' score in the Comparative Manifesto Project Dataset (Volkens et al., 2021). For the Liberals/Conservatives, I use the average position of the two parties.

(the aspiring middle class). In relation to Figure 12.3, it is worth noticing the convergence between the Social Democrats and the Liberals/Conservatives in Denmark since 1973. This is visible from the thick black line that descends over time towards the horizontal zero line. Amidst the Social Democrats shift, the Liberals and Conservatives had to accept that the large welfare state was highly popular and therefore there to stay (Pierson, 1996; Arndt, 2014). This is a common trend across Western countries, and it was no different in Denmark (Mair et al., 2004; Green and Hobolt, 2007). Although difficult to causally disentangle, it is easy to imagine that the shorter distance between the major parties of the left and the right made it easier and more appealing for voters to switch party, and this convergence therefore amplified the increasing electoral volatility. The intensification of volatility (and each party's erosion of their core voter base) further pushed the major parties to moderate their positions to appeal to more voters.

The result of declining class-based voting and a more volatile electorate was a shift in the nature of political competition and, I argue, the nature of political accountability. Issue-based voting came to surpass class-based voting because voters became concerned with a diverse and constantly changing array of issues (immigration most importantly) but also because parties competed on promoting issues that concerned the voters (as competition on positions had become less attractive; Green-Pedersen, 2007; 2010; 2011; 2019). This led voters to increasingly decide on an election-to-election basis which party they deemed most competent to handle their issues of greatest concern (Petrocik, 1996; Andersen et al., 1999; 2003; 2007; Stubager, Hansen et al. 2013; Hansen and Stubager 2017; 2021). Hence, the saliency of issues together with parties' issue competence became pivotal to elections (Mair et al., 2004).

In such a post-class political landscape, we should expect a much closer correspondence between the economy and executive approval. Workers, for example, no longer automatically vote for the Social Democrats, but instead actively and critically assess the party's performance on key issues of concern, including the economy, and would be prepared to punish and sack the party for poor performance (to vote for, e.g. the Danish People's Party instead). I capture this changed relationship between the economy and government approval in the second hypotheses:

> H2: As class voting diminishes, the impact of the economy on executive approval increases.

These developments completely changed the political landscape and the political agenda (Jones and Baumgartner, 2005) nearly turned upside-down. Yet, theoretically, this is a separate process to class voting and H2 in terms of the impact of the economy on executive approval that leads to contrasting expectations. I will elaborate in the following. The Danish economy was improving in the early 1990s and new issues were knocking on the door alongside the immigrant issue. A growing and increasingly well-educated middle class was not primarily concerned with the economy, but rather with non-economic issues such as the environment and global issues (Stubager et al., 2021). Environmental disasters became difficult to ignore (Green-Pedersen and Wolfe, 2009), the integration of a large group of guest workers started to become a real challenge (Green-Pedersen and Krogstrup, 2008), violence in the streets escalated (Seeberg, 2013), and the pressure on the health system became intense (Green-Pedersen and Wilkerson, 2006). Hence, the political agenda widened beyond the issue of the economy and became more dynamic as new issues replaced previously dominating issues such as the economy. As is clearly visible in Figure 12.1, the economy was now (in the post-class political landscape) suddenly just one issue among many, and new issues (marked in grey in Figure 12.1) continuously intruded on the agenda and replaced old issues. The economy did not vanish completely, but its prominence on the political agenda, like that of other issues, began to wax during times of distress and wane during periods of progress (see also Figure 12.5, below). According to the 'economic saliency hypothesis' (Singer, 2011; 2013), the decline in saliency of the economic issue is expected to make the economy less important to the vote choice and therefore less influential on voters' executive approval. Hence, from this saliency perspective, we should expect to see a declining impact of the economy on executive approval over time in Denmark:

> H3: As attention to the economy decreases, the impact of the economy on executive approval decreases.

Notice, that there are two separate processes ongoing: the demise of class politics unfolded alongside a decline in the saliency of the economy on the political agenda. These are opposing mechanisms. The decline in class politics is expected to increase the impact of the economy on executive approval whereas the decline in economic saliency is expected to decrease the impact of the economy on executive approval.

A further implication of the argument is that the moderation of welfare state opinions of the Social Democrats and the Liberals/Conservatives invites voters' to further focus on assessing parties' performance, e.g. on the economy, and thereby further amplifies the weakening ties between voters and parties (Green and Hobolt, 2007; Finseraas and Vernby, 2011). This is the case because the moderation makes party competition and therefore voters' criteria for supporting a party turn to parties' competences rather than (very similar) positions (Mair et al., 2004; Green and Hobolt, 2007). The underlying logic is that parties need to differentiate themselves from their rivals, and when they become ideologically less distinguishable, they find other ways to compete, namely towards delivering high-quality services and handling problems. Similarly, voters need to differentiate the parties and if they cannot use positions, they turn to evaluating them on competence. The bottom line is that we can expect an improved correspondence between the economy and executive approval over time in Denmark from the early 1970s to the 1990s onwards due to class voting decline (H2) and decreased position competition (increased competence competition) between the parties:

> H4: As parties converge in their ideological positions, the impact of the economy on executive approval increases.

Data and Measures

For the analysis of executive approval in Denmark, an uninterrupted time series of quarterly observations is available from 1948 to 2021. Yet the analysis also relies on the consumer confidence indicator to measure the economy, and the longest consistent data series on consumer confidence is only available for 1974–2016 in the form of quarterly observations from the Danish statistical bureau. Hence, the analysis covers a still impressive forty-two years.

The data on executive approval were collected by the author for the Executive Approval Database. Executive approval in Denmark consists of respondents' evaluations of the performance of the prime minister, the prime minister's party, or the government as such. Most questions are concerned with approval of the government. Before 1990, data stems mainly from the Gallup digital archive. The data covering the period after 1990 was collected from survey marginals reported in the major Danish newspapers. Trained student coders searched the Danish media database *Infomedia* and manually checked the physical archive of surveys printed in Danish newspapers collected by Jørgen Goul Andersen, who kindly shared his impressive archive. Most of these surveys on executive approval are based on representative samples of more than a thousand respondents. Approval is typically but not always measured on an ordinal 1–5 Likert scale. In cases where the sample average is reported (e.g. 3.2 on a 1–5 scale or −0.7 on a −2 to +2 scale), I re-scale the score to run between 0 and 100. In cases where the percentage distribution across the five categories is reported, I calculate the mean and again re-scale the score to run between 0 and 100.[2] Hence, executive approval runs on a 0–100 scale (100 is the highest level of approval). For the data series, I apply a smoothed version based on the Wcalc procedure (Stimson, 1999).

To measure the economy, the analysis uses the consumer confidence indicator rather than, for example, unemployment or inflation rates because the latter two indicators have proven more subject to partisan reasoning (Hibbs, 1977; Powell and Whitten, 1993; de Boef and Kellstedt, 2004; Anderson, 2007). The consumer confidence indicator available from the Danish Statistical Bureau uses quarterly, representative surveys of roughly 1,500 consumers to measure their perceptions of the country's economy as well as their own private finances. This includes a battery of questions about consumers' private

[2] For example, if 7 per cent answered 1, 43 per cent answered 2, 15 per cent answered 3, 17 per cent answered 4, and 3 per cent answered 5 (15 per cent did not now), the average score is $0.07\times1 + 0.43\times2 + 0.15\times3 + 0.17\times4 + 0.03\times5 = 2.21$.

financial situations compared to a year ago, their assessments of the economic situation in the country compared to a year ago, the prospects of the financial and economic situation, and their plans for major investments in a car or home improvements and for savings. The indicator ranges from −100 (very pessimistic about the financial and economic situation) to +100 (very optimistic).

Table 12.1 shows that consumer confidence in the period has fluctuated quite substantively around a mean of −1 (σ is 8.3). It has been at a low of −21 and a high of 12.6. On the 0–100 scale, the approval rating has averaged 37 (σ is 8.8), with a low of 16.5 and a high of 71.0.[3] Figure 12.4 charts executive approval and consumer confidence in Denmark over time. The lines reveal the deep economic recession in the mid-1980s and the long spell of recovery and growth until the financial crisis in 2007–2008. Government approval in large part parallels this development, though far from in perfect correspondence.

To test H2 on the impact of decreasing class voting, we used the predicted scores from Stubager et al. (2021). For each election since 1970, the authors calculated how well voters' class membership predicts their vote choice in the election using R^2. To test H3, the study relies on previous research on political attention (Green-Pedersen and Mortensen, 2010; Green-Pedersen, 2011: 2019). Acknowledging that no actor sets the political agenda single-handedly (Green-Pedersen and Mortensen, 2010), this research maintains that the political agenda cannot simply be reduced to either government or opposition communication. Rather, it must include both, and reflect the major issues—say transportation, agriculture, or energy—debated on the floor of parliament at any point in time. Like previous research (Green-Pedersen and Mortensen, 2010), the measure uses all annual bill/law debates, interpellations, accounts, questions to the minister, and the annual executive speech to arrive

Table 12.1 Descriptive statistics, Denmark, 1974–2016

	Obs	Mean	St.D.	Min	Max
Executive approval	172	36.8	8.8	16.5	71.0
Consumer confidence	169	−0.99	8.27	−21	12.6
Political attention to the economy	168	18.4	5.4	9.1	30.5
Political attention diversity	172	2.6	0.1	2.4	2.8

Source: Attention (CAP data; Baumgartner et al., 2019), consumer confidence (Danish Statistical Bureau), executive approval (EAP).

[3] A few observations were missing on the approval variables, and these were interpolated linearly.

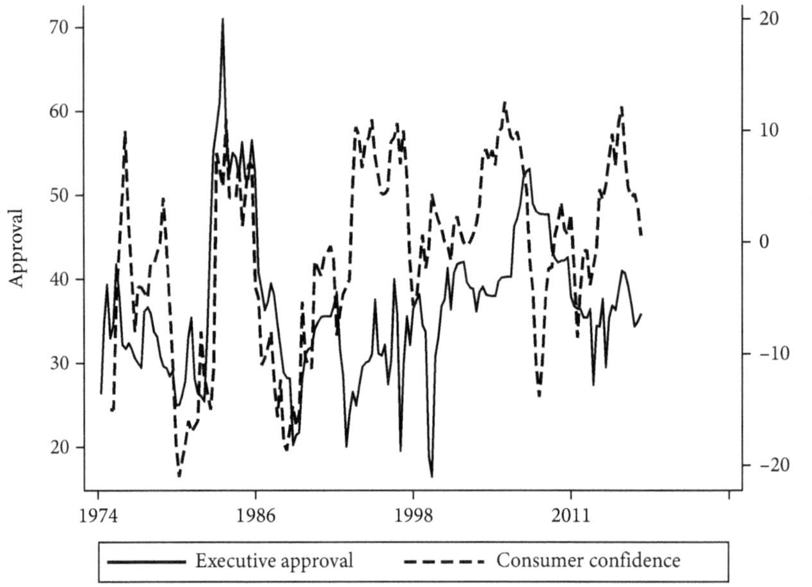

Figure 12.4 Executive approval and consumer confidence in Denmark, 1974–2016

Source: Consumer confidence (right axis, Danish Statistical Bureau), executive approval (left axis, EAP).

at an indicator of the political agenda that is not in the pocket of either the government or the opposition.

The data come from the Danish part of the Comparative Agendas Project (CAP; Baumgartner et al., 2019), in which the author is a co-investigator (together with Christoffer Green-Pedersen and Peter Mortensen). This is based on thousands of observations of parliamentary activities which have been manually issue-classified by trained research assistants consistently over time through an elaborate coding scheme. To test H3, I measure the relative political attention to the economy.[4] To indicate attention to non-economic issues like the environment, immigration, crime, as an alternative way to test H3, we measure the diversity of attention. If political attention does centre on the economy, then the issue diversity in attention will typically be low(er) (although this is not always the case in the rare event that all parties centre on a non-economic issue such as the COVID-19-pandemic or the Russian invasion in Ukraine). I employ an established diversity measure based on Shannon's entropy score (Boydstun et al., 2014; see also Jennings et al., 2011; Bækgaard et al., 2018).

[4] The 'economy' here refers to growth, inflation, exchange rate, prices, and the unemployment rate, all of which are items in Major Topic One in the CAP codebook.

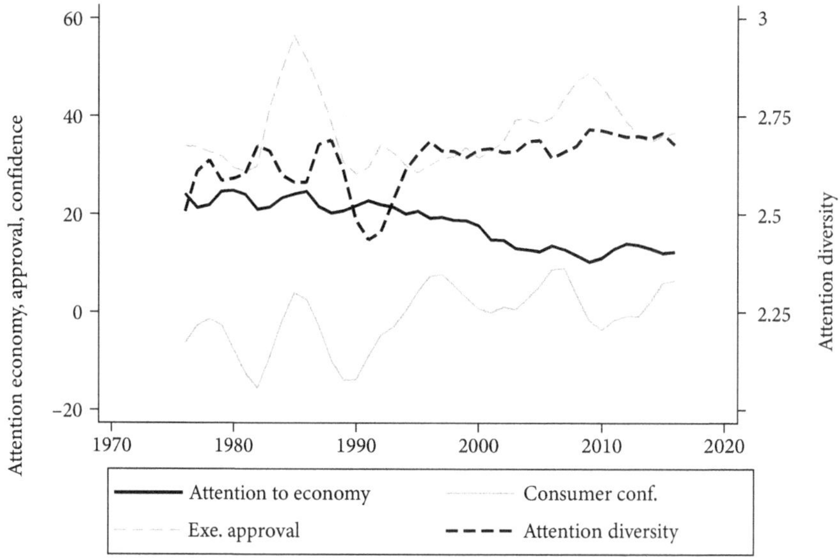

Figure 12.5 Government attention diversity and government attention to the economy in Denmark, 1974–2016

Source: Attention (CAP data), consumer confidence (Danish Statistical Bureau), executive approval (EAP).

Note: Each line reports three-year moving averages.

As a reflection of the face validity of these connected measures of the political agenda, Figure 12.5 shows the political attention to the economy and the political attention diversity. The lines move nearly opposite each other, suggesting that when attention to the economy wanes, attention diversifies. Attention to the economy has generally declined over time, subject to noticeable variation, whereas attention diversity has gradually increased. Moreover, the figure shows that political attention to the economy seems to reflect the actual state of the economy, though there is far from a perfect correspondence. To test H4 on party convergence, I use the CMP rile score (Volkens et al., 2021) to measure the ideological positions of the mainstream left parties and the mainstream right parties in Denmark over time. I refer to distance rather than convergence and measure the absolute distance between the positions of the left and right parties. Since these positions are measured only at elections through content-coding of the party manifestos, the distance measure has been interpolated to the quarterly level of analysis.

The analysis includes a set of control variables. These are an election dummy, a right-wing government dummy (0 is left-wing), a dummy for the type of government (single-party, coalition, minority, majority, etc.; variable 'gov_type' in Armingeon et al., 2020), and a dummy for the quarter of the year to account for seasonal effects. In the main analysis, I do not control for political attention or ideological distance in the analysis of how class conditions the influence of consumer confidence on executive approval (or vice versa). However, the results do not change when all variables are included.

A challenge in estimating the influence of the economy on executive approval is the autoregressive nature of the data. A Breusch-Godfrey test for higher-order serial correlation in the disturbance term indeed indicates autocorrelation ($Chi^2 = 137.38, p < 0.00$). To address this, the estimation relies on an OLS regression with a lagged dependent variable. We also include robust standard errors. An Augmented Dickey-Fuller test rejects that the executive approval variable contains a unit root ($z < —3.408$, $p < 0.01$). The analysis is concerned with the extent to which the level of consumer confidence at t-1 systematically predicts the level of executive approval at t0. To be consistent in the time order of causality, political attention to the economy and political attention diversity also enter the estimation at t-1. The unit of analysis is a quarter in a year (4 quarters x 42 years) because consumer confidence and executive approval are measured at this unit. The annual political agenda measures are therefore repeated every quarter within a year.

Analysis

The analysis is first concerned with the overall cross-time stability in the relationship between consumer confidence and government approval in Denmark between 1974 and 2016. Hypothesis 1 stipulates a persistent impact in the sense that less confidence decreases citizens' government approval. This is tested in Table 12.2 Model 1. The coefficient is positive, as expected in H1, but does not reach conventional levels of statistical significance. This suggests that there is no overall systematic relationship between consumer confidence and executive approval in Denmark, 1974–2016. This invites testing Hypotheses 2 and 4, which stipulate that the impact of consumer confidence on executive approval has increased over time as class voting has declined over time (H2) and party competition on competence has inclined (H4), as well as H3, which stipulates a decrease in the impact of consumer confidence owing to a decline in political attention to the economy.[5]

The remaining columns in Table 2 provide evidence to suggest that the impact of the economy, as gauged by consumer confidence, on executive

[5] As noted, this result may also stem from the low level of clarity of responsibility in Denmark.

Table 12.2 Modelling the effect of consumer confidence on executive approval in Denmark, 1974–2016

		(1)	(2)	(3)	(4)	(5)
	$Approval_{t-1}$	0.857* (0.057)	0.862* (0.057)	0.865* (0.062)	0.858* (0.057)	0.846* (0.065)
H1	Consumer $confidence_{t-1}$	0.049 (0.044)	0.360* (0.154)	0.447* (0.186)	−9.860* (2.645)	−0.047 (0.114)
	Class $vote_t$		0.193 (0.241)			
	Gov. attention $economy_{t-1}$			−0.031 (0.094)		
	Gov. attention $diversity_{t-1}$				11.515° (6.420)	
	Ideological distance between $parties_t$					−0.012 (0.032)
H2	Consumer $confidence_{t-1}$ x class $vote_t$		−0.051° (0.027)			
H3	Consumer $confidence_{t-1}$ x govt attn $economy_{t-1}$			−0.029* (0.014)		
	Consumer $confidence_{t-1}$ x govt attn $diversity_{t-1}$				3.512* (0.934)	
H4	Consumer $confidence_{t-1}$ x $distance_t$					0.002 (0.003)
	party in government (right = 1)	0.675 (0.733)	0.645 (0.708)	0.986 (0.752)	0.727 (0.744)	0.504 (0.905)
	Election (= 1)	−0.305 (1.063)	−0.630 (1.097)	−0.455 (1.089)	−0.570 (1.028)	−0.280 (1.045)
	Government type					
	Minimal winning coalition	−2.692° (1.564)	−2.916° (1.633)	−2.906° (1.626)	−2.713 (1.679)	−2.994° (1.636)
	Single-party minority		−1.785 (1.242)	−1.079 (0.922)	−1.175 (0.800)	−0.309 (0.901)
	Multi-party minority	0.274 (0.895)				

Continued

Table 12.2 *Continued*

	(1)	(2)	(3)	(4)	(5)
Constant	4.906* (2.224)	4.112 (2.784)	5.244 (3.233)	−27.267 (17.803)	6.298° (3.429)
R^2	0.791	0.797	0.796	0.803	0.792
Observations	176	176	164	168	164

Source: Attention (CAP data; Baumgartner et al., 2019), consumer confidence (Danish Statistical Bureau), executive approval (EAP), ideological distance (Comparative Manifesto Project; Volkens et al., 2021), class voting (Stubager et al. (2021).
Note: Cells report OLS regression coefficients with standard errors in parentheses. Models also include quarterly fixed effects (not reported). ° $p < 0.10$, * $p < 0.05$ (two-tailed test)

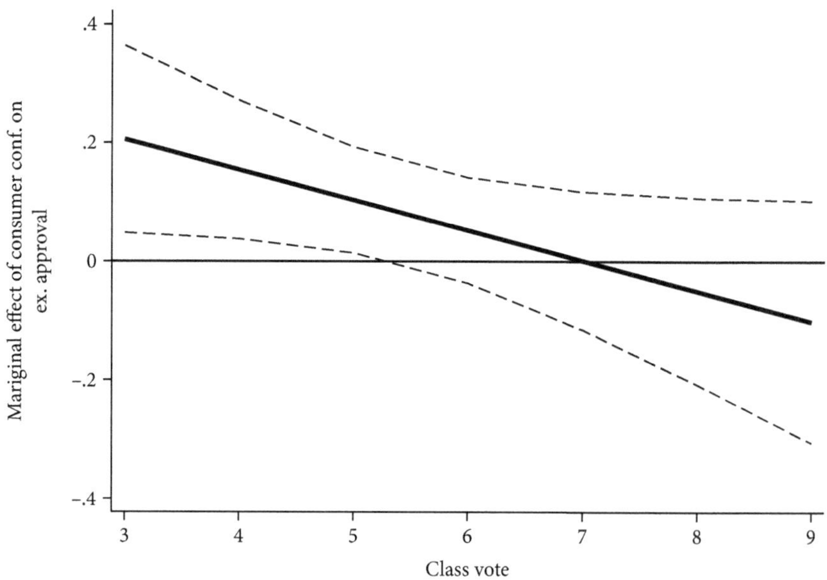

Figure 12.6 Marginal effect of consumer confidence across values of class vote
Source: Author.
Note: The graph is based on Table 12.2, Model 2. Ninety-five per cent confidence interval (dashed line).

approval has indeed changed over time. As the Danish political landscape has changed, the impact of consumer confidence has changed too. In support of Hypothesis 2 (class voting), the coefficient in the interaction term in Model 2 of Table 12.2 is negative, and the marginal effect curve displayed in Figure 12.6 is decreasing. The curve is only above the zero-line and distinguishable from zero at low levels of class voting to the left in Figure 12.6. This suggests that decreasing consumer confidence only systematically lowers executive approval after the breakdown of the class-vote during the 1980 and 1990s (see Figure 12.2). At high levels of class voting, the confidence interval overlaps with the zero-axis. Thus, in the early part of the period 1974–2016 when class voting was high, voters relied more on their ideology and class-identity to approve or disapprove of the executive regardless of the actual state of the economy.

Hypothesis 3 on economic saliency is tested in columns 3–4 of Table 12.2. Defying expectations, the coefficient for economic attention is negative and statistically significant. Thus, as economic attention increases, the impact of consumer confidence on executive approval diminishes. This is also visible in Figure 12.7, which shows the decreasing marginal effect of consumer confidence on executive approval on the *y*-axis as the political attention to the economy increases along the *x*-axis. Increasing consumer confidence only increases executive approval systematically in the left part of the figure. In this case when political attention to the economy is low (post-class era), the confidence interval (dashed line) escapes the zero-line. During high economic attention in the right part of Figure 12.7, the confidence interval overlaps with the *x*-axis leaving no systematic impact of consumer confidence on executive approval. Hence, we do not find support for the 'economic saliency hypothesis'. Yet, the result fits the development in Denmark that we saw in Figures 12.1

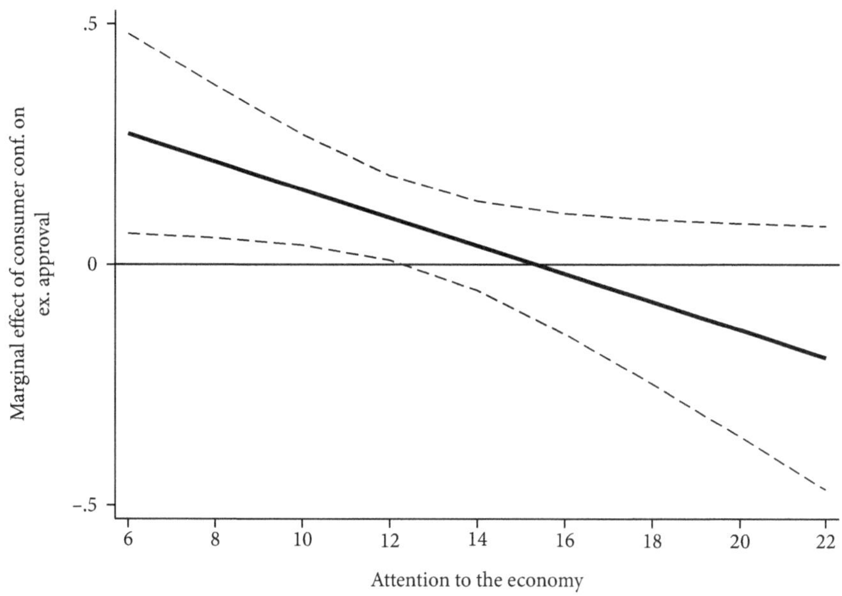

Figure 12.7 Marginal effect of consumer confidence across values of attention to the economy

Source: Author.

Note: The graph is based on Table 12.2, Model 3. Ninety-five per cent confidence interval (dashed line).

and 12.5 and therefore also the result on H2 on class voting. During high economic saliency in the 1970s and 1980s, class voting rather than economic performance and evaluations decided executive approval (towards the right end of Figure 12.7). Alongside the demise of class voting especially through the 1990s, attention to the economy generally waned in Denmark. Meanwhile, the impact of consumer confidence on executive approval ramped up because parties increasingly competed on problem-handling competence and voters increasingly evaluated the parties critically on their performance (towards the left end of the figure).

To get a sense of the substantial impact, a 1 standard deviation decrease in consumer confidence (0.25 x 8.3) at the lowest level of political attention to the economy is associated with a 2.1-point decrease in executive approval. This is a large, but not unusual drop in consumer confidence. From the early part of 2015 to the start of 2016, consumer confidence in Denmark, for example, dropped from 12.2 to 4.1 (at generally low levels of political attention to the economy). The 2.1 drop in executive approval is 23 per cent of a standard deviation in executive approval which varies from 16.5 to 71 in the period. Hence, not a dramatic effect, but still surely noticeable. It is further evidence of this mechanism (less attention, greater influence of consumer confidence) that the estimation in column 4 in Table 12.2 is positively signed and statistically significant. Hence, as diversity in political attention to more issues increases, so does the influence of consumer confidence. The results do not suggest that decreased ideological distance between the parties increases the impact of consumer confidence on executive approval as hypothesized in H4. The coefficient for the interaction between consumer confidence and ideological distance in column 5 in Table 12.2 is not statistically significant.

In sum, the influence of consumer confidence on executive approval is not stable over time, but has evolved. I reject H1 (stability), find support for H2 (class), and reject H3 (saliency) and H4 (ideological convergence). The fact that the estimation of saliency runs counter to H3 and is statistically significant speaks rather strongly against the saliency hypothesis. However, the interpretation might more likely be that decreased economic attention does indeed reduce voters' focus on the economy when evaluating the executive (H3). However, other countervailing forces were stronger, namely the dismantling of the class vote (H2). As a consequence, the voters' overall focus on the executive's competence increased, even if political attention had dropped. The rejection of H4 deducts from this conclusion though since H4 was a close companion to H2 and a further implication of the argument. Further research therefore needs to dig deeper into the implications of the demise of the class society in Denmark and probably come up with more fine-grained measures, e.g. of changes to party competition and the ideological distance between parties.

Conclusion

Taking a long-term perspective, the analysis reveals that there is no systematic, persistent impact of the economy on executive approval in Denmark. Rather, in the early part of the period characterized by class-and-ideology-based voting, a weakening of the economy is not associated with decreased executive approval. Yet, as class voting diminished and voters became more volatile, voters became less loyal to the parties and more critical in terms of evaluating parties' performance on the economy. In this more recent period characterized by issue voting, a weakening of the economy is indeed associated with decreased executive approval. Thus, the key take-away from this analysis is that we need to adopt a (more) dynamic view of the political relevance of the economy. This is an important update—if not corrective—to the pioneering studies of the economy and executive approval in Denmark by Nannestad and Paldam in the early 1990s (Paldam, 1991; Nannestad and Paldam, 1994; 1995; 1997a; 1997b). Based on a much shorter period of analysis, their work finds that executive approval to a large extent—and consistently—hinges on the well-being of the economy.

This chapter aims to put the impact of the economy on executive approval into a broader context of political developments in Denmark which might inspire future comparative research. The main aim is to integrate the economy–approval mechanism into the well-known diminishing of rather static class-based politics and an increase in more dynamic issue politics. The analysis relies on three different indicators of this transition—the level of class voting, political attention to the economy, and the ideological distance between the parties—to capture its impact on the economy–approval nexus. Admittedly, the analysis does apply a rather rough brush, and it will be up to future studies to add more nuance to this mechanism.

The results have important implications for our understanding of the impact of the economy on executive approval. The argument and results in this chapter help to put the economy into context. The findings in this chapter indicate that scholars of the economy–executive connection might easily overrate the importance of the economy for executive approval by only studying the economy in isolation, or only studying the economy during a (too) short time period. The advancement in the voluminous literature on the economy–executive connection has certainly added much detail to how exactly the economy matters (e.g. local versus national, egotropic versus sociotropic), but this does not make the economy more important to executive approval in the broader picture. In order to further understand the economy–approval nexus, this chapter points to the advantages of drawing more heavily on other literatures on, for instance, political agenda-setting, parties' issue competition, and issue voting.

Acknowledgement

This chapter was not possible without Jørgen Goul Andersen kindly sharing his rich archive of historical Danish executive approval data with the author. Moreover, thorough and generous comments from the editors of this volume have much improved this chapter.

References

Andersen, J., Borre, O., Andersen, J. G., and Nielsen, H. J. (1999). *Vælgere med omtanke*. Aarhus: Systime.

Andersen, J. G., and Borre, O. (2003). Politisk forandring. *Værdipolitik and nye skillelinjer ved folketingsvaget 2001*. Aarhus: Systime.

Andersen, J. G., Borre, O., Hansen, K. M., and Nielsen H. J. (2007). Det nye politiske landskab. *Folketingsvalget 2005 i perspektiv*. Aarhus: Academica.

Anderson, C. (2007). The end of economic voting? *Annual Review of Political Science*, *10*(1), 271–96.

Ansell, B. (2019). The politics of housing. *Annual Review of Political Science*, *22*(1), 165–85.

Armingeon, K., Engler, S., Isler, C., Knöpfel, L., and Weisstanner, D. (2020). *Comparative Political Data Set 1960–2014*. Bern: University of Bern.

Arndt, C. (2014). Beating social democracy on its own turf. *Scandinavian Political Studies*, *37*(2), 149–70.

Bille, L., and Pedersen, M. (2004). Electoral fortunes and responses of the social democratic party and liberal party in Denmark. In *Political Parties and Electoral Change*, P. Mair, W. Müller, and F. Plasser, eds. London: Sage. 207–33.

Bisgaard, M. (2015). Bias will find a way: Economic perceptions, attributions of blame, and partisan-motivated reasoning during crisis. *Journal of Politics*, *77*(3), 849–60.

Bisgaard, M., Dinesen, P., and Sønderskov, K. (2015). Reconsidering the neighborhood effect: Does exposure to residential unemployment influence voters' perceptions of the national economy? *Journal of Politics*, *78*(3), 719–32.

Baumgartner, F. R., Breunig, C., and Grossman, E. (eds) (2019). *Comparative Policy Agenda: Theory, Tools, Data*. Oxford: Oxford University Press.

Borre, O. (1997). Economic voting in Danish electoral surveys 1987–94. *Scandinavian Political Studies*, *20*(4), 347–365.

Boydstun, A., Bevan, S., and Thomas, H. (2014). The importance of attention diversity and how to measure it. *Policy Studies Journal*, *42*(2), 173–96.

Baekgaard, M., Mortensen, P., and Seeberg, H. B. (2018). The bureaucracy and the policy agenda. *Journal of Public Administration Research and Theory*, *28*(2), 239–53.

Dalton, R. (2002). The decline of party identifications. In *Parties without Partisans*, R. Dalton and M. Wattenberg, eds. Oxford: Oxford University Press. 19–36.

Damstra, A., and Boukes, M. (2019). The economy, the news, and the public: A longitudinal study of the impact of economic news on economic evaluations and expectations. *Communication Research*, *48*(1), 26–50.

Dassonneville, R., and Lewis-Beck, M. (2019). A changing economic vote in Western Europe? Long-term vs. short-term forces. *European Political Science Review*, *11*(1), 91–108.

De Boef, S., and Kellstedt, P. (2004). The political (and economic) origins of consumer confidence. *American Journal of Political Science*, *48*(4), 633–49.

de Vries, C., and Giger, N. (2014). Holding governments accountable? *European Journal of Political Research*, *53*, 345–62.

Duch, R., and Falcó-Gimeno, A. (2022). Collective decision-making and the economic vote. *Comparative Political Studies*, *55*(5), 757–88.

Edwards, G., Mitchell, W., and Welch, R. (1995). Explaining presidential approval: The significance of issue salience. *American Journal of Political Science*, *39*(1), 108–34.

Finseraas, H., and Vernby, K. (2011). What parties are and what parties do: Partisanship and welfare state reform in an era of austerity. *Socio-Economic Review*, *9*(4), 613–38.

Green, J., and Hobolt, S. (2007). Owning the issue agenda: Party strategies and vote choices in British elections. *Electoral Studies*, *27*, 460–76.

Green-Pedersen, C. (2007). The growing importance of issues. *Political Studies*, *55*(4), 608–28.

Green-Pedersen, C. (2010). Bringing parties into parliament. *Party Politics*, *16*(3), 347–69.

Green-Pedersen, C. (2011). *Partier i nye tider. Den politiske dagsorden i Danmark*. Aarhus: Aarhus University Press.

Green-Pedersen, C. (2019). *The Reshaping of West European Party Politics: Agenda-Setting and Party Competition in Comparative Perspective.* Oxford: Oxford University Press.

Green-Pedersen, C., and Krogstrup, J. (2008) Immigration as a political issue in Denmark and Sweden. *European Journal of Political Research, 47,* 610–34.

Green-Pedersen, C., and Mortensen, P. (2010). Who sets the agenda and who responds to it in the Danish Parliament? *European Journal of Political Research, 49*(2), 257–81.

Green-Pedersen, C., and Wilkerson, J. (2006). How agenda-setting attributes shape politics: Basic dilemmas, problem attention and health politics developments in Denmark and the US. *Journal of European Public Policy, 13*(7), 1039–52.

Green-Pedersen, C. and Wolfe, M. (2009). The institutionalization of environmental attention in the United States and Denmark: Multiple- versus single-venue systems. *Governance, 22*(4), 625–46.

Hansen, K., and Stubager, R. (2017). *Oprør fra udkanten. Folketingsvalget 2015.* Copenhagen: Jurist- and Økonomforbundets Forlag.

Hansen, K. and Stubager, R. (2021). *Klimavalget. Folketingsvalget 2019.* Copenhagen: Jurist- and Økonomforbundets Forlag.

Hart, A. (2013). Can candidates activate or deactivate the economic vote? Evidence from two Mexican elections. *The Journal of Politics, 75*(4), 1051–63.

Hellwig, T. (2012). Constructing accountability: Party position taking and economic voting. *Comparative Political Studies, 45*(1), 91–118.

Hibbs, D. (1977). Political parties and macroeconomic policy. *American Political Science Review, 71*(4), 1467–87.

Hobolt, S., Tilley, J., and Banducci, S. (2012). Clarity of responsibility: How government cohesion conditions performance voting. *European Journal of Political Research, 52*(2), 164–87.

Jennings, W. et al. (2011). The effects of core functions of government on the diversity of executive agendas. *Comparative Political Studies, 44,* 1001–30.

Jones, B. and Baumgartner, F. (2005). *The Politics of Attention: How Government Prioritizes Problems.* Chicago, IL: University of Chicago Press.

Kitschelt, H. (1994). *The Transformation of European Social Democracy.* Cambridge: Cambridge University Press.

Kitschelt, H. (2001). Partisan competition and welfare state retrenchment. In *The New Politics of the Welfare State,* P. Pierson ed. Oxford: Oxford University Press. 265–302.

Kölln, A.-K. (2016). Party membership in Europe: Testing party-level explanations of decline. *Party Politics, 22*(4), 465–77.

Kriesi, H. et al. (2008). *West European Politics in the Age of Globalization.* Cambridge: Cambridge University Press.

Larsen, M. (2016). Economic conditions affect support for prime minister parties in Scandinavia. *Scandinavian Political Studies, 39*(3), 226–41.

Larsen, M., (2021). How do voters hold politicians accountable for personal welfare? Evidence of a self-serving bias. *Journal of Politics*, *83*(2), 740–52.

Larsen, M., Hjorth, F., Dinesen, P., and Sønderskov, K. (2019). When do citizens respond politically to the local economy? Evidence from registry data on local housing markets. *American Political Science Review*, *113*(2), 499–516.

Lewis-Beck, M., and Paldam, M. (2000). Economic voting: An introduction. *Electoral Studies*, *19*(2), 113–21.

Lewis-Beck, M., Stubager, R., and Nadeau, R. (2013). The Kramer problem: Micro-macro resolution with a Danish pool. *Electoral Studies*, *32*(3), 500–5.

Mair, P., Müller, W., and Plasser, F. (2004). *Political Parties and Electoral Change*. London: Sage.

Nannestad, P., and Paldam, M. (1994). The VP-function: A survey of the literature on vote and popularity functions after 25 years. *Public Choice*, *79*(3–4), 213–45.

Nannestad, P., and Paldam, M. (1995). It's the governments fault! A cross-section study of economic voting in Denmark, 1990/93. *European Journal of Political Research*, *28*, 33–62.

Nannestad, P., and Paldam, M. (1997a). The grievance asymmetry revisited: A micro study of economic voting in Denmark, 1986–1992. *European Journal of Political Economy*, *13*(1), 81–99.

Nannestad, P., and Paldam, M. (1997b). From the pocketbook of the welfare man: A pooled cross-section study of economic voting in Denmark, 1986–92. *British Journal of Political Science*, *27*(1), 111–55.

Paldam, M. (1991). How robust is the vote function? In *Economics and Politics: The Calculus of Support*, H. Norpoth and M. Lewis-Beck, eds. Ann Arbor, MI: University of Michigan Press. 9–32.

Pardos-Prado, S. and Sagarzazu, I. (2014). The political conditioning of subjective economic evaluations: The role of party discourse. *British Journal of Political Science*, *46*(4), 799–823.

Petrocik, J. (1996). Issue ownership in presidential elections: With a 1980 case study. *American Journal of Political Science*, *40*(3), 825–50.

Pierson, P. (1996). The new politics of the welfare state. *World Politics*, *48*(2), 143–79.

Powell, G. B., and Whitten, G. (1993). A cross-national analysis of economic voting: Taking account of the political context. *American Journal of Political Science*, *37*(2), 391–414.

Rommetvedt, H., Thesen, G., Christiansen, P., and Nørgaard, A. (2013). Coping with corporatism in decline and the revival of parliament interest group lobbyism in Denmark and Norway, 1980–2005. *Comparative Political Studies*, *46*(4), 457–85.

Seeberg, H. B. (2013). Parties and policies: On the oppositions influence on policy through issue politicization. *Journal of Public Policy*, *33*(1), 89–117.

Seeberg, H. B. (2018). The impact of opposition criticism on the public's evaluation of government competence. *Party Politics*, *26*(4), 484–95.

Seeberg, H. B., and Christiansen, F. (2016). Cooperation between counterparts in parliament from an agenda-setting perspective: Legislative coalitions as a trade of criticism and policy. *West European Politics*, *39*(6), 1160–80.

Singer, M. (2011). Who says 'It's the economy'? Cross-national and cross-individual variation in the salience of economic performance. *Comparative Political Studies*, 44, 284–312.

Singer, M. (2013). The global economic crisis and domestic political agendas. *Electoral Studies*, *32*(2), 404–10.

Soroka, S., Stecula, D., and Wlezien, C. (2015). Its (change in) the (future) economy, stupid: Economic indicators, the media, and public opinion. *American Journal of Political Science*, *59*(2), 457–74.

Stimson, J. A. (1999). *Public Opinion in America: Moods, Cycles, and Swings*, second edn. Boulder, CO: Westview Press.

Stubager, R., Botterill, N. W., Lewis-Beck, M. S., and Nadeau, R. (2014). Scope conditions of economic voting: The Danish exception? *Electoral Studies*, *34*(1), 16–26.

Stubager, R., Hansen K., and Andersen, J. G. (2013). *Krisevalg. Økonomien and folketingsvalget 2011*. Copenhagen: Jurist- and Økonomforbundets Forlag.

Stubager, R., Hansen, K., Lewis-Beck, M., and Nadeau, R. (2021). *The Danish Voter: Democratic Ideals and Challenges*. Ann Arbor, MI: University of Michigan Press.

Stubager, R., Lewis-Beck, M., and Nadeau, R. (2013). Reaching for profit in the welfare state: Patrimonial economic voting in Denmark. *Electoral Studies*, *32*(3), 438–44.

Thau, M. (2019). The social divisions of politics: How parties' group-based appeals influence social group differences in vote choice. *Journal of Politics*, *83*(2), 675–88.

Volkens, A. et al. (2021) *The Manifesto Project Database*. Berlin: WZB.

13

Weakened Ties

The Economy and Presidential Approval in the Twenty-First-Century United States

Kathleen M. Donovan, Paul M. Kellstedt, Ellen M. Key, and Matthew J. Lebo

Few concepts in political science are as ubiquitous as presidential approval. The body of work on approval reaches into many areas of political science—public opinion, the presidency and institutions, foreign policy and international relations, political economy, and political methodology, to name a few. The common thread among these diverse literatures is that approval is a powerful predictor: it is critical for predicting and forecasting election results, explaining the passage of legislation, and understanding how wars are fought or ended.

Regarding the American president, Neustadt (1990, 150) wrote that 'his power is the product of his vantage points in government, together with his reputation in the Washington community and his prestige outside'. The empirical evidence in support of this perspective has been clear: higher approval increases the chances of presidential-backed legislation being passed (Edwards, 1976; Rivers and Rose, 1985; Canes-Wrone and De Marchi, 2002; Lebo and O'Geen, 2011); as well as votes on election day (Abramowitz, 1988; Lewis-Beck and Rice, 1992; Abramowitz and Saunders, 1998; Holbrook, 1996; Lewis-Beck and Tien, 1996). In other words, approval is a desirable commodity for executives if they want to increase their chances of implementing preferred policy changes, and to continue doing so through re-election.

This also means that the question of what drives approval is an imperative one. In the United States, as with other countries in this volume, approval can be conceptualized as a function of the 'e-fraction' or economic input, and the 'p-fraction' or the political component in the popularity function (Paldam, 1991). During the twentieth century, the e-fraction was dominant. In context, this seemed reasonable: the American system features conditions that make it easier to attribute responsibility for national conditions (Lewis-Beck, 1988),

Kathleen M. Donovan et al., *Weakened Ties*. In: *Economics and Politics Revisited*. Edited by: Timothy Hellwig and Matthew Singer, Oxford University Press. © Kathleen M. Donovan et al. (2023). DOI: 10.1093/oso/9780192871664.003.0013

such as a two-party system and having a presidential rather than a parliamentary system (Hellwig and Samuels, 2008). However, despite these institutional features, the strength of the correlation between the economy and executive approval fluctuates over time as demonstrated by the preliminary analyses in Chapter 1.

As discussed in Chapter 1, while other countries may see the relative strength of the e-and p-fractions change due to institutions and clarity of responsibility or issue salience, the story here is one of political predispositions. The United States has increasingly grappled with a common public enemy: partisan polarization. There is no doubt that elites have polarized (McCarty, Poole, and Rosenthal, 2016), a phenomenon that is common in countries with higher income inequality (Pontusson and Rueda, 2008). And given the widely assumed level of elite leadership of mass opinion, it is not surprising to find that countries with more polarized parties tend to exhibit and foster mass polarization (Lupu, 2015).

However, American mass polarization largely manifests itself affectively rather than ideologically (Iyengar, Sood, and Lelkes, 2012; Lelkes, 2016; Mason, 2018). Indeed, Iversen and Soskice (2015) have argued that the same institutional features that cause income inequality also undermine information flows, and thus clarity of responsibility. As a result, economically unequal democracies, such as the United States, tend to exhibit low levels of mass ideological polarization.

When considering the overall level of affective polarization—how socially and emotionally apart the parties are perceived to be—America is relatively average. But the rate at which affective polarization has increased in the United States since the 1990s has been greater than in most Western liberal democracies (Gidron, Adams, and Horne, 2020). As the standard bearer of the party, attitudes towards the president have become a prime target for 'partisan cheerleading'—regardless of the state of the economy. The result is the p-fraction supplanting the e-fraction as the prime driver of presidential approval.

Our aim in this chapter is to integrate the study of US politics into the study of executive approval in other democracies. To that end, we extend our previous analysis (Donovan et al., 2020)—which highlighted the increasing detachment of economic evaluations from approval—through the end of the Trump presidency. In addition, we take a deeper look at approval among political Independents, as one might be tempted to point to their growing prominence as a potential source for depolarization. Perhaps unfortunately, our results support the conclusions of recent work emphasizing their closet partisan nature (Klar and Krupnikov, 2016): like partisans, their views of the president are shaped not by perceptions of economic reality, but by whether the president is a member of their partisan team or not. Finally, we conclude with a discussion of how the pattern we find fits (or doesn't) with the patterns observed in other countries and with some thoughts about where the United States may be headed.

The normative implications of this for democratic accountability are substantial, presenting an ominous warning of a future in which citizens eschew objective information about executive performance and instead base all of their evaluations on an unchanging factor: partisan loyalty. It also raises the question of whether future executives will be motivated by *overall* approval, or merely by approval among their co-partisan supporters. If they cannot win over out-partisans, the key to success may lie more in catering to their partisan supporters rather than pursuing policies—such as good economic performance—that benefit everyone. Absent a jolt to the American political system that motivates elites and citizens to depolarize, these troubling outcomes strike us as likely to continue.

The Long Literature on Presidential Approval

Before presenting the analyses, we first review the literature on predictors of presidential approval in the United States. Following Gronke and Newman (2003), we organize this discussion in three chronological waves: the first generation focused on clear and objective factors, specifically war casualties, major foreign conflicts and events, and economic conditions. As the sophistication of time-series methodologies increased through the 1980s and 1990s, a second generation of researchers was able to ask and answer questions about the duration of an event's impact or changes in the economy on approval. A great deal of interest also focused on which aspects of the economy mattered most, a strand of inquiry that continued into the third generation, commencing roughly around the turn of the century. More substantively, however, this third wave of scholarship replaced questions of 'when' and 'what' factors matter with questions of 'why' and 'for whom'—questions with which we likewise engage. The literature thus evolves from simple analyses of events and economic indicators to nuanced explorations of heterogeneity in terms of time and voters.

First Generation Studies

As with any review of presidential approval, we begin with the seminal work of Mueller (1970), who was the first to examine it as a dependent variable. There are several noteworthy aspects of his findings and his approach, as they launched various strands of research. For one, he found that foreign crises and important events had strong impacts on presidential approval. This implied that presidents might seek to create events in order to generate positive ratings. Early research, however, found that events readily within the president's control, such as foreign travel and televised speeches, played a limited role at best in approval (Simon and Ostrom, 1989).

A second finding was that approval decayed linearly over a president's term, otherwise known as the inexorable decline thesis. This spurred interest in the dynamics of approval, and subsequent work argued for a cyclical pattern of decay (e.g. Presser and Converse, 1976; Stimson, 1976), decay as a function of political and economic events (Kernell, 1978; Monroe, 1979), and as a combination of cycles and events (Norpoth and Segal, 1994).

Mueller (1973), however, attributed the observed decline in popularity to the fragmenting of the coalition of support created during the presidential term. The theory was that presidents lose support over time because uninformed citizens come in with high expectations that are built up during an election. But after the honeymoon is over, they become increasingly disillusioned with his performance. Other research at the time indicated support for this theory, but across partisan groups. Not only did the level of approval vary across partisan groups, but the decline over time (Presser and Converse, 1976) and response to events (Edwards, 1983) was also subject to partisan variation.

Partisanship was not the only variable to exhibit asymmetry, however. A third insight from Mueller's work was that economic prosperity and decline had very different effects on approval, with poor economic conditions decreasing approval but no corresponding effect for economic prosperity (Mueller, 1973). In addition to humans' natural tendency to focus on negative information, negative economic conditions are harder to ignore, and are thus more salient in the media (Stein, 1975), and in individuals' lives (Bloom and Price, 1975).

Second Generation Studies

Given the importance of the economy to approval, the second wave of research focused on which aspects mattered most. Interest initially focused on objective indicators, such as unemployment, inflation, and GDP (Kernell, 1978; Tufte, 1978; Kinder and Kiewiet, 1979; 1981; (Fiorina, 1981; Hibbs, Rivers, and Vasilatos, 1982; Hibbs, 1987; Lewis-Beck, 1988; Haller and Norpoth, 1994). However, it became clear over time that perceptions of the economy mattered more for political attitudes than the economy itself (MacKuen, Erikson, and Stimson, 1992; (Clarke and Stewart, 1994; Norpoth, 1996; Erikson, MacKuen, and Stimson, 2002; De Boef and Kellstedt, 2004).

At the same time, cross-national comparisons revealed the importance of clarity of responsibility (Powell and Whitten, 1993). Divided control of government, for example, sends a murkier signal to the public about who is responsible (Rudolph, 2003), a signal that is further perturbed by elites exploiting the situation to blame each other. Similarly, majoritarian institutions tend to foster greater attributions of responsibility (Nadeau et al., 2002). Although many of these studies focused on institutional factors, the implications are similar to those based on the literature debating subjective and objective indicators: the relationship between the economy and approval is one that is moderated by key variables (Anderson, 2007).

Research during this era was also spurred by increasing methodological sophistication, as more advanced time-series techniques were imported from economics. Unfortunately, results from empirical investigations often changed depending on time-series diagnostics (Clarke and Stewart, 1994), lag structure, time period, or choice of economic variables (Lewis-Beck and Nadeau, 2000). On the bright side, these methodologies allowed for an increased acknowledgement of group-based variation in approval. The focus had switched from macro to individual determinants, an acknowledgement that individuals may respond differently to common shocks. Heterogeneity in the electorate sparked debate about the most appropriate level of analysis and variation within aggregate groups, paving the way for the third generation of presidential approval research, which asked: when does the economy matter (Lebo and Box-Steffensmeier, 2008; Parker-Stephen, 2013) and for whom does it matter (Duch, Palmer, and Anderson, 2000; Gomez and Wilson, 2001; Lebo and Cassino, 2007)?

Third Generation Studies

Building on the work on objective-versus-subjective indications, research in this era shifted from studying the effect of the objective economy on approval to the study of the effects of *perceptions* of the economy on presidential job performance ratings. Consumer confidence is not merely a result of objective economic conditions but also contains other information not found in economic variables (Keynes, 1936; Katona, 1975).

There is disagreement in the literature, however, regarding the relationship between consumer sentiment and politics. Consumer sentiment has been found to affect many aspects of economic (Key and Donovan, 2017) and political life including macropartisanship (Erikson, MacKuen, and Stimson, 2002) as well as presidential and congressional approval (MacKuen, Erikson, and Stimson, 1992; Durr, Gilmour, and Wolbrecht, 1997; Box-Steffensmeier and Tomlinson, 2000). Politics has also been shown to affect consumer sentiment at the aggregate (Norpoth, 1996; De Boef and Kellstedt, 2004; Evans and Pickup, 2010), leading to the conclusion that the relationship between the ICS and presidential approval is one of reciprocal causality.

The relative importance of economic and political factors may also be nonconstant over time (Lebo and Box-Steffensmeier, 2008). In some instances, subjective economic evaluations may be more closely correlated with presidential approval than in others, with consumer sentiment containing information not readily available in other indicators in extreme cases, such as the attack on the World Trade Center on 11 September 2001, but not for more quotidian events. Similarly, the relationship between political or economic events and public opinion is filtered through a partisan lens. Citizens engage in motivated reasoning when evaluating presidential performance (Donovan et al., 2020) and economic indicators (Parker-Stephen, 2013) to reconcile their experiences with their partisan predispositions. Their ability to do so, however, is at least somewhat constrained by reality, at least during extreme periods of economic prosperity or crisis (Parker-Stephen, 2013).

The media may contribute to these time-varying relationships by highlighting different aspects of presidential performance depending on the political circumstances (Brody, 1991; Mutz, 1992; Nadeau et al., 1999). Lewis-Beck and Nadeau (2000) found evidence that voters have asymmetric responses to economic news, punishing the president more for economic decline than rewarding him for economic prosperity (see also Campbell et al., 1960; Mueller, 1973; Bloom and Price, 1975; Lebo and O'Geen, 2011; Lewis-Beck, Nadeau, and Elias, 2008). The same is true for media coverage of the president, with the electorate increasing support for the president when coverage is positive and withdrawing support when the tone of presidential coverage is negative (Nadeau et al., 1999; Key, 2011).

Our previous research had found not only that economic perceptions are increasingly detached from approval, but also that this was driven, at least initially, by out-partisans. Our analysis stopped in 2008, however, and here we extend it through the end of the Trump presidency, once again separating out- and in-partisans from one another. We also analyse Independents as a group. On one hand, polarization increases the salience of party identification, and thus we might expect to see Independents immune from its distorting effects.

On the other hand, recent research has shown convincingly that many Independents are, in fact, closet partisans, who behave in a similar fashion when it comes to politics (Klar and Krupnikov, 2016). Our analysis unfortunately supports this view, indicating that polarization has supplanted the economy as the driving force when it comes to evaluations of the executive.

Time Series and Presidential Approval

Figure 13.1 shows presidential approval from the Eisenhower administration through the end of 2020 from the Executive Approval Database (EAD, Carlin et al., 2019) with vertical lines marking changes in administrations. Some predictable patterns are evident. Approval is high during the honeymoon period at the start of a new administration and declines as the term progresses. This decrease isn't monotonic, however, as approval spikes around rally events like the first Gulf War and the 9/11 terrorist attacks, and declines during crises like the second half of the Iran Hostage Crisis.

Viewing overall, or aggregate, approval obscures the effect of partisanship. When approval is disaggregated by partisanship, a different pattern emerges and the approval gap is visible. Figure 13.2 displays data from Gallup, which allows us to disaggregate approval by partisanship. The graphs chart separate

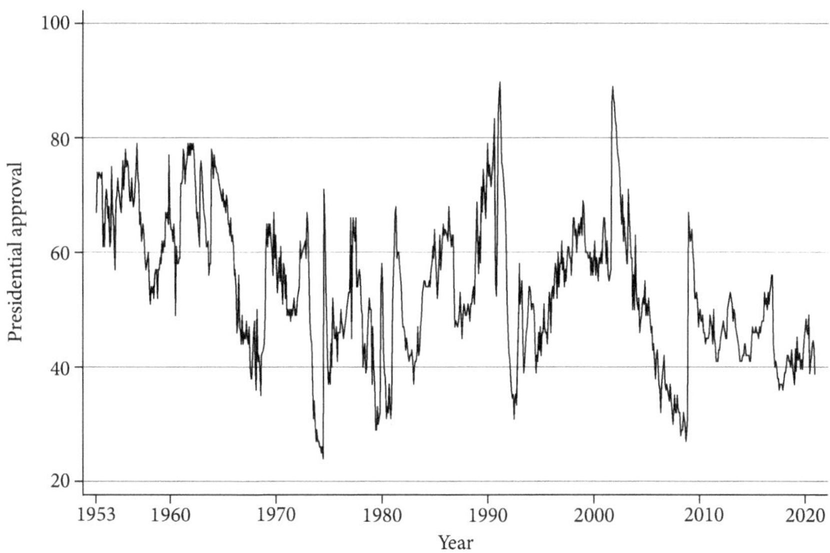

Figure 13.1 US presidential approval, 1953–2020
Source: Executive Approval Database (EAD, Carlin et al., 2019).

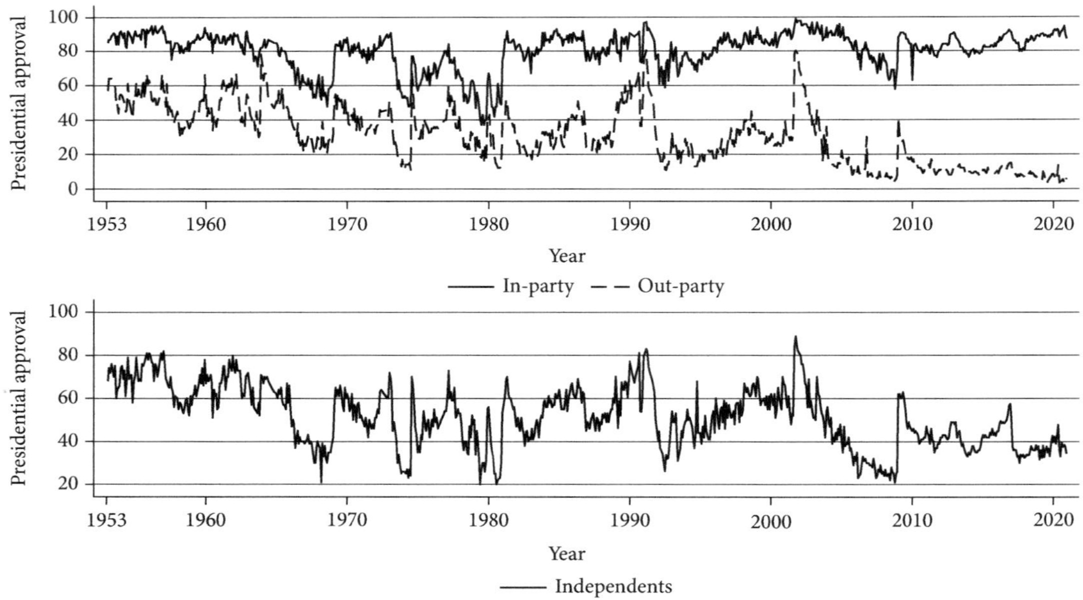

Figure 13.2 Approval among in-party, out-party, and independents, 1953–2020

Source: Gallup.

approval series for respondents who identify with the president's party (in-party), those who identify with the other party (out-party), and Independents. The upper panel shows the obvious fact that the adherents to the in-party are consistently more favourable towards the president than are members of the out-party. Although we can see the approval gap narrowing in response to an extraordinary event like the 9/11 attacks, the series become less dynamic and the gap more stable as partisan polarization increases, with each series becoming relatively flatter after 2010. The approval series for Independents (lower panel of Figure 13.2), on the other hand, remains much more dynamic than the partisan series. Independents not only respond to extraordinary events but also to events that do not shift partisan approval, providing evidence of the power of partisan-motivated reasoning to shape the contours of executive approval.

Hypotheses and Data

Consistent with the literature surveyed above, we expect that more bullish economic perceptions will lead to more positive evaluations of presidential performance. As citizens become more optimistic about economic performance, that optimism should spill over into presidential approval. We expect that the strong correlation between the economy and approval, however, should weaken in the twenty-first century for all partisan groups due to rising polarization (Donovan et al., 2020). As in- and out-partisans increasingly engage in motivated reasoning to confirm their partisan prior beliefs, economic perceptions will be divorced from political evaluations. Independents—roughly one-third of the American electorate—may behave in a more traditional manner by updating their presidential performance evaluations in response to changing economic perceptions. But based on the findings of Klar and Krupnikov (2016) that Independents are covert partisans, we expect they, too, will see a weakening of the ties between the economy and politics.

To explore the contours of executive approval and see how the relative importance of the e-fraction has changed over time, we examine presidential approval using monthly data from the EAD and from Gallup Analytics beginning in 1978 and extending through the end of the Trump administration in 2020. This corresponds to the period for which the University of Michigan's monthly Index of Consumer Sentiment (ICS) is available, which we use as our indicator of subjective economic perceptions. In addition to including economic perceptions in the form of the ICS, the model also contains interventions to account for relevant political events (Newman and Otto, 2022). We estimate approval in Equation (1)[1]

$$\Delta y_t = \alpha_0 + \alpha_1^* y_{t-1} + \beta_0^* \Delta ICS_t + \beta_1^* ICS_{t-1} + \beta_k^* Events_{kt} + e_t \quad (1)$$

Results

Because polarization in the United States has increased in recent decades, accounting for the dynamics of American presidential approval requires us to examine these relationships separately at different time periods. To begin, Figure 13.3 shows EAD data for US approval and the ICS from 1978 to 2000. The display seems to indicate Americans' subjective evaluations of the economy were indeed tied to their ratings of the president. For example, in the late 1990s, even as partisan warfare and impeachment were the main story in national politics, a steadily improving economy was met with increases in President Clinton's approval rating. As late as the end of the twentieth century, in other words, an argument could be made that a 'rational public' existed

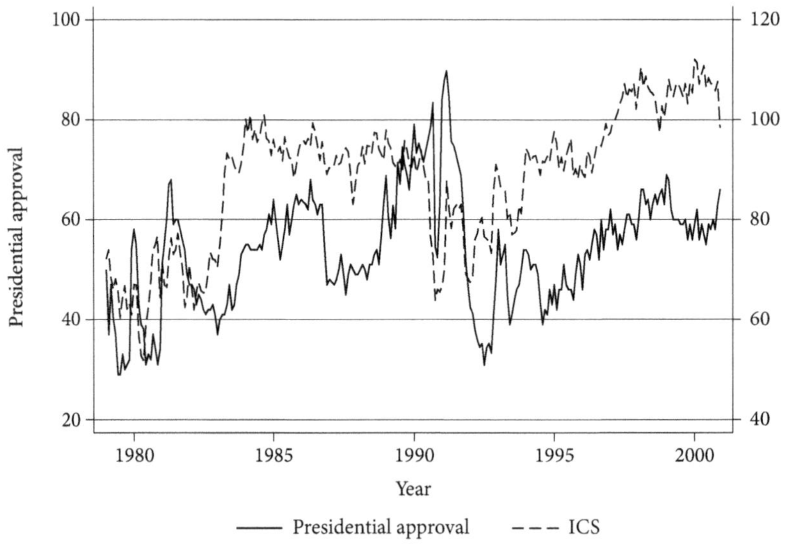

Figure 13.3 Presidential approval and ICS, 1978–2000
Source: EAD and University of Michigan.

[1] In this generalized error correction model we use asterisks on the estimated parameters to differentiate them from parameters in an autoregressive distributed lag model (Kraft, Key, and Lebo, 2022).

in terms of rewards and punishments for economic performance (Page and Shapiro, 1992).

Analyses of the data bear that out as well. Table 13.1 applies a generalized error correction model to both the EAD (left) and Gallup (right) presidential approval series for the years 1978–2000, and includes interventions to control for the effects of major events such as Operation Desert Storm, the Iran Hostage Crisis, and so on.[2] Our main focus is on the effect of the Index of Consumer Sentiment, which we find to have significant effects in both its lagged-level and differenced forms. With uncertainty about the time-series characteristics of the data (e.g. Lebo, Walker, and Clarke, 2000; Kellstedt, Linn, and Hannah 2015), interpretation of those coefficients is potentially complicated. To avoid uncertain unit root testing, we calculate the value of the long-run multiplier (LRM) for the cumulative effect of the ICS on presidential

Table 13.1 The effects of consumer sentiment on presidential approval, 1978–2000

Independent variable	**Executive Approval data**		**Gallup data**	
$Approval_{t-1}$	−0.132*		−0.149*	
	(0.025)		(0.027)	
Δ ICS_t	0.083*		0.237*	
	(0.028)		(0.071)	
ICS_{t-1}	0.033*		0.084*	
	(0.009)		(0.023)	
Constant	3.316		0.439	
	(1.035)		(1.878)	
Long-run multipliers				
	LRM (SE)	LRM *t* (inference)	LRM (SE)	LRM *t* (inference)
ICS	0.249	4.025	0.562	4.042
	(0.062)	(above)	(0.139)	(above)
N	275		275	
R^2	0.225		0.284	

Source: Approval data from Executive Approval Database (EAD, Carlin et al., 2019) and Gallup. Consumer sentiment data from University of Michigan's Survey of Consumers.
Notes: *p≤0.05 (two-tailed test). Standard errors are in parentheses. Standard errors of the LRMs are calculated using the delta method. The lower bound for the *t*-statistic is 1.01 and the upper bound is 3.65. The effects of interventions are not shown.

[2] The complete list follows Lebo and Cassino (2007) and includes Operation Desert Storm, missile strikes on Iraq, the assassination attempt on President Reagan, the bombing of Libya, the Deng visit to the United States, Three Mile Island, gas lines, and the Iran hostage crisis. The only interventions used in the data beyond 2001 are the Iraq War and COVID-19.

approval. This is Equation 1 in the GECM: $\Delta y_t = \alpha_0 + \alpha_1^* y_{t-1} + \beta_0^* \Delta ICS_t + \beta_1^* ICS_{t-1} + \beta_k^* Events_{kt} + e_t$. The t-statistic for the LRM is 4.02 for the EAD data and 4.04 for the Gallup data, which we compare to the critical value bounds provided in Webb, Linn, and Lebo (2019; 2020). Using those bounds, a test-statistic above 3.65 means we are able to safely reject the null hypothesis that the ICS has no cumulative effect on presidential approval, and this conclusion holds regardless of what the underlying univariate properties of the time series might be. Thus, prior to 2001, consumer sentiment was a significant predictor of presidential approval.[3]

The economic story of approval dynamics does not continue into the twenty-first century, however. Our second analysis covers January 2002 until the end of President Trump's term—data highlighted in Figure 13.4.[4]

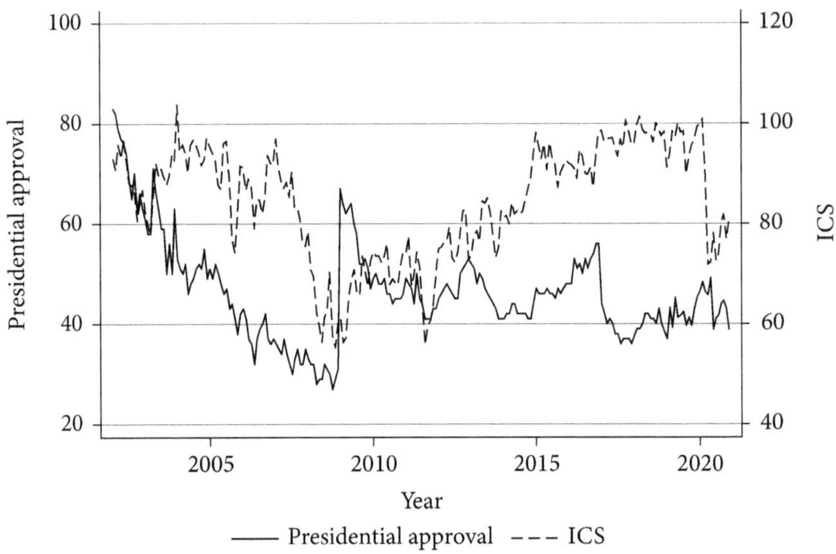

Figure 13.4 Presidential approval and ICS, 2002–2020
Source: EAD and University of Michigan.

[3] When objective economic indicators—inflation and unemployment—are added to the equation, their coefficients fail to achieve statistical significance and their LRMs are between the bounds. Since the effects of these objective indicators work through the public's subjective views of the economy, we have both theoretical and statistical reasons to exclude them from our analyses here.

[4] The terrorist attacks of September 2001 wreak havoc on models like these. For one, the spike in presidential approval is the largest in the nearly seventy years of data and, thus, represents a large proportion of the variance in approval. Second, the rally-around-the-flag effect coincided with an immediate drop in Americans' subjective views of the present and future prospects for the economy, which counteracts the expected effects of economic judgements. For our purposes, therefore, it is desirable to leave 2001 out of our models to get a cleaner look at the link between the ICS and approval over the 2002–2020 period.

Table 13.2 presents two more models with the EAD and Gallup data, where we see that neither of the effects of the ICS—the instantaneous effects nor the cumulative effects—is statistically significant. The t-statistics of the LRM for the ICS are 1.36 and 0.77 in the models. The latter falls below the 0.05-level lower bound (1.01 with k=1 and T=150) of Webb, Linn, and Lebo (2020). This tells us that we fail to reject the null hypothesis that the ICS has no effect on presidential approval, and that this would be true regardless of what conclusions we might make about the time-series properties of the variables. The value of 1.36 for the EAD approval series is just above the lower bound meaning that we are uncertain if we can reject the null hypothesis.

A perplexing part of this story is that it is not simply Democratic and Republican identifiers who have stopped rewarding and punishing presidents based on the outlook of the economy. As Table 13.3 shows, in the latter time period the aggregate level of approval among self-identifying Independents is not following the ICS, either. The LRM t-statistic of 0.82 falls below both bounds and we fail to reject the null hypothesis again. This comports with the work

Table 13.2 The effects of consumer sentiment on presidential approval, 2002–2020

Independent variable	Executive Approval data		Gallup data	
$Approval_{t-1}$	−0.070*		−0.108*	
	(0.017)		(0.024)	
$\Delta\ ICS_t$	0.032		0.054	
	(0.020)		(0.057)	
ICS_{t-1}	−0.011		−0.017	
	(0.008)		(0.021)	
Iraq War	3.553*		13.942*	
	(1.310)		(3.655)	
Constant	3.903*		6.159	
	(0.924)		(1.995)	
Long-run multipliers				
	LRM (SE)	LRM t (inference)	LRM (SE)	LRM t (inference)
ICS	0.162	1.356	0.155	0.763
	(0.120)	(between)	(0.203)	(below)
N	228		228	
R^2	0.120		0.143	

Source: Approval data from Executive Approval Database (EAD, Carlin et al., 2019) and Gallup. Consumer sentiment data from University of Michigan's Survey of Consumers.
Notes: *p≤0.05 (two-tailed test). Standard errors are in parentheses. Standard errors of the LRMs are calculated using the delta method. The lower bound for the t-statistic is 1.01 and the upper bound is 3.65.

Table 13.3 Presidential approval among independents, 2002–2020

Approval$_{t-1}$	**−0.119***	
	(0.032)	
Δ ICS$_t$	0.106	
	(0.067)	
ICS$_{t-1}$	−0.021	
	(0.025)	
Iraq War	20.276*	
	(4.314)	
Constant	6.453	
	(2.275)	
Long-run multiplier		
	LRM (SE)	LRM *t* (inference)
ICS	−0.176 (0.216)	0.821 (below)
N	228	
R^2	0.180	

Source: Approval data from Gallup. Consumer sentiment data from University of Michigan's Survey of Consumers.
Notes: *$p \leq 0.05$ (two-tailed test). Standard errors are in parentheses.

by Klar and Krupnikov (2016) showing most Independents are really undercover partisans. One might look at the partisan gap in approval and hope that perhaps the reality of the economy might at least register with Independents and thereby guide approval—and even elections—in a more objective way. But these data provide no evidence that this happens.

Nothing Seems to Matter Anymore: Obama and Trump Years

In particular, looking at the Obama and Trump presidencies, it is hard to see what factors beyond partisanship might matter. Certainly, aggregate opinions relating to the economy do not affect approval and are themselves greatly influenced by partisanship-motivated reasoning leads Democrats and Republicans to view the state of the economy very differently. As Figure 13.5 shows, after President Obama's honeymoon wore off, his approval mostly moved within a narrow band between the low-40s and low-50s. President Trump's approval was similarly constrained, never going above 48 per cent or below 36 per cent in Gallup's ratings.

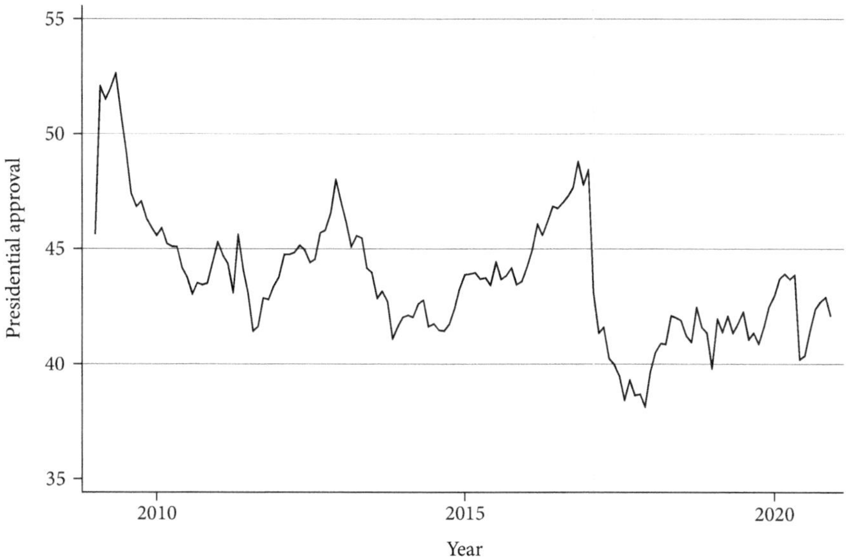

Figure 13.5 Presidential approval, 2009–2020
Source: EAD.

Table 13.4 Obama administration approval, 2009–2016

	In-Party		**Out-Party**		**Independents**	
$Approval_{t-1}$	−0.303*		−0.220*		−0.125*	
	(0.067)		(0.031)		(0.033)	
Δ ICS_t	0.043		0.098*		0.161*	
	(0.086)		(0.041)		(0.059)	
ICS_{t-1}	0.031		0.003		0.037	
	(0.032)		(0.017)		(0.022)	
Constant	22.703*		2.251		2.458	
	(5.967)		(1.569)		(2.438)	
Long-run multipliers						
	LRM	LRM *t*	LRM	LRM *t*	LRM	LRM *t*
	(SE)	(inference)	(SE)	(inference)	(SE)	(inference)
ICS	0.104	0.98	0.013	0.17	0.298	1.46
	(0.106)	(below)	(0.078)	(below)	(0.204)	(between)
N	95		95		95	
R^2	0.127		0.395		0.120	

Source: Approval data from Gallup. Consumer sentiment data from University of Michigan's Survey of Consumers.
*p≤0.05 (two-tailed test). Standard errors are in parentheses.

Table 13.5 Trump administration approval, 2017–2020

	In-Party		Out-Party		Independents	
$Approval_{t-1}$	−0.279*		−0.550*		−0.600*	
	(0.080)		(0.112)		(0.098)	
$\Delta\ ICS_t$	−0.034		0.095		−0.064	
	(0.069)		(0.061)		(0.107)	
ICS_{t-1}	−0.045		0.010		−0.088	
	(0.038)		(0.033)		(0.054)	
COVID-19	2.107		5.422*		3.312	
	(1.496)		(1.476)		(2.330)	
Constant	28.634*		2.839		29.853*	
	(9.248)		(2.841)		(6.789)	
Long-run multipliers						
	LRM (SE)	LRM *t* (inference)	LRM (SE)	LRM *t* (inference)	LRM (SE)	LRM *t* (inference)
ICS	−0.162	1.33	0.019	0.32	0.148	1.68
	(0.123)	(between)	(0.058)	(below)	(0.088)	(between)
N	47		47		47	
R^2	0.104		0.574		0.458	

Source: Approval data from Gallup. Consumer sentiment data from University of Michigan's Survey of Consumers.
Notes: *p≤0.05 (two-tailed test). Standard errors are in parentheses.

To break down what was happening—or, more accurately, what was not happening—during these presidencies, we estimated a seemingly unrelated regression, where the effects of the ICS are measured on the three partisan groups—the in-party and out-party partisans as well as Independent identifiers. Table 13.4 shows that for the ninety-six months of Obama's presidency, the ICS did not significantly predict changes in approval among Democrats, Republicans, or Independents. That is, lower economic sentiments did not lead to Democrats abandoning him, and higher ones did not engender support among Republicans. The story is similar for President Trump. As Table 13.5 shows, the movement of the ICS had no effect on approval for any of the three partisan groups. An update of the advice once given to candidate Bill Clinton might be: 'It's not the economy anymore, stupid.'

Discussion and Conclusion

Beyond any statistical analyses of the data, some simple facts about the popularity of recent presidents go a long way to demonstrate how partisanship is seemingly all that matters anymore. Barack Obama came into office in 2009 and oversaw solid economic and jobs growth for all but the first few months after he took office. On the foreign policy side, Obama undertook no new major armed conflicts, but managed the gradual drawdown of wars in Iraq and Afghanistan, as well as the assassination of Osama Bin Laden. No major scandals shook his administration and no Cabinet members or prominent figures needed to resign in disgrace. Nevertheless, Republicans' approval level of President Obama hovered around 10 per cent in our data for most of his two terms. Nothing he did—or didn't do—could please them.

By comparison, President Trump's four years in office were incredibly tumultuous. Still, Republican approval of his job performance was roughly 90 per cent, and indeed unshakeable for his last two years in office—a period which included countless scandals, two impeachments, a deep and sudden recession, and a pandemic that killed 400,000 Americans during his last year in office. Indeed, in Trump's second impeachment, ten Republican Members of Congress voted to impeach him, and seven Republican Senators joined the Democrats in voting to convict him for inciting an insurrection against Congress on 6 January 2021. Nevertheless, the last few polls of his presidency showed that even an insurrection could not shake Republicans' approval of Trump—Gallup's rating among them dropped from 87 per cent in December 2020 to 82 per cent after the attack on the Capitol in January of 2021.

Perhaps that is all one needs to know about the forces shaping executive approval in the contemporary United States; among his partisan supporters, endangering American democracy and even his own vice president cost President Trump just a bit more than the poll's margin of error.

In the era of American politics where the economy most clearly affected approval, scholars investigated the political business cycle and attempts by the president to influence the economy. As in the Danish case discussed in Chapter 12, the relative importance of the e- and p-fractions in the United States have changed over time. Yet in contrast to Denmark, where partisan convergence has shifted the public's attention to performance, growing affective polarization in the United States has anchored executive approval. Now, in an age of American hyper-partisanship, we see that economic evaluations are untethered from reality, and the president's best hopes of electoral success lie in the power and motivations of partisanship—a strategy Trump pursued. Indeed, he won 10 million more votes in 2020 than he did in 2016. Does this mean that future presidents will similarly pursue a 'red meat' strategy, with less emphasis on the national economy and its sociotropic impacts, and more emphasis on the policies and ideas that activate a core, partisan constituency? If bipartisanship in policymaking is impossible, that might be the only strategy.

Is the polarization of American presidential approval irreversible? Time will tell. On the one hand, it is notable that no president has entered office with as much wind at their back as did Joe Biden. In the first half of 2021, with vaccinations for COVID-19 rolling out, and with the economy bouncing back from a deep recession, Biden's presidency produced objective numbers—jobs and jabs—that might have led even motivated reasoners to have a hard time not seeing. On the other hand, as we move into the second half of 2022, his approval ratings appear to be settling into the now familiar pattern. Although his highest ratings among in-partisans and Independents were higher than Trump's initially, Biden's lows have become similar across all groups, indicating the United States is likely to experience more 'partisanship as usual'.

References

Abramowitz, A. I. (1988). Explaining Senate election outcomes. *American Political Science Review, 82*(2), 385–403.

Abramowitz, A. I., and Saunders, K. (1998). Ideological realignment in the US electorate. *Journal of Political Science, 60*(3), 634–52.

Anderson, C. J. (2007). The end of economic voting? Contingency dilemmas and the limits of democratic accountability. *Annual Review of Political Science, 10*, 271–96.

Bloom, H. S., and Price, H. D. (1975). Voter response to short-run economic conditions: The asymmetric effect of prosperity and recession. *American Political Science Review, 69*(4), 1240–54.

Box-Steffensmeier, J. M., and Tomlinson, A. R. (2000). Fractional integration methods in political science. *Electoral Studies, 19*(1), 63–76.

Brody, R. A. (1991). *Assessing the President: The Media, Elite Opinion, and Public Support*. Stanford, CA: Stanford University Press.

Campbell, A., Converse, P. E., Miller, W. E., and Stokes, D. E. (1960). *The American Voter*. Chicago, IL: University of Chicago Press.

Canes-Wrone, B., and De Marchi, S. (2002). Presidential approval and legislative success. *Journal of Politics, 64*(2), 491–509.

Carlin, R. E., Hartlyn, J., Hellwig, T., Love, G. J., Martinez-Gallardo, C., and Singer, M. M. (2019). Executive Approval Database 2.0. Available for download at www.executiveapproval.org.

Clarke, H. D., and Stewart, M. C. (1994). Prospections, retrospections, and rationality: The 'bankers' model of presidential approval reconsidered. *American Journal of Political Science*, *38*(4), 1104–23.

De Boef, S., and Kellstedt, P. M. (2004). The political (and economic) origins of consumer confidence. *American Journal of Political Science*, *48*(4), 633–49.

Donovan, K. M., Kellstedt, P. M., Key E. M., and Lebo, M. J. (2020). Motivated reasoning, public opinion, and presidential approval. *Political Behavior*, *42*(4), 1201–21.

Duch, R. M., Palmer, H. D., and Anderson, C. J. (2000). Heterogeneity in perceptions of national economic conditions. *American Journal of Political Science*, *44*(4), 635–52.

Durr, R. H., Gilmour, J. B., and Wolbrecht, C. (1997). Explaining congressional approval. *American Journal of Political Science*, *41*(1), 175–207.

Edwards, G. C. (1976). Presidential influence in the House: Presidential prestige as a source of presidential power. *American Political Science Review*, *70*(1), 101–13.

Edwards, G. C. III. (1983). *The Public Presidency: The Pursuit of Popular Support*. New York: St. Martins.

Erikson, R. S., MacKuen, M. B., and Stimson, J. A. (2002). *The Macro Polity*. Cambridge: Cambridge University Press.

Evans, G., and Pickup, M. (2010). Reversing the causal arrow: The political conditioning of economic perceptions in the 2000–2004 US presidential election cycle. *The Journal of Politics*, *72*(4), 1236–51.

Fiorina, M. P. (1981). *Retrospective Voting in American National Elections*. New Haven, CT: Yale University Press.

Gidron, N., Adams, J., and Horne, W. (2020). *American Affective Polarization in Comparative Perspective*. Cambridge: Cambridge University Press.

Gomez, B. T., and Wilson, J. M. (2001). Political sophistication and economic voting in the American electorate: A theory of heterogeneous attribution. *American Journal of Political Science*, *45*(4), 899–914.

Gronke, P., and Newman, B. (2003). FDR to Clinton, Mueller to? A field essay on presidential approval. *Political Research Quarterly*, *56*(4), 501–12.

Haller, H. B., and Norpoth, H. (1994). Let the good times roll: The economic expectations of US voters. *American Journal of Political Science*, *38*(3), 625–50.

Hellwig, T., and Samuels, D. (2008). Electoral accountability and the variety of democratic regimes. *British Journal of Political Science*, *38*(1), 65–90.

Hibbs Jr, D. A., Rivers, R. D., and Vasilatos, N. (1982). The dynamics of political support for American presidents among occupational and partisan groups. *American Journal of Political Science*, *26*(2), 312–32.

Hibbs, D. A. Jr. (1987). *The American Political Economy: Macroeconomics and Electoral Politics in the United States.* Cambridge, MA: Harvard University Press.

Holbrook, T. M. (1996). *Do Campaigns matter?* Thousand Oaks, CA: Sage.

Iversen, T., and Soskice, D. (2015). Information, inequality, and mass polarization: Ideology in advanced democracies. *Comparative Political Studies*, *48*(13), 1781–813.

Iyengar, S., Sood, G., and Lelkes, Y. (2012). Affect, not ideology: social identity perspective on polarization. *Public Opinion Quarterly*, *76*(3), 405–31.

Katona, G. (1975). *Psychological Economics.* New York: Elsevier.

Kellstedt, P. M., Linn, S., and Hannah, A. L. (2015). The usefulness of consumer sentiment: Assessing construct and measurement. *Public Opinion Quarterly*, *79*(1), 181–203.

Kernell, S. (1978). Explaining presidential popularity: How ad hoc theorizing, misplaced emphasis, and insufficient care in measuring one's variables refuted common sense and led conventional wisdom down the path of anomalies. *American Political Science Review*, *72*(2), 506–22.

Key, E. M. (2011). The dynamic relationship between media sentiment and presidential approval. Paper presented at the Annual Meeting of the Midwest Political Science Association. Chicago, IL.

Key, E. M. and Donovan, K. M. (2017). The political economy: Political determinants of the macroeconomy. *Political Behavior*, *39*(3), 763–86.

Keynes, J. M. (1936). *The General Theory of Employment, Interest, and Money.* New York: Harcourt, Brace, and World.

Kinder, D. R., and Kiewiet, D. R. (1979). Economic discontent and political behavior: The role of personal grievances and collective economic judgments in congressional voting. *American Journal of Political Science*, *23*(3), 495–527.

Kinder, D. R., and Kiewiet, D. R. (1981). Sociotropic politics: The American case. *British Journal of Political Science*, *11*(2), 129–61.

Klar, S., and Krupnikov, Y. (2016). *Independent Politics: How American Disdain for Parties Leads to Political Inaction.* New York: Cambridge University Press.

Kraft, P. W., Key, E. M., and Lebo, M. J. (2022). Hypothesis testing with error correction models. *Political Science Research and Methods*, *10*(4), 870–8.

Lebo, M. J., and Box-Steffensmeier, J. M. (2008). Dynamic conditional correlations in political science. *American Journal of Political Science*, *52*(3), 688–704.

Lebo, M. J., and Cassino, D. (2007). The aggregated consequences of motivated reasoning and the dynamics of partisan presidential approval. *Political Psychology*, *28*(6), 719–46.

Lebo, M. J., and O'Geen, A. J. (2011). The president's role in the partisan congressional arena. *The Journal of Politics, 73*(3), 718–34.

Lebo, M. J., Walker, R. W., and Clarke, H. D. (2000). You must remember this: Dealing with long memory in political analyses. *Electoral Studies, 19*(1), 31–48.

Lelkes, Y. (2016). Mass polarization: Manifestations and measurements. *Public Opinion Quarterly, 80*(S1), 392–410.

Lewis-Beck, M. S. (1988). *Economics and Elections: The Major Western Democracies.* Ann Arbor, MI: University of Michigan Press.

Lewis-Beck, M. S., and Tien, C. (1996). The future in forecasting: Prospective presidential models. *American Politics Quarterly, 24*(4), 468–91.

Lewis-Beck, M. S., and Nadeau, R. (2000). French electoral institutions and the economic vote. *Electoral Studies, 19*(2–3), 171–82.

Lewis-Beck, M. S., Nadeau, R., and Elias, A. (2008). Economics, party, and the vote: Causality issues and panel data. *American Journal of Political Science, 52*(1), 84–95.

Lewis-Beck, M. S., and Rice, T. W. (1992). *Forecasting Elections.* Washington, DC: Congressional Quarterly Press.

Lupu, N. (2015). Party polarization and mass partisanship: A comparative perspective. *Political Behavior, 37*(2), 331–56.

MacKuen, M. B., Erikson, R. S., and Stimson, J. A. (1992). Peasants or bankers? The American electorate and the US economy. *American Political Science Review, 86*(3), 597–611.

Mason, L. (2018). *Uncivil Agreement: How Politics Became our Identity.* Chicago, IL: University of Chicago Press.

McCarty, N., Poole, K. T., and Rosenthal, H. (2016). *Polarized America: The Dance of Ideology and Unequal Riches.* Cambridge, MA: MIT Press.

Monroe, K. R. (1979). Econometric analyses of electoral behavior: A critical review. *Political Behavior, 1*(2), 137–73.

Mueller, J. E. (1970). Presidential popularity from Truman to Johnson. *American Political Science Review, 64*(1), 18–34.

Mueller, J. E. (1973). *War, Presidents and Public Opinion.* New York: Wiley.

Mutz, D. C. (1992). Mass media and the depoliticization of personal experience. *American Journal of Political Science, 36*(2), 483–508.

Nadeau, R., Niemi, R. G., Fan, D. P., and Amato, T. (1999). Elite economic forecasts, economic news, mass economic judgments, and presidential approval. *The Journal of Politics, 61*(1), 109–35.

Nadeau, R., Niemi, R. G., and Yoshinaka, A. (2002). A cross-national analysis of economic voting: taking account of the political context across time and nations. *Electoral Studies, 21*(3), 403–23.

Neustadt, R. E. (1990). *Presidential Power and the Modern Presidents: The Politics of Leadership from Roosevelt to Reagan.* New York: John Wiley and Sons.

Newman, B., and Otto, A. (2022). Polls and elections: The economy and events still matter (at least a little): Partisans' presidential approval in the Trump era. *Presidential Studies Quarterly*, *52*(1), 208–23.

Norpoth, H. (1996). Presidents and the prospective voter. *The Journal of Politics*, *58*(3), 776–92.

Norpoth, H., Segal, J. A., Mishler, W., and Sheehan, R. S. (1994). Popular influence on Supreme Court decisions. *American Political Science Review*, *88*(3), 711–24.

Page, B. I., and Shapiro, R. Y. (1992). *The Rational Public: Fifty Years of Trends in Americans' Policy Preferences*. Chicago, IL: University of Chicago Press.

Paldam, M. (1991). How robust is the vote function? A study of seventeen nations over four decades. In *Economics and Politics: The Calculus of Support*, H. Norpoth and M. Lewis-Beck, eds. Ann Arbor, MI: University of Michigan Press. 9–31.

Parker-Stephen, E. (2013). Tides of disagreement: How reality facilitates (and inhibits) partisan public opinion. *The Journal of Politics*, *75*(4), 1077–88.

Pontusson, J., and Rueda, D. (2008). Inequality as a source of political polarization: A comparative analysis of twelve OECD countries. In *Democracy, Inequality, and Representation in Comparative Perspective*, Pablo Beremendi and Christopher J. Anderson, eds. New York, NY: Russell Sage Foundation. 312–53.

Powell Jr, G. B., and Whitten, G. D. (1993). A cross-national analysis of economic voting: Taking account of the political context. *American Journal of Political Science*, *37*(2), 391–414.

Presser, S., and Converse, J. M. (1976). On Stimson's interpretation of declines in presidential popularity. *Public Opinion Quarterly*, *40*(4), 538–41.

Rivers, D., and Rose, N. L. (1985). Passing the president's program: Public opinion and presidential influence in Congress. *American Journal of Political Science*, *29*(2), 183–96.

Rudolph, T. J. (2003). Who's responsible for the economy? The formation and consequences of responsibility attributions. *American Journal of Political Science*, *47*(4), 698–713.

Simon, D. M., and Ostrom Jr, C. W. (1989). The impact of televised speeches and foreign travel on presidential approval. *Public Opinion Quarterly*, *53*(1), 58–82.

Stein, H. (1975). Media distortions: A former official's view. *Columbia Journalism Review*, *13*(6), 37–41.

Stimson, J. A. (1976). On disillusion with the expectation/disillusion theory: A rejoinder. *Public Opinion Quarterly*, *40*(4), 541–3.

Tufte, E. R. 1978. *Political Control of the Economy*. Princeton, NJ: Princeton University Press.

Webb, C., Linn, S., and Lebo, M. (2019). A bounds approach to inference using the long-run multiplier. *Political Analysis*, *27*(3), 281–301.

Webb, C., Linn, S., and Lebo, M. J. (2020). Beyond the unit root question: Uncertainty and inference. *American Journal of Political Science*, *64*(2), 275–92.

14

Economics, Politics, and the Popularity Function

Past, Present, and Future

Mary Stegmaier, Brandon Beomseob Park, and Michael S. Lewis-Beck

In an essential way, the writing of the volume at hand began about thirty-five years ago, at a conference in Bellagio, Italy. Participants went on to compose a collection entitled *Economics and Politics: The Calculus of Support* (Norpoth, Lewis-Beck, and Lafay, 1991). The focus on the volume was vote and popularity functions, which hold government support to be shaped by economic and political outcomes. Martin Paldam (1991, 9) claimed in his chapter that the 'two functions are so alike that I shall speak of VP-functions'. This current volume makes more of that distinction, homing in on the P-function, which provides for more frequent measurement of government popularity than elections.

Research on popularity functions spans back to the seminal work of Goodhart and Bhansali (1970). With over fifty years of country and cross-national studies, the general proposition of the popularity function is well established. But over the years, scholars have questioned why some studies find strong economic effects on approval ratings, while others find it is weak or even nonexistent. In other words, as Lewis-Beck and Paldam (2000, 114) ask, 'is the instability of the VP-function apparent or inherent?' Over decades of research, scholars have found that accounting for the political and economic contexts reduces instability and contributes to more solid theory and findings.

Given the accumulated VP-function research tested in a wide range of democracies (Nannestad and Paldam, 1994; Lewis-Beck and Stegmaier, 2013; Stegmaier et al., 2017; 2021), one might ask: what does this current book contribute? First, it provides a comprehensive cross-national assessment of the economy–popularity link. Second, Lijphart's (1971) classic work on the comparative method and the role of country case studies sheds a special light on

Mary Stegmaier, Brandon Beomseob Park, and Michael S. Lewis-Beck, *Economics, Politics, and the Popularity Function*. In: *Economics and Politics Revisited*. Edited by: Timothy Hellwig and Matthew Singer, Oxford University Press. © Mary Stegmaier, Brandon Beomseob Park, and Michael S. Lewis-Beck (2023). DOI: 10.1093/oso/9780192871664.003.0014

the value of the country-centred chapters. He writes that by focusing intensively on a single case, the study 'can make an important contribution to the establishment of general propositions and thus to theory building in political science' (Lijphart, 1971, 691). As we will see, hypothesis-generating and deviant cases can provide the basis for future research that can contribute to the refinement of generalizable theory. Furthermore, most of the country chapters (10 of the 11) provide full or partial confirmation of the established general proposition that *the economy matters for approval ratings, but sometimes it matters more than others.* In essence, there is a relationship between the economy and popularity, but the magnitude of that relationship is impacted in predictable ways.

In this closing chapter, we first provide a select review of widely recognized cross-national VP-function studies. We do so with an eye towards how certain contextual features impact the strength of the economy in VP-functions, and we will attempt to assess a question that Paldam (1991) asked: how large is the e-fraction (the economy) compared to the p-fraction (politics)? Then we turn to the country case-study chapters in this volume, characterizing them according to Lijphart's typology: theory-confirming, theory-infirming, hypothesis-generating, and deviant case studies. As we will see, the hypothesis-generating and deviant case studies provide insights that deserve greater study. In addition to these, we provide further avenues for research in our concluding section on the future agenda.

What Do We Already Know about VP-Functions?

VP-functions focus on changes over time with an explanatory emphasis on previous support and macroeconomic conditions. For example, in one of the earliest of these time-series studies, Kramer (1971) set out to understand short-term fluctuations in US congressional elections, a vote function, and found that elections are impacted by objective changes—especially economic changes—that took place under the incumbent party's watch. Such vote functions help us understand changes in election results over time, but statistically they generally suffer from a small sample size. This finds a remedy in the study of approval ratings or 'popularity', since these variables are measured more frequently than actual election results.

These popularity functions operate much like vote functions, upon consideration of the actual specification of the equations under investigation. The earliest popularity function study was conducted in Britain by Goodhart and

Bhansali (1970). They used monthly polls that asked citizens which party they would vote for 'if an election were held tomorrow'. They found that inflation and unemployment significantly impacted popularity. Additionally, they identified the pattern known as the honeymoon effect—the elevated popularity of a newly elected government. One important lesson from the ensuing VP-function studies is that the electorate largely focuses on incumbent or leader performance (Lewis-Beck and Stegmaier, 2013; Stegmaier et al., 2017; 2021). When the country is prospering, the electorate will reward the government. But, when times are tough, the incumbent will be punished. Further, that sense of reward or punishment, meted out by the electorate in opinion polls and on the ballot, is present across the electoral cycle. Indeed, in the words of a recent study on the subject, the economic voter abides, responding over a long time horizon (Stiers et al., 2020).

However, an astute reader of the VP-function literature will notice that the magnitude of the economic impact appears to vary from study to study, country to country. This is a question that scholars have worked to understand—is it really unstable, or are there generalizable institutional or contextual features that help explain why the e-part is strong in some places and relatively weak in others?

One answer lies in a country's policymaking environment, which shapes the clarity of responsibility and, hence, influences the economy's impact on approval. Studies have shown, for example, that the magnitude of the economic vote is reduced when more parties are in the government (Lewis-Beck, 1986). Further, when we look at support for parties separately within a ruling coalition, analysis shows that voters mostly reward or punish the prime minister and his or her party (Debus et al., 2014; Williams et al., 2017). Party stability, rather than number of parties, is another relevant institutional feature albeit with two opposing expectations. On the one hand, it is argued that with more parties to choose from, the probability of switching parties increases (Dassonneville et al., 2015), so creating a stronger accountability mechanism based on the economy (Rowe, 2015). On the other hand, citizens may be less likely to punish the incumbent when it is harder to identify viable alternatives from a fragmented party system (Anderson, 2000; Bengtsson, 2004). Hence, '[e]conomic effects are only found in elections when there were clearly available alternatives—in party systems with a relatively low number of effective parties' (Bengtsson, 2004, 757).

One of the most prominent cross-national studies on how the political context impacts the relationship between the economy and support is by Powell and Whitten (1993). In measuring clarity of responsibility, they developed an index that accounted for factors such as minority governments, number of parties, party cohesion, and divided government/executives. They 'find very sharp differences in the impact of economic performance on voters' support for the government' (p. 410). In countries where responsibility is clear, the economic effects are strong and consistent. In contrast, when policymaking responsibility is typically blurred, the economic effects are weak, and the political factors—previous government support and previous government vote swing—dominate in the model. Returning, then, to Paldam's (1991) question about the relative size of the e- and p-parts, Powell and Whitten's results show that in contexts where policymaking responsibility is unclear, the p-part is greater than the e-part. In countries with clear assignment of responsibility, the e-part also matters in statistically and substantively significant ways, both independently and through interaction effects (Powell and Whitten, 1993, Table 3).

In addition to political institutions and policymaking contexts, the domestic and international economic context has also been investigated. Pacek and Radcliff (1995) considered the impact of the level of welfare-state development and how this might mediate the relationship between the economy and vote. Their study, spanning seventeen countries, demonstrated that when the economy is good, the government receives a strong reward in countries with lower levels of welfare spending. In countries with highly developed welfare programmes, the electoral reward is much weaker—in other words, the p-part is larger than the e-part.

Before the era of globalization, governments had greater control over their own economies through fiscal and monetary policies. With increased trade, a country's economy becomes more intertwined with the economies of their trading partners and more susceptible to global fluctuations. This can reduce the amount of control a government has over the direction of the nation's economy, so weakening the economic vote. In a comparative study reaching beyond Europe, across seventy-five countries, Hellwig and Samuels (2007) examine the extent to which exposure to the global economy conditions the impact of economic growth on incumbent vote shares. Looking at their fully specified model, which includes both political variables (such as previous vote, re-election, and the effective number of parties) and economic variables, they show that greater trade openness reduces the positive impact of GDP on incumbent vote share. While it is challenging to assess the relative weight of the p-part (which performs well) to the e-part, the authors walk the reader through scenarios. In closed economies, 'the effect of a 5 per cent increase in per capita economic growth increases the vote share of the incumbent by more than 4 per cent' (p. 294). At the other extreme, when exposure to trade 'exceeds 77 per cent of GDP, the positive effects of the economy on incumbent vote are no longer statistically significant' (p. 294). They note that around one-third of elections in their study took place under high levels of trade openness. In these elections then, the p-part would dominate the e-part.

In addition to the institutional and economic contexts, non-economic issues and events can enter into citizen's assessment of their leaders. While the economy is often 'top-of-mind' for most voters, other crises, events, and issues can reach high levels of public concern—a point emphasized in many of the single case studies in this volume. Rally-round-the-flag events, scandals, votes of no confidence, new party leadership, by-election results, and other political shocks can affect popularity ratings and thus ought to be included for more precise popularity model specification (Mueller, 1970; Anderson, 1995; Stegmaier and Lewis-Beck, 2011; Williams et al., 2017). Furthermore, non-economic issues such as foreign policy or abortion can impact voting and approval ratings, and, as the salience of non-economic issues increases, they can reduce the influence of the economy (Abramowitz, 1995; Edwards et al., 1995; Singer, 2011).

Partisanship and the strength of citizens' party attachments have long been known to shape elections and approval. The authors of *The American Voter* (Campbell et al., 1960) recognized the importance of this in their theoretical 'funnel of causality' explaining vote choice. Partisanship serves as an anchor that orients voters to the political world. For those who hold strong attachments, their vote decision is less swayed by more proximate factors such as issue positions and candidate evaluations. Thus, we may expect in contexts where more people strongly identify with a party, economic conditions will have less sway in influencing approval ratings (see, e.g. Chapter 13 in this volume).

These highlights from fifty years of VP-function research cover a range of factors that might lead to a stronger or weaker relationship between the economy and approval. What more can we say about this relationship and the size of the p- and e-parts? Paldam (1991, 14) assessed a series of studies in terms of the amount of variation the two parts explained and concluded 'the average orders of magnitudes are about one to three for the e-fraction relative to the p-fraction'. In the studies we have highlighted, under certain conditions, the economic effects are strong and stable, but under other conditions—such as obscured clarity of responsibility, strong welfare states, salient non-economic issues, rally-round-the-flag events, and a high degree of partisan attachments—political factors loom large compared to economic factors in accounting for government support.

The Current Volume

In this section, we move on to assess the contemporary country studies of executive approval from this volume, case by case. A case study can be defined as 'an intensive study of a single unit for the purpose of understanding a larger class of (similar) units' (Gerring 2004, 342). It enables scholars to delve deeply into the workings of a country's political system, policy issues, critical events, and the electorate to better understand the factors that shape public approval of leaders and 'may bring to light significant factors and variables neglected in many comparisons' (Dogan and Pelassy, 1990, 123). These insights contribute to the 'establishment of general propositions and thus to theory-building in political science' (Lijphart 1971, 691) and can later serve as the basis for research comparing a small number of cases through 'structured focused comparisons' (George and Bennett, 2005; Stegmaier and Marcinkiewicz, 2019) or in large-*N* cross-national studies.

A single case study, by itself, cannot be the basis for confirming or disproving a valid generalization. As Gerring (2004, 350) notes, even when 'crucial' cases are selected 'we are unlikely to reject a hypothesis, or to consider it definitively proved, on the basis of the study of a single unit, particularly if the hypothesis has behind it a corpus of scholarly work'. Thus, while the case studies in this book illuminate aspects of the economy–approval relationship that will improve our hypotheses, given the vast literature on vote and popularity functions, no single case study can fully disprove or confirm the general theory that the economy plays a role in shaping public approval of political leaders.

We assess the individual country studies collected in this volume utilizing the case study typology that Lijphart (1971) put forward: theory-confirming, theory-infirming, hypothesis-generating, and deviant case studies. Theory-confirming and theory-infirming case analyses are of single cases within the framework of an established generalization. Each case can strengthen or weaken the generalizations of a theory depending on its own finding, although the impact would be marginal if the generalization is based on many studies. Hypothesis-generating case analyses aim to develop a theoretical generalization in areas where no theory exists yet. Though they may start out with a vague hypothesis, these studies contribute to theory-building by uncovering a potential hypothesis that can be tested subsequently in large *N* analyses. Deviant case analyses are selected to 'uncover relevant additional variables—that were not considered previously, or to refine the (operational) definitions of some or all of the variables' (Lijphart 1971, 692); in this way, they serve to refine and sharpen existing hypotheses.

In our assessment of the case studies—a narrative meta-analysis—we note the challenge of comparing across case studies for purposes of categorization and generalization. Even in a volume where all authors model executive approval, differences in how 'the economy' is measured, which control variables are included, the time period under study, and the frequency of the time series (monthly, quarterly, yearly) affect the results and impose limits on direct and systematic comparisons. With this in mind, we take on the challenge of placing each study into one or more of Lijphart's categories.

Theory-Confirming Cases

The theory-confirming case study is a test of the established proposition, which turns out to be confirmed by the specific case. This means that the findings should align with previous findings on how the economy affects executive popularity. We consider cases to be confirming if they show that the economy directly explains approval ratings, and that if the magnitude of the economic effect varies, it does so in ways that are theoretically predictable.

Four case studies—Japan, Britain, Portugal, and France—demonstrate a consistent or increasing role of the economy on executive approval. Chapter 6 on Japan examines the impact of subjective economic indicators and partisanship on approval of the cabinet before and after a major electoral system reform in 1993. Ohmura and Hino note this reform was 'intended to increase the clarity of responsibility for voters by redirecting their attention to political parties and policies'. The analysis finds that sociotropic economic evaluations have an impact both before and after the electoral shift, but that they are more pronounced in the post-reform era.

The British case study pays special attention to the influence of prospective evaluations—both egocentric and sociotropic—on government approval between 1980 and 2015. Bartle, Dellepiane-Avellaneda, and McGann find strong support for their argument that 'governments are rewarded for making people feel optimistic about their economic futures and punished for making them feel bad'. Of the objective economic measures included in their estimation, only the stock market has the expected positive impact. Their analysis also includes a policy advantage measure that covers a range of economic and non-economic issues, and they find that this also contributes to approval. While these economic effects are strong, political factors such as months in power, terrorist attacks, scandals, and wars also shaped approval.

In Portugal, Aguiar-Conraria, Fernandes, and Magalhães show the popularity of both prime minister and president are affected by GDP growth, but the pattern of reward-punishment differs across the two political leaders. The economy seems to affect Portuguese presidents symmetrically—they are rewarded with a good economy and punished with a bad one—while only a negative economy affects Portuguese prime ministers. However, the e-part loses its relevance (importance) during the second term of cohabitation when a conflictual relationship between prime minister and president occurs. During this 'conflictual cohabitation', according to the authors, presidents make more extensive use of their legislative and oversight powers to check the executive office. Consequently, the line of responsibility for policy outcomes between president and prime minister becomes murky, making it difficult for the public to discern whom to blame for a weak economy.

In the French case, Grossman and Guinaudeau observe a pattern of substantial decline in support over each presidential term in data spanning over sixty years. While they argue that the dominant factor that moves presidential popularity is time in office, or the cost of ruling, they also consider the role of economic conditions by including measures of GDP growth, unemployment rates, inflation, and consumer confidence. Of these, inflation and consumer confidence have the strongest impact in the expected directions. A 1-point increase in inflation leads to a 2.5-point decline in approval, while a 1-point increase in consumer confidence results in an increase of somewhat less than 1 point in approval (i.e. 0.6). When they examine the impacts of these variables over time, they further note that the impact of consumer confidence on approval has increased and is highest in the most recent period. By these measures, then, the economic effects are confirming. That said, the relative explanatory power of 'p' far outweighs that of 'e' in France.

Partially Confirming Cases

Besides the foregoing cases, several of the case studies provide partial confirmation of the economy–approval link. We consider these in two different groupings. The first group of 'partially confirming cases' are studies that show a significant impact of the economy on popularity over the entire time series, but when studied in shorter intervals, the economy matters in some but not all eras. Chapter 8, on government approval in Spain, is a nice example of this. Romero-Vidal, Orriols, and Riera find that higher unemployment rates reduce government approval ratings over the full period of the study (1986–2019). But when the analysis is stratified into three different time periods, they find that while unemployment impacted approval in the first and last period, it was not significant in the 2001–2008 period. They argue that because unemployment was relatively low during this middle period, other issues were more salient to voters, thereby erasing its impact on government approval during that time. In the Spanish context, one salient non-economic issue that has had a significant impact on approval rating is concern about terrorism. As terrorism concern increased, approval ratings increased in a manner consistent with a rally-round-the-flag effect.

Additionally, while the German case study in Chapter 10 could be fitted to the 'deviant' category (discussed below), the popularity function based on 'real-time' economic growth data over the full period under study shows a statistically significant and positive economic effect. However, when modelled in decade intervals, the relationship, while holding for the earlier part of the time series, declines in recent years due to lack of clarity of responsibility (i.e. the grand coalition). In the most recent decade (2010–2019) the coefficient indicates a negative relationship, which Kayser and Leininger note is 'theoretically puzzling and deserves more extensive analysis'.

Koliastasis and Yfantopoulos examine the impact of the economy and economic polarization on approval in Greece. Economic polarization refers to the ideological distinctions among the parties on economic issues including the controversial bailouts and austerity measures implemented between 2010 and 2018. In the initial models, unemployment and subjective economic assessments have the expected impact on approval in the full sample and in the pre-bailout period. But when economic polarization is included, it trumps the economy and has a stronger impact in the post-bailout era. However, we should be cautious with these results because the strong impact of economic polarization was likely fuelled by the economic consequences of the policies which deepened the recession. The authors note that 'had the economy been in good shape, the negative impact of economic polarization on the premiers' popularity would probably not have been evident'.

In Bélanger and Jacques' analysis of the Canadian case, it appears that the economy registers significant effects on the prime ministers' approval. However, from a divided sample, before and after the 1993 election (which marks a shift of government fiscal policy), the effects of the economy appear to decline. Thus, the weight of the e-part has decreased, relative to the p-part that has held steady over time.

Italy is also a partially confirming case study, in that the linear impact of economic sentiment is statistically significant in the baseline estimation between 1995 and 2018. Nevertheless, Bellucci and Memoli's models show the economy becomes statistically insignificant as the model specification adds political variables (p-part) such as corruption, inequality, and political communications. This result could shade the classification to 'infirming'. However, the authors point out that perhaps political populism together with political communication may have magnified the salience of inequality among the Italian public, and thus led these political variables to dominate economic measures in explaining popularity.

Next, we introduce another type of 'partially confirming' study—one where no economic effects appear in the entire time-series analysis, but when examining different eras, economic effects emerge, and can be both theoretically and empirically explained. The appearance of these economic effects (after the imposition of era controls) statistically speaking are an example of 'suppressor effects' which, though rare, do occur. The Danish case study in Chapter 12 falls into this category. Seeberg examines the impact of the economy on approval from 1974 to 2016 and over this full time series, the economy appears to have no significant effect. However, this result appears to be masking an underlying trend associated with the decline in class-based voting and greater party system ideological convergence. The study finds that, in fact, Danish voters became more critical in evaluating parties' economic performance because of a decline in traditional class-based voting. For instance, the working class no longer automatically votes for the leftist party (i.e. Social Democrats), but is likely to evaluate parties' competence on various policy areas including the economy, which eventually makes the link between the economy and executive approval stronger. Furthermore, the analysis supports the hypothesis that as the party positions have become more similar, ideological-based voting declines and is replaced by economic evaluations.

All in all, the country case studies from ten countries confirm or partially confirm the received wisdom that the economy drives variation in executive approval at least in some ways. Acknowledging that the proposition of the popularity function is solidly based on a great number of large-*N* studies, confirming the theory with additional case studies does not strengthen it a great deal (Lijphart, 1971). However, having confirming country cases from nearly all these cases studies implies that the influence of the economy on popularity has remained robust.

Theory-Infirming Cases

Not all country cases confirm the conventional wisdom, as the case study of the United States demonstrates. While the economy mattered for presidential approval in the past, the findings suggest that over the past two decades, the economy has no longer been a predictor of variation in executive popularity. Donovan et al. expected that economic evaluations would be disconnected from political evaluations due to rising polarization along partisan lines. Although the subjective economy was a significant predictor of president approval ratings before 2001, the effect completely disappears with the hyper-polarization of current US politics. Notably, commenting on the Obama and Trump presidencies, the authors state that 'it is hard to see what factors beyond partisanship might matter'.

Hypothesis-Generating Cases

As noted earlier, the motivation of hypothesis-generating case studies is to formulate new testable hypotheses. Some of the case studies reach beyond the traditional explanations and delve into newer hypotheses about the role of government responsiveness and economic inequality in shaping the economy–approval relationship.

One of the implicit implications of this volume is to assess if citizens hold their representatives accountable for economic performance in particular and government performance in general. Thus, it is important to understand to what extent governments are responsive to public opinion and mass preferences, because their level of responsiveness will affect their approval ratings down the road. The Spanish chapter, in addition to its focus on unemployment and approval, considers government responsiveness by studying how changes in the distance between general mass opinion (i.e. policy mood) and the government's policy stance shape incumbent approval ratings. The empirical findings suggest that 'popularity grows when mood moves in the direction of the government's ideology. Hence, when mood moves to the left, approval increases if the incumbent is the Socialist Party, but the opposite takes place with People's Party governments.'

While the Spanish case shows the impact of proximity between public opinion and government ideology on approval, the Canadian case study further investigates how governments are rewarded or punished by the public when their performance is in line with, or deviates from, mass preferences, particularly on the federal government deficits. According to the country chapter authors, a big shift in the fiscal policy mood among Canadian citizens occurred around the early 1990s. Before 1993, citizens tended to be tolerant of the budget deficit, and indeed they rewarded the government for spending more. However, citizens' views of the deficit dramatically changed after the early 1990s recession, which hit the Canadian economy hard. For instance, the proportion of Canadians saying that it is very important to reduce the deficit rose from 50 per cent in the 1980s to 75 per cent the early 1990s. Such a dramatic change in mass preference offers an ideal setting to test the link between public opinion and executive popularity. From the Canadian case study, we learned that ordinary citizens tend to reward their executives when governments are more responsive to the collective preference of the public.

While the previous two studies focus on aspects of government responsiveness, the Italian case study explores another understudied influence on approval ratings—economic inequality. Indeed, inequality is everywhere and is becoming an increasingly pressing social issue. According to a Pew Research Center survey (2014), the gap between the rich and the poor is considered as a major challenge by more than 60 per cent of respondents worldwide. In line with this concern, the authors of the Italian case examine whether governments are held accountable for the rising gap in wealth distribution. Their findings support this expectation: a 1-standard-deviation increase in inequality during the 2012–2018 period resulted in a 5.6-point drop in popularity. This effect is more substantial than in the earlier period (1995–2011) when it resulted in a drop of 1.7 points.

In a similar vein, inequality serves as a possible answer to one of the puzzling findings in the German case (Ch.10) that economic growth became 'associated with a *decline* in chancellor approval in the decade from 2010' (emphasis in original). The authors speculate that 'if more of the benefits of growth are captured by the wealthy than in the past, such growth corresponds to rising inequality that most voters might punish'. Put simply, growth in the economy does not help incumbents unless the 'trickle-down effect' is observed across all segments of the population.

Deviant Cases

The last type of case study is the deviant case. According to Lijphart (1971, 692), deviant cases allow us to 'uncover relevant additional variables that were not considered previously, or to refine the (operational) definitions of some or all of the variables'. These studies have the potential to lead to more precise or nuanced theory and/or measurements, that can ultimately strengthen the general theory. The German case study provides an excellent example of this. The initial analysis *deviates* from the received wisdom in that the economy does not affect chancellor approval ratings. However, Kayser and Leininger suggest this may be due to the type of economic data used. They identify two different types of economic data: the real-time information (i.e. the data initially released to the public) and the updated/revised information. When real-time economic data are released, the media immediately report on it to inform the public about the current state of the economy. The data are then later revised by national statistical offices. These revisions are rarely mentioned by the media, and even when they are, the public doesn't pay much attention since that quarter has passed. The real-time data, together with media coverage, is delivered to ordinary citizens, while the revised data are widely used in academia, including in VP-functions—since these are the standard 'most accurate' data sets of the economy. If substantial revisions to the economic data occur, then we as social scientists using the 'most accurate' economic data series—the revised data—are not accurately capturing the information that citizens had at hand at the time they evaluated their leader. This creates a discrepancy, which could be substantial enough to taint the analysis to lead us to believe that the economy doesn't matter for chancellor approval in Germany.

The authors of the German case study test whether their deviant results are a result of using the revised economic data set rather than the real-time data which voters have at hand when evaluating the chancellor. Their results show that chancellor approval corresponds to real-time growth estimates but not to revised growth when the growth is measured over short periods (i.e. quarterly to quarterly). However, when growth is measured over a full year (i.e. year to year), approval responds to both estimates of growth, suggesting 'that media reporting on the economy may only have short-term effects on individuals' assessments of the economy and subsequent approval of the chancellor's party'. Since the German case has demonstrated that the type of economic data series used in the popularity function makes a difference, the next step, according to Lijphart (1971) would be to test the validity of this refinement in other contexts (Kayser and Leininger, 2015).

The Future Agenda

The country cases studies have largely demonstrated that the basic tenets of popularity functions remain intact. Politics and the economy matter for executive approval—though in some cases, we see that the power of the relationships changes over time or depends on the type of measures included in the model. The hypothesis-generating and deviant case studies have pointed to understudied factors such as the type of economic data used, government responsiveness and income inequality. But, as Lijphart (1971, 691) notes, 'A single case can constitute neither the basis for a valid generalization nor the ground for disproving an established generalization.' So, the next step towards generalizable propositions is to test these findings in other countries and cross-national research.

Considering the multitude of challenges modern democracies face, what factors beyond those studied in this volume are we overlooking in our VP-function studies? Are there issues that might become more salient down the road that deserve a spot on our research agenda? Possibilities include the pandemic, climate change, migration, and threats to democracy.

COVID-19 Pandemic

Building on much ongoing research, one area for future analysis is the impact of the COVID-19 pandemic on incumbent support and vote shares. There are a variety of ways in which the pandemic could impact public support for leaders. First, especially at the onset of the pandemic, scholars have examined whether the public rallied-around-the-flag as leaders attempted to combat the new threat. For example, studies in Denmark (Baekgaard et al., 2020) and Austria (Kritzinger et al., 2021) demonstrated strong rally effects at the onset of the pandemic and the initial government responses. However, in France, no such effect was found, due to stark partisan divisions (Kritzinger et al., 2021).

A second way the pandemic may impact approval ratings is through evaluations of how the government is managing the crisis. Lockdowns, restrictions on gatherings and restaurant capacity, and other measures designed to protect the public's health, also limited people's personal and economic freedoms. Bol et al. (2021), studied the impact that the initial lockdowns in March 2020 had on political support in Western Europe and found that the lockdowns increased support for the executive's party by 4 points, and they note that there is 'little evidence that this effect is simply due to a rally-around-the-flag effect brought about by the health crisis itself (p. 502).

Another angle is whether the pandemic, as a non-economic issue, overpowered economic evaluations in shaping government approval. Singer (2021) examined this question using US survey data from July 2020 and finds that while differences in personal economic conditions during the first months of the pandemic did not result in meaningful differences in evaluations of President Trump, the COVID-19 experience did. Those who reported having COVID-19, knew someone who caught COVID-19, or were afraid of getting sick expressed lower approval of Trump on average than other respondents. But there is also evidence showing that an economic effect on government support seems still to persist. Clarke et al. (2021) look at how the pandemic impacted the outcome of the November 2020 presidential election. In October 2020, 39 per cent of Americans said that COVID-19 was the most important issue facing the country, while 17 per cent said the economy (Clarke et al., 2021, 2198). Their analysis of vote choice shows that concern about the pandemic negatively impacted Trump support, but that the economic effects persist. Notably, the change in probability of voting for Trump according to the issue importance of COVID-19 and the economy is nearly equivalent (see Table 5, p. 2202).

The pandemic could also have lingering effects on two contextual measures we have considered in our study: trade and inequality. The pandemic shined the light on detrimental consequences of relying exclusively on other countries for key supplies and goods. Will this lead to a push in some countries for more national self-reliance, turning inward, rather than deepening international economic integration? And when it comes to inequality, the pandemic had a disproportionate impact on low-wage earners who were more likely to lose their jobs, than those in professional positions who could shift to working virtually from home. This may exacerbate economic inequality and increase its salience as a societal issue.

Climate Change

Another increasingly important research question is whether voters blame their leaders for environmental problems and policies. Since climate change undermines the future economy (Burke et al., 2015) and affects citizen's well-being (Doherty and Clayton, 2011), we might expect that some voters will respond. And indeed, recent scholarship points to direct and indirect effects. For example, Obradovich's (2017) analysis of data from over 4,800 constituency-level electoral contests held in nineteen countries between 1925 and 2011 finds that increases in annual temperatures above 21°C (70°F) significantly reduce incumbent electoral performance. Using individual-level survey data from twenty-four countries, Cin (2012) finds similar, albeit distinct, results in that people who believe the quality of environment is poor tend to trust their government less.

Although these findings imply that all citizens agree on the green policy goals, for instance, combating global warming (i.e. valence issue), it is also likely that they disagree on a particular environment policy if such policy incurs concentrated losses (i.e. positional issue). This is because the benefits of the climate policies are consumed by the entire population, but only certain segments of the population incur costs. For instance, Stokes (2016) finds that local environmental policies can negatively impact incumbents if those policies harm their communities. Arndt et al. (forthcoming) also show that citizens' attitudes towards climate policy are not homogeneous across individuals and regions. Instead, they find that the poor and residents of rural regions are reluctant to support climate-change policies compared to well-off urban counterparts, suggesting a potential centre–periphery cleavage in public opinion and party competition.

As countries increasingly feel the impact of climate change and move towards cleaner energy policies, will these climate conditions and policy decisions begin to carry greater weight in the executive approval calculus? How should climate change be considered? Is it a valence issue or a position issue? If citizens become polarized about climate change and policy options (e.g. the level of taxation on fuel) how does this cleavage channel into executive popularity functions?

Migration and Refugees

Migration and refugee issues have challenged modern democracies. The arrival of new people, especially those who practice different religions and customs, place new pressures on governments. As the composition of society begins to change—or is perceived by the public to change—anti-immigration movements and parties build support. Does this emerging issue divide the electorate and political parties, and consequently alter election outcomes?

Stubager et al. (2021) show that immigration issues have increased political contestation and polarized the Danish electorate. In Denmark, the public splits itself into two groups—those with favourable and unfavourable views on immigration—and the distinction is more apparent across different levels of education: people with lower levels of education are more likely to approve of anti-immigrant stances compared to their more educated counterparts. As Danish voters have become more polarized, so have the political parties. For instance, since 1990 the newer far-right party, the Danish People's Party, has garnered support from blue-collar workers. Stubager et al. (2021) suggest that this counter-intuitive trend may have resulted from blue-collar workers perceiving that the arrival of unskilled workers from Eastern Europe was an imminent threat to their job security, and hence, they switched their party support from the Social Democrats (centre-left) to the Danish People's Party, as the latter offers policies alleviating these fears.

Similar patterns of public polarization and success of far-right parties are observed in Central European countries (Bustikova and Guasti, 2017). The introduction of EU quotas for the allocation of refugees in 2016 resulted in significant opposition in Hungary, Slovakia, Poland, and the Czech Republic. Populist and far-right parties appealed to voters whose concerns were rooted in threats to sovereignty, by strengthening their anti-establishment rhetoric and developing negative narratives about the outcomes of accepting asylum-seekers. And, in turn, this resulted in increased vote shares for the far-right parties in the 2015 Polish, the 2016 Slovakian, and 2017 Czech elections (Bustikova and Guasti, 2017). And, it has continued to be a cornerstone of Hungarian Prime Minister Victor Orbán's successful re-election campaigns.

Although the issue of migration and asylum-seekers raises challenges to the public and political parties, it is also important to know what consequences would emerge once the new arrivals assimilate to their new country. Will they emerge as a different voting bloc by reinforcing their ethnic/religious identity, or simply expand the existing composition of the society by assimilating to new political environments? Lewis-Beck and Stegmaier (2016) show that the Hispanic immigrants in the United States exhibit voting behaviour that is similar to other American voters in that they evaluate the president based on egocentric and sociotropic economic assessments. And, although patterns of participation differ across immigrant generations, voters whose family has been in the United States the longest (third-generation immigrants) are likely to mimic what other Americans do when it comes to political engagement (Potochnick and Stegmaier, 2020).

All in all, as immigration and refugees become salient issues, will this non-economic issue reduce the impact of the economy on approval? If more people strongly identify with a party which better appeals to their policy preference on migration and refugee issues, will economic conditions have less sway in influencing incumbent popularity?

Threats to Democracy

Fourth, fundamental tenets of democracy have come under threat in the advanced democracies in ways that erode the conditions necessary for the public to hold their leaders accountable. Threats to democracy have come from extremist and populist leaders who, among other things, restrict the independence of courts, curtail independent media, weaken civil society and political opposition, and spread disinformation, in order to undermine free and fair democratic processes. Over the past decade, the proposals and actions of Prime Minister Victor Orban in Hungary, the far-right Law and Justice party in Poland, and President Donald Trump in the United States (to name just a few) have prompted much debate about the health of both newer and established democracies (Bustikova and Gausti, 2017; Marcinkiewicz and Stegmaier 2017; 2018; Levitsky and Ziblatt, 2018). Whether these illiberal examples are temporary 'swerves' or a lasting 'turn' on the liberal–illiberal continuum remains to be seen. However, even temporary shifts can impact the functioning of elections, and throw off long-established patterns of accountability.

In the United States, the insurrection on 6 January 2021 was a direct result of President Trump undermining the legitimacy of the election. His continued and unsubstantiated attacks on the US election process have resulted in a dramatically divided public. Polls show that while approximately 91 per cent of Democrats believe Joe Biden's victory in 2020 was legitimate, a mere 21 per cent of Republicans believe this (Cuthbert and Theodoridis, 2022). This polling result portends serious problems for the functioning of democracy and the role that elections play in holding leaders accountable.

The threat to democracy, as a non-economic issue, may come to rival the role of the economy in shaping executive approval ratings. Recent polls suggest that most Americans are now concerned about the state of democracy (Schaeffer, 2022) and that 'threats to democracy' has become a leading salient issue to the electorate, even surpassing economic concerns (Schonfeld, 2022). This non-economic issue cuts to the heart of what it means to be one of the world's oldest democracies. Whether this will independently impact US presidential approval may depend on how clearly this issue divides along party lines.

Another dimension of the threat to democracy is the vast divide in media coverage of politics and the tendency for people to associate only with like-minded people. These ideological echo-chambers insulate voters from other perspectives and affect how they understand politics (Leiter et al., 2020). If portions of society consume media that report only political propaganda and false information, how will it be possible for the traditional VP-function—built around the economic reward/punishment of the incumbent—to hold? While we hope that this is not the way of the future, it is another factor that might appear on our field's future research agenda.

References

Abramowitz, A. I. (1995). It's abortion, stupid: Policy voting in the 1992 presidential election. *The Journal of Politics*, *57*(1), 176–86.

Anderson, C. J. (1995). *Blaming the Government: Citizens and the Economy in Five European Democracies.* Armonk, NY: M. E. Sharpe.

Anderson, C. J. (2000). Economic voting and political context: A comparative perspective. *Electoral Studies*, *19*(2–3), 151–70.

Arndt, C., Halikiopoulou, D., and Vrakopoulos, C. (forthcoming). The centre–periphery divide and attitudes towards climate change measures among Western Europeans. *Environmental Politics.*

Baekgaard, M., Christensen, J., Madsen, J. K., and Mikkelsen, K. S. (2020). Rallying around the flag in times of COVID-19: Societal lockdown and trust in democratic institutions. *Journal of Behavioral Public Administration*, *3*(2), 1–12.

Bengtsson, A. (2004). Economic voting: The effect of political context, volatility and turnout on voters' assignment of responsibility. European *Journal of Political Research, 43*, 749–67.

Bol, D., Giani, M., Blais, A., and Loewen, P. J. (2021). The effect of COVID-19 lockdowns on political support: Some good news for democracy? *European Journal of Political Research*, *60*(2), 497–505.

Burke, M., Hsiang, S., and Miguel, E. (2015). Global non-linear effect of temperature on economic production. *Nature*, *527*, 75–77.

Bustikova, L., and Guasti, P. (2017). The illiberal turn or swerve in Central Europe? *Politics and Governance*, *5*(4), 166–76.

Campbell, A., Converse, P. E., Miller, W. E., and Stokes, D. E. (1960). *The American Voter.* New York: Wiley.

Cin, C. K. (2012). Blaming the government for environmental problems: A multilevel and cross-national analysis of the relationship between trust in government and local and global environmental concerns. *Environment and Behavior*, *45*(8), 971–92.

Clarke, H., Stewart, M. C., and Ho, K. (2021). Did COVID-19 kill Trump politically? The pandemic and voting in the 2020 presidential election. *Social Science Quarterly*, *102*(5), 2195–209.

Cuthbert, L., and Theodoridis, A. (2022). Do Republicans really believe Trump won the 2020 election? Our research suggests that they do. Washington Post Monkey Cage, 7 January. https://www.washingtonpost.com/politics/2022/01/07/republicans-big-lie-trump/.

Dassonneville, R., Blais, A., and Dejaeghere, Y. (2015). Staying with the party, switching or exiting? A comparative analysis of determinants of party switching and abstaining. *Journal of Election, Public Opinion and Parties*, *25*(3), 387–405.

Debus, M., Stegmaier, M., and Tosun, J. (2014). Economic voting under coalition governments: Evidence from Germany. *Political Science Research and Methods, 2*(1), 49–67.

Dogan, M., and Pelassy, D. (1990). *How to Compare Nations: Strategies in Comparative Politics*, second edition. Chatham, NJ: Chatham House Publishers.

Doherty, T. J., and Clayton, S. (2011). The psychological impacts of global climate change. *Annual Psychology, 66*(4), 265–76.

Edwards III, G. C., Mitchell, W., and Welch, R. (1995). Explaining presidential approval: The significance of issue salience. *American Journal of Political Science, 39*(1), 108–34.

George, A. L., and Bennett, A. (2005). *Case Study and Theory Development in the Social Sciences*. Cambridge, MA: MIT Press.

Gerring, J. (2004). What is a case study and what is it good for? *American Political Science Review, 98*(2), 341–54.

Goodhart, C. A. E., and Bhansali, R. J. (1970). Political economy. *Political Studies, 18*(1), 43–106.

Hellwig, T., and Samuels, D. (2007). Voting in open economies: The electoral consequences of globalization. *Comparative Political Studies, 40*(3), 283–306.

Kayser, M. A., and Leininger, A. (2015). Vintage errors: Do real-time economic data improve election forecasts? *Research & Politics, 2*(3), 2053168015589624.

Kramer, G. H. (1971). Short-term fluctuations in US voting behavior, 1896–1964. *The American Political Science Review, 65*(1), 131–43.

Kritzinger, S., Foucault, M., Lachat, R., Partheymüller, J., Plescia, C., and Brouard, S. (2021). 'Rally round the flag': the COVID-19 crisis and trust in the national government. *West European Politics, 44*(5–6), 1205–31.

Leiter, D., Reilly, J. L., and Stegmaier, M. (2020). Echoing certainty in uncertain times: Network partisan agreement and the quality of citizen forecasts in the 2015 Canadian election. *Electoral Studies, 63*, 102115.

Levitsky, S., and Ziblatt, D. (2018). *How Democracies Die*. New York, NY: Crown Publishing Group.

Lewis-Beck, M. S. (1986). Comparative economic voting: Britain, France, Germany, Italy. *American Journal Political Studies, 30*(2), 315–46.

Lewis-Beck, M. S., and Paldam, M. (2000). Economic voting: An introduction. *Electoral Studies, 19*(2–3), 113–21.

Lewis-Beck, M. S., and Stegmaier, M. (2013). The VP-function revisited: A survey of the literature on vote and popularity functions after over 40 years. *Public Choice, 157*, 367–85.

Lewis-Beck, M. S., and Stegmaier, M. (2016). The Hispanic immigrant voter and the classic American voter: Presidential support in the 2012 election. *RSF: The Russell Sage Foundation Journal of the Social Sciences, 2*(3), 165–81.

Lijphart, A. (1971). Comparative politics and the comparative method. *American Political Science Review, 65*(3), 682–93.

Marcinkiewicz, K., and Stegmaier, M. (2017). Poland appears to be dismantling its own hard-won democracy. Washington Post Monkey Cage, 21 July. https://www.washingtonpost.com/news/monkey-cage/wp/2017/07/21/poland-appears-to-be-dismantling-its-own-hard-won-democracy/.

Marcinkiewicz, K., and Stegmaier, M. (2018). Democratic elections in Poland face a new threat. Washington Post Monkey Cage, 11 January. https://www.washingtonpost.com/news/monkey-cage/wp/2018/01/11/free-elections-in-poland-face-new-threats-from-a-new-electoral-reform-bill/.

Mueller, J. (1970). Presidential popularity from Truman to Johnson. *American Political Science Review*, *64*(1), 18–34.

Nannestad, P., and Paldam, M. (1994). The VP function: A survey of the literature on vote and popularity functions after 25 years. *Public Choice*, *79*, 213–45.

Norpoth, H., Lewis-Beck, M. S., and Lafay, J.-D. (eds). (1991). *Economics and Politics: The Calculus of Support*. Ann Arbor, MI: University of Michigan Press.

Obradovich, N. (2017). Climate change may speed democratic turnover. *Climatic Change*, *140*, 135–47.

Pacek, A. C., and Radcliff, B. (1995). Economic voting and the welfare state: A cross-national analysis. *The Journal of Politics*, *57*(1), 44–61.

Paldam, M. (1991). How robust is the vote function? A study of seventeen nations over four decades. In *Economics and Politics: The Calculus of Support*, H. Norpoth and M. Lewis-Beck, eds. Ann Arbor, MI: University of Michigan Press. 9–31.

Potochnick, S., and Stegmaier, M. (2020). Latino political participation by citizenship status and immigrant generation. *Social Science Quarterly*, *101*(2), 527–44.

Powell, G. B., Jr., and Whitten, G. D. (1993). A cross-national analysis of economic voting: Taking account of the political context. *American Journal of Political Science*, *37*(2), 391–414.

Rowe, K. (2015). Making voice count: Economic voting and the number of parties. *Party Politics*, *21*(5), 803–21.

Schaeffer, K. (2022). On July Fourth, how Americans see their country and their democracy. Pew Research Center, 30 June. https://www.pewresearch.org/fact-tank/2022/06/30/how-americans-see-their-country-and-their-democracy/.

Schonfeld, Z. (2022). Threats to democracy top list of issues facing US: poll. *The Hill*, 22 August. https://thehill.com/homenews/campaign/3610753-threats-to-democracy-top-list-of-issues-facing-us-poll/.

Singer, M. (2011). Who says 'it's the economy'? Cross-national and cross-individual variation in the salience of economic performance. *Comparative Political Studies*, *44*(March), 284–312.

Singer, M. (2021). It's NOT the economy when people are dying: Accountability for household economic and health outcomes during the pandemic. *Journal of Elections, Public Opinion and Parties*, *31*(1), 155–66.

Stegmaier, M., and Lewis-Beck, M. S. (2011). Shocks and oscillations: The political economy of Hungary. *Electoral Studies, 30*(3), 462–7.

Stegmaier, M., & Marcinkiewicz, K. (2019). Networks, expertise, and research design: A structured focused comparison of electoral rules and election results. In *SAGE Research Methods Cases Part 2.* SAGE Publications, Ltd. https://dx.doi.org/10.4135/9781526466655

Stegmaier, M., Lewis-Beck, M. S., and Brown, L. (2021). The economic voter decides. In *Oxford Encyclopedia of Political Decision Making*, D. Redlawsk, ed. Oxford: Oxford University Press. 477–90.

Stegmaier, M., Lewis-Beck, M. S., and Park, B. (2017). The VP-function: A review. In *SAGE Handbook of Electoral Behaviour, 2v*, K. Arzheimer, J. Evans, and M. S. Lewis-Beck, eds. Thousand Oaks, CA: Sage. 584–605.

Stiers, D., Dassonneville, R., and Lewis-Beck, M. S. (2020). The abiding voter: The lengthy horizon of retrospective evaluations. *European Journal of Political Research, 59*(3), 646–68.

Stokes, L. (2016). Electoral backlash against climate policy: A natural experiment on retrospective voting and local resistance to public policy. *American Journal of Political Science, 60*(4), 958–74.

Stubager, R., Hansen, K. M., Lewis-Beck, M. S., and Nadeau, R. (2021). *The Danish Voter: Democratic Ideals and Challenges.* Ann Arbor, MI: University of Michigan Press.

Williams, L. K., Stegmaier, M., and Debus, M. (2017). Relaxing the constant economic vote restriction: Economic evaluations and party support in Germany. *Party Politics, 23*(3), 286–96.

15

Executive Approval from the 1990s to the 2010s

A Pooled Analysis of Twenty Countries

Timothy Hellwig and Matthew Singer

This volume is concerned with how the economy affects government popularity and how this economics–politics connection has evolved from the late twentieth to the early twenty-first century.[1] What do the country studies tell us about the dynamics of executive approval over these thirty-plus years? Our working hypothesis has been that the drivers of approval—economic or otherwise—are not the same today as in times past. Grappling with this question, chapter authors have examined how changes in national environments—structural, political, and economic—bear on the public's evaluations. In some countries, these changes have elevated a set of new non-valence factors as salient (Canada, Greece, and Spain are examples) or have raised the costs of ruling in ways that recast the basic dynamics of approval (France and Portugal). In other nations, such as Germany, the United Kingdom, and the United States, the economy's impact on political evaluations has fallen from decades past. In still other settings, the economy's influence has held steady (e.g. Italy) or even increased (e.g. Denmark; Japan).

On the one hand, findings presented in this volume reinforce those from previous efforts. Chapter authors find that economic indicators, particularly subjective assessments of economic performance, can help us make sense of popular evaluations of governments, prime ministers, and presidents. As Stegmaier, Park, and Lewis-Beck note in the previous chapter, nearly all the cases examined are theory-confirming in some way. However, unlike relationships in the physical sciences, the impact of an exogenous force

[1] Thanks to Jonathan Hartlyn for detailed feedback on this chapter. For research assistance, we are grateful to Katherine Smith and Calista Stafford and to funding from the Alan R. Bennett Professorship at the University of Connecticut and to the Office of the Vice Provost of International Affairs at Indiana University.

Timothy Hellwig and Matthew Singer, *Executive Approval from the 1990s to the 2010s*. In: *Economics and Politics Revisited*. Edited by: Timothy Hellwig and Matthew Singer, Oxford University Press. © Timothy Hellwig and Matthew Singer (2023). DOI: 10.1093/oso/9780192871664.003.0015

(ups and downs in the economy) on our response series (political popularity) is not fixed but varies across time and over space. Preceding chapters identified multiple drivers governing the economy's impact. Contributors show that the economy's influence has been suppressed due to policy changes (variously, Canada, Spain, and Greece), issue salience (Denmark), media effects (Germany), the polarization of mass partisanship (United States), and divided government, or cohabitation (France, Portugal), among other factors. Importantly, chapters show how factors beside the economy—including but not limited to the electoral cycle—also directly bear on leader popularity. Individually, the details in these country chapters highlight how factors specific to each of these political systems are reflected in public opinion. Collectively, this set of eleven case studies offers the most comprehensive treatment of approval dynamics to date in the advanced democracies. Overall, these analyses show that while the economy is often important, it is not universally so. In fact, the number of cases that Stegmaier et al. classify as only partially confirming (six) is greater than the number that they deem fully confirming (four). Further, even in the confirming cases the magnitude of the economy's effect varies over time.

In this chapter we take a step back to re-examine the broad contours of the political economy of mass politics in advanced capitalist democracies. Our concerns are two-fold. First, to what extent are the factors identified as drivers of approval by the preceding country case studies replicated in a pooled popularity function? Second, to what extent do cross-country differences identified in the introduction to this volume—political context, issue salience, and political dispositions—interfere, facilitate, or otherwise condition the economics–politics connection? This second question brings us back to the field-defining matter of the instability dilemma (Paldam, 1991) introduced in the original *Economics and Politics* volume (Norpoth, Lewis-Beck, and Lafay, 1991). Indeed, the lion's share of research on political accountability for economic conditions over the ensuing thirty-plus years has sought to solve this instability puzzle. This comparative literature has brought into greater relief the process by which the public evaluates responsibility and weighs government performance. As Stegmaier, Park, and Lewis-Beck (Chapter 14) remind us, 'accounting for the political and economic contexts that cause this instability contributes to more solid theory and findings'.

As reviewed in the introduction to this volume, proposed solutions to the instability problem are of three types. The first asks how the public makes sense of who is responsible for economic outputs. When clarity of responsibility is high, then the transition between a buoyant economy and a popular leader is strong and transparent. But when responsibility assignments are blurred, public assessments of politicians are de-linked from economic conditions. Research in this tradition initially looked to formal institutions as contexts shaping responsibility attributions but has since expanded to consider a range of factors, including the nature of party competition, the organization of labour markets, and the economy's integration into world markets. A second approach informing the strength of the economy–popularity connection emphasizes what we might call the issue agenda. This approach identifies broader aspects of political discourse that may move approval. If non-economic issues only tenuously linked to economic matters become more salient to the electorate or receive greater attention in elite discourse, then the public's attention to the economy should decline. The economy may regain its privileged position, however, when hard times draw the public's attention back to jobs, prices, and other gauges of the economic performance. A third path is charted by partisanship. The retrospective accountability model assumes that the public's opinion of the incumbent can be changed by their performance in office. But not all countries have the same share of persuadable citizens or swing voters. As partisanship and polarization wax and wane, so too will the opportunities for performance indicators like the economy to affect approval.

Chapter 1 proposed a set of arguments for how these kinds of dynamics might be systematically reshaping the economics–politics relationship over time. Underlying many of these changes are changes in the structure of national economies themselves. Advanced capitalism is characterized by the decline of manufacturing, the expansion of the service sector and of the knowledge economy within it, and the rise in atypical and temporary work. These trends imply there may no longer be a single 'economy' to which the public is attuned (Anson, 2023; Hellwig and Marinova, 2023). Further, globalization relocates production outside national borders, a shift which makes economic management less central to how leaders are evaluated. Structural shifts also may contribute to shifts in party competition, with new single-issue parties coming onto the scene and older parties refashioning their identities on social or environmental concerns rather than economic ones (e.g. Kriesi et al., 2012). Finally, growing fragmentation and polarization may reduce the size of the electorate whose views of the executive can be swung by their performance in office. We might expect that in countries where these trends are most pronounced that the economy's *political* impact has diminished. Yet to the extent these trends are not universal, we should find countries where the economy–popularity connection, aka popularity function, remains unchanged.

In this, the volume's ultimate chapter, we move from in-depth studies of macro-opinion in separate countries to a cross-national analysis. To date, statistical models for weighing potential solutions to the instability dilemma have employed data either from public opinion surveys or from election returns.[2] Both designs come with shortcomings. While useful for leveraging time-invariant variables, pooled analyses of public opinion surveys are ill-equipped for understanding whether and how factors that vary over time—such as the party system or the issue agenda—affect the vote. On the other hand, analyses of election returns make over-time analyses possible but are of limited use if we want to understand accountability as a continual, dynamic process between elections. Thanks to the Executive Approval Project (EAP), the analyses reported in this chapter eschew both these limitations.

We proceed as follows. We first focus on the evolution of approval across twenty countries from the 1990s through 2019. Multivariate analyses show that the economy–popularity relationship varies across time and space. Regarding the former, we report evidence that the magnitude of the economy's effect has diminished since the turn of the twenty-first century. But the size of this effect is also systematically stronger in some countries than others. Seeking to understand the sources of this variation, we return to the three perspectives introduced in Chapter 1: responsibility attributions, issue salience, and political dispositions. Chapter findings point to the importance of political issues—both in terms of which issues dominate elite messaging and (issue salience) and in terms of the diversity of positions taken (political polarization). Party elites, we show, can suppress the political consequences of economic performance by reducing its salience in the election campaigns. In contrast, political contexts associated with responsibility attributions register little effect. We conclude by drawing out the implications of chapter findings for understanding the economic and non-economic bases of government approval going forward.

[2] Cross-national research has been greatly facilitated by such collaborations as the Comparative Study for Electoral Systems, the European Social Survey, World Values Survey, Eurobarometer, and AmericasBarometer, to name a few.

Perils and Promises of Pooling Popularity Functions

The country chapters advance several mechanisms that explain the up-and-down cycles of government, prime ministerial, or presidential approval. Leveraging over-time changes in political and economic environments, analyses draw on rich and detailed data series to improve on previous studies in their countries. Single-country research designs, however, may make it difficult to isolate the effect of slowly changing variables or to disentangle the effect of two variables that are changing simultaneously in a country. Here we pool country series for executive approval to leverage both temporal *and* spatial variation. In doing so, our objective is to draw out the general from the particular; to identify commonalities across countries. Doing so serves to reconnect this volume with earlier comparative research on how context conditions economic voting and electoral accountability more generally (e.g. Powell and Whitten, 1993; van der Brug et al., 2007; Duch and Stevenson, 2008; Hellwig and Samuels, 2008; Hobolt et al., 2013; Singer and Carlin, 2013).

Understanding whether broader environments impinge on political-economic relationships requires comparison. Meta-analyses compare the direction, magnitude, and precision of X on Y across a range of studies. However, isolating the *bases* of comparison requires particular research designs, either well-designed comparative case studies or pooled analyses whereby the effect of X on Y varies according to some Z which we can include in our data—substituting variables for country names (Przeworski and Teune, 1970). The latter design is more common in research on how public opinion is shaped by contexts (Anderson and Singer, 2008), and we adopt this 'pooled' approach here, which allows us to examine broad trends and how they differ across contexts.

However, it is important to recognize the limits of pooling as a strategy for estimating the effects of contextual factors cross-nationally. Three points of caution are germane here. First and foremost, the returns to pooling data are larger if the effect of X on Y varies across contexts. Pooling data from different contexts can help estimate X's effect more precisely even if that effect does not vary, but pooling data will not necessarily demonstrate that the context matters unless the effect does indeed vary and there is sufficient divergence between contexts, and a significant number of contexts, to isolate that effect. Second, we must have valid and reliable measures of theoretical concepts. While this is always true in empirical research, meeting this requirement is often more challenging when pooling disparate observations (Bartels, 1996). To relate this to our interest in executive approval, Chapter 13 in this volume by Donovan et al. identifies partisanship as a critical conditioning factor linking business sentiment to presidential approval in the United States. Most other chapters, however, grant little attention to partisan dispositions. The reason for such omissions, however, are due less to theoretical scepticism and more to the absence of valid and reliable measures. Pooling across contexts often gives rise to a 'lowest common denominator' problem wherein our ability to test a particular hypothesis is limited by the availability of measures. And third, unless proper conditions are met, pooling can produce biased estimates of regression parameters (Green, Kim, and Yoon, 2001). $T > N$ designs where there are more observations over time than there are country units—such as the ones we employ below—also require corrections to adjust for different dynamic processes.

Our point is not to shun pooled analyses but to recognize their limits and the strengths of single-country relative to cross-national designs. A signature strength of this volume is our ability to pair the pooled analyses here with evidence from the country-specific chapters. The former design takes advantage of cross-case differences in contextual factors and of larger numbers of cases to gain statistical power. This complements earlier chapters which examine factors that are excluded from the pooled analyses due to space constraints, dearth of data, or both, and uncover exceptions to the general patterns identified here.

Variation across Time *and* Space

To investigate what moves approval, we analyse data from the EAP. As discussed in the introduction to this volume, we take as our universe of cases countries that have been members of the Organisation for Economic Cooperation and Development (OECD) group of advanced capitalist democracies since the 1990s. From this set of twenty-nine countries, the EAP contains comparable measures of executive approval of sufficient length for twenty countries: Australia, Austria, Canada, the Czech Republic, Denmark, France, Germany, Greece, Ireland, Italy, Japan, South Korea, Mexico, New Zealand, Poland, Portugal, Spain, Sweden, the United Kingdom, and the United States. Long-term OECD countries that are not represented due to a lack of rich approval data are Belgium, Finland, Hungary, Iceland, Luxembourg, the Netherlands, Norway, Switzerland, and Turkey. We rely in the main on a temporal frame of 1990 to 2019.[3] Data are aggregated at quarterly intervals: this

[3] Data exist from 1990q1 through 2018q4 for all countries examined. Exceptions are the Czech Republic (series begins in 1998q1), Italy (1995q3), and Poland (1992q4).

enables us to strike a balance between density of coverage that comes from less granularity and higher frequency data produced by shorter intervals.

Our outcome variable of primary interest is *Executive approval.* The executive refers to the prime minister or government in parliamentary or parliament-dominant hybrid regimes and to the president in (semi-)presidential regimes. Practically speaking, this means that our measure pertains to approval of the job of the prime minister or government in all but four of the twenty countries: France, Korea, Mexico, and the United States.[4]

Figure 15.1 reports individual country time series. These displays suggest how approval dynamics differ across national contexts. Countries are broadly similar in terms of 'average' approval ratings, with most having mean-reverting values in the mid-40s. Only two cases—New Zealand and Mexico—can boast average approval ratings of above 50 per cent. More intriguing is to consider the volatility of approval in different national contexts. In some countries, like Germany, public assessments fluctuate in a very narrow band: over thirty years, approval of the federal government never exceeds two-thirds nor does it plummet below one-third. Publics in Austria, Poland, and Sweden also exhibit stable ratings, an attribute that may be due to their multi-party systems in parliamentary regimes (see below). On the other hand, sentiment towards leaders in the Czech Republic, Ireland, and South Korea is volatile. During the best of times, three in four citizens in these countries voice approval for their executives; in the worst of times only one in five do.

Most of the variation in approval rates is within countries instead of between them; three-quarters (77 per cent) of the variation in our pooled sample stems from differences within countries over time, a result that lends credence to this volume's focus on change over time. Yet nearly one quarter (23 per cent) of the variation in executive approval levels is attributable to cross-country differences. Furthermore, cross-country variation as a share of the total *increases* with time: during the 1990s it accounts for 30 per cent of the variance, 41 per cent for the period 2000–2008, and nearly half (48 per cent) between 2009 and 2018. The implication is that differences both over time and across space must be considered to arrive at a satisfactory understanding of what moves approval.

[4] For the French and the Portuguese cases, we follow the respective chapters in the volume showing that the French president and the Portuguese prime minister are the dominant target of economic accountability, even while acknowledging that the other office can be held accountable for economic fluctuations as well, as the Portuguese case illustrates.

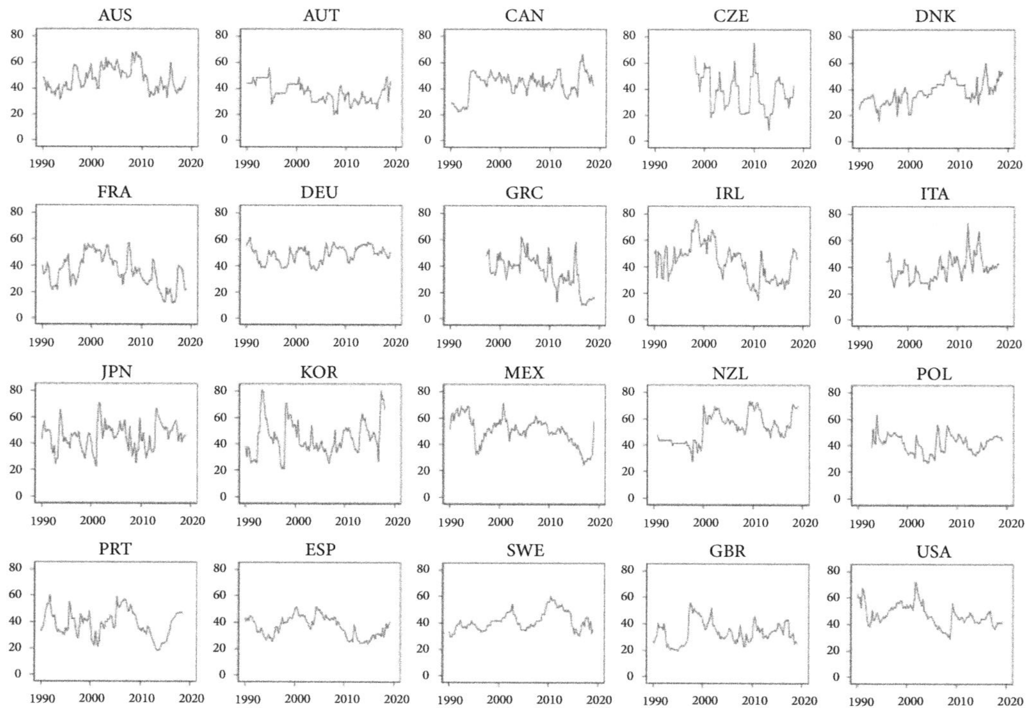

Figure 15.1 Executive approval in twenty countries

Source: Executive Approval Project.

Note: Graphs report *executive approval* on vertical axes with time in quarters on horizontal axes.

Temporal and Spatial Heterogeneity in the Economy–Approval Relationship

We now model government popularity as a function of the economy. A growing body of evidence challenges the universality of the conventional macroeconomic indicators (for a review, see Duch and Stevenson, 2013). The indicators typically used to gauge macroeconomic well-being are partial, may be incompletely measured (Kayser and Leininger, 2015; this volume), fail to capture the economy that matters for different socio-economic segments (Hibbs, Rivers, and Vasilatos, 1982), change in their relative salience over time (Singer, 2013), and in some cases may be misleading (e.g. rising employment may coexist with rising prices). Relying on macroeconomic indicators may thus lead to incomplete inferences (see Table 15.A1).[5]

To measure economic performance, we therefore rely on a subjective indicator as provided by consumer confidence indices.[6] National indices combine aggregate responses to various questions asking about business confidence and economic expectations. For the thirteen EU member states in our sample, the battery consists of four items pertaining to the household's financial situation over the last year, the expected financial situation of the household over the next year, the country's economic situation over the next year, and anticipated major purchases over the next twelve months. For Canada, we use an index provided by the Conference Board of Canada. The index contains four items, two of which pertain to family finances (comparing current to six months prior and to expectations six months ahead), one on the overall employment situation six months from now, and one assessing the current environment for making major purchases. For the United States, we use the University of Michigan's index of consumer sentiment, a five-item index consisting of the household's financial situation since last year, business conditions currently and at present, and a pair of prospective items pertaining to the direction of the national economy and to household finances. For the remaining cases—Australia, Japan, Korea, Mexico, and New Zealand—we rely on the consumer confidence index collected and standardized by the OECD (OECD, 2021). We combine and standardize the series to create a common measure with a possible range of −100 to +100.

[5] Appendix Table 15.A1 reports estimates that show that the impact of objective macroeconomic indicators on executive approval runs through the public's economic evaluations.

[6] See Kellstedt, Linn, and Hannah (2015) for a discussion of the reliability and validity of consumer sentiment measures in the United States. See Carlin et al. (2021) for a cross-national discussion.

Regarding series properties, both an Augmented Dickey-Fuller test and an Im-Pesaran-Shin test that all panels do not have a unit root. However, because our time series are relatively long relative to the number of countries (i.e. $T > N$), we know that time-correlated errors can bias our estimates. To account for significant heterogeneity in the autocorrelation structure across panels, we use a panel-specific AR(1) correction. The estimated AR(1) correction varies considerably between panels, suggesting that a single pooled time correction, either a lagged dependent variable or pooled AR(1) term, would not adequately capture the serial correlation in the data.

In Table 15.1 we report results from a series of feasible generalized least-squares regression models which consider the subjective effect of the economy in the context of elections and subsequent honeymoons. The first column indicates that positive shocks to *Consumer confidence*$_t$ increase support for elected executives. Results imply the economy is generally a driver of leader approval. Leaving aside dynamics, we can posit that a three-point rise in consumer sentiment accounts for a 1 per cent gain in the approval ratings of the average president or prime minister. But how stable is this effect across our twenty democracies? And is this relationship robust over the nearly three decades which comprise our time frame?

With respect to stability across nations—the main basis of Paldam's 'instability dilemma' and subsequent comparative research—we compare the effects of the subjective economy on approval for each of the twenty country cases. We do so by re-estimating Model 1 separately for each case and then comparing the economy's influence by way of coefficients on *Consumer confidence*.[7] Figure 15.2 displays these parameter estimates with 95 per cent confidence intervals. The median coefficient across the twenty countries is 0.35, or very close to the 0.29 estimate reported in Table 15.1. Estimates on consumer confidence are positive in all cases, with around two-thirds estimated as statistically different from zero.

The *range* of effects displayed in Figure 15.2 is also notable: job approval of presidents of France and Korea are highly sensitive to economic sentiment, close to a one-to-one relationship. Elsewhere, notably Canada, chief executives are unaffected by the public's perception of the economy in these

[7] Models are estimated using Prais-Winsten generalized least-squares procedures to account for first-order serial correlation. These simple models improve upon the bivariate correlations in Chapter 1 by including electoral cycles. This becomes particularly important in the case of Italy, where the non-conditional models found a negative correlation between consumer confidence and approval when not accounting for electoral cycles.

Table 15.1 The effect of consumer confidence on executive approval over time

	(1) All 1990q1-2019q1	(2) Period 1 1990q1-2001q3	(3) Period 2 2001q4-2008q3	(4) Period 3 2008q4-2019q1
Consumer confidence$_t$	0.29*	0.43*	0.30*	0.23*
	(0.03)	(0.04)	(0.05)	(0.04)
Election$_{t+1}$	−0.71*	−0.70	−0.63	−0.23
	(0.31)	(0.46)	(0.53)	(0.48)
Election$_t$	0.63	0.49	0.72	0.73
	(0.33)	(0.54)	(0.56)	(0.49)
Honeymoon$_t$	3.61*	1.82*	3.92*	3.71*
	(0.45)	(0.70)	(0.83)	(0.66)
Honeymoon$_{t-1}$	3.29*	1.92*	4.85*	3.04*
	(0.46)	(0.71)	(0.87)	(0.65)
Honeymoon$_{t-2}$	3.04*	2.70*	3.02*	2.78*
	(0.44)	(0.78)	(0.85)	(0.62)
Honeymoon$_{t-3}$	2.28*	0.37	2.44*	2.76*
	(0.43)	(0.73)	(0.84)	(0.60)
Constant	43.03*	44.76*	46.65*	42.24*
	(0.73)	(0.79)	(1.00)	(1.05)
N countries	20	19	19	19
N observations	2,002	636	532	767

Source: Executive Approval Project.
Notes: Model 1 includes all twenty country cases noted above; Models 2–4 exclude Canada. Cells report generalized least-squares estimates with panel-specific AR1 correction and heteroskedastic consistent standard errors in parentheses; * $p < 0.05$ (two-tailed test).

simple models. The economy's effect varies significantly across countries—the cross-country instability dilemma that Paldam observed some thirty years ago remains present today.

Yet the economy–country relationship also appears unstable over time, a point not emphasized by Paldam. To illustrate, we stratify the time series into three periods demarcated by using two critical events of global import: the 11 September 2001 attack on the World Trade Center in New York, and the September 2008 bankruptcy of Lehman Brothers. These events defined the political landscape across the advanced capitalist democracies in ways that could well affect conventional links between economics and politics. September 11th was a critical juncture insomuch as security concerns trumped material ones (e.g. Matsaganis and Payne, 2005). The collapse of Lehman

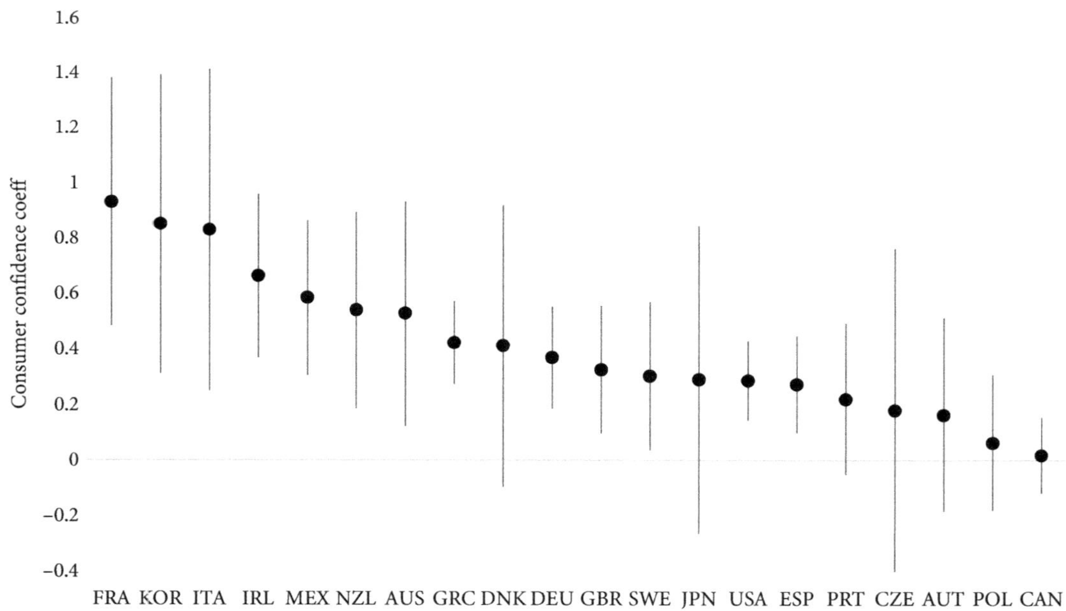

Figure 15.2 Average effects of consumer confidence on executive approval by country, 1990–2019

Source: Executive Approval Project.

Note: Dots represent coefficients on *Consumer confidence*$_t$ from estimating the specification of Table 15.1 Model 1 separately by country. Vertical bars represent 95 per cent confidence intervals.

signalled the high-water point of the subprime mortgage crisis. The ensuing Global Financial Crisis (GFC) reshaped views on the role of the state in the economy for years afterwards. With the GFC the economy regained its place at the top of the public's concerns.[8]

Accordingly, in the remaining table columns we report models separately for 1990 to the third quarter of 2001, the last quarter of 2001 to the third quarter of 2008, and quarter four of 2008 to the end of our time series. To make the bases of comparison more reliable, models exclude Canada as the one country case for which we lack consumer confidence data in all periods.[9] Results show that while the influence of subjective economic assessments on approval is significant and positive in each period, its substantive effect declined from the initial period to the second, and again from the second to the third.[10] The multivariate analysis, which incorporates the electoral cycle and honeymoon effects, confirms that the economy–approval relationship weakened in the early 2000s and has remained weak ever since.

Results reported in Table 15.1 and Figure 15.2 confirm that while economic performance generally has a positive and substantively meaningful effect on approval, the magnitude, and even direction, of its impact in public opinion varies across countries and time periods in the era since the publication of *Economics and Politics: The Calculus of Support* (Norpoth, Lewis-Beck, and Lafay, 1991). The economy–executive support relationship remains unstable, both across and within countries.

Solving the Instability Dilemma Redux

What accounts for this variation? In our quest to understand the economy's role, we now model the influence of the subjective economy on approval as dependent, or conditional, on other features of the larger environment. Returning the theoretical framework introduced in Chapter 1 and reviewed above, we examine three bases of heterogeneity: the political context, the

[8] For discussions of how crisis events shape public opinion and their impact on political support, see Wlezien, 2005; Singer, 2011; Kosmidis, 2018; Hellwig, Kweon, and Vowles, 2020.

[9] Dropping Canada from the twenty-country model reported in Table 15.1 Model 1 produces nearly identical estimates.

[10] Interactive modelling (not shown) reveals that the decline between periods 1 and 2 is statistically significant while the decline between periods 2 and 3 is not statistically different from zero.

salience of economic messages, and political polarization. Each of these varies across and within countries, making them possible drivers of these instabilities.

Trends

We start by looking at factors that should condition the clarity of responsibility. A central focus in the literature is on party-system fragmentation. The more parties represented in legislatures, the more difficult it is for any single party to control the policymaking process. Anderson (2000) also equates the (effective) number of parties with the idea of 'available alternatives', reasoning that dissatisfaction with the sitting incumbent is a function of whether there are other credible actors to take over that the public can coordinate around.

Party-system complexity varies from one country to the next for institutional and social reasons. However, as shown in Figure 15.3, the (effective) number of parties represented in national parliaments also ebbs and flows within countries.[11] In some cases the number of party competitors has remained stable (Australia and the United States) or declined (e.g. Japan and New Zealand, reverting from electoral-system-induced increases in the 1990s). In many countries, however, fragmentation has increased. In some places this is due to the rise of extremist and populist parties that are mobilizing (De Vries and Hobolt, 2020) or responding to (Kriesi et al., 2012) new cleavages. In other cases, forces of identity and geography fuel support for regional parties. Out of necessity, fragmented parliaments tend to be associated with multi-party governments. Indeed, in our data, for each party added to the legislature, the probability of having a coalition government increases by over 25 per cent, while the share of coalition governments increases from 44 per cent during the 1990s to 53 per cent during the 2000s to 58 per cent in the 2010s. Inasmuch as these political contexts impede the capacity of voters to assess responsibility for economic outcomes, we should see that party-system fragmentation and multi-party governments reduce the economy's impact.

The economic context may also affect responsibility attributions. The globalization of formerly national markets reduces the share of economic variation that is domestic in origin and, with it, may reduce blame attributed to national political actors. Countries that rely on consumers overseas to support national

[11] The effective number of parliamentary parties is calculated following Laasko and Taagepera (1979). Data are from Borman and Golder (2013) and updated by the authors. We exclude the first democratic election in Poland to make the graph easier to read.

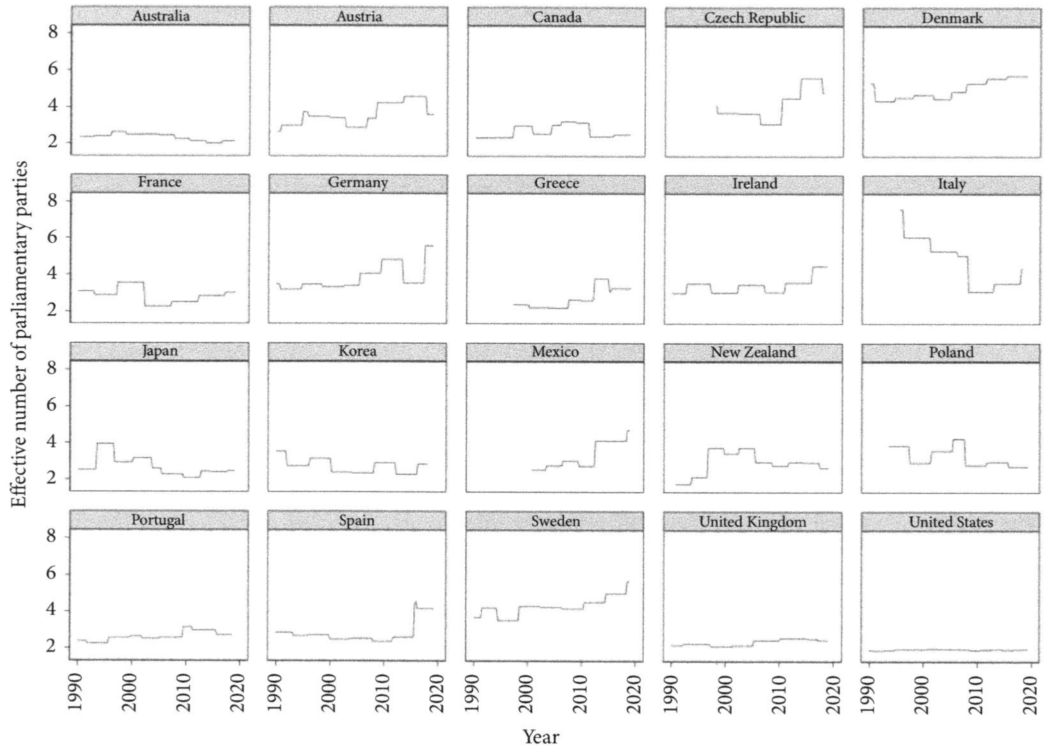

Figure 15.3 The effective number of parliamentary parties by country, 1990–2019

Source: Bormann and Golder (2013), updated by authors.

Note: Graphs report the effective number of parliamentary parties on vertical axes with time in quarters on horizontal axes.

industries are partially dependent on robust demand from foreigners. The politics of globalization may be even more salient for countries dependent on goods and services produced abroad (Colatone and Stanig, 2018). Figure 15.4 tracks changes in country exposure to exports and imports measured as a share of gross domestic product.[12] On average, levels of exports and imports have increased over time. Yet there is substantial variation in the trends, with trade increasing dramatically in some countries while remaining relatively flat in others. These differences in the types and composure of trade may condition how the public responds to the economy. As economies rely more on trade, the extent to which national policymakers are held to account for economic conditions may shrink (Hellwig, 2015). Yet, this may depend on the balance of payments. Reliance on imports places the economy in foreigners' hands, but export-driven economies may be seen as being domestic-led, particularly where finished manufactured goods dominate the export sector.

The second set of factors that may shape the relationship between the economy and government popularity is the changing nature of the public agenda. Parties differ with respect to the issues they choose to emphasize within a crowded policy agenda. The changing weight that political parties place on economic and non-economic issues is particularly apparent in their party programmes. Parties that emphasize their strategies for addressing economic matters like growth and inequality tend to compete along older class-based divides, while parties that play up their solutions to such matters as the environment, law and order, and values relate to each other along a post-material divide. Drawing on manifesto mentions compiled by the Manifesto Research on Political Representation project (MARPOR, Volkens et al., 2020), we create a pair of measures of issue salience. Economic messages are equal to the sum of items in the economic domain; the measure of non-economic messages combines a broader set of items on peace and human rights, the environment, corruption, law and order, and culture and values.[13] We create country-level scores by summing parties' scores on these measures, weighting parties according to seat size.

[12] To facilitate presentation, we exclude Ireland from Figure 15.3 because it has the highest levels of exports and imports in the sample (each averages greater than 100 per cent of GDP.

[13] Specifically, *Economic messages* combines per codes 401–405, 408–410, and 412–414. *Non-economic messages* include per codes 104–107, 109, 201–204, 301, 302, 304, 305, 501, 502, 506, 507, 601–608, 705, and 706.

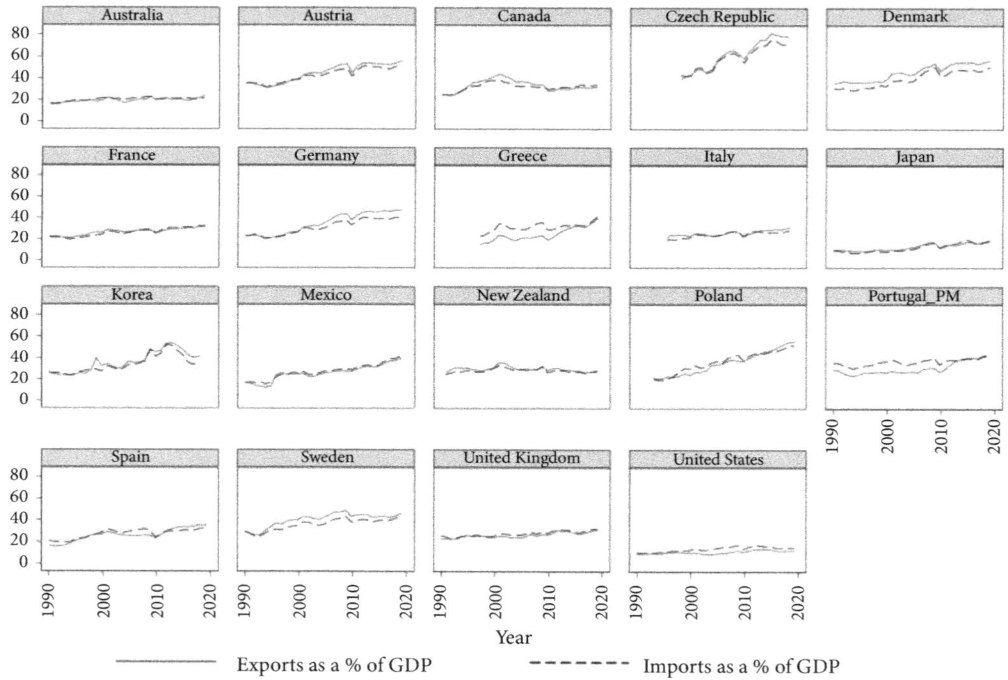

Figure 15.4 Exports and imports as a percentage of GDP by country, 1990–2019

Source: OECD.

Note: Graphs report the exports and imports as share of GDP on vertical axes with time in quarters on horizontal axes. Ireland excluded to facilitate presentation.

Charting these measures, Figure 15.5 shows that in the post-1990 era, non-economic issues have tended to be more salient than economic ones. Notably, in roughly half the countries in the sample, the gap between economic and non-economic issues grew substantially during the 1990s and 2000s. Whether this is due to parties faithfully responding to changing citizen preferences, to the strategic calculations of vote-seeking parties, or both is beyond the scope of this volume. Our interest is with the consequences of these demonstrable shifts. Campaigns in these countries are less about economics today than they were in the past, and this may translate into a more tenuous link between economic performance and government performance. The post-2008 economic crisis appears as something of a return to the past, as elites in many countries (re)engaged with economic concerns, thereby creating a possible return of economic-based executive evaluations.

Finally, the ability of performance factors of all sorts—both economic and non-economic—to move the executive's job approval ratings may be declining due to growing polarization among voters and party elites. Focusing on the latter, we measure polarization as the average deviation of parties from the country's mean position on a given issue dimension, weighting the deviation by seat share. As with issue salience, we separate polarization into economic and non-economic issue dimensions, using the same MARPOR coding convention as for the salience measures described above. While there is little evidence that overall polarization measured on the left-right scale in political manifestos has systematically increased (see Appendix, Figure 15.A1), Figure 15.6 shows that party positions on non-economic issues have tended to diverge more than positions on economic issues.[14] Further, where polarization has increased, that increase has tended to be driven by increased disagreements about non-economic issues. The United States is one of few countries where the increase in polarization has occurred in parallel in both policy domains. While clarity of choice may bolster economic accountability, the high level of division on non-economic issues, combined with their salience documented above, may anchor public evaluations of leaders to their social positions and prevent the public from sanctioning leaders for economic performance.

[14] Portugal is the clearest of several exceptions.

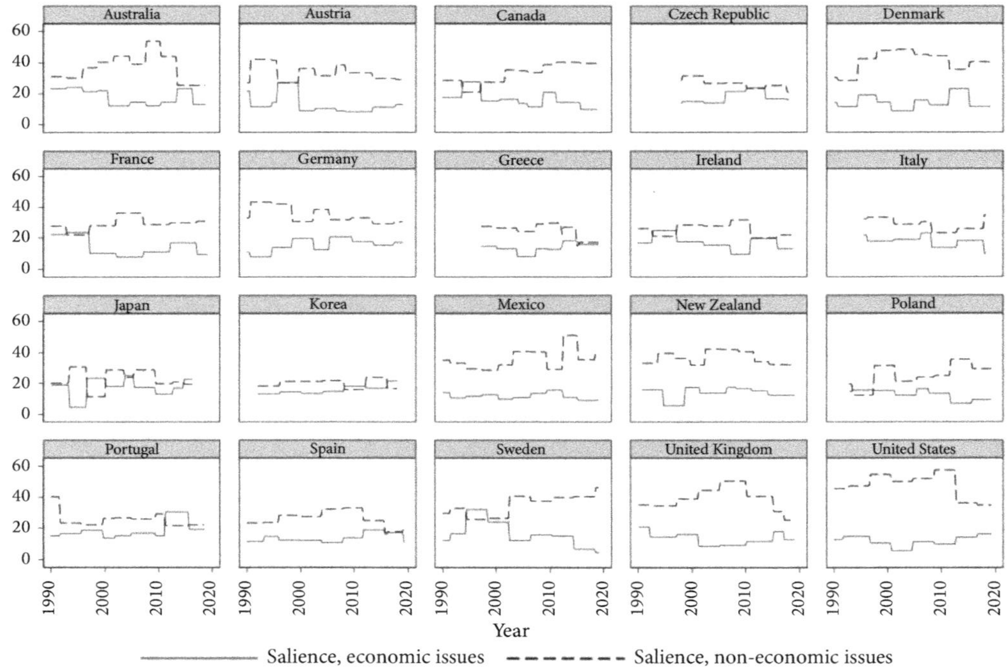

Figure 15.5 Salience of economic and non-economic issues, 1990–2019

Source: Volkens et al. (2020).

Note: Graphs report the issue salience on economic and non-economic areas, as defined in the text.

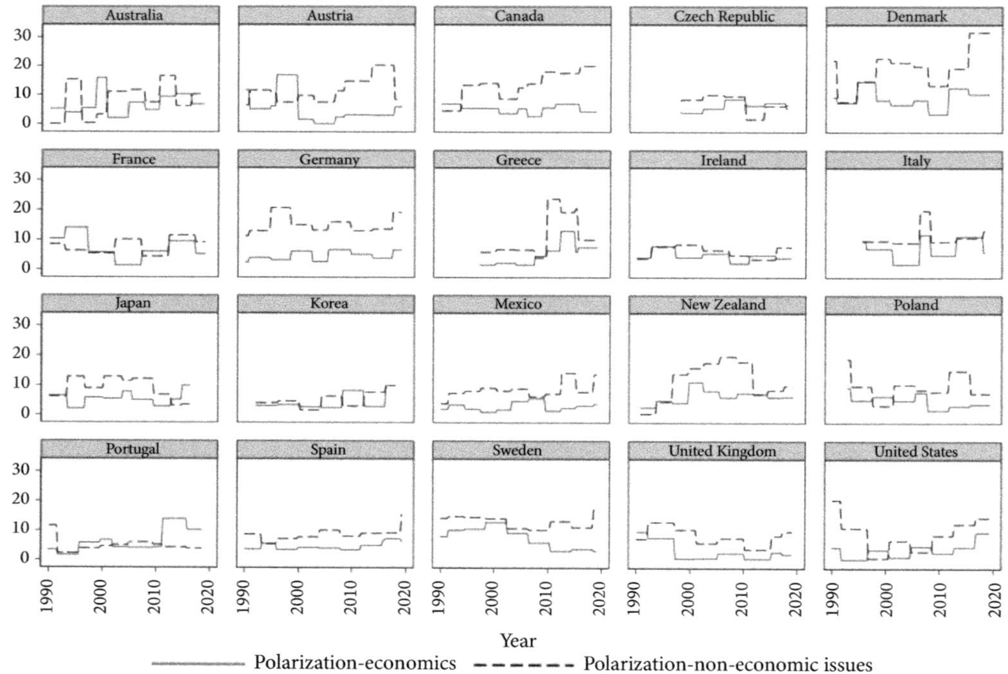

Figure 15.6 Polarization of parties on economic and non-economic issues, 1990–2019

Source: Volkens et al. (2020).

Note: Graphs report the issue polarization on economic and non-economic areas, as defined in the text.

Multivariate Analyses

To examine whether the clarity of responsibility, salience, and polarization influence the relationship between the economy and approval, we sequentially interact indicators of these concepts described above with consumer confidence in a model of leader approval. As above, we estimate models using generalized least squares with panel-specific AR1 correction and heteroskedastic consistent standard errors. Model estimates are reported in Table 15.2 with substantively meaningful conditional effects displayed in Figures 15.7–15.9.

The first two models examine indicators of clarity of responsibility: the effective number of parliamentary parties with seats in the legislature and, as a proxy for government control in global markets, exposure to the world economy. Despite expectations derived from the large literature showing that institutional and party-system complexity regulate the transmission between the economy and the vote for incumbents, we find little evidence that these variables matter for the economy–popularity connection. Model 1 shows that executives in fragmented party systems are, on average, less popular than those in systems with fewer parties. The impact of economic perceptions, however, is unaffected.[15] Model 2 shows that coalition governments also register no effects.

The third column in the table examines a different sort of clarity of responsibility: diffusion of policy control in the form of economic globalization. As per Figure 15.4, globalization is measured as exports and imports, both as share of GDP. Model 3 includes trade openness, measured as the sum of all exports and imports of goods and services as share of GDP. Parameter estimates show that on average, executives in more globalized economies are less popular, a finding consistent with the appeals of protectionist rhetoric.[16] We find no evidence, however, that total trade flows moderate the impact of subjective economic evaluations. The reason for that null effect is apparent in Model 4, which separates exports from imports. The two bases of trade carry different meanings. Exports fuel growth and raise national profiles; imports signal

[15] In results not reported here we tested whether other measures of diffuse/fragmented authority such as the number of parties in the coalition or electoral volaility influence the economy–approval connection but also found no significant effects.

[16] Analyses employing of a broader globalization indicator, combining data on trade flows with foreign direct investments, foreign debt, and foreign reserves (Gygli et al., 2019), produce similar results.

Table 15.2 Consumer confidence and executive approval: conditional effects

	(1)	(2)	(3)	(4)	(5)	(6)	(7)	(8)
Consumer confidence$_t$	0.263*	0.263*	0.273*	0.396*	0.260*	0.256*	0.256*	0.414*
	(0.088)	(0.030)	(0.063)	(0.080)	(0.066)	(0.039)	(0.039)	(0.049)
Election$_{t+1}$	−0.762*	−0.695*	−0.704*	−0.704*	−0.697*	−0.701*	−0.701*	−0.711*
	(0.317)	(0.314)	(0.316)	(0.315)	(0.315)	(0.315)	(0.315)	(0.317)
Election$_t$	0.698*	0.647*	0.638	0.620	0.640	0.688*	0.688*	0.607
	(0.330)	(0.328)	(0.328)	(0.327)	(0.328)	(0.329)	(0.329)	(0.330)
Honeymoon$_t$	3.664*	3.653*	3.624*	3.625*	3.632*	3.638*	3.638*	3.591*
	(0.449)	(0.448)	(0.449)	(0.448)	(0.448)	(0.448)	(0.448)	(0.449)
Honeymoon$_{t-1}$	3.337*	3.348*	3.301*	3.315*	3.298*	3.328*	3.328*	3.296*
	(0.459)	(0.459)	(0.459)	(0.458)	(0.459)	(0.458)	(0.458)	(0.459)
Honeymoon$_{t-2}$	3.074*	3.067*	3.056*	3.096*	3.048*	3.089*	3.089*	3.034*
	(0.444)	(0.443)	(0.444)	(0.442)	(0.444)	(0.443)	(0.443)	(0.444)
Honeymoon$_{t-3}$	2.315*	2.317*	2.286*	2.310*	2.302*	2.298*	2.298*	2.253*
	(0.432)	(0.432)	(0.432)	(0.431)	(0.431)	(0.431)	(0.431)	(0.432)
Effective No. of Parl. Parties$_t$	−1.234*							
	(0.455)							
Cons. conf$_t$ × ENPP$_t$	0.010							
	(0.028)							
Coalition government$_t$		−0.515						
		(0.794)						
Cons. conf$_t$ × coalition$_t$		0.065						
		(0.042)						

Trade $openness_t$	−0.047*				
	(0.019)				
Cons. $conf_t$ × trade $openness_t$	0.000				
	(0.001)				
$Exports_t$		−0.044			
		(0.148)			
Cons. $conf_t$ × $exports_t$		0.014*			
		(0.006)			
$Imports_t$		−0.051			
		(0.177)			
Cons. $conf_t$ × $imports_t$		−0.017*			
		(0.007)			
Economic $messages_t$			0.039		
			(0.068)		
Cons. $conf_t$ × Econ. $messages_t$			0.002		
			(0.004)		
Non-economic $messages_t$				−0.008	
				(0.047)	
Cons. $conf_t$ × Non-econ. $msgs_t$				−0.006*	
				(0.002)	
Economic $polarization_t$					−0.169
					(0.105)
Cons. $conf_t$ × Econ. $polarization_t$					0.006
					(0.006)

Continued

Table 15.2 *Continued*

	(1)	(2)	(3)	(4)	(5)	(6)	(7)	(8)
Non-economic polarization$_t$								−0.008
								(0.070)
Cons. conf$_t$ × Non-econ. polar$_t$								−0.011**
								(0.004)
Constant	46.787*	43.437*	46.235*	45.867*	42.582*	43.809*	43.911*	43.248*
	(1.613)	(0.816)	(1.474)	(1.703)	(1.250)	(2.109)	(0.923)	(1.008)
N countries	20	20	20	20	20	20	20	20
N observations	2,002	2,002	2,002	2,002	2,002	2,002	1,992	1,992

Source: Executive Approval Project.
Notes: Cells report generalized least-squares estimates with panel-specific AR1 correction and heteroskedastic consistent standard errors in parentheses; * $p < 0.05$ (two-tailed test).

dependence. We see that as exports grow as a share of GDP, the economy–popularity connection strengthens. In countries that are import dependent, in contrast, the economy's marginal effect is significantly reduced. Figure 15.7 graphs the conditional effects. The implication is the economy plays a stronger role in approval ratings in countries that run trade surpluses.[17]

Taken together, Models 1–4 lend some insights into the utility of isolating clarity of responsibility effects as a solution to the instability dilemma. Unlike previous studies (e.g. Powell and Whitten, 1993; Hobolt, Tilley, and Banducci, 2013), we find political institutions offer little guidance; However, the case of globalization and its influence on the 'e-fraction' hints that *economic* contexts may offer a path forward. While this parts way with much of the previous work, the dynamic analyses afforded by high-frequency time-series data should push us to identify and examine factors that change over time and not (just) across space.

Moving away from responsibility attributions, another cause for a reduced role of economic signals stems from shifts in salience of issues, away from the economy and onto non-economic, or cultural concerns. Accordingly, we next incorporate information on the public agenda and elite messaging by interacting consumer confidence with measures of economic- and non-economic-focused content in party manifestos (see Figure 15.5). Since messaging from party platforms is formed in advance of the election and persists thereafter, we enter the MARPOR-based series at two quarters in advance of the election quarter to allow for campaign effects. Regression results show that while the economic-messages coefficient is imprecisely estimated (Model 5), the negatively signed coefficient on *Consumer confidence*$_t$ × *Non-economic messages*$_t$ implies the public gives less weight to economic outcomes where elites focus their messages on matters outside the economy (Model 6). The marginal effects in Figure 15.8 highlight the strong correspondence of non-economic messaging with shifts in how the public holds leaders accountable. Results suggest that shifts in political discourse away from economic issues to social ones in the last few decades contribute to the reduced impact of economic considerations on government popularity.

Lastly, these days political polarization is often blamed for much of what ails contemporary democracies, and this extends to the economy–popularity linkage. The last two columns of Table 15.2 present estimates from interacting

[17] We see the same pattern if we interact the consumer confidence measure with a direct measure of the trade surplus; controlling for the overall level of trade, greater trade surpluses see the public give greater weight to the economy when evaluating leaders.

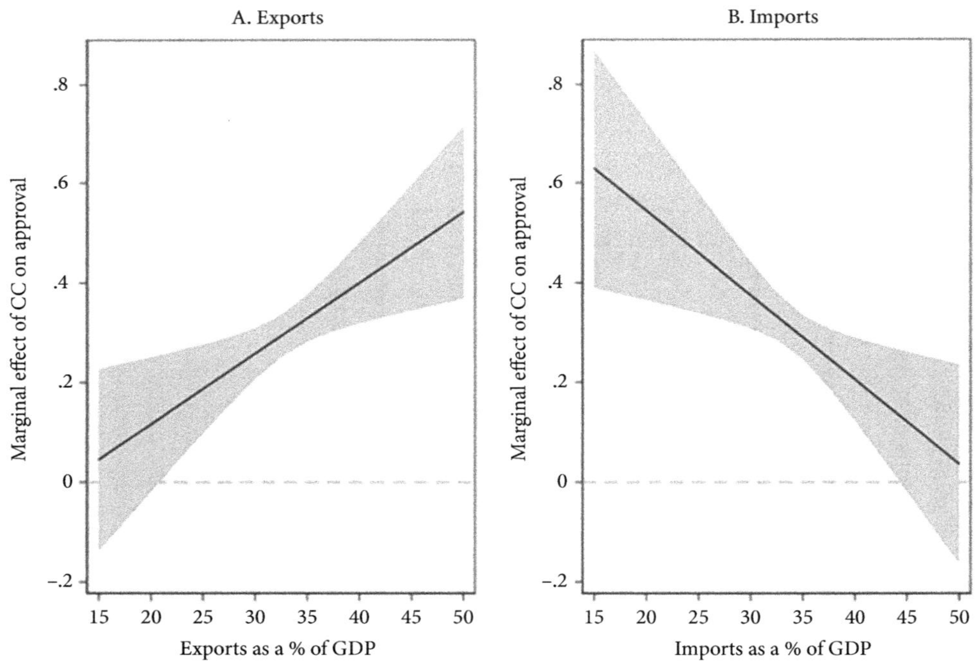

Figure 15.7 The effect of consumer confidence on approval, conditional upon exports and imports

Source: Executive Approval Project.

Note: Figure produced from Table 15.2 Model 4 estimates. Shaded area displays 90 per cent confidence intervals.

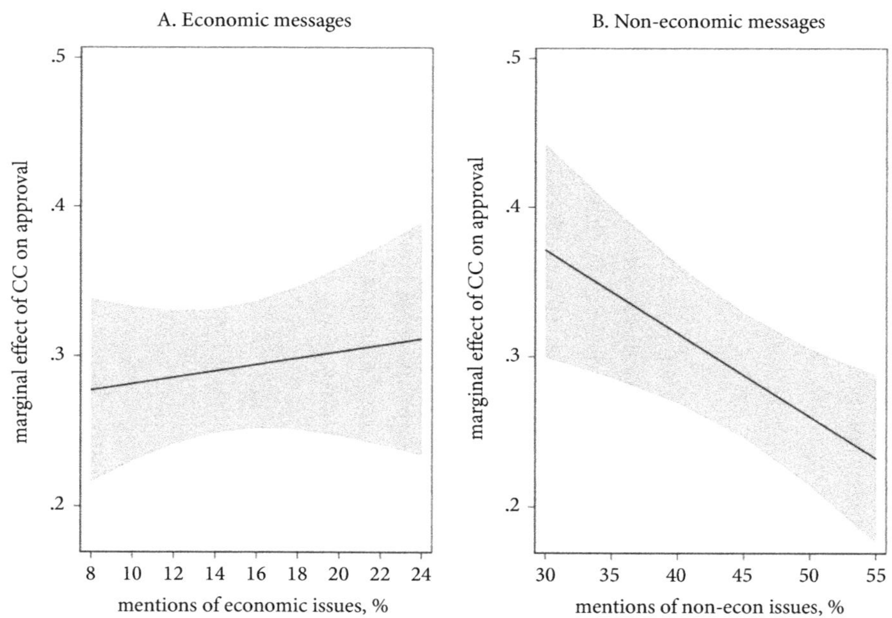

Figure 15.8 The effect of consumer confidence on approval, conditional on elite messaging strategies

Source: Executive Approval Project.
Note: Figure produced from Table 15.2 Models 5 and 6 estimates. The range displays 90 per cent confidence intervals.

the measure of consumer confidence with the indicators of political polarization described above (see Figure 15.6). Estimates show that the effect of polarization depends on issue type. For economic issues, the unconditional coefficient on the interaction of consumer confidence with polarization is positively signed but imprecisely measured (Model 7; Figure 15.9a). In contrast, for elite polarization on non-economic matters the coefficient on the interaction term is precisely estimated and carries a negative sign (Model 8; Figure 15.9b). This implies that the public discounts evaluations of the economy as a gauge of political performance when party competitors distinguish themselves on non-economic issues. The implication is that it is not just polarization writ large that changes the pattern of economic accountability but the *type* of polarization (cf. Hellwig, 2012; Gélineau and Singer, 2015, Stiers and Dassonneville, 2020).

In summary, evidence from time-series analyses of executive approval from an unparalleled twenty countries indicates that the shifting *political content* of the last decade—manifested both in a rising importance of non-economic issues and greater polarization around them—has reduced the importance of the economy in popularity functions. In countries where parties continue to emphasize economics over other issues and present clearly distinct visions about how to manage the economy, publics evaluate their leaders based on economic performance. In contrast, we find weak to no impact of the political-institutional *context* with respect to understanding over-time changes. Neither partisan fragmentation nor the presence of multi-party governments influences how the public reacts to the economy. A possible exception is exposure to the world economy: import dependence makes the public less likely to sanction governments for economic conditions.

Conclusion: Plus ça change?

As noted in Chapter 1, the study of approval of governments and, especially, presidents has an esteemed pedigree. Yet social science must not become complacent but instead re-assess received wisdoms under changing political and economic environments. With respect to the structuring effect of economic conditions on macro evaluations of political executives, findings reported in this and in previous chapters reveal that while some things have changed, others have remained the same. In many countries, the economy remains an important driver of government approval. For a majority of our twenty

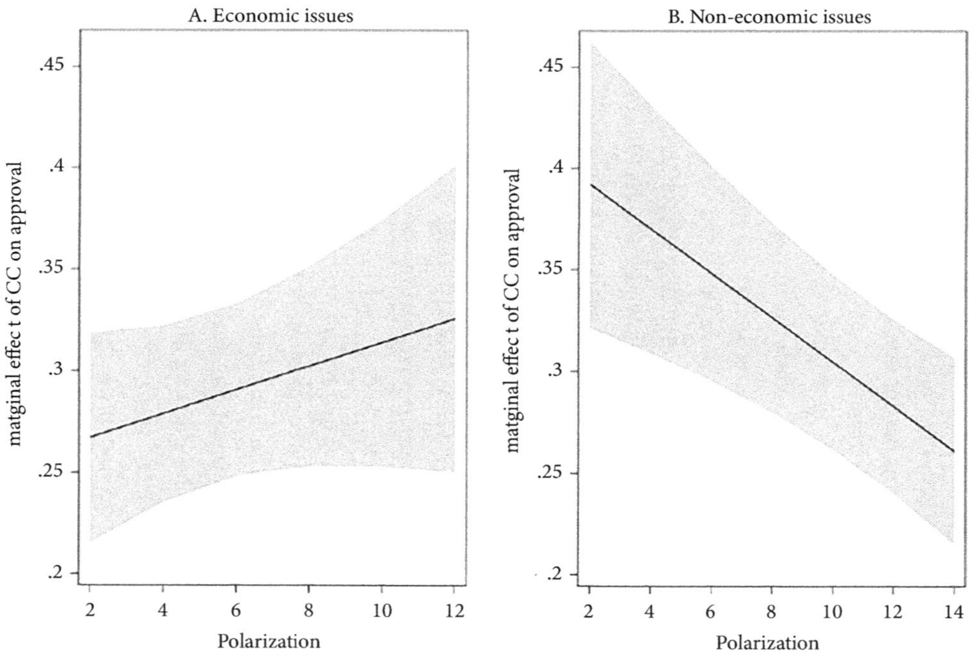

Figure 15.9 The effect of consumer confidence on approval, conditional on party-system polarization

Source: Executive Approval Project.
Note: Figure produced from Table 15.2 Models 7 and 8 estimates. The range displays 90 per cent confidence intervals.

country cases, subjective economic evaluations have a positive impact on assessments of the political executive's job approval, and in no case is the relationship reversed (see Figure 15.2). Even though governments are being held accountable for non-economic factors (e.g. Singer, 2011; De Vries and Giger, 2014), and even though the importance of the economy in many cases is changing over time, the economy remains important to understand leader popularity.

However, our panel investigations find the effect of the economy varies across national contexts. Then, as earlier chapters in this volume detail, we uncover evidence of change over time as well. Of the factors we examine in our pooled-data design, the most consistent explanations for differences in the economy–approval relationship reflect the importance of the economy in elite political competition. Elite messaging on non-economic issues and policy polarization on non-economic issues have increased in many countries in this period, and each have significant moderating effects on the economy. Even with a return to economic concerns following the Great Recession, the continued salient polarization over non-economic issues largely prevented the economy's influence on government popularity from increasing.

Findings also send a cautionary note about the importance of national-specific contexts. Research on the clarity of responsibility predicts that national contexts, like the party system, should reduce the capacity of the public to link performance outcomes to government support. Yet none of the institutional variables we considered yielded results consistent with the argument. The reason, we hasten to say, is that when it comes to executive approval, time matters more than space.[18] This conclusion should push scholars to examine how politics has changed within countries over time. On this point, we show that changes in elite communications, realized in terms of issue salience and by party polarization, may be affecting the political role of the economy. For each of these, the general trend is an increase in the importance of non-material considerations and decline in the material bases of political debate. The upshot is that as scholars look to understand the vagaries of accountability, they should look less at how more-or-less rigid national contexts affect policy responsibility and more at how parties structure the choices available to the public.

[18] The absence of strong effects of economic globalization fits this conclusion as well: in our sample, 76 per cent of the variation in economic openness occurs between countries. Future research should trace the temporal relationships between such changes in economic structures, elite messages, and the public's response.

Traditionally, a strong correspondence between economic outcomes and government approval has been held up as evidence of strong accountability. Does the weakening that we document in many countries here signal that accountability is becoming attenuated in developed democracies? The answer depends upon the mechanism under consideration. The downward trend in the economy's role in countries where polarization has increased is troubling for those looking to the public to provide a continual accountability check on the actions of elected policymakers. If polarization means the public will stick with poorly performing leaders from their side despite that poor performance, then the results presented here are indeed troubling for democracy. We have seen this dynamic at play in Germany, the United States, and elsewhere, not only with regards to the economy but with regards to the COVID-19 pandemic, where partisans have continued to back the leader of their party despite negative outcomes.

Yet if the public's attention—and the political campaigns seeking to attract it—has turned away from the economy because of long-term value change (e.g. Inglehart, 1990), then the economy's decline as a driver of popular support does not represent the weakening of accountability but instead its evolution. Leaders pursue policy on numerous issues and the willingness of the electorate to focus on other areas beyond the economy may deepen accountability instead of limiting it, even as it makes it more difficult to model. The ability of policymakers to react to an expanding set of issues while also delivering peace and prosperity will determine if democratic accountability is strengthened or stymied.

References

Anderson, C. J. (2000). Economic voting and political context: A comparative perspective. *Electoral Studies, 19*(2–3), 151–70.

Anderson, C. J., and Singer, M. M. (2008). The sensitive left and the impervious right: Multilevel models and the politics of inequality, ideology, and legitimacy in Europe. *Comparative Political Studies, 41*(4–5), 564–99.

Anson, I. G. (2023). *Following the Ticker: The Political Origins and Consequences of Americans' Stock Market Perceptions.* New York: SUNY Press.

Bartels, L. M. (1996). Pooling disparate observations. *American Journal of Political Science, 40*(3), 905–42.

Bormann, N. C., and Golder, M. (2013). Democratic electoral systems around the world, 1946–2011. *Electoral Studies, 32*(2), 360–9.

Carlin, R. E., Hellwig, T., Love, G. J., Martínez-Gallardo, C., and Singer, M. M. (2021). When does the public get it right? The information environment and the accuracy of economic sentiment. *Comparative Political Studies, 54*(9), 1499–533.

Colantone, I., and Stanig, P. (2018). The trade origins of economic nationalism: Import competition and voting behavior in Western Europe. *American Journal of Political Science, 62*(4), 936–53.

De Vries, C. E., and Giger, N. (2014). Holding governments accountable? Individual heterogeneity in performance voting. *European Journal of Political Research, 53*(2), 345–62.

De Vries, C. E., and Hobolt, S. B. (2020). *Political Entrepreneurs: The Rise of Challenger Parties in Europe*. Princeton, NJ: Princeton University Press.

Duch, R., and Stevenson, R. (2008). *The Economic Vote*. New York: Cambridge University Press.

Duch, R., and Stevenson, R. (2013). Voter perceptions of agenda power and attribution of responsibility for economic performance. *Electoral Studies, 32*(3), 512–16.

Gélineau, F., and Singer, M. M. (2015). The economy and incumbent support in Latin America. In *The Latin American Voter: Pursuing Representation and Accountability in Challenging Contexts*, Ryan E. Carlin, Matthew M. Singer, and Elizabeth Zechmeister, eds. Ann Arbor, MI: University of Michigan Press. 281–99.

Green, D. P., Kim, S. Y., and Yoon, D. H. (2001). Dirty pool. *International Organization, 55*(2), 441–68.

Gygli, S., Haelg, F., Potrafke, N., and Sturm, J. E. (2019). The KOF globalisation index-revisited. *Review of International Organizations 14*(3): 543–74.

Hellwig, T. (2012). Constructing accountability: Party position taking and economic voting. *Comparative Political Studies, 45*(1), 91–118.

Hellwig, T. (2015). *Globalization and Mass Politics: Retaining the Room to Maneuver*. New York: Cambridge University Press.

Hellwig, T., Kweon, Y., and Vowles, J. (2020). *Democracy under Siege? Parties, Voters, and Elections after the Great Recession*. Oxford: Oxford University Press.

Hellwig, T., and Marinova, D. M. (2023). Evaluating the unequal economy: Poverty risk, economic indicators, and the perception gap. *Political Research Quarterly, 76*(1), 253–66.

Hellwig, T., and Samuels, D. (2008). Electoral accountability and the variety of democratic regimes. *British Journal of Political Science, 38*(1), 65–90.

Hibbs Jr, D. A., Rivers, R. D., and Vasilatos, N. (1982). The dynamics of political support for American presidents among occupational and partisan groups. *American Journal of Political Science, 26*(2),312–32.

Hobolt, S., Tilley, J., and Banducci, S. (2013). Clarity of responsibility: How government cohesion conditions performance voting. *European Journal of Political Research, 52*(2), 164–87.

Inglehart, R. (1990). *Culture Shift in Advanced Industrial Society.* Princeton, NJ: Princeton University Press.

Kayser, M. A., and Leininger, A. (2015). Vintage errors: Do real-time economic data improve election forecasts? *Research & Politics, 2*(3), 2053168015589624.

Kellstedt, P. M., Linn, S., and Hannah, A. L. (2015). The usefulness of consumer sentiment: Assessing construct and measurement. *Public Opinion Quarterly, 79*(1), 181–203.

Kosmidis, S. (2018). International constraints and electoral decisions: Does the room to maneuver attenuate economic voting? *American Journal of Political Science, 62*(3), 519–34.

Kriesi, H., Grande, E., Dolezal, M., Helbling, M., Höglinger, D., Hutter, S., and Wüst, B. (2012). *Political Conflict in Western Europe.* Cambridge: Cambridge University Press.

Laakso, M., and Taagepera, R. (1979). 'Effective' number of parties: A measure with application to West Europe. *Comparative Political Studies, 12*(1), 3–27.

Laver, M. J., and Budge, I. (eds). (1992). *Party Policy and Government Coalitions.* New York, NY: St. Martin's Press.

Matsaganis, M. D., and Payne, J. G. (2005). Agenda setting in a culture of fear: The lasting effects of September 11 on American politics and journalism. *American Behavioral Scientist, 49*(3), 379–92.

Norpoth, H., Lewis-Beck, M. S., and Lafay, J.-D. (eds). (1991). *Economics and Politics: The Calculus of Support.* Ann Arbor, MI: University of Michigan Press.

OECD. (2021). Consumer Confidence Index (CCI) (indicator). DOI: 10.1787/46434d78-en (Accessed on 2 June 2021).

Paldam, M. (1991). How robust is the vote function? A study of seventeen nations over four decades. In *Economics and Politics: The Calculus of Support*, H. Norpoth, M. S. Lewis-Beck, and J.-D. Lafay, eds. Ann Arbor, MI: University of Michigan Press. 9–31.

Powell Jr, G. B., and Whitten, G. D. (1993). A cross-national analysis of economic voting: Taking account of the political context. *American Journal of Political Science, 37*(2), 391–414.

Przeworski, A., and Teune, H. (1970). *The Logic of Comparative Social Inquiry.* New York: John Wiley and Sons.

Singer, M. M. (2011). Who says 'it's the economy'? Cross-national and cross-individual variation in the salience of economic performance. *Comparative Political Studies, 44*(3), 284–312.

Singer, M. M. (2013). Economic voting in an era of non-crisis: The changing electoral agenda in Latin America, 1982–2010. *Comparative Politics, 45*(2), 169–85.

Singer, M. M., and Carlin, R. E. (2013). Context counts: The election cycle, development, and the nature of economic voting. *The Journal of Politics, 75*(3), 730–42.

Stiers, D., and Dassonneville, R. (2020). Retrospective voting and the polarization of available alternatives. *Canadian Journal of Political Science/Revue canadienne de science politique*, *53*(1), 99–115.

Van der Brug, W., Van der Eijk, C., and Franklin, M. (2007). *The Economy and the Vote: Economic Conditions and Elections in Fifteen Countries*. Cambridge: Cambridge University Press.

Volkens, A., Burst, T., Krause, W., Lehmann, P., Theres, M., Merz, N., Regel, S., Weßels, B., and Zehnter, L. (2020). The Manifesto Data Collection. Manifesto Project (MRG/CMP/MARPOR). Version 2020b. Berlin: Wissenschaftszentrum Berlin für Sozialforschung (WZB). https://doi.org/10.25522/manifesto.mpds.2020b.

Wlezien, C. (2005). On the salience of political issues: The problem with 'most important problem'. *Electoral Studies*, *24*(4), 555–79.

APPENDIX

Modeling Consumer Confidence

Table 15.A1 The effect of objective economic indicators on consumer confidence and executive approval in twenty countries, 1990–2019

	(1) **Consumer confidence**	(2) **Executive approval**	(3) **Executive approval**	(4) **Executive approval**
GDP growth$_t$	0.57*	0.07		−0.11
	(0.05)	(0.07)		(0.07)
Unemployment$_t$	−1.20*	−0.79*		−0.44*
	(0.10)	(0.09)		(0.10)
Ln(Inflation)$_t$	−7.44*	−0.53		1.26
	(1.13)	(1.78)		(1.78)
Consumer			0.29*	0.27*
confidence$_t$			(0.03)	(0.03)
Election$_{t+2}$	0.54*			
	(0.21)			
Election$_{t+1}$	0.94*	−0.74*	−0.82*	−0.79*
	(0.27)	(0.33)	(0.32)	(0.32)
Election$_t$	1.82***	0.79*	0.49	0.54
	(0.28)	(0.34)	(0.33)	(0.33)
Election$_{t-1}$	1.12***			
	(0.27)			
Election$_{t-2}$	0.27			
	(0.21)			
Honeymoon$_t$		3.57*	3.55*	3.49*
		(0.47)	(0.45)	(0.46)
Honeymoon$_{t-1}$		3.34*	3.30*	3.24*
		(0.47)	(0.46)	(0.46)
Honeymoon$_{t-2}$		3.09*	3.10*	3.05*
		(0.46)	(0.44)	(0.45)
Honeymoon$_{t-3}$		2.17*	2.20*	2.13*
		(0.45)	(0.44)	(0.44)
Constant	20.41*	49.43*	43.05*	43.90*
	(2.91)	(4.61)	(0.74)	(4.64)
N Countries	20	20	20	20
N Observations	1,972	1,972	1,972	1,972

Source: Executive Approval Project.
Note: Cells report generalized least-squares estimates with panel-specific AR1 correction and hetero-skedastic consistent standard errors in parentheses; * $p < 0.05$.

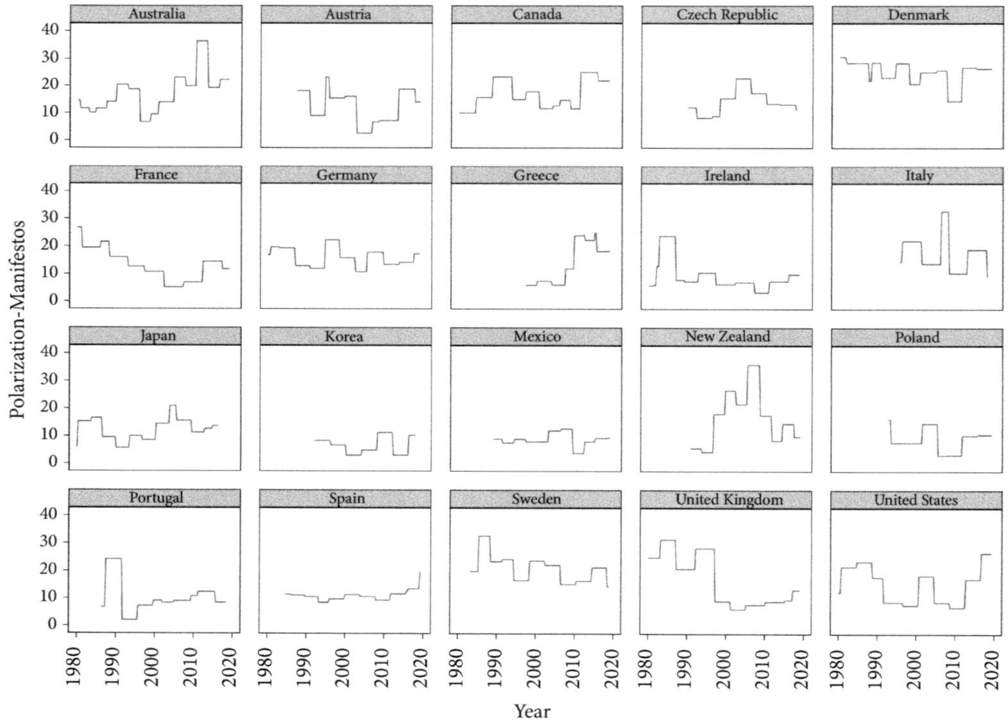

Figure 15.A1 Left-right polarization by country, 1980–2019

Source: Volkens et al. (2020), based on Laver and Budge's (1992) RILE coding.

Note: Graphs report the issue polarization on economic and non-economic areas, as defined in the text.

Index